The Swastika

The Swastika

The Earliest Known Symbol, and Its Migrations

by

Thomas Wilson

Curator, Department of Prehistoric Anthropology,
U.S. National Museum

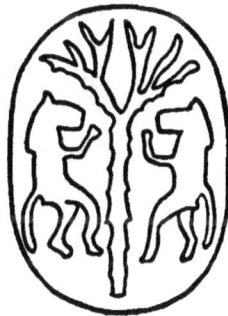

Symbolon Press   San Francisco

Symbolon Press, San Francisco

This is a facsimile edition of Thomas Wilson's, *The Swastika, the Earliest Known Symbol, and Its Migrations; with Observations on the Migration of Certain Industries in Prehistoric Times*. It was first published in *Report of the United States National Museum for the Year Ending June 30, 1894*, Part 2, Number 6: 757–1011, Washington, DC, by the Government Printing Office, in 1896.

Printed in the United States of America
17 16 15 14 13 12 11 10   1 2 3 4 5 6 7 8

ISBN: 978-0-9824034-7-1   (paperback)
Library of Congress Control Number: 2010941280

Published 2010

⊗ The paper used in this publication meets the minimum requirements of the American National Standard for Information Sciences—Permanence of Paper for Printed Library Materials, ANSI Z39.48-1992.

www.SymbolonPress.com

TABLE OF CONTENTS.

THE SWASTIKA,

THE EARLIEST KNOWN SYMBOL, AND ITS MIGRATIONS; WITH OBSERVATIONS ON THE MIGRATION OF CERTAIN INDUSTRIES IN PREHISTORIC TIMES.

By THOMAS WILSON,

Curator, Department of Prehistoric Anthropology, U. S. National Museum.

PREFACE.

An English gentleman, versed in prehistoric archæology, visited me in the summer of 1894, and during our conversation asked if we had the Swastika in America. I answered, "Yes," and showed him two or three specimens of it. He demanded if we had any literature on the subject. I cited him De Mortillet, De Morgan, and Zmigrodzki, and he said, "No, I mean English or American." I began a search which proved almost futile, as even the word Swastika did not appear in such works as Worcester's or Webster's dictionaries, the Encyclopædic Dictionary, the Encyclopædia Britannica, Johnson's Universal Cyclopædia, the People's Cyclopædia, nor Smith's Dictionary of Greek and Roman Antiquities, his Greek and Roman Biography and Mythology, or his Classical Dictionary. I also searched, with the same results, Mollett's Dictionary of Art and Archæology, Fairholt's Dictionary of Terms in Art, "L'Art Gothique," by Gonza, Perrot and Chipiez's extensive histories of Art in Egypt, in Chaldea and Assyria, and in Phenicia; also "The Cross, Ancient and Modern," by W. W. Blake, "The History of the Cross," by John Ashton; and a reprint of a Dutch work by Wildener. In the American Encyclopædia the description is erroneous, while all the Century Dictionary says is, "Same as fylfot," and "Compare *Crux Ansata* and *Gammadion*." I thereupon concluded that this would be a good subject for presentation to the Smithsonian Institution for "diffusion of knowledge among men."

The principal object of this paper has been to gather and put in a compact form such information as is obtainable concerning the Swastika, leaving to others the task of adjustment of these facts and their arrangement into an harmonious theory. The only conclusion sought to be deduced from the facts stated is as to the possible migration in prehistoric times of the Swastika and similar objects.

No conclusion is attempted as to the time or place of origin, or the primitive meaning of the Swastika, because these are considered to be lost in antiquity. The straight line, the circle, the cross, the triangle, are simple forms, easily made, and might have been invented and re-invented in every age of primitive man and in every quarter of the globe, each time being an independent invention, meaning much or little, meaning different things among different peoples or at different times among the same people; or they may have had no settled or definite meaning. But the Swastika was probably the first to be made with a definite intention and a continuous or consecutive meaning, the knowledge of which passed from person to person, from tribe to tribe, from people to people, and from nation to nation, until, with possibly changed meanings, it has finally circled the globe.

There are many disputable questions broached in this paper. The author is aware of the differences of opinion thereon among learned men, and he has not attempted to dispose of these questions in the few sentences employed in their announcement. He has been conservative and has sought to avoid dogmatic decisions of controverted questions. The antiquity of man, the locality of his origin, the time of his dispersion and the course of his migration, the origin of bronze and the course of its migration, all of which may be more or less involved in a discussion of the Swastika, are questions not to be settled by the dogmatic assertions of any individual.

Much of the information in this paper is original, and relates to prehistoric more than to modern times, and extends to nearly all the countries of the globe. It is evident that the author must depend on other discoverers; therefore, all books, travels, writers, and students have been laid under contribution without scruple. Due acknowledgment is hereby made for all quotations of text or figures wherever they occur.

Quotations have been freely made, instead of sifting the evidence and giving the substance. The justification is that there has never been any sufficient marshaling of the evidence on the subject, and that the former deductions have been inconclusive; therefore, quotations of authors are given in their own words, to the end that the philosophers who propose to deal with the origin, meaning, and cause of migration of the Swastika will have all the evidence before them.

Assumptions may appear as to antiquity, origin, and migration of the Swastika, but it is explained that many times these only reflect the opinion of the writers who are quoted, or are put forth as working hypotheses.

The indulgence of the reader is asked, and it is hoped that he will endeavor to harmonize conflicting statements upon these disputed questions rather than antagonize them.

I.—DEFINITIONS, DESCRIPTION, AND ORIGIN.

DIFFERENT FORMS OF THE CROSS.

The simple cross made with two sticks or marks belongs to prehistoric times. Its first appearance among men is lost in antiquity. One may theorize as to its origin, but there is no historical identification of it either in epoch or by country or people. The sign is itself so simple that it might have originated among any people, however primitive, and in any age, however remote. The meaning given to the earliest cross is equally unknown. Everything concerning its beginning is in the realm of speculation. But a differentiation grew up in early times among nations by which certain forms of the cross have been known under certain names and with specific significations. Some of these, such as the Maltese cross, are historic and can be well identified.

The principal forms of the cross, known as symbols or ornaments, can be reduced to a few classes, though when combined with heraldry its use extends to 385 varieties.[1]

 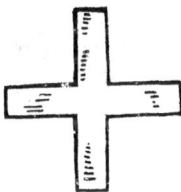 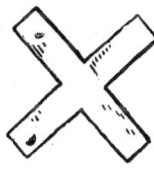

Fig. 1.   Fig. 2.   Fig. 3.

LATIN CROSS (*Crux immissa*).   GREEK CROSS.   ST. ANDREW'S CROSS (*Crux decussata.*)

It is not the purpose of this paper to give a history of the cross, but the principal forms are shown by way of introduction to a study of the Swastika.

The Latin cross, *Crux immissa*, (fig. 1) is found on coins, medals, and ornaments anterior to the Christian era. It was on this cross that Christ is said to have been crucified, and thus it became accepted as the Christian cross.

The Greek cross (fig. 2) with arms of equal length crossing at right angles, is found on Assyrian and Persian monuments and tablets, Greek coins and statues.

The St. Andrew's cross, *Crux decussata*, (fig. 3) is the same as the Greek cross, but turned to stand on two legs.

---

[1] William Berry, Encyclopædia Heraldica, 1828–1840,

The *Crux ansata* (fig. 4) according to Egyptian mythology, was Ankh, the emblem of Ka, the spiritual double of man. It was also said to indicate a union of Osiris and Isis. and was regarded as a symbol of the generative principle of nature.

The Tau cross (fig. 5), so called from its resemblance to the Greek letter of that name, is of uncertain, though ancient, origin. In Scandinavian mythology it passed under the name of "Thor's hammer," being therein confounded with the Swastika. It was also called St. Anthony's cross for the Egyptian hermit of that name, and was always colored blue. Clarkson says this mark was received by the Mithracists on their foreheads at the time of their initiation. O. W. King, in his work entitled "Early Christian Numismatics" (p. 214), expresses the opinion that the Tau cross was placed on the foreheads of men who cry after abominations. (Ezekiel ix, 4.) It is spoken of as a phallic emblem.

Fig. 4.

EGYPTIAN CROSS (*Crux ansata*).

The Key of Life.

Another variety of the cross appeared about the second century, composed of a union of the St. Andrew's cross and the letter P (fig. 6), being the first two letters of the Greek word $XPI\Sigma T\grave{O}\Sigma$ (Christus). This, with another variety containing all the foregoing letters, passed as the monogram of Christ (fig. 6).

As an instrument of execution, the cross, besides being the intersection of two beams with four projecting arms, was frequently of compound forms as Y, on which the convicted person was fastened by the feet and hung head downward. Another form Π, whereon he was

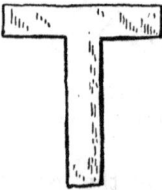

Fig. 5.

TAU CROSS, THOR'S HAMMER, OR ST. ANTHONY'S CROSS.

Fig. 6.

MONOGRAM OF CHRIST.
Labarum of Constantine.

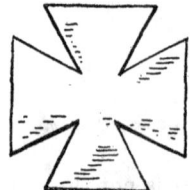

Fig. 7.

MALTESE CROSS.

fastened by one foot and one hand at each upper corner; still another form Ψ, whereon his body was suspended on the central upright with his arms outstretched upon the cross beams.

Fig. 7 represents the sign of the military order of the Knights of Malta. It is of medieval origin.

Fig. 8 (*a* and *b*) represents two styles of Celtic crosses. These belong chiefly to Ireland and Scotland, are usually of stone, and frequently set up at marked places on the road side.

Higgins, in his "Anacalypsis," a rare and costly work, almost an encyclopedia of knowledge,[1] says, concerning the origin of the cross, that
the official name of the governor of Tibet, Lama, comes from the ancient
Tibetan word for the cross. The original spelling was L-a-m-h. This
is cited with approval in Davenport's
"Aphrodisiacs" (p. 13).

Of the many forms of the cross,
the Swastika is the most ancient.
Despite the theories and speculations
of students, its origin is unknown. It
began before history, and is properly
classed as prehistoric. Its description is as follows: The bars of the
normal Swastika (frontispiece and
fig. 9) are straight, of equal thickness
throughout, and cross each other at

Fig. 8.

CELTIC CROSSES.

right angles, making four arms of equal size, length, and style. Their
peculiarity is that all the ends are bent at right angles and in the same

Fig. 9.

NORMAL SWASTIKA.

Fig. 10.

SUAVASTIKA.

direction, right or left. Prof. Max
Müller makes the symbol different
according as the arms are bent to the
right or to the left. That bent to the
right he denominates the true Swastika, that bent to the left he calls
Suavastika (fig. 10), but he gives no
authority for the state-
ment, and the author has
been unable to find, ex-

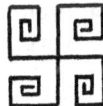

Fig. 11.

SWASTIKA.

Meander.

cept in Burnouf, any justification for a difference of names.
Professor Goodyear gives the title of "Meander" to that
form of Swastika which bends two or more times (fig. 11).

The Swastika is sometimes represented with dots or
points in the corners of the intersections (fig. 12a), and occasionally
the same when without bent ends (fig. 12b), to which Zmigrodzki gives

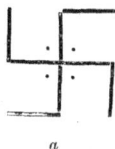

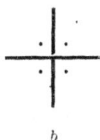

a

b

c

Fig. 12.

CROIX SWASTICALE (ZMIGRODZKI).

the name of *Croix Swasticale.* Some Swastikas have three dots placed
equidistant around each of the four ends (fig. 12c).

[1] Higgins, "Anacalypsis," London, 1836, I, p. 230.

There are several varieties possibly related to the Swastika which have been found in almost every part of the globe, and though the relation may appear slight, and at first sight difficult to trace, yet it will appear more or less intimate as the examination is pursued through its ramifications. As this paper is an investigation into and report upon facts rather than conclusions to be drawn from them, it is deemed wise to give those forms bearing even possible relations to the Swastika. Certain of them have been accepted by the author as related to the Swastika, while others have been rejected; but this rejection

Fig. 13a.
OGEE AND SPIRAL SWASTIKAS.
Tetraskelion (four-armed).

Fig. 13b.
SPIRAL AND VOLUTE.
Triskelion (three-armed).

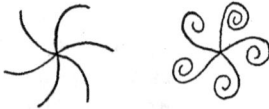

Fig. 13c.
SPIRAL AND VOLUTE.
(Five or many armed.)

Fig. 13d.
OGEE SWASTIKA, WITH
CIRCLE.

PECULIAR FORMS OF SWASTIKA.

has been confined to cases where the known facts seemed to justify another origin for the symbol. Speculation has been avoided.

NAMES AND DEFINITIONS OF THE SWASTIKA.

The Swastika has been called by different names in different countries, though nearly all countries have in later years accepted the ancient Sanskrit name of Swastika; and this name is recommended as the most definite and certain, being now the most general and, indeed, almost universal. It was formerly spelled s-v-a-s-t-i-c-a and s-u-a-s-t-i-k-a, but the later spelling, both English and French, is s-w-a-s-t-i-k-a. The definition and etymology of the word is thus given in Littre's French Dictionary:

Svastika, or Swastika, a mystic figure used by several (East) Indian sects. It was equally well known to the Brahmins as to the Buddhists. Most of the rock inscriptions in the Buddhist caverns in the west of India are preceded or followed by the holy (sacramentelle) sign of the Swastika. (Eug. Burnouf, "Le Lotus de la bonne loi." Paris, 1852, p. 625.) It was seen on the vases and pottery of Rhodes (Cyprus) and Etruria. (F. Delaunay, Jour. Off., Nov. 18, 1873, p. 7024, 3d Col.)

Etymology: A Sanskrit word signifying happiness, pleasure, good luck. It is composed of Su (equivalent of Greek εὖ), "good," and asti, "being," "good being," with the suffix ka (Greek κα, Latin co).

In the "Revue d'Ethnographie" (ɪᴠ, 1885, p. 329), Mr. Dumoutier gives the following analysis of the Sanskrit *swastika*:

Su, radical, signifying *good, well, excellent*, or *suvidas*, prosperity.
Asti, third person, singular, indicative present of the verb *as*, to be, which is *sum* in Latin.
Ka, suffix forming the substantive.

Professor Whitney in the Century Dictionary says, Swastika—[Sanskrit, lit., "of good fortune." Svasti (*Su*, well, + *asti*, being), welfare.] Same as fylfot. Compare *Crux ansata* and *gammadion*.

In "Ilios" (p. 347), Max Müller says:

Ethnologically, *svastika* is derived from *srasti*, and *svasti* from *su*, "well," and *as*, "to be." *Svasti* occurs frequently in the Veda, both as a noun in a sense of happiness, and as an adverb in the sense of "well" or "hail!" It corresponds to the Greek εὐεστώ. The derivation *Svasti-ka* is of later date, and it always means an auspicious sign, such as are found most frequently among Buddhists and Jainas.

M. Eugène Burnouf[1] defines the mark Swastika as follows:

A monogrammatic sign of four branches, of which the ends are curved at right angles, the name signifying, literally, the sign of benediction or good augury.

The foregoing explanations relate only to the present accepted name "Swastika." The *sign* Swastika must have existed long before the *name* was given to it. It must have been in existence long before the Buddhist religion or the Sanskrit language.

In Great Britain the common name given to the Swastika from Anglo-Saxon times by those who apparently had no knowledge whence it came, or that it came from any other than their own country, was Fylfot, said to have been derived from the Anglo-Saxon *fower fot*, meaning four-footed, or many-footed.[2]

George Waring, in his work entitled "Ceramic Art in Remote Ages" (p. 10), says:

The word [Fylfot] is Scandinavian and is compounde᷉ of Old Norse *fïel*, equivalent to the Anglo-Saxon *fela*, German *viel*, many, and *fotr*, foot, the many-footed figure. * * * It is desirable to have some settled name by which to describe it· we will take the simplest and most descriptive, the "Fylfot."

He thus transgresses one of the oldest and soundest rules of scientific nomenclature, and ignores the fact that the name Swastika has been employed for this sign in the Sanskrit language (the etymology of the word naturally gave it the name Svastika, *sv*—good or well, *asti*—to be or being, or it is) and that two thousand and more years of use in Asia and Europe had sanctioned and sanctified that as its name. The use of Fylfot is confined to comparatively few persons in Great Britain

---

[1] "Des Sciences et Religion," p. 256.

[2] R. P. Greg, "The Fylfot and Swastika," Archæologia, xʟᴠɪɪɪ, part 2, 1885, p. 298; Goblet d'Alviella, "Migration des Symboles," p. 50.

and, possibly, Scandinavia. Outside of these countries it is scarcely known, used, or understood.

The Swastika was occasionally called in the French language, in earlier times, *Croix gammée* or *Gammadion,* from its resemblance to a combination of four of the Greek letters of that name, and it is so named by Count Goblet d'Alviella in his late work, "La Migration des Symboles." It was also called *Croix cramponnée, Croix pattée, Croix à crochet.* But the consensus even of French etymologists favors the name Swastika.

Some foreign authors have called it Thor's hammer, or Thor's hammer-mark, but the correctness of this has been disputed.[1] Waring, in his elaborate work, "Ceramic Art in Remote Ages,"[2] says:

The ⌐┴ used to be vulgarly called in Scandinavia the hammer of Thor, and Thor's hammer-mark, or the hammer-mark, but this name properly belongs to the mark Y.

Ludwig Müller gives it as his opinion that the Swastika has no connection with the Thor hammer. The best Scandinavian authors report the "Thor hammer" to be the same as the Greek tau (fig. 5), the same form as the Roman and English capital T. The Scandinavian name is Miölner or Mjolner, the crusher or mallet.

The Greek, Latin, and Tau crosses are represented in Egyptian hieroglyphics by a hammer or mallet, giving the idea of crushing, pounding, or striking, and so an instrument of justice, an avenger of wrong,[3] hence standing for Horus and other gods.[4] Similar symbolic meanings have been given to these crosses in ancient classic countries of the Orient.[5]

SYMBOLISM AND INTERPRETATION.

Many theories have been presented concerning the symbolism of the Swastika, its relation to ancient deities and its representation of certain qualities. In the estimation of certain writers it has been respectively the emblem of Zeus, of Baal, of the sun, of the sun-god, of the sun-chariot of Agni the fire-god, of Indra the rain-god, of the sky, the sky-god, and finally the deity of all deities, the great God, the Maker and Ruler of the Universe. It has also been held to symbolize light or the god of light, of the forked lightning, and of water. It is believed by some to have been the oldest Aryan symbol. In the estimation of others it represents Brahma, Vishnu, and Siva, Creator, Preserver, Destroyer. It appears in the footprints of Buddha, engraved upon the

---

[1] Stephens, "Old Northern Runic Monuments," part II, p. 509; Ludwig Müller, quoted on p. 778 of this paper; Goblet d'Alviella, "La Migration des Symboles," p. 45; Haddon, "Evolution in Art," p. 288.

[2] Page 12.

[3] "La Migration des Symboles," pp. 21, 22.

[4] "Le Culte de la Croix avant Jésus-Christ," in the Correspondant, October 25, 1889, and in Science Catholique, February 15, 1890, p. 163.

[5] Same authorities.

solid rock on the mountains of India (fig. 32). It stood for the Jupiter Tonans and Pluvius of the Latins, and the Thor of the Scandinavians. In the latter case it has been considered—erroneously, however—a variety of the Thor hammer. In the opinion of at least one author it had an intimate relation to the Lotus sign of Egypt and Persia. Some authors have attributed a phallic meaning to it. Others have recognized it as representing the generative principle of mankind, making it the symbol of the female. Its appearance on the person of certain goddesses, Artemis, Hera, Demeter, Astarte, and the Chaldean Nana, the leaden goddess from Hissarlik (fig. 125), has caused it to be claimed as a sign of fecundity.

In forming the foregoing theories their authors have been largely controlled by the alleged fact of the substitution and permutation of the Swastika sign on various objects with recognized symbols of these different deities. The claims of these theorists are somewhat clouded in obscurity and lost in the antiquity of the subject. What seems to have been at all times an attribute of the Swastika is its character as a charm or amulet, as a sign of benediction, blessing, long life, good fortune, good luck. This character has continued into modern times, and while the Swastika is recognized as a holy and sacred symbol by at least one Buddhistic religious sect, it is still used by the common people of India, China, and Japan as a sign of long life, good wishes, and good fortune.

Whatever else the sign Swastika may have stood for, and however many meanings it may have had, it was always ornamental. It may have been used with any or all the above significations, but it was always ornamental as well.

The Swastika sign had great extension and spread itself practically over the world, largely, if not entirely, in prehistoric times, though its use in some countries has continued into modern times.

The elaboration of the meanings of the Swastika indicated above and its dispersion or migrations form the subject of this paper.

Dr. Schliemann found many specimens of Swastika in his excavations at the site of ancient Troy on the hill of Hissarlik. They were mostly on spindle whorls, and will be described in due course. He appealed to Prof. Max Müller for an explanation, who, in reply, wrote an elaborate description, which Dr. Schliemann published in "Ilios.'"

He commences with a protest against the word Swastika being applied generally to the sign Swastika, because it may prejudice the reader or the public in favor of its Indian origin. He says:

I do not like the use of the *word svastika* outside of India. It is a *word* of Indian origin and has its history and definite meaning in India. * * * The occurrence of such crosses in different parts of the world may or may not point to a common origin, but if they are once called *Svastika* the *vulgus profanum* will at once

---

[1] Page 346, et seq.

jump to the conclusion that they all come from India, and it will take some time to weed out such prejudice.

Very little is known of Indian art before the third century B. C., the period when the Buddhist sovereigns began their public buildings.[1]

The name Svastika, however, can be traced (in India) a little farther back. It occurs as the name of a particular sign in the old grammar of Pânani, about a century earlier. Certain compounds are mentioned there in which the last word is *karna*, "ear." * * * One of the signs for marking cattle was the Svastika [fig. 41], and what Pânani teaches in his grammar is that when the compound is formed, *svastika-karna*, i. e., "having the ear marked with the sign of a Svastika," the final *a* of Svastika is not to be lengthened, while it is lengthened in other compounds, such as *datra-karna*, i. e., "having the ear marked with the sign of a sickle."

D'Alviella[2] reinforces Max Müller's statement that Panini lived during the middle of the fourth century, B. C. Thus it is shown that the word Swastika had been in use at that early period long enough to form an integral part of the Sanskrit language and that it was employed to illustrate the particular sounds of the letter *a* in its grammar.

Max Müller continues his explanation:[3]

It [the Swastika] occurs often at the beginning of the Buddhist inscriptions, on Buddhist coins, and in Buddhist manuscripts. Historically, the Svastika is first attested on a coin of Krananda, supposing Krananda to be the same king as Xandrames, the predecessor of Sandrokyptos, whose reign came to an end in 315 B. C. (See Thomas on the Identity of Xandrames and Krananda.) The paleographic evidence, however, seems rather against so early a date. In the footprints of Buddha the Buddhists recognize no less that sixty-five auspicious signs, the first of them being the *Svastika* [see fig. 32], (Eugene Burnouf, "Lotus de la bonne loi," p. 625); the fourth is the *Suavastika*, or that with the arms turned to the left [see fig. 10]; the third, the *Nandyâvarta* [see fig. 14], is a mere development of the *Svastika*. Among the Jainas the *Svastika* was the sign of their seventh Jina, Supârsva (Colebrooke "Miscellaneous Essays," II, p. 188; Indian Antiquary, vol. 2, p. 135).

In the later Sanskrit literature, *Svastika* retains the meaning of an auspicious mark; thus we see in the Râmâyana (ed. Gorresio, II, p. 348) that Bharata selects a ship marked with the sign of the Svastika. Varâhamihira in the Brihat-samhitâ (Med. Sæc., VI, p. Ch.) mentions certain buildings called Svastika and Nandyâvarta (53.34, seq.), but their outline does not correspond very exactly with the form of the signs. Some Sthûpas, however, are said to have been built on the plan of the Svastika. * * * Originally, *svastika* may have been intended for no more than two lines crossing each other, or a cross. Thus we find it used in later times referring to a woman covering her breast with crossed arms (Bâlarâm, 75.16), *svahastas-vastika-stani*, and likewise with reference to persons sitting crosslegged.

Dr. Max Ohnefalsch-Richter[4] speaking of the Swastika position, either of crossed legs or arms, among the Hindus,[5] suggests as a possible explanation that these women bore the Swastikas upon their

---

[1] The native Buddhist monarchs ruled from about B. C. 500 to the conquest of Alexander, B. C. 330. See "The Swastika on ancient coins," Chapter II of this paper, and Waring, "Ceramic Art in Remote Ages," p. 83.

[2] "La Migration des symboles," p. 104.

[3] "Ilios," pp. 347, 348.

[4] Bulletins de la Sociètè d'Anthropologie, 1888, p. 678.

[5] Mr. Gandhi makes the same remark in his letter on the Buddha shell statue shown in pl. 10 of this paper.

arms as did the goddess Aphrodite, in fig. 8 of his writings, (see fig. 180 in the present paper), and when they assumed the position of arms crossed over their breast, the Swastikas being brought into prominent view, possibly gave the name to the position as being a representative of the sign.

Max Müller continues[1]:

Quite another question is, why the sign ⊔⌐ should have had an auspicious meaning, and why in Sanskrit it should have been called Svastika. The similarity between the group of letters *sv* in the ancient Indian alphabet and the sign of Svastika is not very striking, and seems purely accidental.

A remark of yours [Schliemann] (Troy, p. 38) that the Svastika resembles a wheel in motion, the direction of the motion being indicated by the crampons, contains a useful hint, which has been confirmed by some important observations of Mr. Thomas, the distinguished Oriental numismatist, who has called attention to the fact that in the long list of the recognized devices of the twenty-four Jaina Tirthankaras the sun is absent, but that while the eighth Tirthankara has the sign of the half-moon, the seventh Tirthankara is marked with the Svastika, i. e., the sun. Here, then, we have clear indications that the Svastika, with the hands pointing in the right direction, was originally a symbol of the sun, perhaps of the vernal sun as opposed to the autumnal sun, the *Suavastika*, and, therefore, a natural symbol of light, life, health, and wealth.

But, while from these indications we are justified in supposing that among the Aryan nations the Svastika may have been an old emblem of the sun, there are other indications to show that in other parts of the world the same or a similar emblem was used to indicate the earth. Mr. Beal * * * has shown * * * that the simple cross (+) occurs as a sign for earth in certain ideographic groups. It was probably intended to indicate the four quarters—north, south, east, west—or, it may be, more generally, extension in length and breadth.

That the cross is used as a sign for "four" in the Bactro-Pali inscriptions (Max Müller, "Chips from a German Workshop," Vol. II, p. 298) is well known; but the fact that the same sign has the same power elsewhere, as, for instance, in the Hieratic numerals, does not prove by any means that the one figure was derived from the other. We forget too easily that what was possible in one place was possible also in other places; and the more we extend our researches, the more we shall learn that the chapter of accidents is larger than we imagine.

The "Suavastika" which Max Müller names and believes was applied to the Swastika sign, with the ends bent to the left (fig. 10), seems not to be reported with that meaning by any other author except Burnouf.[2] Therefore the normal Swastika would seem to be that with the ends bent to the right. Burnouf says the word Suavastika may be a derivative or development of the Svastikaya, and ought to signify "he who, or, that which, bears or carries the Swastika or a species of Swastika." Greg,[3] under the title Sôvastikaya, gives it as his opinion that there is no difference between it and the Swastika. Colonel Low[4] mentions the word Sawattheko, which, according to Burnouf[5] is only a variation of

---

[1] "Ilios," p. 348.

[2] "Lotus de la Bonne Loi," App. VIII, p. 626, note 4.

[3] Archæologia, p. 36.

[4] Transactions of the Royal Asiatic Society of Great Britain, III, p. 120.

[5] "Lotus de la Bonne Loi," App. VIII, p. 625, note 2.

the Pali word Sotthika or Suvatthika, the Pali translation of the San-skrit Swastika. Burnouf translates it as Svastikaya.

M. Eugene Burnouf[1] speaks of a third sign of the footprint of Çakya, called Nandâvartaya, a good augury, the meaning being the "circle of fortune," which is the Swastika inclosed within a square with avenues radiating from the corners (fig. 14). Burnouf says the above sign has many significations. It is a sacred temple or edifice, a species of laby-rinth, a garden of diamonds, a chain, a golden waist or shoulder belt, and a conique with spires turning to the right.

Colonel Sykes[2] concludes that, according to the Chinese authorities Fa-hian, Soung Young, Hiuan thsang, the "Doctors of reason,'Tao-sse, or followers of the mystic cross ⊞ were diffused in China and India before the advent of Sakya in the sixth century B. C. (according to Chinese, Japanese, and Buddhist authorities, the eleventh century B. C.), continuing until Fa-hian's time; and that they were professors of a qualified Buddhism, which, it is stated, was the universal religion of Tibet before Sakya's advent,[3] and continued until the introduction of orthodox Buddhism in the ninth century A. D.[4]

Klaproth[5] calls attention to the frequent men-tion by Fa-hian, of the Tao-sse, sectaries of the mystic cross ⊞ (Sanskrit Swastika), and to their existence in Central Asia and India; while he says they were diffused over the countries to the west and southwest of China, and came annually from all kingdoms and countries to adore Kassapo, Buddha's predecessor.[6] Mr. James Burgess[7] mentions the Tirthanka-ras or Jainas as being sectarians of the Mystic Cross, the Swastika.

Fig. 14.

NANDÂVARTAYA, A THIRD SIGN OF THE FOOTPRINT OF BUDDHA.

Burnouf, "Lotus de la Bonne Loi," Paris, 1852, p. 626.

The Cyclopædia of India (title Swastika), coinciding with Prof. Max Müller, says:

The Swastika symbol is not to be confounded with the Swastika sect in Tibet which took the symbol for its name as typical of the belief of its members. They render the Sanskrit Swastika as composed of su "well" and asti "it is," meaning, as Professor Wilson expresses it, "so be it," and implying complete resignation under all circumstances. They claimed the Swastika of Sanskrit as the *suti* of Pali, and that the Swastika cross was a combination of the two symbols *sutti-suti*. They are rationalists, holding that contentment and peace of mind should be the only objects of life. The sect has preserved its existence in different localities and under different names, Thirthankara, Ter, Musteg, Pon, the last name meaning purity, under which a remnant are still in the farthest parts of the most eastern province of Tibet.

---

[1] "Lotus de la Bonne Loi," p. 626.

[2] "Notes on the Religious, Moral, and Political state of India," Journ. Asiatic Soc. Great Britain, VI, pp. 310–334.

[3] Low, Trans. Roy. Asiatic Soc. of Great Britain III, pp. 334, 310.

[4] Ibid., p. 299.

[5] Ibid., p. 299.

[6] Low, Trans. Royal Asiatic Soc. of Great Britain, III, p. 310.

[7] Indian Antiquary, II, May, 1873, p. 135.

General Cunningham[1] adds his assertion of the Swastika being the symbol used by the Buddhist sect of that name. He says in a note:

The founder of this sect flourished about the year 604 to 523 B. C., and that the mystic cross is a symbol formed by the combination of the two Sanskrit syllables *su* and *ti-suti*.

Waring[2] proceeds to demolish these statements of a sect named Swastika as pure inventions, and " consulting Professor Wilson's invaluable work on the Hindoo religious sects in the 'Asiatic Researches,' we find no account of any sect named Swastika."

Mr. V. R. Gandhi, a learned legal gentleman of Bombay, a representative of the Jain sect of Buddhists to the World's Parliament of Religions at Chicago, 1893, denies that there is in either India or Tibet a sect of Buddhists named "Swastika." He suggests that these gentlemen probably mean the sects of Jains (of which Mr. Gandhi is a member), because this sect uses the Swastika as a sign of benediction and blessing. This will be treated further on. (See p. 804.)

Zmigrodzki, commenting on the frequency of the Swastika on the objects found by Dr. Schliemann at Hissarlik, gives it as his opinion[3] that these representations of the Swastika have relation to a human cult indicating a supreme being filled with goodness toward man. The sun, stars, etc., indicate him as a god of light. This, in connection with the idol of Venus, with its triangular shield engraved with a Swastika (fig. 125), and the growing trees and palms, with their increasing and multiplying branches and leaves, represent to him the idea of fecundity, multiplication, increase, and hence the god of life as well as of light. The Swastika sign on funeral vases indicates to him a belief in a divine spirit in man which lives after death, and hence he concludes that the people of Hissarlik, in the "Burnt City" (the third of Schliemann), adored a supreme being, the god of light and of life, and believed in the immortality of the soul.

R. P. Greg says:[4]

Originally it [the Swastika] would appear to have been an early Aryan atmospheric device or symbol indicative of both rain and lightning, phenomena appertaining to the god Indra, subsequently or collaterally developing, possibly, into the Suastika, or sacred fire churn in India, and at a still later period in Greece, adopted rather as a solar symbol, or converted about B. C. 650 into the meander or key pattern.

Waring, while he testifies to the extension of the Swastika both in time and area, says:[5]

But neither in the hideous jumble of Pantheism—the wild speculative thought, mystic fables, and perverted philosophy of life among the Buddhists—nor in the equally wild and false theosophy of the Brahmins, to whom this symbol, as distinc-

---

[1] "Bilsa Topes," p. 17.

[2] "Ceramic Art in Remote Ages," p. 12.

[3] Tenth Congress International d'Anthropologie et d'Archæologie Prehistoriques, Paris, 1889, p. 474.

[4] Archæologia, XLVII, pt. 1, p. 159.

[5] "Ceramic Art in Remote Ages," p. 11.

tive of the Vishnavas, sectarian devotees of Vishnu, is ascribed by Moor in his "Indian Pantheon," nor yet in the tenets of the Jains,[1] do we find any decisive explanation of the meaning attached to this symbol, although its allegorical intention is indubitable.

He mentions the Swastika of the Buddhists, the cross, the circle, their combination, the three-foot Y and adds: "They exhibit forms of those olden and widely spread pagan symbols of Deity and sanctity, eternal life and blessing."

Professor Sayce says:[2]

The Cyprian vase figured in Di Cesnola's "Cyprus," pl. XLV, fig. 36 [see fig. 156], which associates the Swastika with the figure of an animal, is a striking analogue of the Trojan whorls on which it is associated with the figures of stags. The fact that it is drawn within the vulva of the leaden image of the Asiatic goddess [see fig. 125] seems to show that it was a symbol of generation. I believe that it is identical with the Cyprian character $\mathcal{J\!f}$ or ⵏ (ne), which has the form)ᛡ in the inscription of Golgi, and also with the Hittite ᚵ or ⵏ which Dr. Hyde Clarke once suggested to me was intended to represent the organs of generation.

Mr. Waller, in his work entitled "Monumental Crosses," describes the Swastika as having been known in India as a sacred symbol many centuries before our Lord, and used as the distinguishing badge of a religious sect calling themselves "Followers of the Mystic Cross." Subsequently, he says, it was adopted by the followers of Buddha and was still later used by Christians at a very early period, being first introduced on Christian monuments in the sixth century. But Mr. Waring says that in this he is not correct, as it was found in some of the early paintings in the Roman catacombs, particularly on the habit of a *Fossor*, or gravedigger, given by D'Agincourt.

Pugin, in his "Glossary of Ornament," under the title "Fylfot," says that in Tibet the Swastika was used as a representation of God crucified for the human race, citing as his authority F. Augustini Antonii Georgii.[3] He remarks:

From these accounts it would appear that the fylfot is a mystical ornament, not only adopted among Christians from primitive times, but used, as if prophetically, for centuries before the coming of our Lord. To descend to later times, we find it constantly introduced in ecclesiastical vestments, * * * till the end of the fifteenth century, a period marked by great departure from traditional symbolism.

Its use was continued in Tibet into modern times, though its meaning is not given.[4] (See p. 802.)

The Rev. G. Cox, in his "Aryan Mythology," says:

We recognize the male and the female symbol in the trident of Poseidon, and in the fylfot or hammer of Thor, which assumes the form of a cross-pattée in the various legends which turn on the rings of Freya, Holda, Venus, or Aphrodite.

---

[1] See explanation of the Swastika by Mr. Gandhi according to the Jain tenets, p. 804.

[2] "Ilios," p. 353.

[3] "Alphabetum Tibetarium," Rome, 1762, pp. 211, 460, 725.

[4] Rockhill, "Diary of a Journey through Mongolia and Tibet," Smithsonian Institution, Washington, 1894, p. 67.

Here again we find the fylfot and cross-pattèe spoken of as the same symbol, and as being emblematic of the reproductive principles, in which view of its meaning Dr. Inman, in his "Ancient Faiths Embodied in Ancient Names," concurs.

Burnouf[1] recounts the myth of Agni (from which comes, through the Latin *ignis*, the English word igneous), the god of Sacred Fire, as told in the Veda:[2]

The young queen, the mother of Fire, carried the royal infant mysteriously concealed in her bosom. She was a woman of the people, whose common name was "Arani"—that is, the instrument of wood (the Swastika) from which fire was made or brought by rubbing. * * * The origin of the sign [Swastika] is now easy to recognize. It represents the two pieces of wood which compose *l'arani*, of which the extremities were bent to be retained by the four nails. At the junction of the two pieces of wood was a fossette or cup-like hole, and there they placed a piece of wood upright, in form of a lance (the Pramantha), violent rotation of which, by whipping (after the fashion of top-whipping), produced fire, as did Prometheus, the *porteur du feu*, in Greece.

And this myth was made, as have been others, probably by the priests and poets of succeeding times, to do duty for different philosophies. The Swastika was made to represent Arani (the female principle); the Pramantha or upright fire stake representing Agni, the fire god (the male); and so the myth served its part to account for the birth of fire. Burnouf hints that the myth grew out of the production of holy fire for the sacred altars by the use of the Pramantha and Swastika, after the manner of savages in all times. Zmigrodzki accepts this myth, and claims all specimens with dots or points—supposed nail holes—as Swastikas.

The Count Goblet d'Alviella[3] argues in opposition to the theory announced by Burnouf and by Zmigrodzki, that the Swastika or croix swasticale, when presenting dots or points, had relation to fire making. He denies that the points represent nails, or that nails were made or necessary either for the Swastika or the Arani, and concludes that there is no evidence to support the theory, and nothing to show the Swastika to have been used as a fire-making apparatus, whether with or without the dots or points.

Mr. Greg[4] opposes this entire theory, saying:

The difficulty about the Swastika and its supposed connection with fire appears to me to lie in not knowing precisely what the old fire drill and chark were like. * * * I much doubt whether the Swastika had originally any connection either with the fire-chark or with the sun. * * * The best authorities consider Burnouf is in error as to the earlier use of the two lower cross pieces of wood and the four nails said to have been used to fix or steady the framework.

He quotes from Tylor's description[5] of the old fire drill used in India

---

[1] "Des Sciences et Religion," pp. 252, 257.
[2] Vol. XI.
[3] "La Migration des Symboles," pp. 61-63.
[4] Archæologia, XLVIII, pt. 2, pp. 322, 323.
[5] "Early History of Mankind," p. 257, note C.

for kindling the sacrificial fire by the process called "churning," as it resembles that in India by which butter is separated from milk. It consists in drilling one piece of Arani wood by pulling a cord with one hand while the other is slackened, and so, alternately (the strap drill), till the wood takes fire. Mr. Greg states that the Eskimos use similar means, and the ancient Greeks used the drill and cord, and he adds his conclusions: "There is nothing of the Swastika and four nails in connection with the fire-churn."

Burton[1] also criticises Burnouf's theory:

If used on sacrificial altars to reproduce the holy fire, the practice is peculiar and not derived from everyday life; for as early as Pliny they knew that the savages used two, and never three, fire sticks.

Burnouf continues his discussion of myths concerning the origin of fire:

According to Hymnes, the discoverer of fire was Atharan, whose name signifies fire, but Bhrigon it was who made the sacred fire, producing resplendent flames on the earthen altar. In theory of physics, Agni, who was the fire residing within the "onction," (?) came from the milk of the cow, which, in its turn, came from the plants that had nourished her; and these plants in their turn grew by receiving and appropriating the heat or fire of the sun. Therefore, the virtue of the "onction" came from the god.

One of the Vedas says of Agni, the god of fire:[2]

> Agni, thou art a sage, a priest, a king,
> Protector, father of the sacrifice;
> Commissioned by our men thou dost ascend
> A messenger, conveying to the sky
> Our hymns and offerings, though thy origin
> Be three fold, now from air and now from water,
> Now from the mystic double *Arani*.[3]

Count Goblet d'Alviella combats the hypothesis of Burnouf that the Swastika when turned to right or left, passed, the one for the male and the other for the female principle, and declares, on the authority of Sir George Birdwood, that it is, in modern India, a popular custom to name objects which appear in couples as having different sexes, so that to say "the male Swastika" and the "female Swastika," indicating them by the pronouns "he" or "she," would be expressed in the same manner when speaking of the hammer and the anvil or of any other objects used in pairs.[4]

Ludwig Müller, in his elaborate treatise, gives it as his opinion that the Swastika had no connection with the Tau cross or with the *Crux ansata*, or with the fire wheel, or with arani, or agni, or with the mystic or alphabetic letters, nor with the so-called spokes of the solar wheel, nor the forked lightning, nor the hammer of Thor. He considers that the tris-

---

[1] "The Book of the Sword," p. 202, note 2.

[2] Burnouf, "Des Sciences et Religion," p. 18.

[3] The two pieces of wood of *Ficus religiosa*, used for kindling fire.

[4] "La Migration des Symboles," p. 63.

kelion might throw light on its origin, as indicating perpetual whirling or circular movement, which, in certain parts of southern Asia as the emblem of Zeus, was assimilated to that of Baal, an inference which he draws from certain Asiatic coins of 400 B. C.

Mr. R. P. Greg[1] opposes this theory and expresses the opinion that the Swastika is far older and wider spread as a symbol than the tris-kelion, as well as being a more purely Aryan symbol. Greg says that Ludwig Müller attaches quite too much importance to the sun in con-nection with the early Aryans, and lays too great stress upon the sup-posed relation of the Swastika as a solar symbol. The Aryans, he says, were a race not given to sun worship; and, while he may agree with Müller that the Swastika is an emblem of Zeus and Jupiter merely as the Supreme God, yet he believes that the origin of the Swastika had no reference to a movement of the sun through the heavens; and he prefers his own theory that it was a device suggested by the forked lightning as the chief weapon of the air god.

Mr. Greg's paper is of great elaboration, and highly complicated. He devotes an entire page or plate (21) to a chart showing the older Aryan fire, water, and sun gods, according to the Brahmin or Buddhist system. The earliest was Dyaus, the bright sky or the air god; Adyti, the infinite expanse, mother of bright gods; Varuna, the covering of the shining firmament. Out of this trinity came another, Zeus, being the descendant of Dyaus, the sky god; Agni, the fire; Sulya, the sun, and Indra, the rain god. These in their turn formed the great Hindu trinity, Brahma, Vishnu, and Siva—creator, preserver, and destroyer; and, in his opinion, the Swastika was the symbol or ordinary device of Indra as well as of Zeus. He continues his table of descent from these gods, with their accompanying devices, to the sun, lightning, fire, and water, and makes almost a complete scheme of the mythology of that period, into which it is not possible to follow him. However, he declines to accept the theory of Max Müller of any difference of form or mean-ing between the Suavastika and the Swastika because the ends or arms turned to the right or to the left, and he thinks the two symbols to be substantially the same. He considers it to have been, in the first instance, exclusively of early Aryan origin and use, and that down to about 600 B. C. it was the emblem or symbol of the supreme Aryan god; that it so continued down through the various steps of descent (according to the chart mentioned) until it became the device and sym-bol of Brahma, and finally of Buddha. He thinks that it may have been the origin of the Greek fret or meander pattern. Later still it was adopted even by the early Christians as a suitable variety of their cross, and became variously modified in form and was used as a charm.

D'Alviella[2] expresses his doubts concerning the theory advanced by Greg[3] to the effect that the Swastika is to be interpreted as a symbol

[1] Archæologia, XLIII, pt. 2, pp. 324, 325.
[2] "La Migration des Symboles," p. 64.
[3] "Fylfot and Swastika," Archæologia, 1885, p. 293.

of the air or of the god who dwells in the air, operating sometimes to produce light, other times rain, then water, and so on, as is represented by the god Indra among the Hindus, Thor among the Germans and Scandinavians, Perkun among the Slavs, Zeus among the Pelasgi and Greeks, Jupiter Tonans, and Pluvius among the Latins. He disputes the theory that the association of the Swastika sign with various others on the same object proves its relationship with that object or sign. That it appears on vases or similar objects associated with what is evidently a solar disk is no evidence to him that the Swastika belongs to the sun, or when associated with the zigzags of lightning that it represents the god of lightning, nor the same with the god of heaven. The fact of its appearing either above or below any one of these is, in his opinion, of no importance and has no signification, either general or special.

D'Alviella says[1] that the only example known to him of a Swastika upon a monument consecrated to Zeus or Jupiter is on a Celto-Roman altar, erected, according to all appearances, by the Daci during the time they were garrisoned at Ambloganna, in Britain. The altar bears the letters I. O. M., which have been thought to stand for Jupiter Optimus Maximus. The Swastika thereon is flanked by two disks or rouelles, with four rays, a sign which M. Gaidoz believes to have been a representative of the sun among the Gaulois.[2]

Dr. Brinton[3] considers the Swastika as being related to the cross and not to the circle, and asserts that the Ta Ki or Triskeles, the Swastika and the Cross, were originally of the same signification, or at least closely allied in meaning.

Waring,[4] after citing his authorities, sums up his opinion thus:

We have given remarks of the various writers on this symbol, and it will be seen that, though they are more or less vague, uncertain, and confused in their description of it, still, with one exception, they all agree that it is a mystic symbol, peculiar to some deity or other, bearing a special signification, and generally believed to have some connection with one of the elements—water.

Burton says:[5]

The Svastika is apparently the simplest form of the Guilloche [scroll pattern or spiral]. According to Wilkinson (11, Chap. IX), the most complicated form of the Guilloche covered an Egyptian ceiling upward of a thousand years older than the objects found at Nineveh. The Svastika spread far and wide, everywhere assuming some fresh mythological and mysterious significance. In the north of Europe it became the Fylfot or Crutched cross.

Count Goblet d'Alviella is of the opinion (p. 57) that the Swastika was "above all an amulet, talisman, or phylactere," while (p. 56) "it is incontestable that a great number of the Swastikas were simply motifs

---

[1] "La Migration des Symboles," p. 65.
[2] "Le Dieu gaulois du Soleil et le symbolisme de la roue," Paris, 1886.
[3] Proc. Amer. Philosoph. Soc., 1889, pp. 177–187.
[4] "Ceramic Art in Remote Ages."
[5] "The Book of the Sword," p. 202.

of ornamentation, of coin marks, and marks of fabrics," but he agrees
(p. 57) that there is no symbol that has given rise to so many interpretations, not even the *tricula* of the Buddhists, and "this is a great deal
to say." Ludwig Müller believes the Swastika to have been used as an
ornament and as a charm and amulet, as well as a sacred symbol.

Dr. H. Colley March, in his learned paper on the "Fylfot and the
Futhorc Tir,"[1] thinks the Swastika had no relation to fire or fire making
or the fire god. His theory is that it symbolized axial motion and not
merely gyration; that it represented the celestial pole, the axis of the
heavens around which revolve the stars of the firmament. This appearance of rotation is most impressive in the constellation of the Great
Bear. About four thousand years ago the apparent pivot of rotation
was at α *Draconis*, much nearer the Great Bear than now, and at that
time the rapid circular sweep must have been far more striking than at
present. In addition to the name Ursa Major the Latins called this
constellation *Septentriones*, "the seven plowing oxen," that dragged
the stars around the pole, and the Greeks called it ἑλίκη, from its vast
spiral movement.[2] In the opinion of Dr. March all these are represented or symbolized by the Swastika.

Prof. W. H. Goodyear, of New York, has lately (1891) published an
elaborate quarto work entitled "The Grammar of the Lotus: A New
History of Classic Ornament as a Development of Sun Worship."[3] It
comprises 408 pages, with 76 plates, and nearly a thousand figures. His
theory develops the sun symbol from the lotus by a series of ingenious
and complicated evolutions passing through the Ionic style of architecture, the volutes and spirals forming meanders or Greek frets, and
from this to the Swastika. The result is attained by the following line
of argument and illustrations:

The lotus was a "fetish of immemorial antiquity and has been wor-
shiped in many countries from Japan to the Straits of Gibraltar;" it
was a symbol of "fecundity," "life," "immortality," and of "resurrec-
tion," and has a mortuary significance and use. But its elementary
and most important signification was as a solar symbol.[4]

He describes the Egyptian lotus and traces it through an innumerable number of specimens and with great variety of form. He mentions many of the sacred animals of Egypt and seeks to maintain their
relationship by or through the lotus, not only with each other but with
solar circles and the sun worship.[5] Direct association of the solar disk
and lotus are, according to him, common on the monuments and on
Phenician and Assyrian seals; while the lotus and the sacred animals,
as in cases cited of the goose representing Seb (solar god, and father
of Osiris), also Osiris himself and Horus, the hawk and lotus, bull and

---

[1] Trans. Lancaster and Cheshire Antiq. Soc., 1886.
[2] Haddon, "Evolution in Art," London, 1895, p 288.
[3] Sampson, Low, Marston & Co., London.
[4] Goodyear, "The Grammar of the Lotus," pp. 4, 5.
[5] Ibid., p. 6.

lotus, the asp and lotus, the lion and lotus, the sphinx and lotus, the gryphon and lotus, the serpent and lotus, the ram and lotus—all of which animals, and with them the lotus, have, in his opinion, some related signification to the sun or some of his deities.[1] He is of the opinion that the lotus motif was the foundation of the Egyptian style of architecture, and that it appeared at an early date, say, the fourteenth century B. C. By intercommunication with the Greeks it formed the foundation of the Greek Ionic capital, which, he says,[2] "offers no

Fig. 15.

TYPICAL LOTUS ON CYPRIAN
VASES.

Fig. 16.

TYPICAL LOTUS ON RHODIAN
VASES.

Fig. 17.

TYPICAL LOTUS ON MELIAN
VASES.

From figures in Goodyear's "Grammar of the Lotus," p. 77.

dated example of the earlier time than the sixth century B. C." He supports this contention by authority, argument, and illustration.

He shows[3] the transfer of the lotus motif to Greece, and its use as an ornament on the painted vases and on those from Cyprus, Rhodes, and Melos (figs. 15, 16, 17).

Chantre[4] notes the presence of spirals similar to those of fig. 17, in

Fig. 18.

DETAIL OF CYPRIAN VASE SHOWING
LOTUSES WITH CURLING SEPALS.

Metropolitan Museum of Art, New York.
Goodyear, "Grammar of the Lotus," pl. 47, fig. 1.

the terramares of northern Italy and up and down the Danube, and his fig. 186 (fig. 17) he says represents the decorating motif, the most frequent in all that part of prehistoric Europe. He cites "Notes sur les torques ou ornaments spirals."[5]

That the lotus had a foundation deep and wide in Egyptian mythology is not to be denied; that it was allied to and associated on the monuments and other objects with many sacred and mythologic characters in Egypt and afterwards in Greece is accepted. How far it extends in the direction contended for by Professor Goodyear, is no part of this investigation. It appears well established that in both countries it became highly conventionalized, and it is quite sufficient for the purpose of this argument that it became thus associated with the Swastika. Figs. 18 and 19

---

[1] Goodyear, "The Grammar of the Lotus," pp. 7, 8.

[2] Ibid., p. 71.

[3] Ibid., pp. 74, 77.

[4] "Age du Bronze," Deuxieme partie, p. 301.

[5] Matériaux pour l'Histoire Primitive et Naturelle de l'Homme, 3d ser., VIII, p. 6.

represent details of Cyprian vases and amphora belonging to the Cesnola collection in the New York Metropolitan Museum of Art, showing

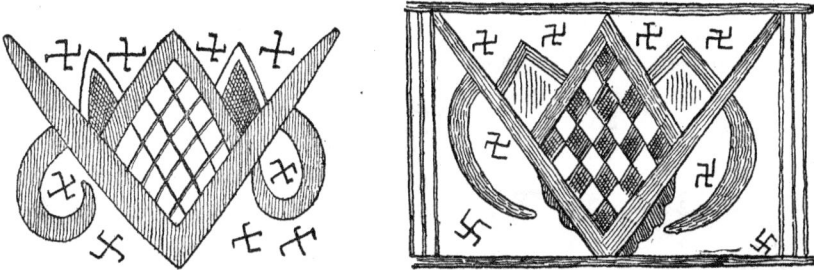

Fig. 19.
DETAIL OF CYPRIAN AMPHORA IN METROPOLITAN MUSEUM OF ART, NEW YORK CITY.
Lotus with curling sepals and different Swastikas.
Goodyear, "Grammar of the Lotus," pl. 47, figs. 2, 3.

the lotus with curling sepals among which are interspersed Swastikas
of different forms.

According to Professor Goodyear,[1] these bent sepals of the lotus were
exaggerated and finally became spir-
als,[2] which, being projected at a
tangent, made volutes, and, continuing one after the other, as shown in
fig. 20, formed bands of ornament;
or,[3] being connected to right and left,
spread the ornament over an extended

Fig. 20.
THEORY OF THE EVOLUTION OF THE SPIRAL
SCROLL FROM LOTUS.
One volute.
Goodyear, "Grammar of the Lotus," fig. 51.

surface as in fig. 21. One of his paths of evolution closed these volutes
and dropped the connecting tangent, when they formed the concentric
rings of which we see so much. Several
forms of Egyptian scarabæi, showing the evolution of concentric rings, are shown in figs.
22, 23, and 24.

By another path of the evolution of his theory, one has only to square the spiral volutes,
and the result is the Greek fret shown in fig.
25.[4] The Greek fret has only to be doubled,
when it produces the Swastika shown in fig.
26.[5] Thus we have, according to him, the origin
of the Swastika, as shown in figs. 27 and 28.[6]

Professor Goodyear is authority for the statement that the earliest dated instances of the
isolated scroll is in the fifth dynasty of Egypt,
and of the lotus and spiral is in the eleventh dynasty. The spiral of
fig. 19 (above) belongs to the twelfth dynasty.[7]

Fig. 21.
THEORY OF LOTUS RUDIMENTS IN
SPIRAL.
Tomb 33, Abd-el Kourneh, Thebes.
Goodyear, "Grammar of the Lotus," p. 96.

---

[1] "Grammar of the Lotus," pl. 8, p. 81.
[2] Ibid., pp. 82–94.
[3] Ibid., p. 96.
[4] Ibid., pl. X, figs. 7–9, p. 97.
[5] Ibid., p. 354.
[6] Ibid., p. 353.
[7] Ibid, p. 354, fig. 174.

Professor Goodyear devotes an entire chapter to the Swastika. On pages 352, 353 he says:

There is no proposition in archæology which can be so easily demonstrated as the assertion that the Swastika was originally a fragment of the Egyptian meander, provided Greek geometric vases are called in evidence. The connection between

EGYPTIAN SCARABÆI SHOWING EVOLUTION OF CONCENTRIC RINGS.

Fig. 22.	Fig. 23.	Fig. 24.
CONCENTRIC RINGS CONNECTED BY TANGENTS.	CONCENTRIC RINGS WITH DISCONNECTED TANGENTS.	CONCENTRIC RINGS WITHOUT CONNECTION.
From a figure in Petrie's "History of Scarabs."	Barringer collection, Metropolitan Museum of Art, New York City. Goodyear, "Grammar of the Lotus," pl 8, fig. 23.	Farman collection, Metropolitan Museum of Art, New York City. Goodyear, "Grammar of the Lotus," pl. 8, fig. 25.

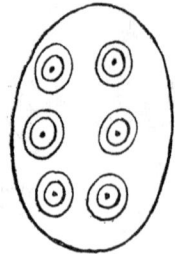

the meander and the Swastika has been long since suggested by Prof. A. S. Murray.[1] Hindu specialists have suggested that the Swastika produced the meander. Birdwood[2] says: "I believe the Swastika to be the origin of the key pattern ornament of Greek and Chinese decorative art." Zmigrodzki, in a recent publication,[3] has not only reproposed this derivation of the meander, but has even connected the Mycenæ spirals with this supposed development, and has proposed to change the name of the spiral ornament accordingly. * * * The equivalence of the Swastika with the meander pattern is suggested, in the first instance, by its appearance in the shape of the meander on the Rhodian (pl. 28, fig. 7), Melian (pl. 60, fig. 8), archæic Greek (pl. 60, fig. 9, and pl. 61, fig. 12), and Greek geometric vases (pl. 56). The appearance in shape of the meander may be verified in the British Museum on one geometric vase of the oldest type, and it also occurs in the Louvre.

Fig. 25.

SPECIAL EGYPTIAN MEANDER.

An illustration of the theory of derivation from the spiral.

Goodyear, "Grammar of the Lotus," pl. 10, fig. 9.

On page 354, Goodyear says:

The solar significance of the Swastika is proven by the Hindu coins of the Jains. Its generative significance is proven by a leaden statuette from Troy. It is an equivalent of the lotus (pl. 47, figs. 1, 2, 3), of the solar diagram (pl. 57, fig. 12, and pl. 60, fig. 8), of the rosette (pl. 20, fig. 8), of concentric rings (pl. 47, fig. 11), of the spiral scroll (pl. 34, fig. 8, and pl.

---

[1] Cesnola, "Cyprus, its Ancient Cities, Tombs, and Temples," p. 410.

[2] "Industrial Arts of India," p. 107.

[3] "Zur Geschichte der Swastika."

39, fig. 2), of the geometric boss (pl. 48, fig. 12), of the triangle (pl. 46, fig. 5), and of the anthemion (pl. 28, fig. 7, and pl. 30, fig. 4). It appears with the solar deer (pl. 60, figs. 1 and 2), with the solar antelope (pl. 37, fig. 9), with the symbolic fish (pl. 42, fig. 1), with the ibex (pl. 37, fig. 4), with the solar sphinx (pl. 34, fig. 8), with the solar lion (pl. 30, fig. 4), the solar ram (pl. 28, fig. 7), and the solar horse (pl. 61, figs. 1, 4, 5, and 12). Its most emphatic and constant association is with the solar bird (pl. 60, fig. 15; fig. 173).

Count Goblet d'Alviella, following Ludwig Müller, Percy Gardner, S. Beal, Edward Thomas, Max Müller, H. Gaidoz, and other authors, accepts their theory that the Swastika was a symbolic representation of the sun or of a sun god, and argues it fully.[1] He starts with the proposition

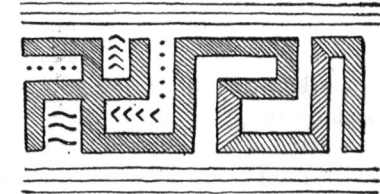

Fig. 26.

DETAIL OF GREEK VASE.

Meander and Swastika.

Goodyear, "Grammar of the Lotus," fig. 174.

that most of the nations of the earth have represented the sun by a circle, although some of them, notably the Assyrians, Hindus, Greeks, and Celts, have represented it by signs more or less cruciform. Examining his fig. 2, wherein signs of the various people are set forth, it is to be remarked that there is no similarity or apparent relationship between the six symbols given, either with themselves or with the sun. Only one of them, that of Assyria, pretends to be a circle; and it may or may not stand for the sun. It has no exterior rays. All the rest are crosses of different kinds. Each of

Fig. 27.

DETAIL OF GREEK GEOMETRIC VASE IN THE BRITISH MUSEUM.

Swastika, right, with solar geese.

Goodyear, "Grammar of the Lotus," p. 353, fig. 173.

the six symbols is represented as being from a single nation of people. They are prehistoric or of high antiquity, and most of them appear to have no other evidence of their representation of the sun than is contained in the sign itself, so that the first objection is to the premises, to wit, that while his symbols may have sometimes represented the sun, it is far from certain that they are used constantly or steadily as such. An objection is made to the theory or hypothesis presented by Count d'Alviella[2] that it is not

Fig. 28.

GREEK GEOMETRIC VASE.

Swastika with solar geese.

Goodyear, "Grammar of the Lotus," p. 353, fig. 172.

[1] "La Migration des Symboles," chap. 2, pt. 3, p. 66.
[2] Ibid., p. 67.

the cross part of the Swastika which represents the sun, but its bent arms, which show the revolving motion, by which he says is evolved the tetraskelion or what in this paper is named the "Ogee Swastika." The author is more in accord with Dr. Brinton and others that the Swastika is derived from the cross and not from the wheel, that the bent arms do not represent rotary or gyratory motion, and that it had no association with, or relation to, the circle. This, if true, relieves the Swastika from all relation with. the circle as a symbol of the sun. Besides, it is not believed that the symbol of the sun is one which required rotary or gyratory motion or was represented by it, but, as will be explained, in speaking of the Assyrian sun-god Shamash (p. 789), it is rather by a circle with pointed rays extending outward.

D'Alviella[1] presents several figures in support of his contention. The first (a) is on a fibula from Etruria (fig. 190 of this paper). His explanation is that the small circle of rays, bent at right angles, on the broad shield of the pin, represents graphically the rotary movement of the sun, and that the bent arms in the Swastikas on the same object are taken from them. It seems curious that so momentous a subject as the existence of a symbol of a great god, the god of light, heat, and thus of life, should be made to depend upon an object of so small importance. This specimen (fig. 190) is a fibula or pin, one of the commonest objects of Etruscan, Greek, or Roman dress. The decorations invoked are on the broad end, which has been flattened to protect the point of the pin, where appears a semicircle of so-called rays, the two Swastikas and two possible crosses. There is nothing about this pin, nor indeed any of the other objects, to indicate any holy or sacred character, nor that any of them were used in any ceremony having relation to the sun, to any god, or to anything holy or sacred. His fig. b is fig. 88 in this paper. It shows a quadrant of the sphere found by Schliemann at Hissarlik. There is a slightly indefinite circle with rays from the outside, which are bent and crooked in many directions. The sphere is of terra cotta; the marks that have been made on it are rough and ill formed. They were made by incision while the clay was soft and were done in the rudest manner. There are dozens more marks upon the same sphere, none of which seem to have received any consideration in this regard. There is a Swastika upon the sphere, and it is the only mark or sign upon the entire object that seems to have been made with care or precision. His third figure (c) is taken from a reliquaire of the thirteenth century A. D. It has a greater resemblance to the acanthus plant than it has to any solar disk imaginable. The other two figures (d and e) are tetraskelions or ogee Swastikas from ancient coins.

D'Alviella's next argument[2] is that the triskelion, formed by the same process as the tetraskelion, is an "incontestable" representation of solar

---

[1] "La Migration des Symboles," p. 69.
[2] Ibid., p. 71.

movement. No evidence is submitted in support of this assertion, and the investigator of the present day is required, as in prehistoric objects, to depend entirely upon the object itself. The bent arms contain no innate evidence (even though they should be held to represent rotary or gyratory motion) representing the sun or sun gods. It is respectfully suggested that in times of antiquity, as in modern times, the sun is not represented as having a rotary motion, but is rather represented by a circle with diminishing rays projecting from the center or exterior. It seems unjustifiable, almost ridiculous, to transform the three flexed human legs, first appearing on the coins of Lycia, into a sun symbol, to make it the reliable evidence of sun worship, and give it a holy or sacred character as representing a god. It is surely pushing the argument too far to say that this is an "incontestable" representation of the solar movement. The illustrations by d'Alviella on his page 71 are practically the same as figs. 224 to 226 of this paper.

Count d'Alviella's further argument[1] is that symbols of the sun god being frequently associated, alternated with, and sometimes replaced by, the Swastika, proves it to have been a sun symbol. But this is doubted, and evidence to sustain the proposition is wanting. Undoubtedly the Swastika was a symbol, was intentional, had a meaning and a degree of importance, and, while it may have been intended to represent the sun and have a higher and holier character, yet these mere associations are not evidence of the fact.

D'Alviella's plate 2, page 80, while divided into sections a and b, is filled only with illustrations of Swastika associated with circles, dots, etc., introduced for the purpose of showing the association of the Swastika therewith, and that the permutation and replacing of these signs by the Swastika is evidence that the Swastika represented the sun. Most of the same illustrations are presented in this paper, and it is respectfully submitted that the evidence does not bear out his conclusion. If it be established that these other symbols are representatives of the sun, how does that prove that the Swastika was itself a representative of the sun or the sun god? D'Alviella himself argues[2] against the proposition of equivalence of meaning because of association when applied to the *Crux ansata*, the circle, the crescent, the triskelion, the lightning sign, and other symbolic figures. He denies that because the Swastika is found on objects associated with these signs therefore they became interchangeable in meaning, or that the Swastika stood for any of them. The Count[2] says that more likely the engraver added the Swastika to these in the character of a talisman or phylactery. On page 56 he argues in the same line, that because it is found on an object of sacred character does not necessarily give it the signification of a sacred or holy symbol. He regards the Swastika as

---

[1] "La Migration des Symboles," pp. 72, 75, 77.
[2] Ibid., p. 61.

a symbol of good fortune, and sees no reason why it may not be employed as an invocation to a god of any name or kind on the principle,
"Good Lord, good devil," quoting the Neapolitan proverb, that it will
do no harm, and possibly may do good.

Prof. Max Müller [1] refers to the discovery by Prof. Percy Gardner of
one of the coins of Mesembria, whereon the Swastika replaces the last
two syllables of the word, and he regards this as decisive that in
Greece the meaning of the Swastika was equivalent to the sun. This
word, Mesembria, being translated *ville de midi*, means town or city
of the south, or the sun. He cites from Mr. Thomas's paper on the
"Indian Swastika and its Western Counterparts"[2] what he considers
an equally decisive discovery made some years ago, wherein it was
shown that the wheel, the emblem of the sun in motion, was replaced
by the Swastika on certain coins; likewise on some of the Andhra
coins and some punched gold coins noted by Sir Walter Elliott.[3] In
these cases the circle or wheel alleged to symbolize the sun was replaced by the Swastika. The Swastika has been sometimes inscribed
within the rings or normal circles representing what is said to be the
four suns on Ujain patterns or coins (fig. 230). Other authorities have
adopted the same view, and have extended it to include the lightning,
the storm, the fire wheel, the sun chariot, etc. (See Ohnefalsch-Richter,
p. 790.) This appears to be a *non sequitur*. All these speculations may be
correct, and all these meanings may have been given to the Swastika,
but the evidence submitted does not prove the fact. There is in the
case of the foregoing coins no evidence yet presented as to which sign,
the wheel or the Swastika, preceded and which followed in point of
time. The Swastika may have appeared first instead of last, and may
not have been a substitution for the disk, but an original design. The
disk employed, while possibly representing the sun in some places, may
not have done so always nor in this particular case. It assumes too
much to say that every time a small circle appears on an ancient object
it represented the sun, and the same observation can be made with
regard to symbols of the other elements. Until it shall have been
satisfactorily established that the symbols represented these elements
with practical unanimity, and that the Swastika actually and intentionally replaced it as such, the theory remains undemonstrated, the
burden rests on those who take the affirmative side; and until these
points shall have been settled with some degree of probability the conclusion is not warranted.

As an illustration of the various significations possible, one has but
to turn to Chapter IV, on the various meanings given to the cross among
American Indians, where it is shown that among these Indians the
cross represented the four winds, the sun, stars, dwellings, the dragon

---

[1] Athenæum, August 20, 1892, p. 266.
[2] Numismatic Chronicle, 1880, xx, pp. 18–48.
[3] Madras Journ. of Lit. and Sci., iii, pl. 9.

fly, midē' society, flocks of birds, human form, maidenhood, evil spirit, and divers others.

. Mr. Edward Thomas, in his work entitled " The Indian Swastika and its Western Counterparts,"[1] says:

As far as I have been able to trace or connect the various manifestations of this emblem [the Swastika], they one and all resolve themselves into the primitive conception of solar motion, which was intuitively associated with the rolling or wheel-like projection of the sun through the upper or visible arc of the heavens, as understood and accepted in the crude astronomy of the ancients. The earliest phase of astronomical science we are at present in position to refer to, with the still extant aid of indigenous diagrams, is the Chaldean. The representation of the sun in this system commences with a simple ring or outline circle, which is speedily advanced toward the impression of onward revolving motion by the insertion of a cross or four wheel-like spokes within the circumference of the normal ring. As the original Chaldean emblem of the sun was typified by a single ring, so the Indian mind adopted a similar definition, which remains to this day as the ostensible device or cast-mark of the modern Sauras or sun worshipers.

The same remarks are made in "Ilios" (pp. 353, 354).

The author will not presume to question, much less deny, the facts stated by this learned gentleman, but it is to be remarked that, on the theory of presumption, the circle might represent many other things than the sun, and unless the evidence in favor of the foregoing statement is susceptible of verification, the theory can hardly be accepted as conclusive. Why should not the circle represent other things than the sun? In modern astronomy the full moon is represented by the plain circle, while the sun, at least in heraldry, is always represented as a circle with rays. It is believed that the "cross or four wheel-like spokes" in the Chaldean emblem of the sun will be found to be rays rather that cross or spokes. A cast is in the U. S. National Museum (Cat. No. 154766) of an original specimen from Niffer, now in the Royal Museum, Berlin, of Shamash, the Assyrian god of the sun. He is represented on this monument by a solar disk, 4 inches in diameter, with eight rays similar to those of stars, their bases on a faint circle at the center, and tapering outwards to a point, the whole surrounded by another faint circle. This is evidence that the sun symbol of Assyria required rays as well as a circle. A similar representation of the sun god is found on a tablet discovered in the temple of the Sun God at Abu-Habba.[2]

Perrot and Chipiez[3] show a tablet from Sippara, of a king, Nabu-abal-iddin, 900 B. C., doing homage to the sun god (identified by the inscription), who is represented by bas-relief of a small circle in the center, with rays and lightning zigzags extending to an outer circle.

In view of these authorities and others which might be cited, it is

---

[1] London, 1880.

[2] Rawlinson, "Cuneiform Inscriptions of Western Asia," v, pl. 60; Trans. Soc. Biblical Archæology, VIII, p. 165.

[3] "History of Art in Chaldea and Assyria," I, p. 200, fig. 71.

questionable whether the plain circle was continuously a representation of the sun in the Chaldean or Assyrian astronomy. It is also doubtful whether, if the circle did represent the sun, the insertion of the cross or the four wheel-like spokes necessarily gave the impression of "onward revolving motion;" or whether any or all of the foregoing afford a satisfactory basis for the origin of the Swastika or for its relation to, or representation of, the sun or the sun god.

Dr. Max Ohnefalsch-Richter[1] announces as his opinion that the Swastika in Cyprus had nearly always a signification more or less religious and sacred, though it may have been used as an ornament to fill empty spaces. He attributes to the *Croix swasticale*—or, as he calls it, *Croix cantonnée*—the equivalence of the solar disk, zigzag lightning, and double hatchet; while to the Swastika proper he attributes the signification of rain, storm, lightning, sun, light, seasons, and also that it lends itself easily to the solar disk, the fire wheel, and the sun chariot.

Greg[2] says:

Considered finally, it may be asked if the fylfot or gammadion was an early symbol of the sun, or, if only an emblem of the solar revolutions or m ovements across the heavens, why it was drawn square rather than curved: The ⌐⌐, even if used in a solar sense, must have implied something more than, or something distinct from, the sun, whose proper and almost universal symbol was the circle. It was evidently more connected with the cross ＋ than with the circle ◯ or solar disk.

Dr. Brinton[3] considers the Swastika as derived from the cross rather than from the circle, and the author agrees that this is probable, although it may be impossible of demonstration either way.

Several authors, among the rest d'Alviella, Greg, and Thomas, have announced the theory of the evolution of the Swastika, beginning with the triskelion, thence to the tetraskelion, and so to the Swastika. A slight examination is sufficient to overturn this hypothesis. In the first place, the triskelion, which is the foundation of this hypothesis, made its first appearance on the coins of Lycia. But this appearance was within what is called the first period of coinage, to wit, between 700 and 480 B. C., and it did not become settled until the second, and even the third period, 280 to 240 B. C., when it migrated to Sicily. But the Swastika had already appeared in Armenia, on the hill of Hissarlik, in the terramares of northern Italy, and on the hut-urns of southern Italy many hundred, possibly a thousand or more, years prior to that time. Count d'Alviella, in his plate 3 (see Chart I, p. 794), assigns it to a period of the fourteenth or thirteenth century B. C., with an unknown and indefinite past behind it. It is impossible that a symbol which first appeared in 480 B. C. could have been the ancestor of one which appeared in 1400 or 1300 B. C., nearly a thousand years before.

---

[1] Bull. Soc. d'Anthrop., Paris, 1888, pp. 674, 675.

[2] Archæologia, XLVIII, pt. 2, p. 326.

[3] Proc. Amér. Philosoph. Soc., 1889, XXIX, p. 180.

William Simpson[1] makes observations upon the latest discoveries regarding the Swastika and gives his conclusion:

* * * The finding of the Swastika in America gives a very wide geographical space that is included by the problem connected with it, but it is wider still, for the Swastika is found over the most of the habitable world, almost literally "from China to Peru," and it can be traced back to a very early period. The latest idea formed regarding the Swastika is that it may be a form of the old wheel symbolism and that it represents a solar movement, or perhaps, in a wider sense, the whole celestial movement of the stars. The Dharmachakra, or Buddhist wheel, of which the so-called "praying wheel" of the Lamas of Thibet is only a variant, can now be shown to have represented the solar motion. It did not originate with the Buddhists; they borrowed it from the Brahminical system to the Veda, where it is called "the wheel of the sun." I have lately collected a large amount of evidence on this subject, being engaged in writing upon it, and the numerous passages from the old Brahminical authorities leave no doubt in the matter. The late Mr. Edward Thomas * * * and Prof. Percy Gardner * * * declared that on some Andhra gold coins and one from Mesembria, Greece, the part of the word which means day, or when the sun shines, is represented by the Swastika. These details will be found in a letter published in the "Athenæum" of August 20, 1892, written by Prof. Max Müller, who affirms that it "is decisive" as to the meaning of the symbol in Greece. This evidence may be "decisive" for India and Greece, but it does not make us quite certain about other parts of the world. Still it raises a strong presumption that its meaning is likely to be somewhat similar wherever the symbol is found.

It is now assumed that the Triskelion or Three Legs of the Isle of Man is only a variant of the Swastika. * * * There are many variants besides this in which the legs, or limbs, differ in number, and they may all be classed as whorls, and were possibly all, more or less, forms intended originally to express circular motion. As the subject is too extensive to be fully treated here, and many illustrations would be necessary, to those wishing for further details I would recommend a work just published entitled "The Migration of Symbols," by Count Goblet d'Alviella, with an introduction by Sir George Birdwood. The frontispiece of the book is a representation of Apollo, from a vase in the Kunsthistorisches Museum of Vienna, and on the middle of Apollo's breast there is a large and prominent Swastika. In this we have another instance going far to show its solar significance. While accepting these new interpretations of the symbol, I am still inclined to the notion that the Swastika may, at the same time, have been looked upon in some cases as a cross—that is, a pre-Christian cross, which now finds acceptance by some authorities as representing the four cardinal points. The importance of the cardinal points in primitive symbolism appears to me to have been very great, and has not as yet been fully realized. This is too large a matter to deal with here. All I can state is, that the wheel in India was connected with the title of a *Chakravartin*—from *Chakra*, a wheel—the title meaning a supreme ruler, or a universal monarch, who ruled the four quarters of the world, and on his coronation he had to drive his chariot, or wheel, to the four cardinal points to signify his conquest of them. Evidence of other ceremonies of the same kind in Europe can be produced. From instances such as these, I am inclined to assume that the Swastika, as a cross, represented the four quarters over which the solar power by its revolving motion carried its influence.

ORIGIN AND HABITAT.

Prehistoric archæologists have found in Europe many specimens of ornamental sculpture and engraving belonging to the Paleolithic age,

---

[1] Quarterly Statement of the Palestine Exploration Fund, January, 1895, pp. 84, 85.

but the cross is not known in any form, Swastika or other. In the Neolithic age, which spread itself over nearly the entire world, with many geometric forms of decoration, no form of the cross appears in times of high antiquity as a symbol or as indicating any other than an ornamental purpose. In the age of bronze, however, the Swastika appears, intentionally used, as a symbol as well as an ornament. Whether its first appearance was in the Orient, and its spread thence throughout prehistoric Europe, or whether the reverse was true, may not now be determined with certainty. It is believed by some to be involved in that other warmly disputed and much-discussed question as to the locality of origin and the mode and routes of dispersion of Aryan peoples. There is evidence to show that it belongs to an earlier epoch than this, and relates to the similar problem concerning the locality of origin and the mode and routes of the dispersion of bronze. Was bronze discovered in eastern Asia and was its migration westward through Europe, or was it discovered on the Mediterranean, and its spread thence? The Swastika spread through the same countries as did the bronze, and there is every reason to believe them to have proceeded contemporaneously—whether at their beginning or not, is undeterminable.

The first appearance of the Swastika was apparently in the Orient, precisely in what country it is impossible to say, but probably in central and southeastern Asia among the forerunners or predecessors of the Bramins and Buddhists. At all events, a religious and symbolic signification was attributed to it by the earliest known peoples of these localities.

M. Michael Zmigrodzki, a Polish scholar, public librarian at Sucha, near Cracow, prepared and sent to the World's Columbian Exposition at Chicago a manuscript chart in French, showing his opinion of the migration of the Swastika, which was displayed in the Woman's Building. It was arranged in groups: The prehistoric (or Pagan) and Christian. These were divided geographically and with an attempt at chronology, as follows:

 I. Prehistoric:
  1. India and Bactria.
  2. Cyprus, Rhodes.
  3. North Europe.
  4. Central Europe.
  5. South Europe.
  6. Asia Minor.
  7. Greek and Roman epoch—Numismatics.
 II. Christian:
  8. Gaul—Numismatics.
  9. Byzantine.
  10. Merovingian and Carlovingian.
  11. Germany.
  12. Poland and Sweden.
  13. Great Britain.

Lastly he introduces a group of the Swastika in the nineteenth century. He presented figures of Swastikas from these localities and representing these epochs. He had a similar display at the Paris Exposition of 1889, which at its close was deposited in the St. Germain Prehistoric Museum. I met M. Zmigrodzki at the Tenth International Congress of Anthropology and Prehistoric Archæology in Paris, and heard him present the results of his investigations on the Swastika. I have since corresponded with him, and he has kindly sent me separates of his paper published in the Archives für Ethnographie, with 266 illustrations of the Swastika; but on asking his permission to use some of the information in the chart at Chicago, he informed me he had already given the manuscript chart and the right to reproduce it to the Chicago Folk-Lore Society. The secretary of this society declined to permit it to pass out of its possession, though proffering inspection of it in Chicago.

In his elaborate dissertation Count Goblet d'Alviella[1] shows an earlier and prehistoric existence of the Swastika before its appearance on the hill of Hissarlik. From this earlier place of origin it, according to him, spread to the Bronze age terramares of northern Italy. All this was prior to the thirteenth century B. C. From the hill of Hissarlik it spread east and west; to the east into Lycaonia and Caucasus, to the west into Mycenæ and Greece; first on the pottery and then on the coins. From Greece it also spread east and west; east to Asia Minor and west to Thrace and Macedonia. From the terramares he follows it through the Villanova epoch, through Etruria and Grand Greece, to Sicily, Gaul, Britain, Germany, Scandinavia, to all of which migration he assigns various dates down to the second century B. C. It developed westward from Asia Minor to northern Africa and to Rome, with evidence in the Catacombs; on the eastward it goes into India, Persia, China, Tibet, and Japan. All this can be made apparent upon examination of the plate itself. It is introduced as Chart I, p. 794.

The author enters into no discussion with Count d'Alviella over the correctness or completeness of the migrations set forth in his chart. It will be conceded, even by its author, to be largely theoretical and impossible to verify by positive proof. He will only contend that there is a probability of its correctness. It is doubted whether he can maintain his proposition of the constant presence or continued appearance of the Swastika on altars, idols, priestly vestments, and sepulchral urns, and that this demonstrates the Swastika to have always possessed the attributes of a religious symbol. It appears to have been used more frequently upon the smaller and more insignificant things of every-day life—the household utensils, the arms, weapons, the dress, the fibulæ, and the pottery; and while this may be consonant with the attributes of the talisman or amulet or charm, it is still compatible with the theory of the Swastika being a sign or symbol for benediction, blessing, good fortune, or good luck; and that it was rather this than a religious symbol.

---

[1] "La Migration des Symboles," pl. 3.

CHART I.—*Probable introduction of the Swastika into different countries, according to Count Goblet d'Alviella.*

["La Migration des Symboles," pl. 3.]

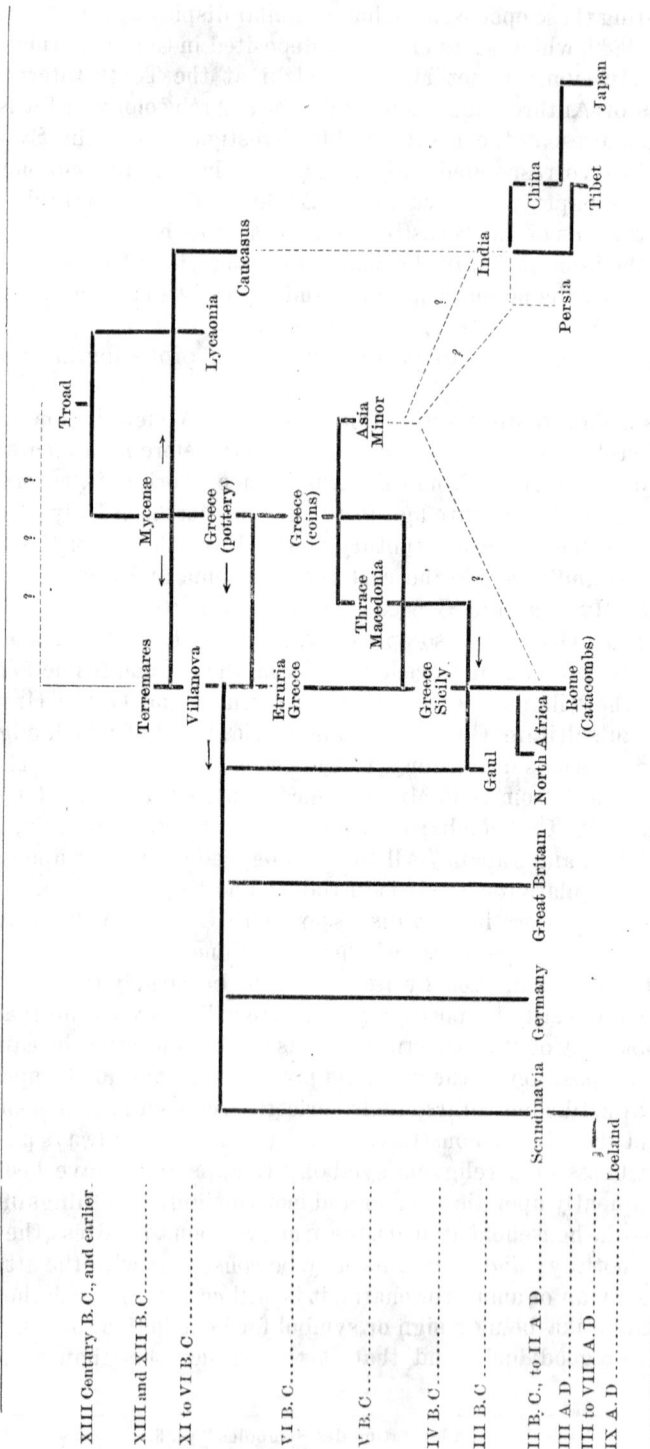

Count Goblet d'Alviella, in the fourth section of the second chapter[1] relating to the country of its origin, argues that the Swastika sign was employed by all the Aryans except the Persians. This omission he explains by showing that the Swastika in all other lands stood for the sun or for the sun-god, while the Aryans of Persia had other signs for the same thing—the *Crux ansata* and the winged globe. His conclusion is[2] that there were two zones occupied with different symbols, the frontier between them being from Persia, through Cyprus, Rhodes, and Asia Minor, to Libya; that the first belonged to the Greek civilization, which employed the Swastika as a sun symbol; the second to the Egypto-Babylonian, which employed the *Crux ansata* and the winged globe as sun symbols.

Professor Sayce, in his preface to "Troja," says:[3]

The same symbol [the Swastika], as is well known, occurs on the Archaic pottery of Cyprus * * * as well as upon the prehistoric antiquities of Athens and Mykênæ [same, "Ilios," p. 353], but it was entirely unknown to Babylonia, to Assyria, to Phœnicia, and to Egypt. It must therefore either have originated in Europe and spread eastward through Asia Minor or have been disseminated westward from the primitive home of the Hittites. The latter alternative is the more probable; but whether it is so or not, the presence of the symbol in the land of the Ægean indicates a particular epoch and the influence of a pre-Phœnician culture.

Dr. Schliemann[4] reports that "Rev. W. Brown Keer observed the Swastika innumerable times in the most ancient Hindu temples, especially those of the Jainas."

Max Müller cites the following paragraph by Professor Sayce:[5]

It is evident to me that the sign found at Hissarlik is identical with that found at Mycenæ and Athens, as well as on the prehistoric pottery of Cyprus (Di Cesnola, Cyprus, pls. 44 and 47), since the general artistic character of the objects with which this sign is associated in Cyprus and Greece agrees with that of the objects discovered in Troy. The Cyprian vase [fig. 156, this paper] figured in Di Cesnola's "Cyprus," pl. 45, which associates the Swastika with the figure of an animal, is a striking analogue of the Trojan whorls, on which it is associated with the figure of the stags. The fact that it is drawn within the vulva of the leaden image on the Asiatic goddess shown in fig. 226 ("Ilios," fig. 125 this paper) seems to show that it was a symbol of generation.

Count Goblet d'Alviella,[6] citing Albert Dumont[7] and Perrot and Chipiez,[8] says:

The Swastika appears in Greece, as well as in Cyprus and Rhodes, first on the pottery, with geometric decorations, which form the second period in Greek ceramics. From that it passes to a later period, where the decoration is more artistic and the appearance of which coincides with the development of the Phœnician influences on the coasts of Greece.

Dr. Ohnefalsch-Richter, in a paper devoted to the consideration of

[1] "La Migration des Symboles," p. 93.
[2] Ibid., p. 107.
[3] "Ilios.," p. XXI."
[4] Ibid, p. 352.
[5] Ibid, p. 353.
[6] "La Migration des Symboles," p. 43.
[7] "Peintures céramiques de la Grèce propre," I, pl. XV, fig. 17.
[8] "Histoire de l'art dans l'antiquité," III, figs. 513, 515, 518.

the Swastika in Cyprus,[1] expresses the opinion that the emigrant or commercial Phenicians traveling in far eastern countries brought the Swastika by the sea route of the Persian Gulf to Asia Minor and Cyprus, while, possibly, other people brought it by the overland route from central Asia, Asia Minor, and Hissarlik, and afterwards by migration to Cyprus, Carthage, and the north of Africa.

Professor Goodyear says:[2]

The true home of the Swastika is the Greek geometric style, as will be immediately obvious to every expert who examines the question through the study of that style. In seeking the home of a symbol, we should consider where it appears in the largest dimension and where it appears in the most formal and prominent way. The Greek geometric vases are the only monuments on which the Swastika systematically appears in panels exclusively assigned to it (pl. 60, fig. 13; and pl. 56, fig. 4). There are no other monuments on which the Swastika can be found in a dimension taking up one-half the height of the entire object (pl. 56, fig. 4). The ordinary size of the Swastika, in very primitive times, is under a third of an inch in diameter. They are found in Greek geometric pottery 2 or 3 inches in diameter, but they also appear in the informal scattering way (pl. 61, fig. 4) which characterizes the Swastika in other styles.

*   *   *   *   *   *   *

The Swastika dates from the earliest diffusion of the Egyptian meander in the basin of the Mediterranean, and it is a profound remark of De Morgan (Mission Scientifique au Caucase) that the area of the Swastika appears to be coextensive with the area of bronze. In northern prehistoric Europe, where the Swastika has attracted considerable attention, it is distinctly connected with the bronze culture derived from the south. When found on prehistoric pottery of the north, the southern home of its beginnings is equally clear.

In seeking the home of a symbol, we should consider not only the nature of its appearance, but also where it is found in the largest amount, for this shows the center of vogue and power—that is to say, the center of diffusion. The vogue of the Swastika at Troy is not as great as its vogue in Cyprian Greek pottery (pl. 60, fig. 15) and Rhodian pottery (pl. 60, fig. 2). * * * It is well known to Melian vases (pl. 60, fig. 8) and to archaic Greek vases (pl. 61, fig. 12), but its greatest prominence is on the pottery of the Greek geometric style (pl. 60, fig. 13; pl. 56, fig. 4; pl. 61, figs. 1 and 4; and figs. 173 and 174). * * *

Aside from the Greek geometric style, our earliest reference for the Swastika, and very possibly an earlier reference than the first, is its appearance on the "hut urns" of Italy. On such it appears rather as a fragment of the more complicated meander patterns, from which it is derived. My precise view is that the earliest and, consequently, imperfect, forms of the Swastika are on the hut urns of Italy, but that, as an independent and definitely shaped pattern, it first belongs to the Greek geometric style. I do not assert that the Swastika is very common on hut urns, which are often undecorated. * * * Our present intermediate link with India for the Swastika lies in the Caucasus and in the adjacent territory of Koban. This last ancient center of the arts in metal has lately attracted attention through the publication of Virchow (Das Gräberfeld von Koban). In the original Coban bronzes of the Prehistoric Museum of St. Germain there is abundant matter for study (p. 351).

Mr. R. P. Greg, in "Fret or Key Ornamentation in Mexico and Peru,"[3] says:

Both the Greek fret and the fylfot appear to have been unknown to the Semitic nations as an ornament or as a symbol.

---

[1] Bull. Soc. d'Anthrop., Paris, December 6, 1888, pp. 669, 679, 680.
[2] "Grammar of the Lotus," p. 348 et seq.
[3] Archæologia, XLVII, pt. 1, p. 159.

In Egypt the fylfot does not occur. It is, I believe, generally admitted or supposed that the fylfot is of early Aryan origin. Eastward toward India, Tibet, and China it was adopted, in all probability, as a sacred symbol of Buddha; westward it may have spread in one form or another to Greece, Asia Minor, and even to North Germany.

Cartailhac says:[1]

Modern Christian archæologists have obstinately contended that the Swastika was composed of four gamma, and so have called it the Croix Gammée. But the Ramâ-yana placed it on the boat of the Rama long before they had any knowledge of Greek. It is found on a number of Buddhist edifices; the Sectarians of Vishnu placed it as a sign upon their foreheads. Burnouf says it is the Aryan sign par excellence. It was surely a religious emblem in use in India fifteen centuries before the Christian era, and thence it spread to every part. In Europe it appeared about the middle of the civilization of the bronze age, and we find it, pure or transformed into a cross, on a mass of objects in metal or pottery during the first age of iron. Sometimes its lines were rounded and given a graceful curve instead of straight and square at its ends and angles. [See letter by Gandhi, pp. 803, 805.]

M. Cartailhac notes[2] several facts concerning the associations of the Swastika found by him in Spain and Portugal and belonging to the first (prehistoric) age of iron: (1) The Swastika was associated with the silhouettes of the duck or bird, similar to those in Greece, noted by Goodyear; (2) the association (in his fig. 41) on a slab from the lake dwellings, of the Maltese cross and reproduction of the triskelion; (3) a tetraskelion, which he calls a Swastika "flamboyant," being the triskelion, but with four arms, the same shown on Lycian coins as being ancestors of the true triskelion (his fig. 412); (4) those objects were principally found in the ancient lake dwellings of Sambroso and Briteiros, supposedly dating from the eighth and ninth centuries B. C. With them were found many ornaments, borders representing cords, spirals, meanders, etc., which had the same appearance as those found by Schliemann at Mycenæ. Cartailhac says:[3]

Without doubt Asiatic influences are evident in both cases; first appearing in the Troad, then in Greece, they were spread through Iberia and, possibly, who can tell, finally planted in a far-away Occident.

A writer in the Edinburgh Review, in an extended discussion on "The pre-Christian cross," treats of the Swastika under the local name of "Fylfot," but in such an enigmatical and uncertain manner that it is difficult to distinguish it from other and commoner forms of the cross. Mr. Waring[4] criticises him somewhat severely for his errors:

He states that it is found * * * in the sculptured stones of Scotland (but after careful search we can find only one or two imperfect representations of it, putting aside the Newton stone inscription, where it is probably a letter or numeral only); that it is carved on the temples and other edifices of Mexico and Central America (where again we have sought for it in vain); that it is found on the cinerary urns of the terramare of Parma and Vicenza, the date of which has been assigned by Italian antiquaries to 1000 B. C. (but there again we have found only the plain

[1] "Ages Prehistorique de l'Espagne et du Portugal," pp. 285–293.
[2] Ibid., p. 286.
[3] Ibid., p. 293.
[4] "Ceramic Art in Remote Ages," p. 13.

cross, and not the fylfot), and, finally, he asserts that "it was the emblem of Libitina or Persephone, the awful Queen of the Shades, and is therefore commonly found on the dress of the tumulorum fossor in the Roman catacombs," but we have only found one such example. "It is noteworthy, too," he continues, "in reference to its extreme popularity, or the superstitious veneration in which it has been also universally held, that the cross pattée, or cruciform hammer (but we shall show these are different symbols), was among the very last of purely pagan symbols which was religiously preserved in Europe long after the establishment of Christianity (not in Europe, but in Scandinavia and wherever the Scandinavians had penetrated). * * * It may be seen upon the bells of many of our parish churches, as at Appleby, Mexborough, Haythersaye, Waddington, Bishop's Norton, West Barkwith, and other places, where it was placed as a magical sign to subdue the vicious spirit of the tempest;" and he subsequently points out its constant use in relation to water or rain.

Mr. Waring continues:

The Rev. C. Boutell, in "Notes and Queries," points out that it is to be found on many mediæval monuments and bells, and occurs—e. g., at Appleby in Lincolnshire (peopled by Northmen)—as an initial cross to the formula on the bell "Sta. Maria, o. p. n. and c." In these cases it has clearly been adopted as a Christian symbol. In the same author's "Heraldry," he merely describes it as a mystic cross.

Mr. Waring makes one statement which, being within his jurisdiction, should be given full credit. He says, on page 15:

It [the Swastika] appears in Scotland and England only in those parts where Scandinavians penetrated and settled, but is not once found in any works of purely Irish or Franco-Celtic art.

He qualifies this, however, by a note:

I believe it occurs twice on an "Ogam" stone in the Museum of the Royal Irish Academy, figured in Wilde's Catalogue (p. 136), but the fylfots are omitted in the wood cut. [See fig. 215.]

Dr. Brinton,[1] describing the normal Swastika, "with four arms of equal length, the hook usually pointing from left to right," says: "In this form it occurs in India and on very early (Neolithic) Grecian, Italic, and Iberian remains." Dr. Brinton is the only author who, writing at length or in a critical manner, attributes the Swastika to the Neolithic period in Europe, and in this, more than likely, he is correct. Professor Virchow's opinion as to the antiquity of the hill of Hissarlik, wherein Dr. Schliemann found so many Swastikas, should be considered in this connection. (See p. 832, 833 of this paper.) Of course, its appearance among the aborigines of America, we can imagine, must have been within the Neolithic period.

---

[1] Proc. Amer. Philosoph. Soc., 1889, XXIX, p. 179.

II.—DISPERSION OF THE SWASTIKA.

EXTREME ORIENT.

JAPAN.

The Swastika was in use in Japan in ancient as well as modern times. Fig. 29 represents a bronze statue of Buddha, one-fifteenth natural size, from Japan, in the collection of M. Cernuschi, Paris. It has eight Swastikas on the pedestal, the ends all turned at right angles to the right. This specimen is shown by De Mortillet[1] because it relates to prehistoric man. The image or statue holds a cane in the form of a "tintin-nabulum," with movable rings arranged to make a jingling noise, and De Mortillet inserted it in his volume to show the likeness of this work in Japan with a number of similar objects found in the Swiss lake dwellings in the prehistoric age of bronze (p. 806).

The Swastika mark was employed by the Japanese on their porcelain. Sir Augustus W. Franks[2] shows one of these marks, a small Swastika turned to the left and inclosed in a circle (fig. 30). Fig. 9 also represents a mark on Japanese bronzes.[3]

KOREA.

The U. S. National Museum has a ladies' sedan or carrying chair from Korea. It bears eight Swastika marks, cut by stencil in the brass-bound corners, two on each corner, one looking each way. The Swastika is normal, with arms crossing at right angles, the ends bent at right angles and to the right. It is quite plain; the lines are all straight, heavy, of equal thickness, and the angles all at 90 degrees. In appearance it resembles the Swastika in fig. 9.

Fig. 29.

BRONZE STATUE OF BUDDHA.

Japan.

Eight Swastikas on pedestal. Cane tintinnabulum with six movable rings or bells.

One fifteenth natural size.

Fig. 30.

JAPANESE POT-TER'S MARK ON PORCELAIN.

De Mortillet, "Musée Préhistorique," fig. 1248.

CHINA.

In the Chinese language the sign of the Swastika is pronounced *wan* (p. 801), and stands for "many," "a great number," "ten thousand," "infinity," and by a synecdoche is construed to mean "long

[1] "Musée Préhistorique," fig. 1230; Bull. Soc. d'Anthrop., Paris., 1886, pp. 299, 313, 314.

[2] "Catalogue of Oriental Porcelain and Pottery," pl. 11, fig. 139.

[3] De Morgan, "Au Caucase," fig. 180.

life, a multitude of blessings, great happiness," etc.; as is said in French, "mille pardons," "mille remercîments," a thousand thanks, etc. During a visit to the Chinese legation in the city of Washington, while this paper was in progress, the author met one of the attachés, Mr. Chung, dressed in his robes of state; his outer garment was of moiré silk. The pattern woven in the fabric consisted of a large circle with certain marks therein, prominent among which were two Swastikas, one turned to the right, the other to the left. The name given to the sign was as reported above, wan, and the signification was "longevity," "long life," "many years." Thus was shown that in far as well as near countries, in modern as well as ancient times, this sign stood for blessing, good wishes, and, by a slight extension, for good luck.

The author conferred with the Chinese minister, Yang Yu, with the request that he should furnish any appropriate information concerning the Swastika in China. In due course the author received the following letter and accompanying notes with drawings:

* * * I have the pleasure to submit abstracts from historical and literary works on the origin of the Swastika in China and the circumstances connected with it in Chinese ancient history. I have had this paper translated into English and illustrated by india-ink drawings. The Chinese copy is made by Mr. Ho Yen-Shing, the first secretary of the legation, translation by Mr. Chung, and drawings by Mr. Li.

With assurance of my high esteem, I am,

Very cordially,		YANG YU.

Buddhist philosophers consider simple characters as half or incomplete characters and compound characters as complete characters, while the Swastika 卍 is regarded as a natural formation. A Buddhist priest of the Tang Dynasty, Tao Shih by name, in a chapter of his work entitled Fa Yuen Chu Lin, on the original Buddha, describes him as having this 卍 mark on his breast and sitting on a high lily of innumerable petals. [Pl. 1.]

Empress Wu (684–704 A. D.), of the Tang Dynasty, invented a number of new forms for characters already in existence, amongst which ⊕ was the word for sun, ②

for moon, ◯ for star, and so on. These characters were once very extensively used in ornamental writing, and even now the word ⊕ sun may be found in many of the famous stone inscriptions of that age, which have been preserved to us up to the present day. [Pl. 2.]

The history of the Tang Dynasty (620–906 A. D.), by Lui Hsu and others of the Tsin Dynasty, records a decree issued by Emperor Tai Tsung (763–779 A. D.) forbidding the use of the Swastika on silk fabrics manufactured for any purpose. [Pl. 3.]

Fung Tse, of the Tang Dynasty, records a practice among the people of Loh-yang to endeavor, on the 7th of the 7th month of each year, to obtain spiders to weave the Swastika on their web. Kung Ping-Chung, of the Sung Dynasty, says that the people of Loh-yang believe it to be good luck to find the Swastika woven by spiders over fruits or melons. [Pl. 4.]

Sung Pai, of the Sung Dynasty, records an offering made to the Emperor by Li Yuen-su, a high official of the Tang Dynasty, of a buffalo with a Swastika on the forehead, in return for which offering he was given a horse by the Emperor. [Pl. 5.]

The Ts'ing-I-Luh, by Tao Kuh, of the Sung Dynasty, records that an Empress in

ORIGIN OF BUDDHA ACCORDING TO TAO SHIH, WITH SWASTIKA SIGN.

From a drawing by Mr. Li, presented to the U. S. National Museum by Mr. Yang Yü, Chinese Minister, Washington, D. C.

唐武后偕羣大周天冊金輪神聖皇帝自
造文字曰為卍月為◑星為○當時馮
善廓造浮圖銘法門寺碑涅槃經信法
寺碑潘尊師碣獲嘉縣浮圖銘王仁
求碑梁師亮墓誌銘小石橋碑嵩岳觀
碑凡日字皆作卍形

SWASTIKA DECREED BY EMPRESS WU (684-704 A. D.) AS A SIGN FOR
SUN IN CHINA.

From a drawing by Mr. Li, presented to the U. S. National Museum by Mr. Yang Yü, Chinese
Minister, Washington, D. C.

晉劉昫等舊唐書代宗紀戊寅詔云綾錦

呪織萬字卍萬即雙勝並宜禁斷

SWASTIKA DESIGN ON SILK FABRICS.

This use of the Swastika was forbidden in China by Emperor Tai Tsung (763–779 A. D.).

From a drawing by Mr. Li, presented to the U. S. National Museum by Mr. Yang Yü, Chinese
Minister, Washington, D. C.

SWASTIKA IN SPIDER WEB OVER FRUIT.

(A good omen in China.)

From a drawing by Mr. Li, presented to the U. S. National Museum by Mr. Yang Yü, Chinese
Minister, Washington, D. C.

宋宋白文苑英華唐鳳閣侍郎李元素
進拍牛一頭額上骨萬字萬即賜馬一匹
李嬌代為表

BUFFALO WITH SWASTIKA ON FOREHEAD.

Presented to Emperor of Sung Dynasty.

From a drawing by Mr. Li. presented to the U. S. National Museum by Mr. Yang Yü, Chinese
Minister, Washington, D. C.

宋陶穀清異錄南唐李煜長秋周氏居
柔儀殿其焚香之器冑卍字

INCENSE BURNER WITH SWASTIKA DECORATION.

South Tang Dynasty.

From a drawing by Mr. Li, presented to the U. S. National Museum by Mr. Yang Yü, Chinese
Minister, Washington D. C.

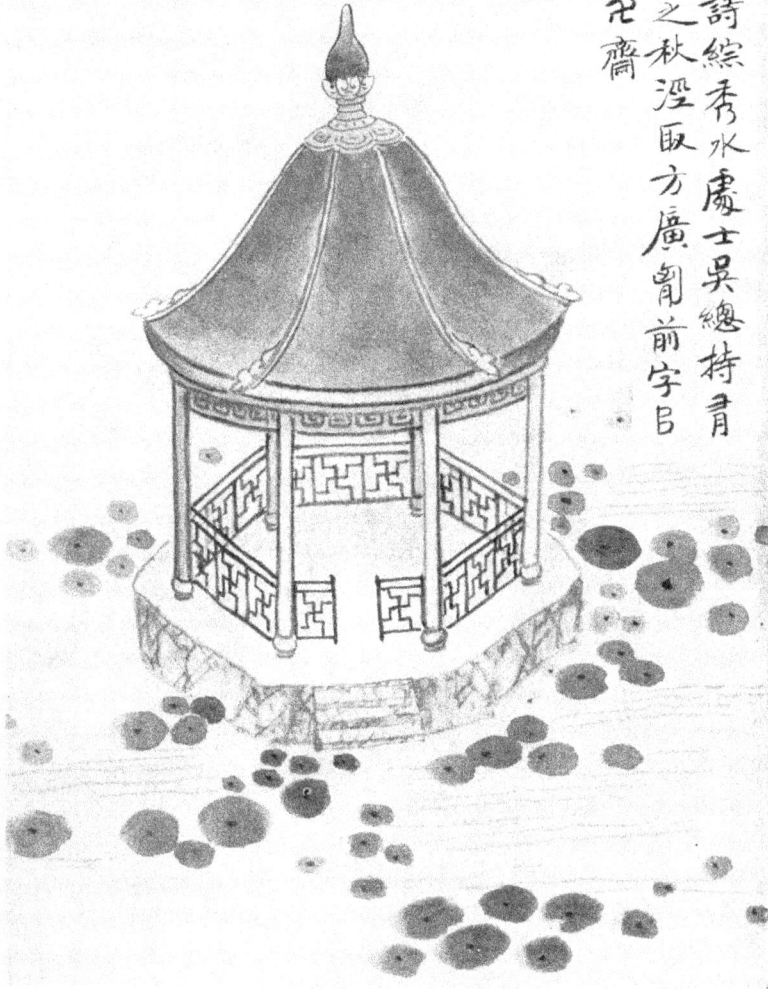

朱彝尊明詩綜秀水處士吳總持胄
大宅在北郭之秋涇取方廣冑前字曰
爲曲闌名曰卍齋

HOUSE OF WU TSUNG-CHIH OF SIN SHUI, WITH SWASTIKA IN RAILING

From a drawing by Mr. Li, presented to the U. S. National Museum by Mr. Yang Yü, Chinese
Minister, Washington, D. C.

PLATE 8.

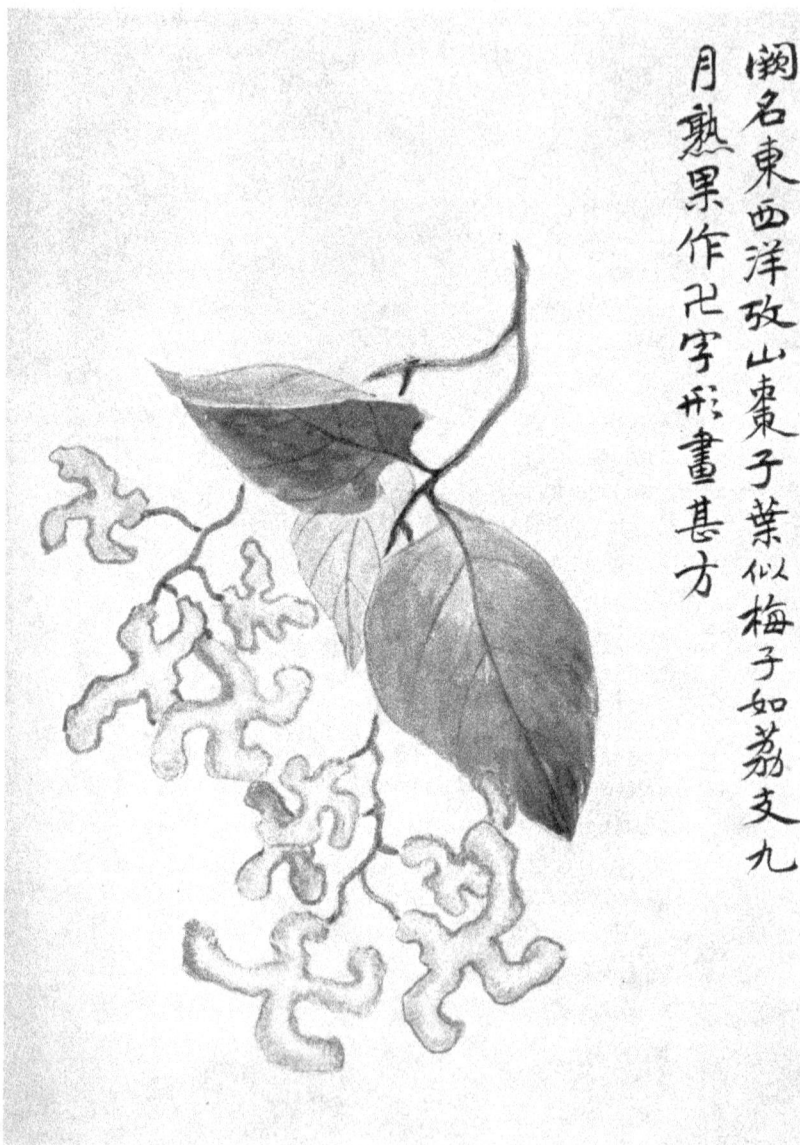

關名東西洋攷山棗子葉似梅子如荔支九月熟果作卍字形畫甚方

MOUNTAIN OR WILD DATE.—FRUIT RESEMBLING THE SWASTIKA.

From a drawing by Mr. Li, presented to the U. S. National Museum by Mr. Yang Yü, Chinese Minister, Washington, D. C.

the time of the South Tang Dynasty had an incense burner the external decoration of which had the Swastika design on it. [Pl. 6.]

Chu I-Tsu, in his work entitled Ming Shih Tsung, says Wu Tsung-Chih, a learned man of Sin Shui, built a residence outside of the north gate of that town, which he named "Wan-Chai," from the Swastika decoration of the railings about the exterior of the house. [Pl. 7.]

An anonymous work, entitled the Tung Hsi Yang K'ao, described a fruit called shan-tsao-tse (mountain or wild date), whose leaves resemble those of the plum. The seed resembles the lichee, and the fruit, which ripens in the ninth month of the year, suggests a resemblance to the Swastika. [Pl. 8.]

The Swastika is one of the symbolic marks of the Chinese porcelain. Prime[1] shows what he calls a "tablet of honor," which represents a Swastika inclosed in a lozenge with loops at the corners (fig. 31). This mark on a piece of porcelain signifies that it is an imperial gift.

Major-General Gordon, controller of the Royal Arsenal at Woolwich, England, writes to Dr. Schliemann:[2] "The Swastika is Chinese. On the breech chasing of a large gun lying outside my office, captured in the Taku fort, you will find this same sign." But Dumoutier[3] says this sign is nothing else than the ancient Chinese character *c h e*, which, according to D'Alviella,[4] carries the idea of perfection or excellence, and signifies the renewal and perpetuity of life. And again,[2] "Dr. Lockyer, formerly medical missionary to China, says the sign ⌐⌐ is thoroughly Chinese."

Fig. 31.

POTTER'S MARK ON PORCELAIN.

China.

Tablet of honor, with Swastika.

Prime, "Pottery and Porcelain," p. 254.

The Swastika is found on Chinese musical instruments. The U. S. National Museum possesses a Hu-Ch'in, a violin with four strings, the body of which is a section of bamboo about 3½ inches in diameter. The septum of the joint has been cut away so as to leave a Swastika of normal form, the four arms of which are connected with the outer walls of the bamboo. Another, a Ti-Ch'in, a two-stringed violin, with a body of cocoanut, has a carving which is believed to have been a Swastika; but the central part has been broken out, so that the actual form is undetermined.

Prof. George Frederick Wright, in an article entitled "Swastika,"[5] quotes Rev. F. H. Chalfont, missionary at Chanting, China, as saying: "Same symbol in Chinese characters 'ouan,' or 'wan,' and is a favorite ornament with the Chinese."

---

[1] "Pottery and Porcelain," p. 254.

[2] "Ilios," p. 352.

[3] "Le Swastika et la roue solaire en Chine," Revue d'Ethnographie, IV, pp. 319, 350.

[4] "La Migration des Symboles," p. 55.

[5] New York Independent, November 16, 1893; Science, March 23, 1894, p. 162.

TIBET.

Mr. William Woodville Rockhill,[1] speaking of the fair at Kumbum, says:

I found there a number of Lh'asa Tibetans (they call them Gopa here) selling pulo, beads of various colors, saffron, medicines, peacock feathers, incense sticks, etc. I had a talk with these traders, several of whom I had met here before in 1889. * * * One of them had a Swastika (yung-drung) tattooed on his hand, and I learned from this man that this is not an uncommon mode of ornamentation in his country.

Count D'Alviella says that the Swastika is continued among the Buddhists of Tibet; that the women ornament their petticoats with it,

Fig. 32.

FOOTPRINT OF BUDDHA WITH SWASTIKA, FROM AMARAVATI TOPE.

From a figure by Fergusson and Schliemann.

and that it is also placed upon the breasts of their dead.[2]

He also reports[3] a Buddhist statue at the Musée Guimet with Swastikas about the base. He does not state to what country it belongs, so the author has no means of determining if it is the same statue as is represented in fig. 29.

INDIA.

Burnouf[4] says approvingly of the Swastika:

Christian archæologists believe this was the most ancient sign of the cross. * * * It was used among the Brahmins from all antiquity. (Voyez mot "Swastika" dans notre dictionnaire sanskrit.) Swastika, or Swasta, in India corresponds to "benediction" among Christians.

The same author, in his translation of the "Lotus de la Bonne Loi," one of the nine Dharmas or Canonical books of the Buddhists of the North, of 280 pages, adds an appendix of his own writing of 583 pages; and in one (No. 8) devoted to an enumeration and description of the sixty-five figures traced on the footprint of Çakya (fig. 32) commences as follows:

1. *Svastikaya:* This is the familiar mystic figure of many Indian sects, represented

---

[1] "Diary of a Journey through Mongolia and Tibet in 1891–92," p. 67.

[2] "La Migration des Symboles," p. 55, citing note I, Journ. Asiatique, 2e série, IV, p. 245, and Pallas, "Sammlungen historischer Nachrichten über die mongolischen Völkerschaften," I, p. 277.

[3] Ibid., p. 55.

[4] "Des Sciences et Religion," p. 256.

thus, ⊔⊓, and whose name signifies, literally, "sign of benediction or of good augury." (Rgya tch'er rol pa, Vol. 11, p. 110.)

* * * The sign of the Swastika was not less known to the Brahmins than to the Buddhists. "Ramayana," Vol. II, p. 348, ed. Gor., Chap. XCVII, st. 17, tells of vessels on the sea bearing this sign of fortune. This mark, of which the name and usage are certainly ancient, because it is found on the oldest Buddhist medals, may have been used as frequently among the Brahmins as among the Buddhists. Most of the inscriptions on the Buddhist caverns in western India are either preceded or followed by the holy (*sacramentelle*) sign of the Swastika. It appears less common on the Brahmin monuments.

Mr. W. Crooke (Bengal Civil Service, director of Eth. Survey, Northwest Provinces and Oudh), says:[1]

The mystical emblem of the Swastika, which appears to represent the sun in his journey through the heavens, is of constant occurrence. The trader paints it on the flyleaf of his ledger, he who has young children or animals liable to the evil eye makes a representation of it on the wall beside his doorpost. It holds first place among the lucky marks of the Jainas. It is drawn on the shaven heads of children on the marriage day in Gujarat. A red circle with Swastika in the center is depicted on the place where the family gods are kept (Campbell, Notes, p. 70). In the Meerut division the worshiper of the village god Bhumiya constructs a rude model of it in the shrine by fixing up two crossed straws with a daub of plaster. It often occurs in folklore. In the drama of the Toy Cart the thief hesitates whether he shall make a hole in the wall of Charudatta's house in the form of a Swastika or of a water jar (Manning, Ancient India, 11, 160).

Village shrines.—The outside (of the shrines) is often covered with rude representations of the mystical Swastika.

On page 250 he continues thus:

Charms.—The bazar merchant writes the words "Ram Ram" over his door, or makes an image of Genesa, the god of luck, or draws the mystical Swastika. The jand tree is reverenced as sacred by Khattris and Brahmins to avoid the evil eye in children. The child is brought at 3 years of age before a jand tree; a bough is cut with a sickle and planted at the foot of the tree. A Swastika symbol is made before it with the rice flour and sugar brought as an offering to the tree. Threads of string, used by women to tie up their hair, are cut in lengths and some deposited on the Swastika.

Mr. Virchand R. Gandhi, a Hindu and Jain disciple from Bombay, India, a delegate to the World's Parliament of Religions at Chicago in 1893, remained for sometime in Washington, D. C., proselyting among the Christians. He is a cultivated gentleman, devoted to the spread of his religion. I asked his advice and assistance, which he kindly gave, supervising my manuscript for the Swastika in the extreme Orient, and furnishing me the following additional information relative to the Swastika in India, and especially among the Jains:

The Swastika is misinterpreted by so-called Western expounders of our ancient Jain philosophy. The original idea was very high, but later on some persons thought the cross represented only the combination of the male and the female principles. While we are on the physical plane and our propensities on the material line, we think it necessary to unite these (sexual) principles for our spiritual growth. On

---

[1] "Introduction to Popular Religion and Folk Lore of North India," p. 58.

the higher plane the soul is sexless, and those who wish to rise higher than the physical plane must eliminate the idea of sex.

I explain the Jain Swastika by the following illustration [fig. 33]: The horizontal and vertical lines crossing each other at right angles form the Greek cross. They represent spirit and matter. We add four other lines by bending to the right each arm of the cross, then three circles and the crescent, and a circle within the crescent. The idea thus symbolized is that there are four grades of existence of souls in the material universe. The first is the lowest state—Archaic or protoplasmic life. The soul evolves from that state to the next—the earth with its plant and animal life. Then follows the third stage—the human; then the fourth stage—the celestial. The word "celestial" is here held to mean life in other worlds than our own. All these graduations are combinations of matter and soul on different scales. The spiritual plane is that in which the soul is entirely freed from the bonds of matter. In order to reach that plane, one must strive to possess the three jewels (represented by the three circles), right belief, right knowledge, right conduct. When a person has these, he will certainly go higher until he reaches the state of liberation, which is represented by the crescent. The crescent has the form of the rising moon and is always growing larger. The circle in the crescent represents the omniscient state of the soul when it has attained full consciousness, is liberated, and lives apart from matter.

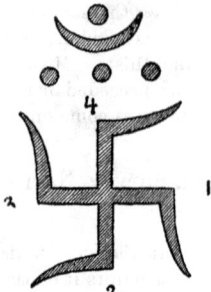

Fig. 33.

EXPLANATION OF THE JAIN SWASTIKA, ACCORDING TO GANDHI.

(1) Archaic or protoplasmic life; (2) Plant and animal life; (3) Human life; (4) Celestial life.

The interpretation, according to the Jain view of the cross, has nothing to do with the combination of the male and female principle. Worship of the male and female principles, ideas based upon sex, lowest even of the emotional plane, can never rise higher than the male and female.

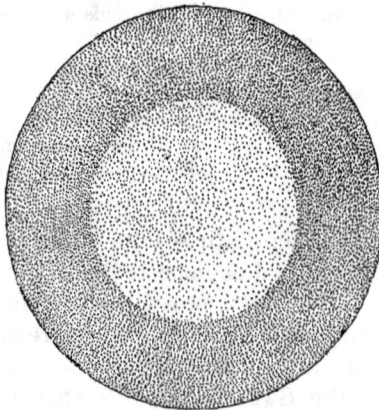

Fig. 34a.

THE FORMATION OF THE JAIN SWASTIKA—FIRST STAGE.

Handful of rice or meal, in circular form, thinner in center.

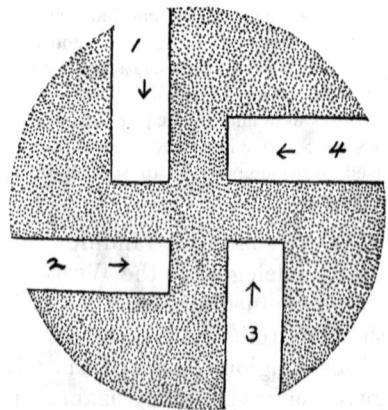

Fig. 34b.

THE FORMATION OF THE JAIN SWASTIKA—SECOND STAGE.

Rice or meal, as shown in preceding figure, with finger marks, indicated at 1, 2, 3, 4.

The Jains make the Swastika sign when we enter our temple of worship. This sign reminds us of the great principles represented by the three jewels and by which we are to reach the ultimate good. Those symbols intensify our thoughts and make them more permanent.

Mr. Gandhi says the Jains make the sign of the Swastika as frequently and deftly as the Roman Catholics make the sign of the cross.
It is not confined to the temple nor to the priests or monks. Whenever
or wherever a benediction or blessing is given, the Swastika is used.
Figs. 34 *a*, *b*, *c* form a series showing how it is made. A handful of
rice, meal, flour, sugar, salt, or any similar substance, is spread over a
circular space, say, 3 inches in diameter and one-eighth of an inch deep
(fig. 34*a*), then commence at the outside of the circle (fig. 34*b*), on its
upper or farther left-hand corner, and draw the finger through the meal
just to the left of the center, halfway or more to the opposite or near
edge of the circle (1), then again to the right (2), then upward (3), finally

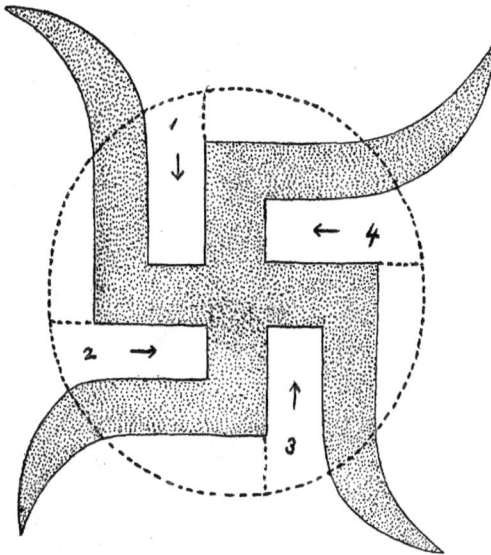

Fig. 34*c*.

THE FORMATION OF THE JAIN SWASTIKA—THIRD STAGE.

Ends turned out, typifying animal, human, and celestial life, as shown in fig. 33.

to the left where it joins with the first mark (4). The ends are swept
outward, the dots and crescent put in above, and the sign is complete
(fig. 34*c*).

The sign of the Swastika is reported in great numbers, by hundreds
if not by thousands, in the inscriptions on the rock walls of the Buddhist caves in India. It is needless to copy them, but is enough to say
that they are the same size as the letters forming the inscription; that
they all have four arms and the ends turn at right angles, or nearly so,
indifferently to the right or to the left. The following list of inscriptions, containing the Swastikas, is taken from the first book coming to
hand—the "Report of Dr. James Burgess on the Buddhist Cave Temples and their Inscriptions, Being a Part of the Result of the Fourth,

Fifth, and Sixth Seasons' Operations of the Archæological Survey of Western India, 1876, 1877, 1878, 1879:"[1]

Plate.		Inscription number.	Direction in which ends are bent.
Bhaja	XLIV	2	To right.
Kuda	XLVI	26	Do.
Do	XLVI	27	To left.
Kol	XLVI	5	To right.
Karle	XLVII	1	Do.
Do	XLVII	3	Do.
Junnar	XLIX	5	Do.
Do	XLIX	6	To left.
Do	XLIX	7	To right.
Do	XLIX	8	To left.
Do	XLIX	9	To right.
Do	XLIX	10	Do.
Do	YLIX	11 (?)	Do.
Do	XLIX	12	Do.
Do	XLIX	13 (?)	Do.
Do	XLIX	13 (?)	To left.
Do	XLIX	14	Do.
Do	L	17	To right.
Do	L	19	Do.
Nasik	LII	5	Do.
Do	LV (Nasik 21)	5 (?)	Do.
Do	LV (Nasik 24)	8 (?)	Do.

Chantre[2] says:

I remind you that the (East) Indians, Chinese, and Japanese employ the Swastika, not only as a religious emblem but as a simple ornament in painting on pottery and elsewhere, the same as we employ the Greek fret, lozenges, and similar motifs in our ornamentation. *Sistres* [the staff with jingling bells, held in the hand of Buddha, on whose base is engraved a row of Swastikas, fig. 29 of present paper] of similar form and style have been found in prehistoric Swiss lake dwellings of the bronze age. Thus the *sistres* and the Swastika are brought into relation with each other. The *sistres* possibly relate to an ancient religion, as they did in the Orient; the Swastika may have had a similar distinction.

De Mortillet and others hold the same opinion.[3]

CLASSICAL ORIENT.

BABYLONIA, ASSYRIA, CHALDEA, AND PERSIA.

Waring[4] says, "In Babylonian and Assyrian remains we search for it [the Swastika] in vain." Max Müller and Count Goblet d'Alviella are of the same opinion.[5]

---

[1] Trubner & Co., London, 1883, pp. 140, pl. 60.

[2] "Âge du Bronze," pt. 1, p. 206.

[3] "Musée Préhistorique," pl. 98; "Notes de l'Origine Orientale de la Métallurgie," Lyon, 1879; "L'Âge de la Pierre et du Bronze dans l'Asie Occidentale," Bull. Soc. d'Anthrop., Lyon, I, fasc. 2, 1882; Bull. Soc. d'Anthrop. de Paris, 1886, pp. 299, 313, and 314.

[4] "Ceramic Art in Remote Ages."

[5] "La Migration des Symboles," pp. 51, 52.

Of Persia, D'Alviella (p. 51), citing Ludwig Müller,[1] says that the Swastika is manifested only by its presence on certain coins of the Arsacides and the Sassanides.

PHENICIA.

It is reported by various authors that the Swastika has never been found in Phenicia, e. g. Max Müller, J. B. Waring, Count Goblet d'Alviella.[2]

Ohnefalsch-Richter[3] says that the Swastika is not found in Phenicia, yet he is of the opinion that their emigrant and commercial travelers brought it from the far east and introduced it into Cyprus, Carthage, and the north of Africa. (See p. 796.)

LYCAONIA.

Lempriere, in his Classical Dictionary, under the above title, gives the following:

A district of Asia Minor forming the southwestern quarter of Phrygia. The origin of its name and inhabitants, the Lycaones, is lost in obscurity. * * * Our first acquaintance with this region is in the relation of the expedition of the younger Cyprus. Its limits varied at different times. At first it extended eastward from Iconium 23 geographical miles, and was separated from Cilicia on the south by the range of Mount Taurus, comprehending a large portion of what in later times was termed Cataonia.

Count Goblet d'Alviella,[4] quoting Perrot and Chipiez,[5] states that the Hittites introduced the Swastika on a bas-relief of Ibriz, Lycaonia, where it forms a border of the robe of a king or priest offering a sacrifice to a god.

ARMENIA.

M. J. de Morgan (the present director of the Gizeh Museum at Cairo), under the direction of the French Government, made extensive excavations and studies into the prehistoric antiquities and archæology of Russian Armenia. His report is entitled "Le Premier Âge de Métaux dans l'Arménie Russe."[6] He excavated a number of prehistoric cemeteries, and found therein various forms of crosses engraved on ceintures, vases, and medallions. The Swastika, though present, was more rare. He found it on the heads of two large bronze pins (figs. 35 and 36) and on one piece of pottery (fig. 37) from the prehistoric tombs. The bent arms are all turned to the left, and would be the Suavastika of Prof. Max Müller.

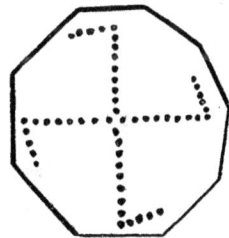

Fig. 35.
BRONZE PIN-HEAD FROM CHEITHAN-THAGH.
De Morgan, " Au Caucase," fig. 177.

---

[1] "Det Saakaldte Hagebors," Copenhagen, 1877.
[2] "La Migration des Symboles," pp. 51, 52.
[3] Bull. de la Soc. d'Anthrop., December 6, 1888, XI, p. 671.
[4] "La Migration des Symboles," p. 51.
[5] "Histoire de l'Art dans l'Antiquité," IV.
[6] "Mission Scientifique au Caucase."

CAUCASUS.

In Caucasus, M. E. Chantre[1] found the Swastika in great purity of form. Fig. 38 represents portions of a bronze plaque from that country, used on a ceinture or belt. Another of slightly different style, but with square cross and arms bent at right angles, is represented in his pl. 8, fig. 5. These belonged to the first age of iron, and much of the art was intricate.[2] It represented animals as well as all geometric forms, crosses, circles (concentric and otherwise), spirals, meanders, chevrons, herring bone, lozenges, etc. These were sometimes cast in the metal, at other times repoussé, and again were engraved, and occasionally these methods were employed together. Fig. 39 shows another form, frequently employed and suggested as a possible evolution of the Swastika, from the same locality and same plate. Fig. 40 represents

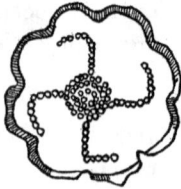

Fig. 36.
BRONZE PIN-HEAD FROM AKTHALA.
De Morgan, "Au Caucase," fig. 178.

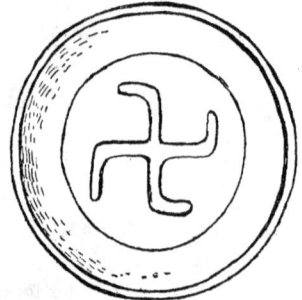

Fig. 37.
SWASTIKA MARK ON BLACK POTTERY.
Cheithan-thagh.
De Morgan, "Au Caucase," fig. 179.

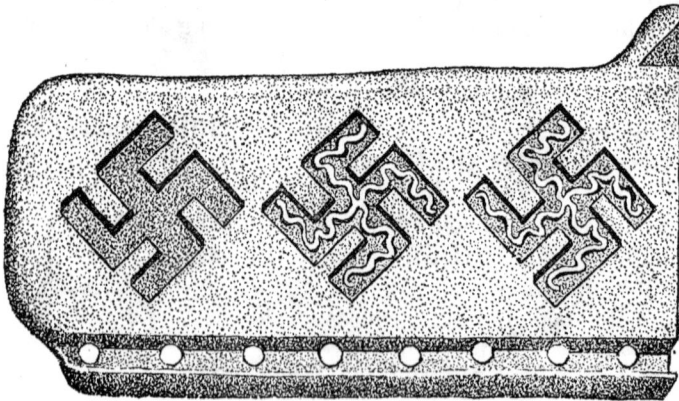

Fig. 38.
FRAGMENT OF BRONZE CEINTURE.
Swastika repoussé.
Necropolis of Koban, Caucasus.
Chantre, " Le Caucase," pl. 11, fig. 3.

signs reported by Waring[3] as from Asia Minor, which he credits, without explanation, to Ellis's "Antiquities of Heraldry."

[1] "Recherches Anthropologiques dans le Caucase," tome deuxième, période protohistorique, Atlas, pl. 11, fig. 3.
[2] Count Goblet d'Alviella, "La Migration des Symboles," p. 51.
[3] "Ceramic Art in Remote Ages," pl. 41, figs. 5 and 6.

The specimen shown in fig. 41 is reported by Waring,[1] quoting Rzewusky,[2] as one of the several branding marks used on Circassian horses for identification.

Mr. Frederick Remington, the celebrated artist and literateur, has an article, "Cracker Cowboy in Florida,"[3] wherein he discourses of the forgery of brands on cattle in that country. One of his genuine brands is a circle with a small cross in the center. The forgery consists in elongating each arm of the cross and turning it with a scroll, forming an ogee Swastika(fig.13d),which, curiously enough, is practically the same brand used on Circassian horses (fig. 41).

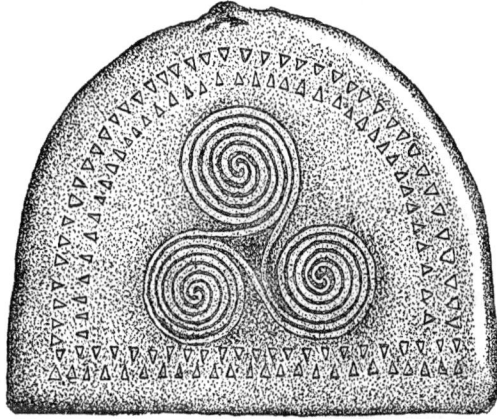

Fig. 39.

BRONZE AGRAFE OR BELT PLATE.

Triskelion in spiral.

Koban, Caucasus.

Chantre, "Le Caucase," pl. 11, fig. 4.

Fig. 40.

SWASTIKA SIGNS FROM ASIA MINOR.

Waring, "Ceramic Art in Remote Ages," pl. 41, figs. 5 and 6.

Max Ohnefalsch-Richter[4] says that instruments of copper (*audumbaroasih*) are recommended in the Atharva-Veda to make the Swastika, which represents the figure 8; and thus he attempts to account for the use of that mark branded on the cows in India (supra, p. 772), on the horses in Circassia (fig. 41), and said to have been used in Arabia.

ASIA MINOR—TROY (HISSARLIK).

Fig. 41.

BRAND FOR HORSES IN CIRCASSIA.

Ogee Swastika, tetraskelion.

Waring, "Ceramic Art in Remote Ages," pl. 42, fig. 20c.

Many specimens of the Swastika were found by Dr. Schliemann in the ruins of Troy, principally on spindle whorls, vases, and bijoux of precious metal. Zmigrodzki[5] made from Dr. Schliemann's great atlas the following classification of the objects found at Troy, ornamented with the Swastika and its related forms:

Fifty-five of pure form; 114 crosses with the four dots, points or alleged nail holes (*Croix swasticale*); 102 with three branches or arms (triskelion); 86 with five branches or arms; 63 with six branches or arms; total, 420.

Zmigrodzki continues his classification by adding those which have

---

[1] "Ceramic Art in Remote Ages," pl. 42, fig. 20c.

[2] "Mines de l'Orient," v.

[3] Harper's Magazine, August, 1895.

[4] Bulletins de la Soc. d'Anthrop., 1888, II, p. 678.

[5] Dixième Congrès International d'Anthropologie et d'Archéologie Préhistorique, Paris, 1889, p. 474.

relation to the Swastika thus: Eighty-two representing stars; 70 representing suns; 42 representing branches of trees or palms; 15 animals non-ferocious, deer, antelope, hare, swan, etc.; total, 209 objects. Many of these were spindle whorls.

Dr. Schliemann, in his works, "Troja" and "Ilios," describes at length his excavations of these cities and his discoveries of the Swastika on many objects. His reports are grouped under titles of the various cities, first, second, third, etc., up to the seventh city, counting always from the bottom, the first being deepest and oldest. The same system will be here pursued. The first and second cities were 45 to 52 feet (13 to 16 meters) deep; the third, 23 to 33 feet (7 to 10 meters) deep; the fourth city, 13 to 17.6 feet (4 to 5½ meters) deep; the fifth city, 7 to 13 feet (2 to 4 meters) deep; the sixth was the Lydian city of Troy, and the seventh city, the Greek Ilium, approached the surface.

First and Second Cities.—But few whorls were found in the first and

Fig. 42.

FRAGMENT OF LUSTROUS BLACK POTTERY.

Swastika, right.

Depth, 23 feet.

Schliemann, "Ilios," fig. 247.

second cities[1] and none of these bore the Swastika mark, while thousands were found in the third, fourth, and fifth cities, many of which bore the Swastika mark. Those of the first city, if unornamented, have a uniform lustrous black color and are the shape of a cone (fig. 55) or of two cones joined at the base (figs. 52 and 71). Both kinds were found at 33 feet and deeper. Others from the same city were ornamented by incised lines rubbed in with white chalk, in which case they were flat.[2] In the second city the whorls were smaller than in the first. They were all of a black color and their incised ornamentation was practically the same as those from the upper cities.[3]

Zmigrodzki congratulated himself on having discovered among Schliemann's finds what he believed to be the oldest representation of the Swastika of which we had reliable knowledge. It was a fragment of a vase (fig. 42) of the lustrous black pottery peculiar to the whorls of the first and second cities. But Zmigrodzki was compelled to recede, which he did regretfully, when Schliemann, in a later edition, inserted the footnote (p. 350) saying, that while he had found this (with a companion piece) at a great depth in his excavations, and had attributed them to the first city, yet, on subsequent examination, he had become convinced that they belonged to the third city.

The Swastika, turned both ways 卐 and 卍, was frequent in the third, fourth, and fifth cities.

The following specimens bearing the Swastika mark are chosen, out of the many specimens in Schliemann's great album, in order to make a fair representation of the various kinds, both of whorls and of Swas-

---

[1] "Ilios," pp. 229, 350, note 1.

[2] Ibid, figs. 63–70, p. 229.

[3] Ibid, p. 303.

tikas. They are arranged in the order of cities, the depth being indicated in feet.

The Third, or Burnt, City (23 to 33 feet deep).—The spindle-whorl shown in fig. 43 contains two Swastikas and two crosses.[1]   Of the one

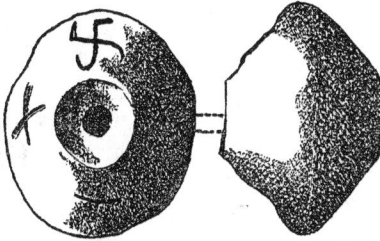

Fig. 43.
SPINDLE-WHORL WITH TWO SWASTIKAS AND TWO
CROSSES.
Depth, 23 feet.
Schliemann, "Ilios," fig. 1858.

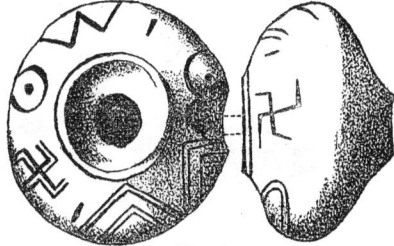

Fig. 44.
SPINDLE-WHORL WITH TWO SWASTIKAS.
Depth, 23 feet.
Schliemann, "Ilios," fig. 1874.

Swastika, two arms are bent to the right at right angles, while the other two are bent to the right in curves.   The other Swastika has but two bends, one at right angles, the other curved, both to the right.   The specimen shown in fig. 44 has two Swastikas, in one of which the four arms are bent at right angles to the left.   The entire figure is traced in double lines, one heavy and one light, as though to represent edges or shadows.   The second Swastika has its ends bent at an

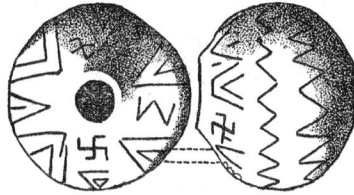

Fig. 45.
SPINDLE-WHORL WITH TWO SWASTIKAS.
Depth, 23 feet.
Schliemann, "Ilios," fig. 1919.

obtuse angle to the left, and at the extremities the lines taper to a point.   The whorl shown in fig. 45 is nearly spherical, with two Swastikas in the upper part.

Fig. 46.
SPINDLE-WHORL WITH TWO
SWASTIKAS.
Depth, 28 feet.
Schliemann, "Ilios," fig. 1826.

The ends of the four arms in both are bent at right angles, one to the right, the other to the left.   Fig. 46 represents a spindle-whorl with two irregular Swastikas; but one arm is bent at right angles and all the arms and points are uncertain and of unequal lengths.

Fig. 47.
SPINDLE-WHORL WITH THREE SWASTIKAS.
Depth, 23 feet.
Schliemann, "Ilios," fig. 1851.

The rest of the field is covered with indefinite and inexplicable marks, of which the only ones noteworthy are points or dots, seven in number.   In fig. 47 the top is surrounded by a line of zigzag

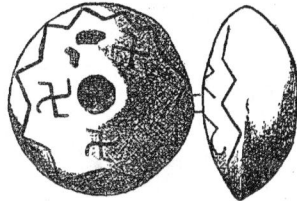

---

[1] All spindle-whorls from the hill of Hissarlik are represented one-half natural size.

or dog-tooth ornaments. Within this field, on the upper part and equidistant from the central hole, are three Swastikas, the ends of all of which turn to the left, and but one at right angles. All three have

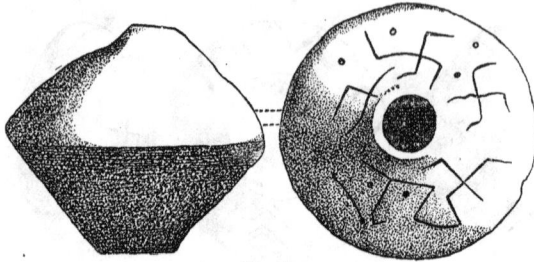

Fig. 48.

SPINDLE-WHORL WITH SWASTIKAS.

Depth, 23 feet.

Schliemann, "Ilios," fig. 1982.

one or more ends bent, not at any angle, but in a curve or hook, making an ogee. Fig. 48 shows a large whorl with two or three Swastikas on its upper surface in connection with several indefinite marks apparently without meaning. The dots are interspersed over the field, the Swastikas all bent to the right, but with uncertain lines and at indefinite angles. In one of them the main line forming the cross is curved toward the central hole; in another, the ends are both bent in the same direction—that is, pointing to the periphery of the whorl. Fig. 49 shows a sphere or globe (see figs. 75, 88) divided by longitudinal lines into four segments, which are again divided by an equatorial line. These segments contain marks or dots and circles, while one segment contains a normal Swastika turned to the left. This terra-cotta ball has figured in a peculiar degree in the symbolic representation of the Swastika. Greg says of it:[1]

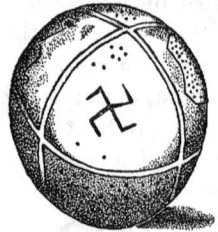

Fig. 49.

SPHERE DIVIDED INTO EIGHT SEGMENTS, ONE OF WHICH CONTAINS A SWASTIKA.

Schliemann, "Ilios," fig. 1999.

We see on one hemisphere the ⊞ standing for Zeus (=Indra) the sky god, and on the other side a rude representation of a sacred (*somma*) tree; a very interesting and curious western perpetuation of the original idea and a strong indirect proof of the ⊞ standing for the emblem of the sky god.

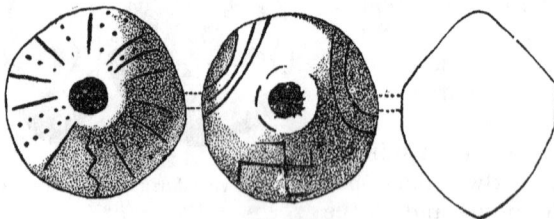

Fig. 50.

BICONICAL SPINDLE-WHORL WITH SWASTIKA.

Schliemann, "Ilios," fig. 1949.

Fig. 50 represents one of the biconical spindle-whorls with various decorations on the two sides, longitudinal lines interspersed with dots, arcs of concentric circles arranged in three parallels, etc. On one of these sides is a normal Swastika, the arms crossing at right angles, the ends bent at right angles to the left.

---

[1] Archæologia, XLVIII, pt. 2, p. 322.

The specimen shown in fig. 51 contains four perfect Swastikas and two inchoate and uncertain. Both of the latter have been damaged by breaking the surface. The four Swastikas all have their arms bent to the right; some are greater than at right angles, and one arm is curved. Several ends are tapered to a point. Fig. 52 shows a whorl of biconical form. It contains two Swastikas, the main arms of which are ogee

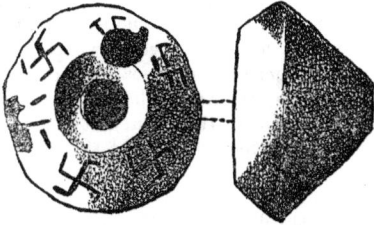

Fig. 51.

BICONICAL SPINDLE-WHORL WITH SIX SWASTIKAS.

Depth, 33 feet.

Schliemann, "Ilios," fig. 1859.

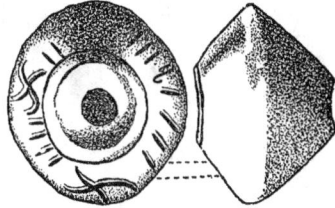

Fig. 52.

BICONICAL SPINDLE-WHORL WITH TWO OGEE SWASTIKAS.

Depth, 33 feet.

Schliemann, "Ilios," fig. 1876.

forms, crossing each other at the center at nearly right angles, the ogee ends curving to the right. In fig. 53 the entire field of the upper surface is filled with, or occupied by, a Greek cross, in the center of which is the central hole of the whorl, while on each of the four arms is represented a Swastika, the main arms all crossing at right angles, the ends all bent to the right at a slightly obtuse angle. Each of these bent ends tapers to a point, some with slight curves and a small flourish. (See figs. 33 and 34 for reference to this flourish.) The specimen shown in fig. 54 has a center field in its upper part, of which the decoration consists of incised parallel lines forming segments of circles, repeated in each one of the four quarters of the field. The center hole is surrounded by two concentric rings of incised lines. In one of

Fig. 53.

SPINDLE-WHORL WITH FOUR SWASTIKAS.

Depth, 33 feet.

De Mortillet, "Musée Préhistorique," fig. 1240.

Fig. 54.

SPINDLE-WHORL WITH ONE SWASTIKA.

Depth, 33 feet.

De Mortillet, "Musée Préhistorique," fig. 1241.

these spaces is a single Swastika; its main arms crossing at right angles, two of its ends bent to the left at right angles, the other two in the same direction and curved.

The Fourth City (13.2 to 17.6 feet deep).—Schliemann says:[1]

We find among the successors of the burnt city the same triangular idols; the same primitive bronze battle-axes; the same terra-cotta vases, with or without tripod feet; the same double-handled goblets (δέπα ἀμφικύπελλα); the same battle-axes of jade, porphyry, and diorite; the same rude stone hammers, and saddle querns of trachyte. * * * The number of rude stone hammers and polished stone axes are fully thrice as large as in the third city, while the masses of shells and cockles

[1] "Ilios," pp. 518, 571.

accumulated in the débris of the houses are so stupendous that they baffle all description. The pottery is coarser and of a ruder fabric than in the third city. * * * There were also found in the fourth city many needles of bone for female handiwork, bear tusks, spit rests of mica schist, whetstones of slate, porphyry, etc., of the usual form, hundreds of small silex saws, and some knives of obsidian. Stone whorls, which are so abundant at Mycenæ, are but rarely found here; all of those which occur are, according to Mr. Davis, of steatite. On the other hand, terra-cotta whorls, with or without incised ornamentation, are found by thousands; their forms hardly vary from those in the third (the burnt) city, and the same may be generally said of their incised ornamentation. * * * The same representation of specimens of whorls are given as in the third city, and the same observations apply.

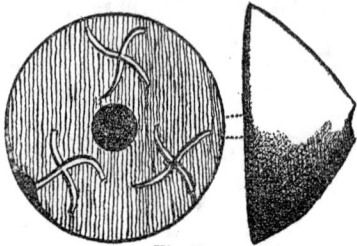

Fig. 55.

CONICAL SPINDLE-WHORL WITH THREE OGEE SWASTIKAS.

Depth, 13½ feet.

Schliemann, "Ilios," fig. 1850.

Fig. 55 shows a simple cone, the upper surface being flat and without other decoration than three Swastikas equidistant from the hole and from each other, all made by the two crossed ogee lines with ends curved to the right. This specimen is much like that of fig. 71 (Madam Schliemann collection in the U. S. National Museum, Cat. No. 149704). Fig. 56 shows a remarkable spindle-whorl. Its marks greatly excited the interest of Dr. Schliemann, and he devoted much space to the discussion of these and similar characters. The whorl is

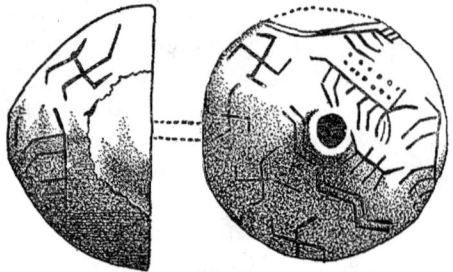

Fig. 56.

CONICAL SPINDLE-WHORL WITH FOUR SWASTIKAS OF VARIOUS KINDS.

Depth, 13½ feet.

Schliemann, "Ilios," fig. 1879.

in the form of a cone. It bears upon its conical surface four Swastikas, the ends of three of which bend to the right and one to the left. There are but two of these ends which bend at right angles. Most of them are at an obtuse angle, while the ends of two are curved. Some taper to a point and finish with a slight flourish. The other marks which so interested Dr. Schliemann were the chevron ornament (zigzag), drawn in parallel lines, which, he strongly argued, and fortified with many authorities, represented lightning. The second series of marks he called a "burning altar." This assertion he also fortified with authorities and with

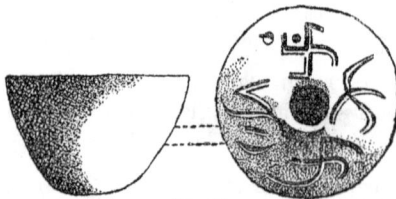

Fig. 57.

CONICAL SPINDLE-WHORL WITH SWASTIKAS.

Depth, 13¼ feet.

Schliemann, "Ilios," fig. 1894.

illustrations of a similar sign from different countries. (See fig. 101.)
The third series of marks represented an animal, name and character

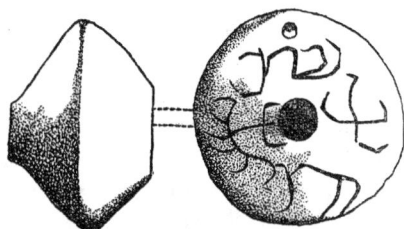

Fig. 58.

BICONICAL SPINDLE-WHORL WITH ONE SWASTIKA.

Depth, 13½ feet.

Schliemann, "Ilios," fig. 1983.

unknown, with a head or tusks
with two large branching horns
or ears, a straight back, a stiff but
drooping tail, four legs, and two
rows of the remarkable dots—
seven in one, six in the other—
placed over the back of the animal.
(See figs. 99 and 100.) Fig. 57
represents another cone-shaped
whorl, the flat surface of which is
engraved with one perfect Swastika, the two arms crossing each
other at right angles and the two ends bending at right angles to
the right; the other two are curved, also to the right. Two of the

other figures Dr.
Schliemann calls
Swastikas, al-
though they are
uncertain in some
of their arms
and angles. The
fourth character
he imagined to
be an inchoate or
attempted Swas-
tika. Fig. 58

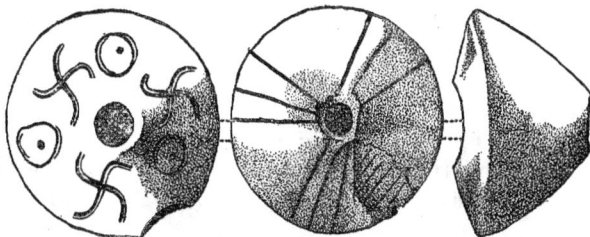

Fig. 59.

BICONICAL SPINDLE-WHORL WITH THREE OGEE SWASTIKAS.

Depth, 13½ feet.

Schliemann, "Ilios," fig. 1990.

shows a biconical whorl with curious and inexplicable characters. One
of them forms a crude Swastika, which, while the main arms cross at

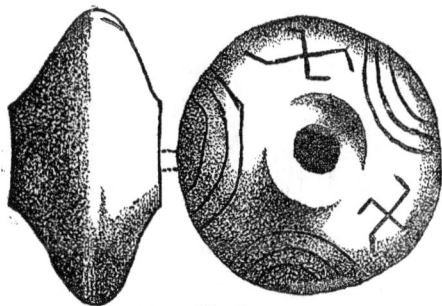

Fig. 60.

BICONICAL SPINDLE-WHORL WITH TWO SWASTIKAS.

Depth, 16½ feet.

Schliemann, "Ilios," fig. 1863.

right angles the ends are bent
at uncertain angles, three to
the left and one to the right.
These characters are so undetermined that it is doubtful
if they could have had any signification, either ornamental
or otherwise. Fig. 59 is almost
conical, the flat surface thereof
being only slightly raised at
the center. It is much the same
form as the whorls shown in
figs. 55 and 71. The nearly flat
surface is the top, and on it,
equidistant from the center
hole and from each other, are three ogee Swastikas of double lines,
with their ends all curved to the right. In the alternate spaces are
small incised circles, with dots in the centers. In fig. 60 a biconical

whorl is shown. It has three of the circle segments marked in equilateral positions, with three or four parallel lines, after the style shown in fig. 54. In the spaces are two Swastikas, in both of which the two

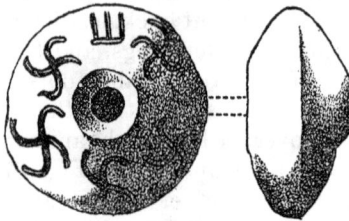

main arms cross at right angles. Some of the ends bend at a right, and others at an obtuse, angle. In one of the Swastikas the bent ends turn toward each other, forming a rude figure 8. The specimen shown in fig. 61 is biconical, but much flattened; it contains five ogee Swastikas, of which the ends of four bend to the right and one to the left. In an interval between them is one of the burning altars. Fig. 62 shows three Swastikas with double

Fig. 61.

BICONICAL SPINDLE-WHORL WITH FIVE OGEE SWASTIKAS.

Depth, 18 feet.

Schliemann, "Ilios," fig. 1905.

parallel lines. The main arms cross each other at right angles; the ends are bent at nearly right angles, one to the left, one to the right, and the other both ways. Fig. 63 represents a spindle-whorl with a cup-shaped depression around the central hole, which is surrounded by three lines in concentric circles, while on the field, at 90 degrees from

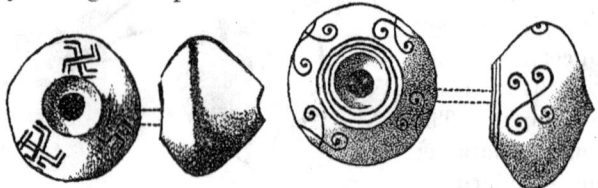

Fig. 62.

SPINDLE-WHORL WITH THREE SWASTIKAS.

Depth, 19.8 feet.

Schliemann, "Ilios," fig. 1855.

Fig. 63.

SPINDLE-WHORL HAVING FOUR OGEE SWASTIKAS WITH SPIRAL VOLUTES.

Depth, 18 feet.

Schliemann, "Ilios," fig. 1868.

each other, are four ogee Swastikas (tetraskelions), the arms all turning to the left and spirally each upon itself. The specimen shown in

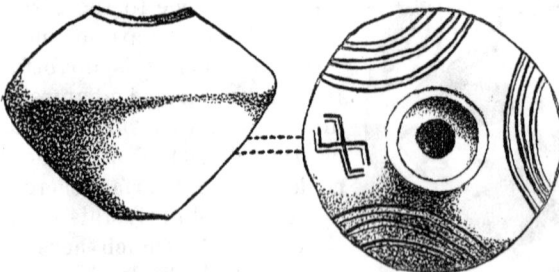

fig. 64 is biconical, though, as usual, the upper cone is the smallest. There are parallel lines, three in a set, forming the segments of three circles, in one space of which appears a Swastika of a curious and unique form, similar to that shown in fig. 60. The two main arms cross each other at very nearly right angles and the ends also bend at right angles toward and approaching each other, so

Fig. 64.

BICONICAL SPINDLE-WHORL WITH ONE SWASTIKA.

Depth, 19.8 feet.

Schliemann, "Ilios," fig. 1865.

that if continued slightly farther they would close and form a decorative figure 8. The specimen shown in fig. 65 is decorated with parallel lines, three in number, arranged in segments of three circles, the periphery of which is toward the center, as in figs. 60 and 64. In one of the spaces is a Swastika of curious form; the main arms cross each other at right angles, but the four ends represent different styles—two are bent square to the left, one square to the right, and the fourth curves to the left at no angle. Fig. 66 shows a biconical whorl, and its top is decorated to represent three Swastikas

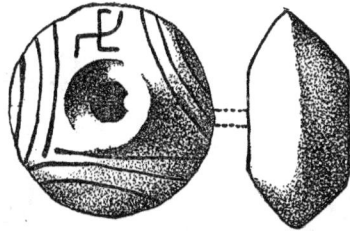

Fig. 65.
BICONICAL SPINDLE-WHORL WITH ONE SWASTIKA.
Depth, 19.8 feet.
Schliemann, "Ilios," fig. 1866.

and three burning altars. The ends of the arms of the Swastikas all bend to the left, some are at right angles and some at obtuse angles,

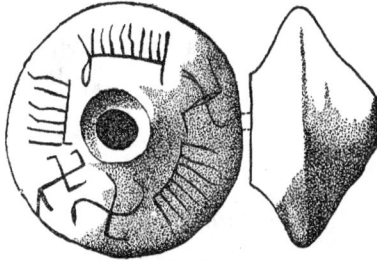

Fig. 66.
BICONICAL SPINDLE-WHORL WITH THREE SWASTIKAS AND THREE BURNING ALTARS.
Depth, 19.8 feet.
Schliemann, "Ilios," fig. 1872.

while two or three are curved; two of them show corrections, the marks at the ends having been changed in one case at a different angle and in another from a straight line to a curve. Fig. 67 shows four specimens of Swastika, the main arms of all of which cross at right angles. The ends all bend to the right, at nearly right angles, tapering to a point and finishing with the slight flourish noted in the Jain Swastika (fig. 34c). They are alternated with a chevron decoration. Fig. 68 shows three Swastikas, the ends of the arms of which are all bent to the left. One Swastika is composed of

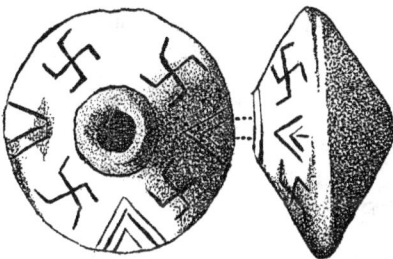

Fig. 67.
BICONICAL SPINDLE-WHORL WITH FOUR SWASTIKAS.
Depth, 19.8 feet.
Schliemann, "Ilios," fig. 1873.

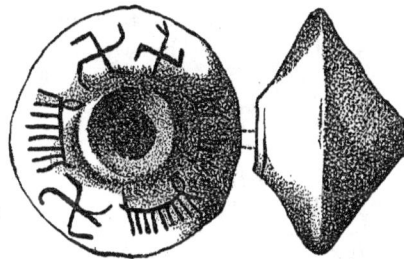

Fig. 68.
BICONICAL SPINDLE-WHORL WITH THREE SWASTIKAS OF DIFFERENT STYLES.
Depth, 19.8 feet.
Schliemann, "Ilios," fig. 1911.

two ogee lines. Two arms of another are curved, but all others are bent at right angles, some of them tapering to points, finishing with a
H. Mis. 90, pt. 2——52

little flourish (figs. 67 and 34c). One of these ends, like that in fig. 66, has been corrected by the maker. Fig. 69 represents one Swastika in which the main arms cross at nearly right angles. Both ends of one

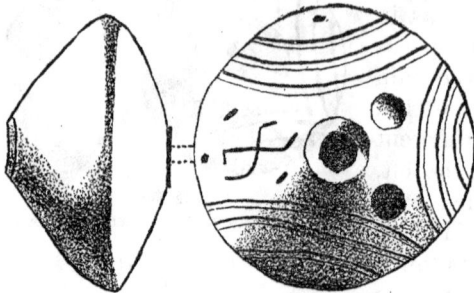

Fig. 69.
BICONICAL SPINDLE-WHORL WITH ONE SWASTIKA OF THE
FIGURE-8 STYLE.
Depth, 19.8 feet.
Schliemann, "Ilios," fig. 1861.

arm turn to the left and those of the other arm turn to the right in figure 8 style. One of the ends is curved, the others bent at different angles. Fig. 70 shows the parallel lines representing segments of a circle similar to figs. 60, 64, 65, and 69, except that it has four instead of three. It has one Swastika; the main arms (of double lines) cross at right angles, the ends all curving to the left with a slight ogee.

The U. S. National Museum was, during 1893, the fortunate recipient of a collection of objects from Madame Schliemann, which her husband, before his death, had signified should be given to the United States as a token of his remembrance of and regard for his adopted country. He never forgot that he was an American citizen, and, preparing for death, made his acknowledgments in the manner mentioned. The collection consisted of 178 objects, all

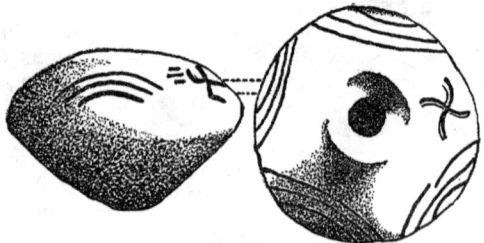

Fig. 70.
BICONICAL SPINDLE-WHORL WITH ONE SWASTIKA, SLIGHTLY OGEE.
Depth, 19.8 feet.
Schliemann, "Ilios," fig. 1864.

from ancient Troy, and they made a fair representation of his general finds. This collection is in the Department of Prehistoric Anthropology. In this collection is a spindle-whorl, found at 13½ feet (4 meters) depth and belonging to the fourth city. It had three Swastikas upon its face, and is here shown as fig. 71.[1]

The Fifth City.—Schliemann says:[2]

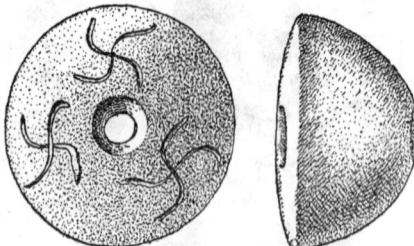

Fig. 71.
CONICAL SPINDLE-WHORL WITH THREE OGEE SWASTIKAS.
Depth, 13.5 feet.
Gift of Madame Schliemann. Cat. No. 149704, U. S. N. M.

* The rude stone hammers found in enormous quantities in the fourth city are no longer found in this stratum, nor did the stone axes, which are so very abundant there, occur again here. In-

[1] "Ilios," fig. 1852.   [2] Ibid, p. 573.

stead of the hundreds of axes I gathered in the fourth city, I collected in all only two
here. * * * The forms of the terra-cotta whorls, too, are in innumerable instances
different here. These objects are of a much inferior fabric, and become elongated
and pointed. Forms of whorls like Nos. 1801, 1802, and 1803 [see figs. 72, 73, and 74],
which were never found before, are here plentiful.

The Sixth and Seventh Cities.—The sixth city is described in "Ilios,"
page 587, and the seventh on pages 608 and 618. Both cities contained
occasional whorls of clay, all thoroughly baked, without incised or
painted ornamentation, and shed no fur-
ther light on the Swastika.

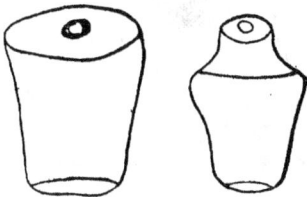

Figs. 72, 73, 74.

FORMS OF WHORLS FROM THE FIFTH BURIED CITY OF
HISSARLIK, FOR COMPARISON.

Schliemann, "Ilios," figs. 1801, 1802, 1803.

Fig. 75 represents the opposite hemispheres of a terra-cotta ball, found at a
depth of 26 feet, divided by incised lines into fifteen zones, of
which two are ornamented with
points and the middle zone, the
largest of all, with thirteen specimens of 卐 and 卍.

Zmigrodzki says[1] that there
were found by Schliemann, at Hissarlik, fifty-five specimens of the Swastika "pure and simple" (pp. 809, 826). It will be perceived by examination that the Swastika "pure and simple" comprised Swastikas of
several forms; those in which the four arms of the cross were at other
angles besides right angles, those in which the ends bent at square
and other angles to the right; then those to the left (Burnouf and Max
Müller's Suavastika); those in which the bends were, some to the right
and some to the left, in the same design; where the points tapered off
and turned outward with a
flourish; where the arms
bent at no angle, but were
in spirals each upon itself,
and turned, some to the
right, some to the left.
We shall see other related
forms, as where the arms
turn spirally upon each
other instead of upon themselves. These will some-
times have three, five, six,
or more arms, instead of

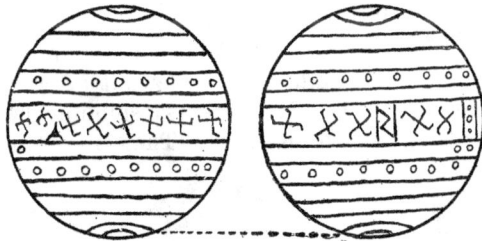

Fig. 75.

TERRA-COTTA SPHERE WITH THIRTEEN SWASTIKAS,
Third city. Depth, 26 feet.

Schliemann, "Ilios," figs. 245, 246.

four (p. 768). The cross and the circle will also appear in connection
with the Swastika; and other designs, as zigzags (lightning), burning
altars, men, animals, and similar representations will be found associated with the Swastika, and are only related to it by the association
of similar objects from the same locality. A description of their patterns will include those already figured, together with Schliemann's

[1] Tenth Congr. Inter. d'Anthrop. et d'Archæol. Prehist., Paris, 1889, p. 474.

comments as to signification and frequency. They become more important because these related forms will be found in distant countries and among distant peoples, notably among the prehistoric peoples of America. Possibly these designs have a signification, possibly not. Dr. Schliemann thought that in many cases they had. Professor Sayce supported him, strongly inclining toward an alphabetic or linguistic, perhaps ideographic, signification. No opinion is advanced by the author on these theories, but the designs are given in considerable numbers, to the end that the evidence may be fully reported, and future investigators, radi-

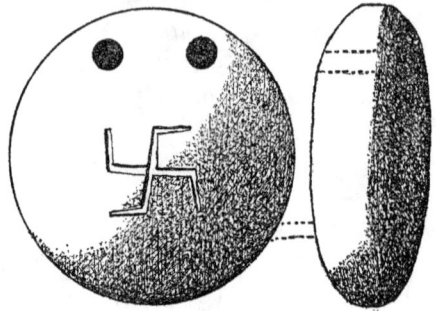

Fig. 76.
TERRA-COTTA DISK WITH ONE SWASTIKA.
Schliemann, " Ilios," fig. 1849.

cal and conservative, imaginative and unimaginative, theorists and agnostics, may have a fair knowledge of this mysterious sign, and an opportunity to indulge their respective talents at length. Possibly these associated designs may throw some light upon the origin or history of the Swastika or of some of its related forms.

Fig. 77.
SPINDLE-WHORL WITH OGEE SWASTIKA.
Third city. Depth, 23 feet.
Schliemann, " Ilios," fig. 1822.

The specimen represented in fig. 76 is not a spindle-whorl, as shown by the number and location of the holes. It bears a good representation of a Swastika the form of which has been noticed several times. The two main arms cross each other at nearly right angles. The ends of the arms all bend to the right at a slightly obtuse angle and turn outward with a flourish somewhat after the style of the Jain Swastika (fig. 34c). Fig. 77 represents a spindle-whorl with a Swastika of the ogee style curved to the right. The center hole of the whorl forms the cen-

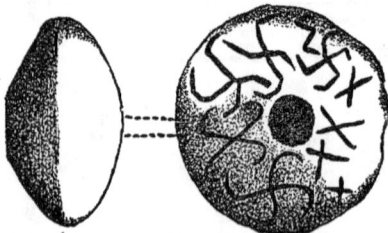

Fig. 78.
BICONICAL SPINDLE-WHORL WITH IRREGULAR SWASTIKAS AND CROSSES.
Fourth city. Depth, 13.6 feet.
Schliemann, " Ilios," fig. 1871.

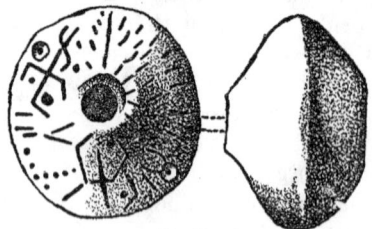

Fig. 79.
BICONICAL SPINDLE-WHORL WITH UNCERTAIN AND MALFORMED SWASTIKAS.
Third city. Depth, 33 feet.
Schliemann, " Ilios," fig. 1870.

ter of the sign. The figure is of double lines, and in the interspaces are four dots, similar to those in figs. 96–98, and others which Dr. Schliemann reports as common, and to which he attributes some special but unknown meaning. Swastikas and crosses of irregular shape and style are shown in the field of fig. 78. Two fairly well formed Swastikas appear, both of the ogee style, with the ends curved to the right. One is of the style resembling the figure 8 (see figs. 60 and 64). Two others are crudely and irregularly formed, and would scarcely be recognized as Swastikas except for their association. Fig. 79 represents uncertain and malformed Swastikas. The arms are bent in different directions in the same line. Two of the main

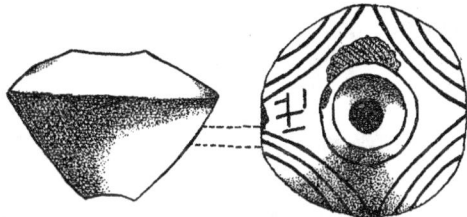

Fig. 80.

BICONICAL SPINDLE-WHORL WITH IRREGULAR AND PARTLY FORMED SWASTIKAS HAVING LARGE DOT IN CENTER.

Fourth city. Depth, 23 feet.

Schliemann, "Ilios," fig. 1875.

arms are not bent. The inexplicable dots are present, and the field is more or less covered with unmeaning or, at least, unexplained marks. Fig. 80 also illustrates the indefinite and inchoate style of decoration. One unfinished Swastika appears which, unlike anything we have yet seen, has a circle with a dot in the center for the body of the Swastika at the crossing of the main arms. Fig. 81 shows two Swastikas, both crossing their main arms at right angles and the ends bending also at right angles—one to the right, the other to the

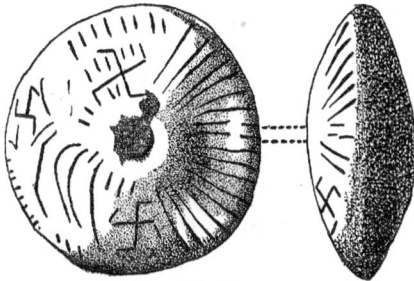

Fig. 81.

BICONICAL SPINDLE-WHORL, FLATTENED, WITH TWO SWASTIKAS AND INDEFINITE DECORATION.

Schliemann, "Ilios," fig. 1947.

left. This specimen is inserted here because of the numerous decorations of apparently unmeaning, or, at least, unexplained, lines. Fig. 82 shows four segmented circles with an indefinite Swastika in one of the spaces. The ends are not well turned, only one being well attached to the main arms. One of the ends is not joined, one overruns and forms a sort of cross; the other has no bend. Fig. 83 contains an unmistakable Swastika, the main arms of which cross at right angles, turning to the

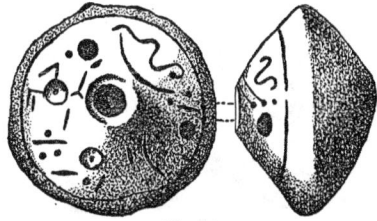

Fig. 82.

BICONICAL SPINDLE-WHORL WITH ONE SWASTIKA AND FOUR SEGMENTS OF CIRCLES.

Third city. Depth, 33 feet.

Schliemann, "Ilios," fig. 1989.

left with an ogee curve. The peculiarity of this specimen is that the center of the sign is inclosed in a circle, thus showing the indifference of the Swastika sign to other signs, whether cross or circle. The outer parts of the field are occupied with the parallel lines of the circle

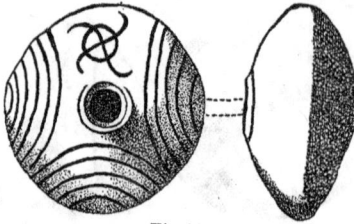

Fig. 83.
BICONICAL SPINDLE-WHORL, FLATTENED.
Ogee Swastika with central circle.
Third city. Depth, 23 feet.
Schliemann, "Ilios," fig. 1987.

segment, as shown in many other specimens. The specimen shown in fig. 84 is similar in style to the last. The bodies of six Swastikas are formed by a circle and dot, while the arms of the cross start from the outside of the circle, extending themselves in curves, all of them to the right. (See fig. 13d.) It has no other ornamentation. The same remark is to be made about the indifferent use of the Swastika in association with cross or circle. We have seen many Swastikas composed of the crossed ogee lines or curves. Figs. 85 and 86 show the same ogee lines and curves not crossed; and thus, while it may be that neither of them are Swastikas, yet they show a relationship of form from which the derivation of a Swastika would be easy.

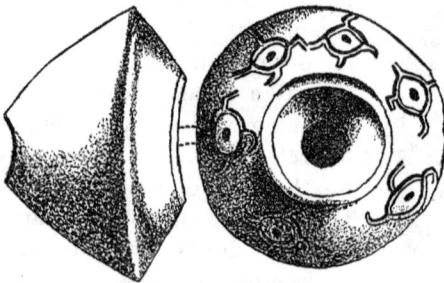

Fig. 84.
BICONICAL SPINDLE-WHORL WITH SIX OGEE SWASTIKAS
HAVING CENTRAL CIRCLE AND DOT.
Third city. Depth, 23 feet.
Schliemann, "Ilios," fig. 1862.

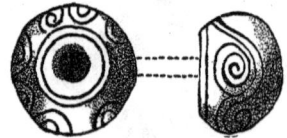

Fig. 85.
SPHERICAL SPINDLE-WHORL WITH
FLATTENED TOP AND OGEE LINES
WHICH DO NOT FORM SWASTIKAS.
Schliemann, "Ilios," fig. 1890.

Attention has been called to decorations comprising segments of the circles incised in these whorls, the periphery of which is toward their centers (figs. 60, 64, 65, 69, 70, 82 and 83). Also to the mysterious dots (figs. 46, 56, 75, 76, 77, 79, 84, 92, 96 and 97). Fig. 87 shows a combination of the segments of three circles, the dots within each, and two Swastikas. Of the Swastikas, one is normal, turning to the right; the other turns to the right, but at an obtuse angle, with one end straight and the

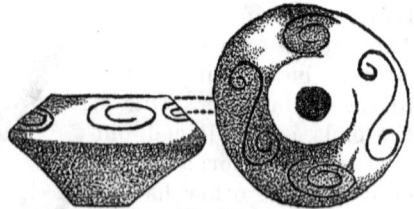

Fig. 86.
BICONICAL SPINDLE-WHORL WITH OGEE CURVES WHICH
ARE NOT CROSSED TO FORM SWASTIKAS.
Schliemann, "Ilios," fig. 1889.

other irregularly curved. Fig. 88 represents two sections of a terracotta sphere divided similar to fig. 49. Each of these sections contains a figure like unto a Swastika and which may be related to it. It is a circle with arms springing from the periphery, which arms turn all to the left, as they do in the ogee Swastika. One has seven, the other nine, arms. One has regular, the other irregular, lines and intervals. Fig. 89 represents a spindle-whorl of terra cotta nearly spherical, with decoration of a large central dot and lines springing thereout, almost like the spokes of a wheel, then all turning to the left as volutes. In some countries this has been called the sun symbol, but there is nothing to indicate that it had any signification at Hissarlik.

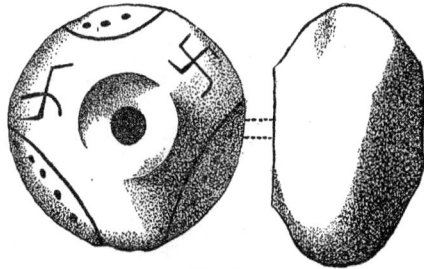

Fig. 87.

SPHERICAL SPINDLE-WHORL, FLATTENED.

Two Swatikas combined with segments and dots.

Schliemann, " Ilios," fig. 1988.

One of the marks resembles the long-backed, four-legged animal (figs. 99 and 100).[1] Figs. 90, 91, 92, and 93 show a further adaptation of the

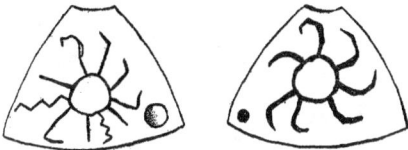

Fig. 88.

SECTIONS OF TERRA-COTTA SPHERE.[2]

Central circles with extended arms turning to the left, ogee and zigzag.

Schliemann, " Ilios," fig. 1993.

ogee curve developed into a Swastika, in which many arms start from the center circle around the central hole in the whorl, finally taking a spiral form. The relation of this to a sun symbol is only mentioned and not specified or declared. The inexplicable and constantly recurring dots are seen in fig. 90.

It is not contended that these are necessarily evolutions of the Swastika. We will see farther on many lines and forms of decoration by incised lines on these Trojan whorls, which may have had no relation to the Swastika, but are inserted here because persons rich in theories and brilliant in imagination have declared that they could see a resemblance, a relation, in this or some other decoration. As objects belonging to the same culture, from the same locality, and intimately associated with unmistakable Swastikas, they

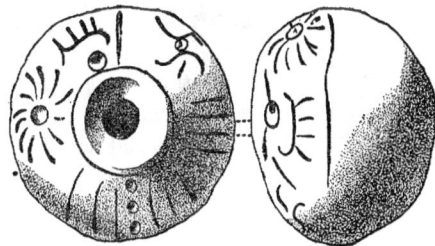

Fig. 89.

SPHERICAL SPINDLE-WHORL.

Large central dot with twelve arms, similar in form to the ogee Swastika.

Schliemann, " Ilios," fig. 1946.

were part of the res gestæ, and as such entitled to admission as evidence in the case. The effect of their evidence is a legitimate subject for discussion and argument. To refuse these figures admission would

---

[1] " Ilios " p. 418.   [2] See p. 786

be to decide the case against this contention without giving the opposing party an opportunity to see the evidence or to be heard in argument. Therefore the objects are inserted.

Fig. 90.

SPINDLE-WHORL.

Central dot with ogee arms radiating therefrom in different directions, but in the form of a Swastika.

Third city. Depth, 29 feet.

Schliemann, "Ilios," fig. 1830.

Fig. 91.

SPINDLE-WHORL WITH CENTRAL HOLE AND RADIATING ARMS.

Third city. Depth, 23 feet.

Schliemann, "Ilios," fig. 1842.

Specimens of other crosses are presented because the Swastika is considered to be a form of the cross. There may have been no evolution or relationship between them; but no person is competent to decide from a mere inspection or by reason of dissimilarity that there was not. We have to plead *ignoramus* as to the growth and evolution of both cross and Swastika, because the origin of both is lost in antiquity. But all are fair subjects for discussion. There certainly is nothing improbable in the relationship and evolution between the Swastika and the cross. It may be almost assumed.

Evidence leading to conviction may be found in associated contemporaneous specimens. M. Montelius, an archæologist of repute in the National Museum at Stockholm, discovered eight stages of culture in the bronze age of that country, which discovery was based solely upon the foregoing principle applied to the fibulæ found in prehistoric graves. In assorting his stock of

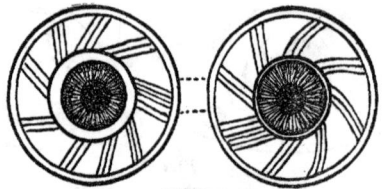

Fig. 92.

SPINDLE-WHORL WITH CENTRAL CIRCLE AND MANY ARMS.

Fourth city. Depth, 19.8 feet.

Schliemann, "Ilios," fig. 1887.

fibulæ, he was enabled to lay out a series of eight styles, each different, but with many presentations. He arranged them seriatim, according to certain differences in size, style, elegance of workmanship, etc.,

Fig. 93.

SPINDLE-WHORL WITH CENTRAL HOLE, LARGE CIRCLE, AND MANY CURVED ARMS.

Third city. Depth, 29 feet.

Schliemann, "Ilios," fig. 1833.

No. 1 being the smallest, and No. 8 the largest and most elaborate. They were then classified according to locality and association, and he discovered that Nos. 1 and 2 belonged together, on the same body or in the same grave, and the same with Nos. 2 and 3, 3 and 4, and so on to No. 8, but that there was no general or indefinite intermixture; Nos. 1 and 3 or 2 and 4 were not found together and were not associated, and so on. Nos. 7 and 8 were associated, but not 6 and 8, nor 5 and 7, nor was there any association beyond adjoining numbers in the series. Thus Montelius was able to determine that each one or each two of the series formed a stage in the culture of these peoples. While the numbers of the series separated from each other, as 1, 5, 8, were never found associated, yet it was conclusively shown that they were related, were the same object, all served a similar purpose, and together formed an evolutionary series showing their common origin, derivative growth and continuous im-provement in art, always by com-munication be-tween their makers or owners.

Thus it may be with the other forms of crosses, and thus it ap-pears to be with the circle and spiral Swastikas and those with ends bent in op-posite and differ-ent directions. Just what their

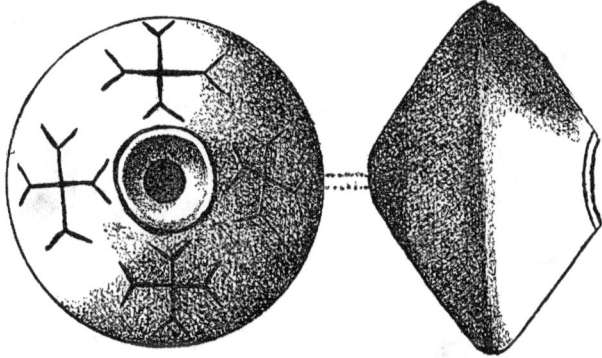

Fig. 94.

LARGE BICONICAL SPINDLE-WHORL.
Four crosses with bifurcated arms.
Third city. Depth, 23 feet.
Schliemann, "Ilios," fig. 1856.

relations are and at which end of the series the evolution began, is not argued. This is left for the theorists and imaginists, protesting, however, that they must not run wild nor push their theories beyond bounds. Fig. 94 represents four crosses, the main arms of which are at right angles, and each and all ends, instead of being turned at an angle which would make them Swastikas, are bifurcated and turn both

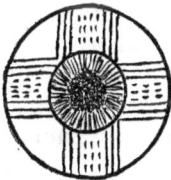

Fig. 95.

SPINDLE-WHORL.

Hole and large circle in center
with broad arms of Greek
cross.

Third city. Depth, 26.4 feet.

Schliemann, "Ilios," fig. 1820.

Fig. 96.

SPINDLE-WHORL.

Hole and large circle in center.
Eextended parallel arms with
dots, forming a Greek cross.

Third city. Depth, 23 feet.

Schliemann, "Ilios," fig. 1817.

Fig. 97.

SPINDLE-WHORL.

Greek cross. Tapering arms
with dots.

Third city. Depth, 23 feet.

Schliemann, "Ilios," fig. 1818.

ways, thus forming a foliated cross similar to the Maya cross, the "Tree of life." Figs. 95, 96, and 97 show Greek crosses. The centers of the crosses are occupied by the central hole of the whorl, while the arms extend to the periphery. In the centers of the respective arms are the ubiquitous dots. The question might here be asked whether these holes, which represented circles, stood for the sun symbol or solar disk. The question carries its own answer and is a refutation of those who fancy they can see mythology in everything. Fig. 98 is the same style of figure with the same dots, save that it has three instead of four arms.

Fig. 98.

SPINDLE-WHORL.

Central hole and three arms with dots.

Third city. Depth, 23 feet.

Schliemann, "Ilios," fig. 1819.

Figs. 99 and 100 each show four of the curious animals heretofore represented (fig. 56) in connection with the Swastika. They are here inserted for comparison. They are all of the same form, and one description will serve. Back straight, tail drooping, four legs, round head showing eye on one side, and long ears resembling those of a rabbit or hare, which, in fig. 56, are called horns. The general remarks in respect to the propriety of inserting crosses and burning altars (p. 824) apply with equal pertinency to these animals and to the unexplained dots seen on so many specimens. Fig. 101 shows both ends of a spindle-whorl, and is here inserted because it represents one of the "burning altars" of Dr. Schliemann, associated with a Swastika, as in figs. 61, 66, and 68, and even those of figure-8 style (figs. 64 and 69).

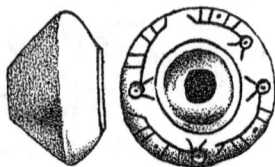

Fig. 99.

BICONICAL SPINDLE-WHORL.

Four animals are shown similar to those found associated with the Swastika.

Third city. Depth, 33 feet.

Schliemann, "Ilios," fig. 1877.

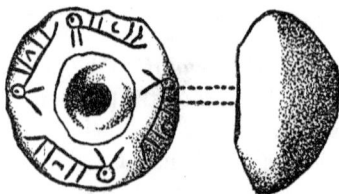

Fig. 100.

BICONICAL SPINDLE-WHORL.

Four animals are shown similar to those found associated with the Swastika.

Fourth city. Depth, 19.6 feet.

Schliemann, "Ilios," fig. 1867.

Dr. Schliemann found, during his excavations on the hill of Hissarlik, no less than 1,800 spindle-whorls. A few were from the first and second cities; they were of somewhat peculiar form (figs. 72 and 74), but the greatest number were from the third city, thence upward in decreasing numbers. The Swastika pure and simple was found on 55 specimens, while its related or suggested forms were on 420 (pp. 809, 819). Many of the other whorls were decorated with almost every imaginable form of dot, dash, circle, star, lozenge, zigzag, with many indefinite and undescribable forms. In presenting the claims of the Swastika as an intentional sign, with intentional, though perhaps

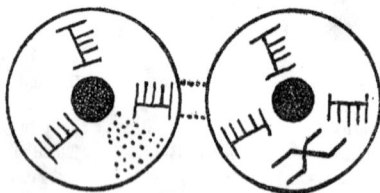

Fig. 101.

SPINDLE-WHORL WITH FIGURE-8 SWASTIKA(?) AND SIX "BURNING ALTARS."

Fourth city. Depth, 19.6 feet.

Schliemann, "Ilios," fig. 1838.

different, meanings, it might be unsatisfactory to the student to omit descriptions of these associated decorative forms. This description is impossible in words; therefore the author has deemed it wiser to insert figures of these decorations as they appeared on the spindle-whorls found at Troy, and associated with those heretofore given with the Swastika. It is not decided, however, that these have any relation to the Swastika, or that they had any connection with its manufacture or existence, either by evolution or otherwise, but they are here inserted to the end that the student and reader may take due account of the association and make such comparison as will satisfy him. (Figs. 102 to 124.)

102.

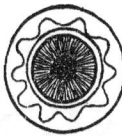

103.

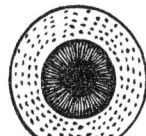

104.

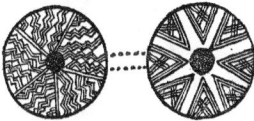

105.

106.

107.

108.

109.

110.

111.

112.

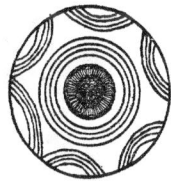

113.

Figs. 102–113.
TROJAN SPINDLE-WHORLS.
Schliemann, " Ilios."

114.

115.

116.

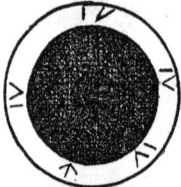

117.

118.

119.

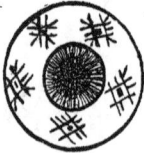

120.

121.

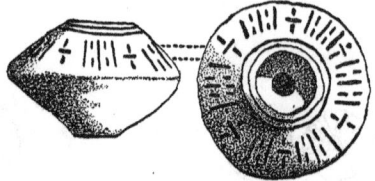

122.

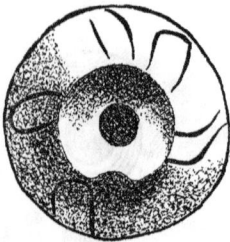

123.

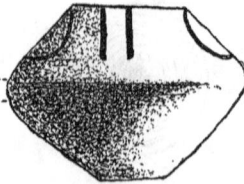

124.

Figs. 114–124.

TROJAN SPINDLE-WHORLS.

Schliemann, "Ilios."

Leaden idol of Hissarlik.—Dr. Schliemann, in his explorations on the hill of Hissarlik, at a depth of 23 feet, in the third, the burnt city, found a metal idol (fig. 125), which was determined on an analysis to be lead.[1] It was submitted to Professor Sayce who made the following report:[2]

> It is the Artemis Nana of Chaldea, who became the chief deity of Carchemish, the Hittite capital, and passed through Asia Minor to the shores and islands of the Ægean Sea. Characteristic figures of the goddess have been discovered at Mycenæ as well as in Cyprus.

In "Troja" Professor Sayce says:

> Precisely the same figure, with ringlets on either side of the head, but with a different ornament (dots instead of Swastika) sculptured on a piece of serpentine was recently found in Mæonia, and published by M. Salmon Reinach in Revue Archæologique. By the side of the goddess stands the Babylonian Bel, and among the Babylonian symbols that surround them is the representation of one of the terra-cotta whorls, of which Dr. Schliemann found such multitudes at Troy.

The chief interest to us of Dr. Schliemann's description of the idol lies in the last paragraph:[3]

> The vulva is represented by a large triangle, in the upper side of which we see three globular dots; we also see two lines of dots to the right and left of the vulva. The most curious ornament of the figure is a Swastika, which we see in the middle of the vulva. * * * So far as we know, the only figures to which the idol before us has any resemblance are the female figures of white marble found in tombs in Attica and in the Cyclades. Six of them, which are in the museum at Athens, * * * represent naked women. * * * The vulva is represented on the six figures by a large triangle. * * * Similar white Parian marble figures, found in the Cyclades, whereon the vulva is represented by a decorated triangle, are preserved in the British Museum. Lenormant, in "Les Antiquités de la Troade" (p. 46), says: "The statuettes of the Cyclades, in the form of a naked woman, appear to be rude copies made by the natives, at the dawn of their civilization, from the images of the Asiatic goddess which had been brought by Phœnician merchants. They were found in the most ancient sepulchers of the Cyclades, in company with stone weapons,

Fig. 125.

LEADEN IDOL OF ARTEMIS NANA OF CHALDEA, WITH SWASTIKA.[4]

Third city. Depth, 23 feet.

Schliemann, " Ilios." fig. 126

1⅓ natural size.

principally arrowheads of obsidian from Milo, and with polished pottery without paintings. We recognize in them the figures of the Asiatic Venus found in such large numbers from the banks of the Tigris to the island of Cyprus, through the whole extent of the Chaldeo-Assyrian, Aramæan, and Phœnician world. Their prototype is the Babylonian Zarpanit, or Zirbanit, so frequently represented on the cylinders and by terra-cotta idols, the fabrication of which begins in the most primitive time of Chaldea and continues among the Assyrians.

---

[1] "Ilios," fig. 226, p. 337.
[2] Ibid, p. 694.
[3] Ibid, p. 338.
[4] See p. 795.

It is to be remarked that this mark is not on the vulva, as declared by Schliemann, but rather on a triangle shield which covers the *mons veneris*.

Professor Sayce is of the opinion, from the evidence of this leaden idol, that the Swastika was, among the Trojans, a symbol of the generative power of man.

An added interest centers in these specimens from the fact that terra-cotta shields of similar triangular form, fitted to the curvature of the body, were worn in the same way in prehistoric times by the aboriginal women of Brazil. These pieces have small holes at the angles, apparently for suspension by cords. The U. S. National Museum has some of these, and they will be figured in the chapter relating to Brazil. The similarity between these distant objects is remarkable, whether they were related or not, and whether the knowledge or custom came over by migration or not.

Owl-shaped vases.—It is also remarkable to note in this connection the series of owl-shaped terra-cotta vases of the ruined cities of Hissarlik and their relation to the Swastika as a possible symbol of the generative power. These vases have rounded bottoms, wide bellies, high shoulders (the height of which is emphasized by the form and position of the handles), the mouth narrow and somewhat bottle-shaped, but not entirely so. What would be the neck is much larger than usual for a bottle, and more like the neck of a human figure,

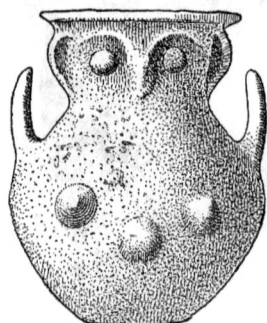

Fig. 126.

TERRA-COTTA VASE WITH MAMELON.

Fourth city. Depth, 16.5 feet.

Cat. No. 149676, U. S. N. M.

⅓ natural size.

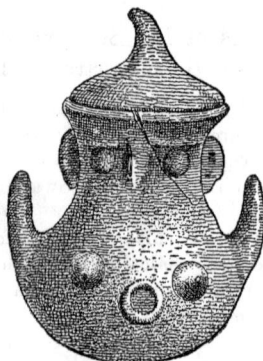

Fig. 127.

TERRA-COTTA VASE WITH CIRCLE OR RING.

Fourth city. Depth, 20 feet.

Schliemann, "Ilios," fig. 988.

⅓ natural size.

which the object in its entirety represents in a rude, but, nevertheless, definite, manner. At the top of the vase are the eyes, eyebrows, and the nose. It is true that the round eyes, the arched eyebrows, and the pointed nose give it somewhat an owlish face, but if we look at fig. 127, the human appearance of which is emphasized by the cover of the vase, which serves as a cap for the head and has the effect of enlarging it to respectable dimensions, we will see how nearly it represents a human being. The U. S. National Museum possesses one of these vases in the Schliemann collection (fig. 126). It has the face as described, while the other human organs are only indicated by small knobs. It and the three figures, 127, 128, and 129, form a series of which the one in the Museum would be the first, the others following in the order named.

No. 2 in the series has the female attributes indefinitely and rudely indicated, the lower organ being represented by a concentric ring. In No. 3 the mammæ are well shown, while the other organ has the concentric ring, the center of which is filled with a Greek cross with four dots, one in each angle, the *Croix swasticale* of Zmigrodzki (fig. 12). No. 4 of the series is more perfect as a human, for the mouth is represented by a circle, the mammæ are present, while in the other locality appears a well-defined Swastika. The first three of these were found in the fourth city at 20 to 22 feet depth, respectively; the last was found in the fifth city at a depth of 10 feet. The leaden idol (fig. 125), with its Swastika mark on the triangle covering the private parts, may properly be considered as part of the series. When to this series is added the *folium vitus* of Brazil (pl. 18), the similarity becomes significant, if not mysterious. But, with all this significance and mystery, it

Fig. 128.

TERRA-COTTA VASE WITH CIRCLE OR RING
AND CROIX SWASTICALE.

Schliemann, "Ilios," fig. 986.
⅕ natural size.

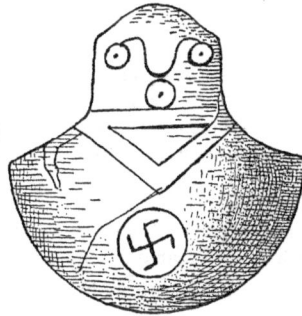

Fig. 129.

TERRA-COTTA VASE WITH CIRCLE OR
RING INCLOSING SWASTIKA.

Schliemann, "Troja," fig. 101.
⅔ natural size.

appears to the author that this sign, in its peculiar position, has an equal claim as a symbol of blessing, happiness, good fortune, as that it represents the generative power.

From the earliest time of which we have knowledge of the thoughts or desires of man we know that the raising up "heirs of his body" constituted his greatest blessing and happiness, and their failure his greatest misery. The first and greatest command of God to man, as set forth in the Holy Bible, is to "Be fruitful, and multiply, and replenish the earth."[1] This was repeated after the Deluge,[2] and when He pronounced the curse in the Garden, that upon the woman[3] was, "In sorrow thou shalt bring forth children." God's greatest blessing to Abraham, when He gave to him and his seed the land as far as he could see, was that his seed should be as the dust of the earth, "so that if a

---

[1] Genesis i, 28.
[2] Genesis viii, 17; ix, 7.
[3] Genesis iii, 16.

man can number the dust of the earth, then shall thy seed also be numbered."[1] " Tell the stars, if thou be able to number them * * * so shall thy seed be. * * * As the father of many nations," etc. We all know the story of Sarai, how, when she and Abraham had all riches and power on earth, it was as naught while they were childless, and how their greatest blessing was the Divine promise of an heir, and that their greatest happiness was over the birth of Isaac. This may be no proof of the symbolism of the Swastika, but it shows how, in high antiquity, man's happiness in his children was such as makes the Swastika mark, in the position indicated, equally a symbol of good fortune and blessing as it was when put on the spindle-whorls of Hissarlik, the vases of Greece, or the fibulæ of Etruria.

The age of the Trojan cities.—It may be well to consider for a moment the age or epoch of these prehistoric Trojan cities on the hill of His-sarlik. Professor Virchow was appealed to by Schliemann for his opinion. He says:[2]

> Other scholars have been inclined to ascribe the oldest cities of Hissarlik to the Neolithic age, because remarkable weapons and utensils of polished stone are found in them. * * * This conception is unjustified and inadmissible. To the third century A. D. belongs the surface of the fortress hill of Hissarlik, which still lies above the Macedonian wall; and the oldest "cities"—although not only polished stones but also chipped flakes of chalcedony and obsidian occur in them—neverthe-less fall within the age of metals, for even in the first city utensils of copper, gold, and even silver were dug up. No stone people, properly so called, dwelt upon the fortress hill of Hissarlik, so far as it has been uncovered.

Virchow's opinion that none of the cities of Hissarlik were in the stone age may be correct, but the reason he gave is certainly doubtful. He says they come within the age of metals, for, or because, "*utensils of copper, gold, and even silver were dug up among the ruins of the first city.*" That the metals, gold, silver, or copper, were used by the abo-rigines, is no evidence that they were in a metal age, as it has been assigned and understood by prehistoric archæologists. The great prin-ciple upon which the names of the respective prehistoric ages—stone, bronze, and iron—were given, was that these materials were used for cutting and similar implements. The use of gold and silver or any metal for ornamental purposes has never been considered by archæol-ogists as synchronous with a metal age. Indeed, in the United States there are great numbers of aboriginal cutting implements of copper, of which the U. S. National Museum possesses a collection of five or six hundred; yet they were not in sufficient number to, and they did not, supersede the use of stone as the principal material for cutting implements, and so do not establish a copper age in America. In Paleolithic times bone was largely used as material for utensils and ornaments. Bone was habitually in use for one purpose or another, yet no one ever pretended that this establishes a bone age. In coun-tries and localities where stone is scarce and shell abundant, cutting

---

[1] Genesis xiii, 16; xv, 5.
[2] "Ilios," preface, p. xi.

implements were, in prehistoric times, made of shell; and chisels or hatchets of shell, corresponding to the polished stone hatchet, were prevalent wherever the conditions were favorable, yet nobody ever called it an agé of shell. So, in the ruined cities of Hissarlik, the first five of them abounded in stone implements peculiar to the Neolithic age, and while there may have been large numbers of implements and utensils of other materials, yet this did not change it from the polished stone age. In any event, the reason given by Virchow—i. e., that the use, undisputed, of copper, gold, and silver by the inhabitants of these cities—is not evidence to change their culture status from that denominated as the polished stone age or period.

Professor Virchow subsequently does sufficient justice to the antiquity of Schliemann's discoveries and says[1] while "it is impossible to assign these strata to the stone age, yet they are indications of what is the oldest known settlement in Asia Minor of a people of prehistoric times of some advance in civilization," and[2] that "no place in Europe is known which could be put in direct connection with any one of the six lower cities of Hissarlik."

Professor Sayce also gives his opinion on the age of these ruins:[3]

The antiquities, therefore, unearthed by Dr. Schliemann at Troy, acquire for us a double interest. They carry us back to the later stone ages of the Aryan race.

AFRICA.

EGYPT.

A consensus of the opinions of antiquarians is that the Swastika had no foothold among the Egyptians. Prof. Max Müller is of this opinion, as is also Count Goblet d'Alviella.[4]

Waring[5] says:

The only sign approaching the fylfot in Egyptian hieroglyphics that we have met is shown in fig. 3, pl. 41, where it forms one of the hieroglyphs of Isis, but is not very similar to our fylfot.

Mr. Greg says:[6] "In Egypt the fylfot does not occur." Many other authors say the same. Yet many specimens of the Swastika have been found in Egypt (figs. 130 to 136). Professor Goodyear,[7] says:

The earliest dated Swastikas are of the third millenium B. C., and occur on the foreign Cyprian and Carian (?) pottery fragments of the time of the twelfth dynasty (in Egypt), discovered by Mr. Flinders Petrie in 1889. (Kahun, Gurob, and Hawara, pl. 27, Nos. 162 and 173.)

---

[1] "Ilios," app. 1, p. 685.

[2] "Ibid.," app. 6, p. 379.

[3] "Troja," p. xii.

[4] "La Migration des Symboles," pp. 51, 52.

[5] "Ceramic Art in Remote Ages," p. 82.

[6] Archæologia, XLVII, pt. 1, p. 159.

[7] "Grammar of the Lotus," pl. 30, figs. 2 and 10, p. 356.

Naukratis.—Figs. 130 to 135, made after illustrations in Mr. W. Flinders Petrie's Third Memoir of the Egypt Exploration Fund (Pt. 1), found by him in Naukratis, all show unmistakable Swastikas. It should be explained that these are said to be Greek vases which have been imported into Egypt. So that, while found in Egypt and so classed geographically, they are not Egyptian, but Greek.

Fig. 130.

GREEK VASE SHOWING DEER, GEESE, AND SWASTIKAS.

Naukratis, Ancient Egypt. Sixth and fifth centuries, B. C.

Petrie, Third Memoir, Egypt Exploration Fund, part 1, pl. 4, fig. 3, and Goodyear, "Grammar of the Lotus," pl. 60, fig. 2.

Coptos (Achmim-Panopolis). — Within the past few years great discoveries have been made in Upper Egypt, in Sakkarah, Fayum, and Achmim, the last of which was the ancient city of Panopolis. The inhabitants of Coptos and the surrounding or neighboring cities were Christian Greeks, who migrated from their country during the first centuries of our era and settled in this land of Egypt. Strabo mentions these people and their ability as weavers and embroiderers. Discoveries have been made of their cemeteries, winding sheets, and grave clothes. These clothes have been subjected to analytic investigation, and it is the conclusion of M. Gerspach, the administrator of the national manufactory of the Gobelin tapestry, Paris,[1] that they were woven in the same way as the Gobelins, and that, except being smaller, they did not differ essentially from them. He adds:

> These Egyptian tapestries and those of the Gobelins are the result of work which is identical except in some secondary details, so that I have been able, without difficulty, to reproduce these Coptic tapestries in the Gobelin manufactory.

On one of these Coptic cloths, made of linen, reproduced in "Die Gräber- und Textilfunde von Achmim-Panopolis," by R. Forrer, occurs

Fig. 130a.

DETAIL OF VASE SHOWN IN THE PRECEDING FIGURE.

[1] "Les Tapisseries Coptes," sec. 4, pp. 5, 6.

a normal Swastika embroidered or woven, tapestry fashion, with woolen thread (fig. 136). It belongs to the first epoch, which includes

Fig. 131.
POTTERY FRAGMENTS WITH TWO MEANDER SWASTIKAS.
Naukratis, Ancient Egypt.
Petrie, Third Memoir of the Egypt Exploration Fund, part 1, pl. 5, figs. 15, 24.

portions of the first and second centuries A. D. There were on these cloths an enormous amount of decoration, representing many figures,

Fig. 132.
FRAGMENT OF GREEK VASE WITH LION AND THREE MEANDER SWASTIKAS.
Naukratis, Ancient Egypt.
Petrie, Sixth Memoir of the Egypt Exploration Fund, part 2, fig. 7, and Goodyear, "Grammar of the Lotus," pl. 30, fig 2.

both natural and geometric. Among them was the Swastika variously applied and in different sizes, sometimes inserted in borders, and

Fig. 133.

FRAGMENT OF GREEK VASE DECORATED WITH FIGURES OF SACRED ANIMALS AND SWASTIKAS, ASSOCIATED
WITH GREEK FRET.

Naukratis, Ancient Egypt.

Petrie, Sixth Memoir of the Egypt Exploration Fund, part 2, pl. 6, fig. 1.

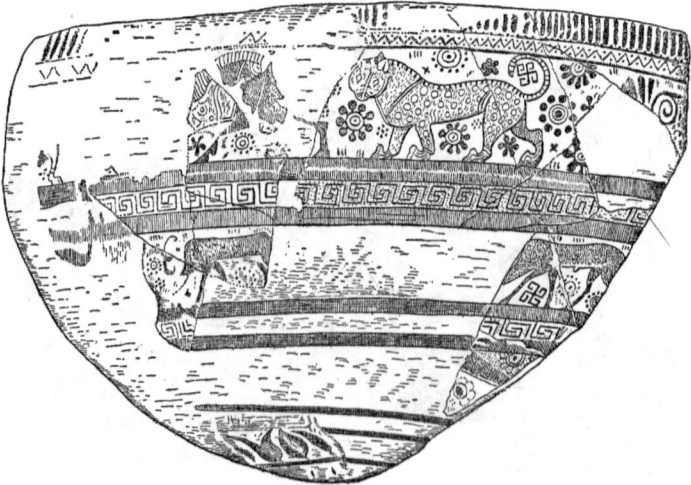

Fig. 134.

FRAGMENT OF GREEK VASE WITH FIGURES OF ANIMALS, TWO MEANDER SWASTIKAS, AND GREEK FRET.

Naukratis, Ancient Egypt.

Petrie, Sixth Memoir of the Egypt Exploration Fund, part 2, pl. 8, fig. 1, and Goodyear, "Grammar of the Lotus," pl. 30, fig. 10.

Fig. 135.

GREEK VASE WITH DEER, AND MEANDER AND FIGURE-8 SWASTIKAS.

Naukratis, Ancient Egypt.

Petrie, Sixth Memoir of the Egypt Exploration Fund, part 2, pl. 5, fig. 1.

Fig. 136.

GREEK TAPESTRY.

Coptos, Egypt. First and second centuries, A. D.

Forrer, "Die Gräber- und Textilfunde von Achmin-Panopolis."

sometimes adorning the corners of the tunics and togas as a large medallion, as shown in the figure.[1]

ALGERIA.

Waring, in his "Ceramic Art in Remote Ages," discoursing upon the Swastika, which he calls fylfot, shows in pl. 43, fig. 2 (quoting from Dela-

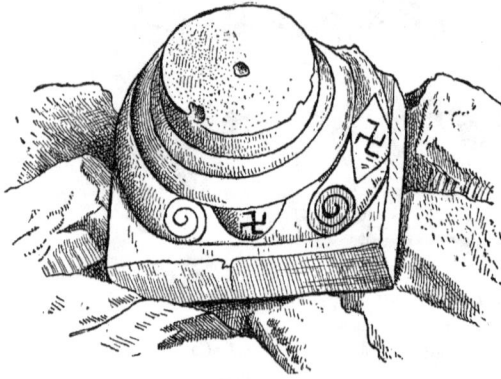

Fig. 137.
TORUS OF COLUMN WITH SWASTIKAS.
Roman ruins, Algeria.
Waring, "Ceramic Art in Remote Ages," pl. 43, fig. 2, quoting from Delamare.

mare), the base of a column from a ruined Roman building in Algeria (fig. 137), on the torus of which are engraved two Swastikas, the arms crossing at right angles, all ends bent at right angles to the left. There are other figures (five and six on the same plate) of Swastikas from a Roman mosaic pavement in Algeria. Instead of being square, however, or at right angles, as might ordinarily be ex-

pected from mosaic, they are ogee. In one of the specimens the ogee ends finish in a point; in the other they finish in a spiral volute turning upon itself. The Swastika has been found on a tombstone in Algeria.[2]

ASHANTEE.

Mr. R. B. Æneas McLeod, of Invergordon Castle, Ross-shire, Scotland, reported[3] that, on looking over some curious bronze ingots captured at Coomassee in 1874, during the late Ashantee war, by Captain Eden,

in whose possession they were at Inverness, he had found some marked with the Swastika sign (fig. 138). These specimens were claimed to be aboriginal, but whether the marks were cast or stamped in the ingot is not stated.

Fig. 138.
BRONZE INGOTS BEARING SWASTIKAS.
Comassee, Ashantee.

---

[1] Forrer, "Die Gräber- und Textilfunde von Achmim-Panopolis," p. 20.
[2] Bull. Soc. Française de numism. et d'archéol., II, pl. 3, p. 3.
[3] "Ilios," p. 353.

CLASSICAL OCCIDENT—MEDITERRANEAN.

GREECE AND THE ISLANDS OF CYPRUS, RHODES, MELOS, AND THERA.

The Swastika has been discovered in Greece and in the islands of the Archipelago on objects of bronze and gold, but the principal vehicle was pottery; and of these the greatest number were the painted vases. It is remarkable that the vases on which the Swastika appears in the

Fig. 139.

VARIATION OF THE GREEK FRET.

Continuous lines crossing each other at right angles forming figures resembling the Swastikas.

Fig. 140.

GREEK GEOMETRIC VASE IN THE LEYDEN MUSEUM, WITH FIGURES OF GEESE AND SWASTIKA IN PANEL.[1]

Smyrna.

Conze, "Anfänge," etc., Vienna, 1870, and Goodyear, "Grammar of the Lotus," pl. 56, fig. 4.

largest proportion should be the oldest, those belonging to the Archaic period. Those already shown as having been found at Naukratis, in Egypt, are assigned by Mr. Flinders Petrie to the sixth and fifth centuries B. C., and their presence is accounted for by migrations from Greece.

The Greek fret and Egyptian meander not the same as the Swastika.—Professor Goodyear says:[2] "There is no proposition in archæology which can be so easily demonstrated as the assertion that the Swastika is originally a fragment of the Egyptian meander, provided Greek geometric vases are called in evidence."

Egyptian meander here means the Greek fret. Despite the ease with which he says it can be demonstrated that the Swastika was originally a fragment of the Egyptian meander,

Fig. 141.

GREEK VASE WITH FIGURES OF HORSES, GEOMETRIC ORNAMENTS AND SWASTIKAS IN PANELS.

Athens.

Denuls, "Etruria," I, p. cxiii.

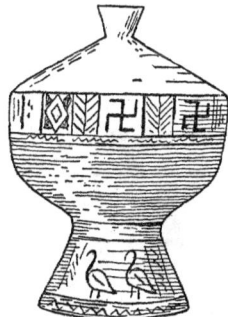

Fig. 142.

GREEK VASE WITH SWASTIKAS IN PANELS.

Conze, "Anfänge," etc., and Goodyear, "Grammar of the Lotus," pl. 60, fig. 13.

and with all respect for the opinion of so profound a student of classic ornament, doubts must arise as to the existence of the evidence necessary to prove his proposition.

---

[1] See p. 845.
[2] "Grammar of the Lotus," p. 352.

Professor Goodyear, and possibly others, ascribe the origin of the Swastika to the Greek fret; but this is doubtful and surely has not been proved. It is difficult, if not impossible, to procure direct evidence on the proposition. Comparisons may be made between the two signs; but this is secondary or indirect evidence, and depends largely on argument. No man is so poor in expedients that he may not argue. Goldsmith's schoolmaster "e'en tho' vanquished, he could argue still." The Greek fret, once established, might easily be doubled or crossed in some of its members, thus forming a figure similar to the Swastika (fig. 139), which would serve as an ornament, but is without any of the characteristics of the Swastika as a symbol. The

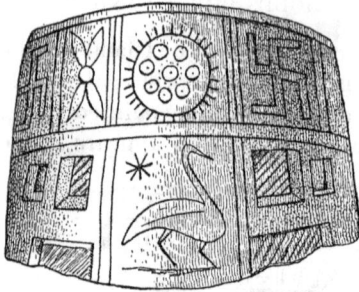

Fig. 143.

DETAIL OF ARCHAIC GREEK VASE WITH FIGURE OF SOLAR GOOSE AND SWASTIKAS IN PANELS.
British Museum.
Waring, "Ceramic Art in Remote Ages," pl. 41, fig. 15.

crossed lines in the Greek fret seem to have been altogether fortuitous. They gave it no symbolic character. It was simply a variation of the fret, and at best was rarely used, and like it, was employed only for ornament and not with any signification—not a sign of benediction, blessing, or good luck, as was the Swastika.

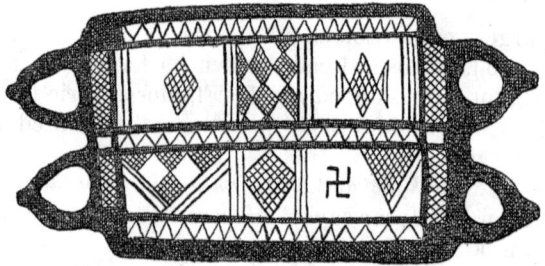

Fig. 144.

CYPRIAN POTTERY PLAQUE WITH SWASTIKA IN PANEL.
Metropolitan Museum of Art, New York City.
Cesnola, "Cyprus, its Ancient Cities, Tombs, and Temples," pl. 47, fig. 40.

The foundation principle of the Greek fret, so far as we can see its use, is its adaptability to form an extended ornamental band, consisting of doubled, bent, and sometimes crossed or interlaced lines, always continuous and never ending, and running between two parallel border lines. Two interlacing lines can be used, crossing each other at certain places, both making continuous meanders and together forming the ornamental band (fig. 139). In the Greek fret the two lines meandered between the two borders back and forth, up and down, but always forming a continuous line. This seems to be the foundation principle of the Greek fret. In all this

Fig. 145.

DETAIL OF CYPRIAN VASE WITH SWASTIKAS IN TRIANGLES.
Goodyear, "Grammar of the Lotus," pl. 1, fig. 11.

Fig. 146.

DETAIL OF ATTIC VASE WITH FIGURE OF ANTELOPE(?) AND SWASTIKA.
British Museum.
Bohlau, Jahrbuch, 1885, p. 50, and Goodyear, "Grammar of the Lotus," pl. 37, fig. 9.

requirement or foundation principle the Swastika fails. A row or band of Swastikas can not be made by continuous lines; each one is and must be separated from its fellows. The Swastika has four arms, each made by a single line which comes to an end in each quarter. This is more imperative with the meander Swastika than with the normal. If the lines be doubled on each other to be carried along to form another Swastika adjoining, in the attempt to make a band, it

Fig. 147.

CYPRIAN VASE WITH SWASTIKAS.

Cesnola, "Cyprus, Its Ancient Cities, Tombs, and Temples," appendix by Murray, p. 404, fig. 15.

Fig. 148.

TERRA COTTA FIGURINE WITH SWASTIKAS IN PANELS.

Cesnola, "Cyprus, Its Ancient Cities, Tombs, and Temples," p. 300, and Ohnefalsch-Richter, Bull. Soc. d'Anthrop., Paris, 1888, p. 681.

will be found impossible. The four lines from each of the four arms can be projected, but each will be in a different direction, and no band can be made. It is somewhat difficult to describe this, and possibly not of great need. An attempt to carry out the project of making a band of Swastikas, to be connected with each other, or to make them travel in any given direction with continuous lines, will be found impossible.

Professor Goodyear attempts to show how this is done by his figure on page 96, in connection with pl. 10, fig. 9, also figs. 173 and 174 (pp. 353 and 354). These figures are given in this paper and are, respectively, Nos. 21, 25, 26, and 27. Exception is taken to the pretended line of evolution in these figures: (1) There

Fig. 150.

BRONZE FIBULA WITH SWASTIKA AND REPRESENTATIONS OF A GOOSE AND A FISH.

Bœotia, Greece.

De Mortillet, "Musée Préhistorique," fig. 1265.

Fig. 149.

TERRA COTTA VASE WITH SWASTIKA AND FIGURE OF HORSE.[1]

is nothing to show any actual relationship between them. There is no evidence that they agreed either in locality or time, or that there was any unity of thought or design in

[1] Goodyear, "Grammar of the Lotus," pl. 61, fig. 1.

the minds of their respective artists. (2) Single specimens are no evidence of custom. This is a principle of the common law which has

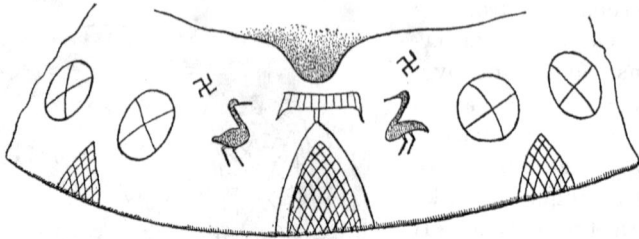

Fig. 151.

DETAIL OF GREEK VASE WITH SWASTIKAS AND FIGURES OF BIRDS.

Waring, "Ceramic Art in Remote Ages," pl. 33, fig. 24, and Goodyear, "Grammar of the Lotus," pl. 46, fig. 5.

still a good foundation, and was as applicable in those days as it is now. The transition from the spiral to the Greek fret and from the

Fig. 152.

DETAIL OF CYPRIAN VASE.

Sunhawk, lotus, solar disk, and Swastikas.

Böhlau, Jahrbuch, 1886, pl. 8 ; Reinach Revue Archæologique, 1885, II, p. 360 ; Perrot and Chipiez, "History of Art in Phenicia and Cyprus," II ; Goodyear, "Grammar of the Lotus," pl. 45, fig. 3.

Greek fret to the Swastika can be shown only by the existence of the custom or habit of the artist to make them both in the same or adjoin-

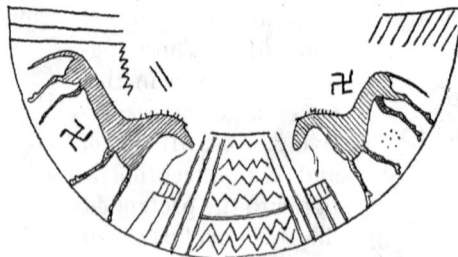

Fig. 153.

DETAIL OF GREEK GEOMETRIC VASE WITH SWASTIKAS AND FIGURES OF HORSES.

Thera.

Leyden Museum.

Goodyear, "Grammar of the Lotus," pl. 61, fig. 4.

ing epochs of time, and this is not proved by showing a single specimen. (3) If a greater number of specimens were produced, the chain of evidence would still be incomplete, for the meander of the Greek fret will, as has just been said, be found impossible of transition into the meander Swastika. It (the Swastika) does not extend itself into a band, but if spread at all, it spreads in each of the four directions (figs. 21 and 25). The transition will be found much easier from the Greek meander fret to the normal Swastika and from that to the meander Swastika than to proceed in the opposite direction. Anyone who doubts this has

Fig. 154.

BRONZE FIBULA WITH LARGE SWASTIKA ON SHIELD.
Greece.
Musée St. Germain.
De Mortillet, "Musée Préhistorique," fig. 1264.
$\frac{1}{2}$ natural size.

Fig. 155.

GREEK VASE, OINOCHOË, WITH
TWO PAINTED SWASTIKAS.
De Mortillet, "Musée Préhistorique,"
fig. 1244.
$\frac{1}{4}$ natural size.

but to try to make the Swastika in a continuous or extended band or line (fig. 26), similar to the Greek fret.

Figs. 133 and 134, from Naukratis, afford palpable evidence of the different origin of the Swastika and the Greek fret. Evidently Grecian vases, though found in Egypt, these specimens bear side by side examples of the fret and the Swastika used contemporaneously, and

Fig. 156.

CYPRIAN VASE WITH SWASTIKAS AND FIGURE
OF ANIMAL.[1]
Cesnola, "Cyprus, its Ancient Cities, Tombs, and Temples,"
pl. 45, fig. 36.

Fig. 157.

ARCHAIC GREEK POTTERY FRAGMENT.
Santorin, Ancient Thera.
Waring, "Ceramic Art in Remote Ages," pl. 42,
fig. 2.

both of them complete and perfect. If one had been parent of the other, they would have belonged to different generations and would not have appeared simultaneously on the same specimen. Another illustration of simultaneous use is in fig. 194, which represents an Etruscan vase[2] ornamented with bronze nail heads in the form of

[1] See p. 795.
[2] Matériaux pour l'Histoire Primitive et Naturelle de l'Homme, XVIII, p. 14.

Swastikas, but associated with it is the design of the Greek fret, showing them to be of contemporaneous use, and therefore not, as Professor

Fig. 158.

CYPRIAN VASE WITH LOTUS AND SWASTIKAS AND FIGURE OF BIRD.

Metropolitan Museum of Art, New York City.

Goodyear, " Grammar of the Lotus, pl. 60, fig. 15.

Goodyear believes, an evolution of one from the other.   The specimen
is in the Museum at Este, Italy.

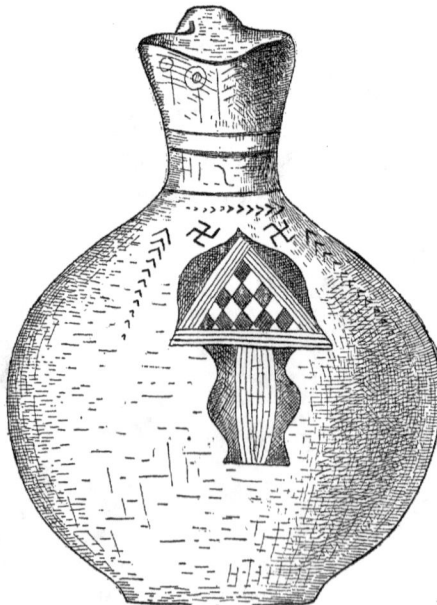

Fig. 159.

CYPRIAN VASE WITH TWO SWASTIKAS.

Cesnola Collection, Metropolitan Museum of Art, New York City.

Goodyear, " Grammar of the Lotus," fig. 151.

The Greek fret has been in common use in all ages and all countries
adopting the Grecian civilization.   Equally in all ages and countries has

appeared the crossed lines which have been employed by every architect and decorator, most or many of whom had no knowledge of the Swastika, either as an ornament or as a symbol.[1]

Swastika in panels.—Professor Goodyear, in another place,[2] argues in a manner which tacitly admits the foregoing proposition, where, in his endeavor to establish the true home of the Swastika to be in the Greek geometric style,

Fig. 160.

FRAGMENT OF TERRA COTTA VASE WITH SWASTIKAS, FROM RUINS OF TEMPLE AT PALEO-PAPHOS.

Depth, 40 feet.

Cesnola, "Cyprus, its Ancient Cities, Tombs, and Temples," p. 210.

he says we should seek it where it appears in "the largest dimension" and in "the most prominent way." In verification of this declaration, he says that in this style the Swastika systematically appears in panels exclusively assigned to it. But he gives only two illustrations of the Swastika in panels. These have been copied, and are shown in figs. 140 and 142. The author has added other specimens, figs. 141 to 148, from Dennis's "Etruria," from Waring's "Ceramic Art," and from Cesnola and Ohnefalsch-Richter. It might be too much to say that these are the only Swastikas in Greece appearing in panels, but it

Fig. 161.

WOODEN BUTTON, CLASP, OR FIBULA COVERED WITH PLATES OF GOLD.

Ogee Swastika, tetraskelion in center.

Schliemann, "Mycenæ," fig. 385.

is certain that the great majority of them do not thus appear. Therefore, Professor Goodyear's theory is not sustained, for no one will pretend that four specimens found in panels will form a rule for the great number which did not thus appear. This argument of Professor Goodyear is destructive of his other proposition

Fig. 162.

DETAIL OF GREEK VASE WITH FIGURE OF GOOSE, HONEYSUCKLE (ANTHEMION), AND SPIRAL SWASTIKA.

Thera.

"Monumenti Inedite," LXV, p. 2, and Goodyear, "Grammar of the Lotus," pl. 46, fig. 7.

that the Swastika sign originated by evolution from the meander or Greek fret, for we have seen that the latter was always used in a band

---

[1] Athenic vases painted by Andokides, about 525 B. C., represent the dress of the goddess, ornamented with Swastika and *Croix swasticale.* Am. Journ. Archæol., January–March, 1896, XI, No. 1, figs. 9, 11.

[2] "Grammar of the Lotus," pp. 348, 353.

and never in panels. Although the Swastika and the Greek fret have
a certain similarity of appearance in that they consist of straight lines
bent at right angles, and this continued many times, yet the similarity

Fig. 163.

DETAIL OF GREEK VASE.

Sphinx with spiral scrolls, and two meander
Swastikas (right).

Melos.

Böhlau, Jahrbuch, 1887, xii, and Goodyear, "Grammar of
the Lotus," pl. 34, fig. 8.

Fig. 164.

DETAIL OF GREEK VASE.

Ibex, scroll, and meander Swastika (right).

Melos.

Böhlau, Jahrbuch, 1887, xii, p. 121, and Goodyear, "Grammar
of the Lotus," pl. 39, fig. 2.

is more apparent than real; for an analysis of the motifs of both show
them to have been essentially different in their use, and so in their
foundation and origin.

Fig. 165.

DETAIL OF A GREEK VASE IN THE BRITISH MUSEUM.

Ram, meander Swastika (left), circles, dots, and crosses.

Salzmann, "Necropole de Camire," ll, and Goodyear, "Grammar of the Lotus," pl. 28, fig. 7.

*Swastikas with four arms, crossing at right angles, with ends bent to
the right.*—The author has called this the normal Swastika. He has
been at some trouble to gather such Swastikas from Greek vases as was

possible, and has divided them according to forms and peculiarities. The first group (figs. 140, 143, 146, 147, 148, and 150) shows the normal Swastika with four arms, all bent at right angles and to the right. In the aforesaid division no distinction has been made between specimens from different parts of Greece and the islands of the Grecian Archi-

Fig. 166.

CYPRIAN VASE WITH SWASTIKAS AND FIGURES OF BIRDS.

Perrot and Chipiez, "History of Art in Phenicia and Cyprus," II, p. 300, fig. 237; Goodyear, "Grammar of the Lotus," pl. 48, figs. 6, 12; Cesnola, "Cyprus, its Ancient Cities, Tombs, and Temples," Appendix by Murray, p. 412, pl. 44, fig. 34.

pelago, and these, with such specimens as have been found in Smyrna, have for this purpose all been treated as Greek.

Swastikas with four arms crossing at right angles, ends bent to the left.— Figs. 141, 142, 144, 149, 151, 152, 153, 154, 156, and 157 represent the normal Swastika with four arms, all bending at right angles, but to the left. The vases on which they have been found are not described as to color or form. It would be difficult to do so correctly; besides, these descriptions are not important in our study of the Swastika. Fig. 155 represents a vase or pitcher (oinochoë, Greek—οἶνος, wine, and χέω, to pour) with painted Swastika, ends turned to the left. It is in the Museum of St. Germain, and is figured by M. De Mortillet in "Musée Préhistorique." Fig. 156 represents a Cyprian vase from Ormidia,

Fig. 167.

CYPRIAN VASE WITH LOTUS, BOSSES, BUDS, SEPALS, AND DIFFERENT SWASTIKAS.

Cesnola Collection, Metropolitan Museum of Art, New York City.

Goodyear, "Grammar of the Lotus," pl. 48, fig. 3.

in the New York Museum. It is described by Cesnola[1] and by Perrot and Chipiez.[2] Fig. 157 is taken from a fragment of archaic Greek pottery found in Santorin (Ancient Thera), an island in the

[1] "Cyprus, its Ancient Cities, Tombs, and Temples," pl. 45, fig. 36.
[2] "History of Art in Phenicia and Cyprus," II, p. 302, fig. 239

Greek Archipelago. This island was first inhabited by the Phenicians, afterwards by the Greeks, a colony of whom founded Cyrene
in Africa. This specimen is cited by Rochette and figured by
Waring.[1]

*Swastikas with four arms crossing at other than right angles, the ends
ogee and to the left.*—Figs. 158, 159, and 160 show Swastikas with four

Fig. 168.

CYPRIAN VASE WITH BOSSES, LOTUS BUDS, AND DIFFERENT
SWASTIKAS.

Cesnola Collection, Metropolitan Museum of Art, New
York City.

Goodyear, "Grammar of the Lotus," pl. 48, fig. 15.

arms crossing at other than
right angles, many of them
ogee, but turned to the left.
Fig. 161 is a representation
of a wooden button or clasp,
much resembling the later
gold brooch of Sweden, classified by Montelius (p. 867),
covered with plates of gold,
from Sepulcher IV, Mycenæ
(Schliemann, Mycenæ, fig. 385,
p. 259). The ornament in its
center is one of the ogee
Swastikas with four arms
(tetraskelion) curved to the
left. It shows a dot in each

of the four angles of the cross similar to the Suavastika of Max
Müller and the *Croix swasticale* of Zmigrodzki, which Burnouf attributed to the four nails which fastened the cross *Arani* (the female
principle), while the *Pramantha* (the male), produced, by rotation,
the holy fire from the sacred cross. An almost exact reproduction

of this Swastika will be found on
the shield of the Pima Indians of
New Mexico (fig. 258).

Dr. Schliemann reports that the
Swastika in its spiral form is represented innumerable times in the
sculptured ceiling of the Thalamos
in the treasury at Orchomenos.
(See figs. 21 and 25.)

He also reports[2] that Swastikas
(turned both ways) may be seen in
the Royal Museum at Berlin incised
on a balustrade relief of the hall

Fig. 169.

DETAIL OF EARLY BŒOTIAN VASE.

Figure of horse, solar diagram, Artemis with
geese, and Swastikas (normal and meander,
right and left).

Goodyear, "Grammar of the Lotus," pl. 61, fig. 12.

which surrounded the temple of Athene at Pergamos. Fig. 162 represents a spiral Swastika with four arms crossing at right angles, the ends
all turned to the left and each one forming a spiral.

---

[1] "Ceramic Art in Remote Ages," pl. 42, fig. 2.
[2] "Troja," p. 123.

Waring[1] figures and describes a Grecian oinochoë from Camirus, Rhodes, dating, as he says, from 700 to 500 B. C., on which is a band of decoration similar to fig. 130. It is about 10 inches high, of cream color, with ornamentation of dark brown. Two ibexes follow each other with an ogee spiral Swastika between the forelegs of one.

Meander pattern, with ends bent to right and left.—Figs. 163, 164, and 165 show the Swastika in meander pattern. Fig. 163 shows two Swas-tikas, the arms of both bent to the right, one six, the other nine times. The Swastika shown in fig. 164 is bent to the right eight times. That shown in fig. 165 bends to the left eight times.

Swastikas of different kinds on the same object.— The next group (figs. 167 to 176) is of importance in that it represents ob-jects which, bearing the

Fig. 170.

DETAIL OF RHODIAN VASE.

Figures of geese, circles and dots, and Swastikas (right and left).

British Museum.

Waring, "Ceramic Art in Remote Ages," pl. 27, fig. 9.

normal Swastika, also show on the same object other styles of Swas-tika, those turned to the left at right angles, those at other than right angles, and those which are spiral or meander. The presence on a single object of different forms of Swastika is considered as evidence of their chronologic identity and their consequent relation to each other, showing them to be all the same sign—that is, they were all Swastikas,

Fig. 171.

DETAIL OF RHODIAN VASE.

Geese, lotus circles, and two Swastikas (right and left).

Goodyear, "Grammar of the Lotus," p. 271, fig. 145.

whether the arms were bent to the right or to the left, ogee or in curves, at right angles or at other than right angles, in spirals or meanders.

Many examples of vases similar to fig. 172 are shown in the London, Paris, and New York museums, and in other collections. (See figs. 149, 159.) Fig. 174 shows an Attic painted vase (*Lebes*) of the Archaic period, from Athens. It is a pale yellowish ground, probably the

---

[1] "Ceramic Art in Remote Ages," frontispiece, fig. 3, and p. 115.

natural color, with figures in maroon. It belongs to the British Museum. It bears on the front side five Swastikas, all of different styles; three turn to the right, two to the left. The main arms cross at right angles, but the ends of four are bent at right angles, while one is curved (ogee). Three have the ends bent (at right angles) four times, making a meander form, while two make only one bend. They seem not to be placed with any reference to each other, or to any other object, and are

Fig. 172.

GREEK VASE OF TYPICAL RHODIAN STYLE.

Ibex, lotus, geese, and six Swastikas (normal, meander, and ogee, all left).

Goodyear, "Grammar of the Lotus," p. 251, pl. 38.[1]

scattered over the field as chance or luck might determine. A specimen of Swastika interesting to prehistoric archæologists is that on a vase from Cyprus (Musée St. Germain, No. 21557), on which is represented an arrowhead, stemmed, barbed, and suspended by its points between the Swastika.[2]

Dr. Max Ohnefalsch-Richter presented a paper before the Société

---

[1] Another Rhodian vase, similar in style, with Swastikas, is shown in the "Grammar of the Lotus," pl. 37, fig. 4.

[2] Matériaux pour l'Histoire Primitive et Naturelle de l'Homme, 1881, XVI, p. 416

d'Anthropologie in Paris, December 6, 1888, reported in the Bulletin of that year (pp. 668–681). It was entitled "La Croix gammée et la Croix cantonnée en Chypre." (The *Croix gammeé* is the Swastika, while the *Croix cantonnée* is the cross with dots, the *Croix swasticale* of Zmigrodzki.) In this paper the author describes his finding the Swastika during his excavations into prehistoric Cyprus. On the first page of his paper the following statement appears:

Fig. 173.

DETAIL OF GREEK VASE.

Deer, solar diagrams, and three Swastikas (single, double, and meander, right).

Melos.

Conze, "Melloche Thongefässe," and Goodyear, "Grammar of the Lotus," pl. 60, fig. 8.

The Swastika comes from India as an ornament in form of a cone (*conique*) of metal, gold, silver, or bronze gilt, worn on the ears (see G. Perrot: "Histoire de l'Art," III, p. 562 et fig. 384), and nose-rings (see S. Reinach: "Chronique d'Orient,"

3ᵉ série, t. IV, 1886). I was the first to make known the nose-ring worn by the goddess Aphrodite-Astarte, even at Cyprus. In the Indies the women still wear these ornaments in their nostrils and ears. The fellahin of Egypt also wear similar jewelry; but as Egyptian art gives us no example of the usage of these ornaments in

Fig. 174.

ARCHAIC GREEK VASE WITH FIVE SWASTIKAS OF FOUR DIFFERENT FORMS.

Athens.

Birch, "History of Ancient Pottery," quoted by Waring in "Ceramic Art in Remote Ages," pl. 41, fig. 15; Dennis, "The Cities and Cemeteries of Etruria," I, p. 91.

antiquity, it is only from the Indies that the Phenicians could have borrowed them. The nose-ring is unknown in the antiquity of all countries which surrounded the island of Cyprus.

The first pages of his memoir are employed in demonstrating that

the specimens of the Swastika found in Cyprus, the most of which are
set forth in this paper (figs. 177–182), show a Phenician influence; and
according to his theory demonstrate their mi-
gration or importation. He does not specify
the evidence on which he bases his assertion
of Phenician influence in Cyprus, except in
one or two par-
ticulars. Speak-
ing of the spec-
imen shown in
fig. 177 of the
present paper,
he says:

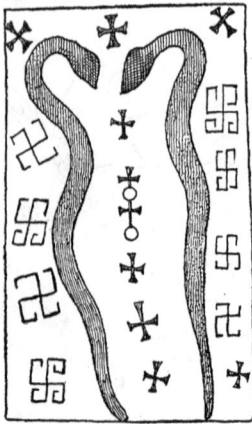

Fig. 175.

DETAIL OF ARCHAIC BŒOTIAN
VASE.

Serpents, crosses, and Swastikas
(normal, right, left, and meander).

Goodyear, "Grammar of the Lotus," pl. 60,
fig. 9.

It represents the
sacred palm under
which Apollo, the
god of light, was
born. * * * At
Cyprus the palm
did not appear
only with the Phe-
nicians; it was
not known prior to
that time (p. 674).

The design shown in fig. 178 he describes as representing two birds in the
attitude of adoration before a Swastika,
all being figured on a Greek cup of the
style Dipylon.[1]

Dr. Ohnefalsch-Richter adds:

Fig. 176.

ATTIC VASE FOR PERFUME, WITH CROIX SWAS-
TICALE AND TWO FORMS OF SWASTIKAS.

Ohnefalsch-Richter, Bull. Soc. d'Anthrop., Paris, 1888,
p. 673, fig. 4.

On the vases of Dipylon the Swastikas are generally transformed into other ornaments, mostly meanders. But this is not the
rule in Cyprus. The Swastika disappeared
from there as it came, in its sacred form, with
the Phenician influence, with the Phenician
inscriptions on the vases, with the concentric
circles without central points or tangents.

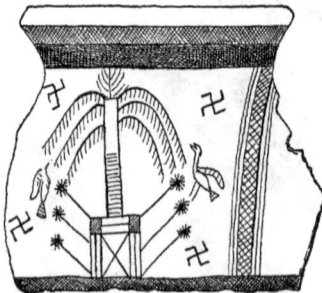

Fig. 177.

DETAIL OF CYPRIAN VASE.

Swastikas with palm tree, sacred to Apollo.
Citium, Cyprus.

Ohnefalsch-Richter, Bull. Soc. d'Anthrop., Paris, 1888, p.
673, fig. 3.

He says[2] that the Swastika as well
as the "Croix cantonnée" (with points
or dots), while possibly not always the
equivalent of the solar disk, zigzag
lightning, or the double hatchet, yet
are employed together and are given
the same signification, and frequently
replace each other. It is his opinion[3]
that the Swastika in Cyprus had nearly

[1] G. Hirschfield, "Vasi archaici Ateniesi," Annali dell' Instituto di corrispondenza
archæologica, 1872, Tav. d'Ag. K. 6, 52.

[2] Bull. Soc. d'Anthrop., Paris, 1888, pp. 674–675.

[3] Ibid., p. 675.

always a signification more or less religious, although it may have been used as an ornament to fill empty spaces. His interpretation of the Swastika in Cyprus is that it will signify *tour à tour* the storm, the lightning, the sun, the light, the seasons—sometimes one, sometimes another of these significations—and that its form lends itself easily (*facilement*) to the solar disk, to the fire wheel, and to the sun chariot. In support of this, he cites a figure (fig. 179) taken from Cesnola,[1] in which the wheels of the chariot are decorated with four Swastikas displayed in each of the four quarters. The chief personage on the car he identifies as the god of Apollo-Resef, and the decoration on his shield represents the solar disk. He is at once the god of war and also the god of light, which identifies him with Helios. The other personage is Herakles-Mecquars, the right hand of Apollo, both of them heroes of the sun.

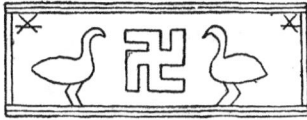

Fig. 178.
CYPRIAN VASE WITH FIGURES OF BIRDS
AND SWASTIKA IN PANEL.
Musée St. Germain.
Ohnefalsch-Richter, Bull. Soc. d'Anthrop., Paris,
1888, p. 674, fig. 6.

Fig. 179.
CHARIOT OF APOLLO-RESEF.
Sun symbol(?) on shield and four Swastikas (two right and two left) on quadrants of chariot wheels.
Cesnola, "Salaminia," p. 240, fig. 226, and Ohnefalsch-Richter,
Bull. Soc. d'Anthrop., Paris, 1888, p. 675, fig. 7.

The supreme goddess of the Isle of Cyprus was Aphrodite-Astarte,[2] whose presence with a preponderating Phenician influence can be traced back to the period of the age of iron, her images bearing signs of the Swastika, being, according to Dr. Ohnefalsch-Richter, found in Cyprus. In fig. 180 the statue of this goddess is shown, which he says was found by himself in 1884 at Curium. It bears four Swastikas, two on the shoulders and two on the forearms. Fig. 181 represents a centaur found by him at the same time, on the right arm of which is a Swastika painted in black, as in the foregoing statue.

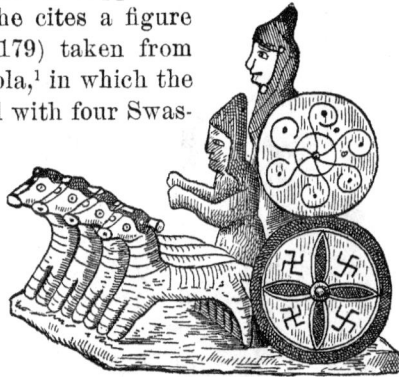

Fig. 180.
TERRA-COTTA STATUE OF THE
GODDESS APHRODITE-ASTARTE
WITH FOUR SWASTIKAS.[3]
Curium. Cyprus.
Ohnefalsch-Richter, Bull. Soc. d'Anthrop.,
Paris, 1888, p. 676, fig. 8.

Fig. 181.
CYPRIAN CENTAUR WITH ONE
SWASTIKA.
Cesnola, "Salaminia," p. 243, fig. 230;
Ohnefalsch-Richter, Bull. Soc. d'Anthrop., Paris, 1888, p. 676, fig. 9.

[1] "Salaminia," p. 240, fig. 226.
[2] Aphrodite=Phenician Ashtoreth, Astarte=Babylonian Ishtar.
[3] See p. 773.

We have found, in the course of this paper, many statues of human figures bearing the mark of the Swastika on some portion of their garments. M. Ohnefalsch-Richter, on page 677, gives the following explanation thereof:

It appears to me that the priests and priestesses, also the boys who performed the services in the sacred places, were in the habit of burning or tattooing Swastikas upon their arms. * * * In 1885, among the votive offerings found in one of the sacred places dedicated to Aphrodite-Astoret, near Idalium, was a stone statuette, representing the young Adonis Kinyras in a squatting posture, with the Swastika tattooed or painted in red color upon his naked arm.

And, says Richter, when, later on, the custom of tattooing had disappeared, they placed the Swastika on the sacerdotal garments. He has found in a Greek tomb in 1885, near Polistis Chrysokon, two statuettes representing female dancers in the service of Aphrodite-Ariadne, one of which (fig. 182) bore six or more Swastikas. In other cases, says he (p. 678), the *Croix cantonnée* (the *Croix swasticale* of Zmigrodzki) replaced the Swastika on the garments, and he cites the statue of Hercules strangling the lion in the presence of Athena, whose robe is ornamented with the *Croix cantonnée*. He repeats that the two signs of the cross represent the idea of light, sun, sacrifice, rain, storm, and the seasons.

Fig. 182.
GREEK STATUE OF APH-
RODITE-ARIADNE.
Six Swastikas (four right and two left).
Polistis Chrysokon.
Ohnefalsch-Richter, Bull. Soc. d'Anthrop., Paris, 1888, p. 677, fig. 10.

EUROPE.

BRONZE AGE.

Prehistoric archæologists claim that bronze was introduced into Europe in prehistoric times from the extreme Orient. The tin mines of the peninsula of Burma and Siam, with their extension into China on the north, Malacca and the islands of the archipelago on the south, are known to have been worked in extremely ancient times and are believed to have furnished the tin for the first making of bronze. The latter may not be susceptible of proof, but everything is consistent therewith. After it became known that copper and tin would make bronze, the discovery of tin would be greatly extended, and in the course of time the tin mines of Spain, Britain, and Germany might be opened. A hundred and more prehistoric bronze foundries have been discovered in western Europe and tens of thousands of prehistoric bronze implements. If bronze came originally from the extreme Orient, and the Swastika belonged there also, and as objects of bronze belonging to prehistoric times and showing connection with the Orient, like the tintinnabulum (fig. 29) have been found in the Swiss lake dwellings of prehistoric times, it is a fair inference that the Swastika mark found on the same objects came also from the Orient. This inference is strengthened by the manufacture and continuous use of the Swastika on both bronze and pottery, until it practically covered, and is to be found over, all Europe wherever the culture of bronze prevailed. Nearly all varieties of the Swastika came into use during the Bronze Age. The objects on which it was placed may have been different in different localities, and so also another variety of form may have prevailed in a given locality; but, subject to these exceptions, the Swastika came into general use throughout the countries wherein the Bronze Age prevailed. As we have seen, on the hill of Hissarlik the Swastika is found principally on the spindle-whorl; in Greece and Cyprus, on the pottery vases; in Germany, on the ceintures of bronze; in Scandinavia, on weapons and on toilet and dress ornaments. In Scotland and Ireland it was mostly on sculptured stones, which are many times themselves ancient Celtic crosses. In England, France, and Etruria, the Swastika appears on small bronze ornaments, principally fibulæ. Different forms of the Swastika, i. e., those to the right, left, square, ogee, curved, spiral and meander, triskelion and tetraskelion, have been found on the same object, thereby showing their interrelationship. No distinction is apparent between the arms bent to the right or to the left. This difference, noted by Prof. Max Müller, seems to fail altogether.

Greg says:[1]

About 500 to 600 B. C., the fylfot, (Swastika) curiously enough begins to disappear as a favorite device of early Greek art, and is rarely, if ever, seen on the regular Etruscan vase.

This indicates that the period of the use of the Swastika during the Bronze Age in Europe lay back of the period of its disappearance in the time of early Greek art, and that it was of higher antiquity than would otherwise be suspected.

Dr. Max Ohnefalsch-Richter says:[2]

The Swastika makes absolute default in Cyprus during all the age of bronze and in all its separate divisions according as the vases were decorated with intaglio or relief, or were painted.

Etruria and Italy.—The Etruscans were a prehistoric people. The country was occupied during the two ages of stone, Paleolithic and Neolithic, and during the Bronze Age. The Etruscans were probably the descendants of the Bronze Age people. The longest continued geographical discussion the world has heard was as to *who were* the Etruscans, and *whence* or *by what* route did they come to their country? It was opened by Herodotus and Dionysius Halicarnassus in the fourth century B. C.; while Dr. Brinton and the late President Welling have made the latest contributions thereto. The culture of the Etruscans

---

[1] Archæologia, XLVIII, pt. 2, p. 305.
[2] Bull. Soc. d'Anthrop., Paris, 1888, p. 679.

was somewhat similar to that of the Bronze Age peoples, and many of the implements had great resemblance, but with sufficient divergence to mark the difference between them. There were different stages of culture among the Etruscans, as can be easily and certainly determined from their tombs, modes of burial, pottery, etc.

The Swastika appears to have been employed in all these epochs or stages. It was undoubtedly used during the Bronze Age, and in Italy it continued throughout the Etruscan and into the Roman and Christian periods.

While it may be doubtful if any specimen of Swastika can be identified as having belonged to the Neolithic Age in Europe, there can be no doubt that it was in common use during the Bronze Age. Professor Goodyear gives it as his opinion, and in this he may be correct, that the earliest specimens of Swastika of which identification can be made are on the hut urns of central Italy. These have been considered as belonging definitely to the Bronze Age in that country. Fig. 183 is a representation of one of these hut urns. It shows upon its roof several specimens of Swastika, as will be apparent from examination. There are other figures, incised and in relief. One of them is the celebrated "burning altar" mark of Dr. Schliemann. This specimen was found in the Via Appia near Rome, and is exhibited in the Vatican Museum. Similar specimens have been found in other parts of Etruria. The author saw in the Municipal Museum at Corneto many of them, which had been excavated from the neighboring cemetery of the prehistoric city of Corneto-Tarquinii. They were of pottery, but made as if to represent rude huts of skin, stretched on cross poles, in general appearance not unlike the cane and rush conical cabins used to this day by the peasants around Rome. They belonged to the Bronze Age, and antedated the Etruscan civilization. This was demonstrated by the finds at Corneto-Tarquinii. Tombs to the number of about 300, containing them, were found, mostly in 1880–81, at a lower level than, and were superseded by, the Etruscan tombs. They contained the weapons, tools, and ornaments peculiar to the Bronze Age—swords, hatchets, pins, fibulæ, bronze and pottery vases, etc., the characteristics of which

Fig. 183.

HUT URN IN THE VATICAN MUSEUM.

"Burning altar" mark associated with Swastikas.

Etruria (Bronze Age).

were different from Etruscan objects of similar purpose, so they could be satisfactorily identified and segregated. The hut urns were receptacles for the ashes of the cremated dead, which, undisturbed, are to be seen in the museum. The vases forming part of this grave furniture bore the Swastika mark; three have two Swastikas, one three, one four, and another no less than eight.

Dennis figures a hut urn from Alba Longa,[1] and another from the Alban Mount.[2] He says (note 1):

These remarkable urns were first found in 1817 at Montecucco, near Marino, and at Monte Crescenzio, near the Lago de Castello, beneath a stratum of *peperino* (tufa) 18 inches thick. They were embedded in a yellowish volcanic ash and rested on a lower and earlier stratum of *peperino*.[3]

Curiously enough, the three or four pronged mark, called "burning altar" by Dr. Schliemann, is on both hut urns in Dennis's "Cities and Cemeteries of Etruria." Dr. Schliemann argues strongly in favor of the relationship between Swastika and the "burning altar" sign, but assigns no other reason than the similarity of the marks on the two objects. He appears unable, in "Ilios," to cite any instance of the Swastika being found on the hut urns in connection with the "burning altar" sign, but he mentions the Swastika five times repeated on one of the hut urns in the Etruscan collection in the museum of the Vatican at Rome.[4] The photograph of the hut urn from the Vatican (fig. 183) supplies the missing link in Schliemann's evidence. The roof of the hut urn bears the "burning altar" mark (if it be a burning altar, as claimed), which is in high relief (as it is in the Dennis specimens), and was wrought in the clay by the molder when the hut was made. Such of the other portions of the roof as are in sight show sundry incised lines which, being deciphered, are found to be Swastikas or parts of them. The parallelogram in the front contains a cross and has the appearance of a labyrinth, but it is not. The other signs or marks, however, represent Swastikas, either in whole or in part. This specimen completes the proof cited by Schliemann, and associates the Swastika with the "burning altar" sign in the Etruscan country, as well as on the hill of Hissarlik and in other localities.

Dennis supposes the earliest Etruscan vases, called by many different names, to date from the twelfth century B. C. to 540 B. C.,[5] the latter being the epoch of Theodoros of Samos, whose improvements marked an epoch in the culture of the country. He says:

These vases were adorned with annular bands, zigzag, waves, meanders, concentric circles, hatched lines, Swastikas, and other geometric patterns.

---

[1] "Cities and Cemeteries of Etruria," I, p. 69.
[2] Ibid., II, p. 457.
[3] Annali dell' Instituto, Rome, 1871, pp. 239–279; Bulletino Instituto, Rome, 1871, pp. 34–52; Pigorini and Sir John Lubbock, "Notes on Hut Urns and other objects from Marino," London, 1869; Virchow, "Die Huttenurnen von Marino," Berlin, 1883.
[4] "Troja," p. 122.
[5] "Cities and Cemeteries of Etruria," I, p. lxxxix.

A fragment of Archaic Greek pottery is reported by Rochette from the necropolis of Cumæ, in the campagna of Italy, and is shown in fig.

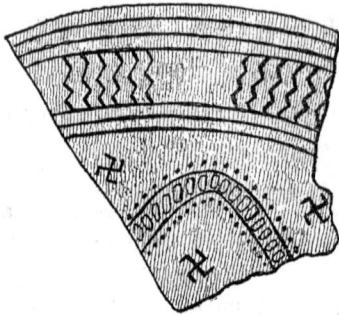

Fig. 184.

FRAGMENT OF ARCHAIC GREEK POTTERY WITH
THREE SWASTIKAS.

Cumæ, Italy.

Waring, "Ceramic Art in Remote Ages," pl. 42, fig. 1.

184. Rochette reports it as an example of a very early period, believed by him to have been Phenician. When we consider the rarity of Phenician pottery in Italy compared with the great amount of Greek pottery found there, and that the Phenicians are not known to have employed the Swastika, this, combined with the difficulty of determining the place of origin of such a fragment, renders it more likely to have been Greek than Phenician. A reason apparently moving Rochette to this decision was the zigzag ornamentation, which he translated to be a Phenician sign for water; but this pattern was used many times and in many places without having any such meaning, and is no proof of his proposition.

Figs. 185 and 186 represent the one-handled cinerary urns peculiar to the Bronze Age in Italy. They are believed to have been contemporaneous with or immediately succeeding the hut urns just shown. The cinerary urn shown in fig. 185 was found at Marino, near Albano, in the same locality and under the same condition as the hut urns

Fig. 186.

CINERARY URN WITH SWASTIKAS
INCLOSED BY INCISED LINES IN
INTAGLIO.

Cervetri, Italy.

"Conestabile due Dischi in Bronzo," pl. 5,
fig. 2.

⅓ natural size.

Fig. 185.

CINERARY URN WITH SWASTIKAS IN PANELS.

San Marino, near Albano, Italy.

Vatican Museum.

The original is in the Vatican Museum and was figured by Pigorini in "Archæologia," 1869. Fig. 186 shows a one-handled urn of pottery with Swastika (left) in intaglio, placed in a band of incised squares around the body of the vessel below the shoulder. A small though good example of Etruscan work is shown in the gold fibula (fig. 187). It is ornamented on the outside with the fine gold filigree work peculiar to the best Etruscan art. On the inside are two Swastikas. It is in the Vatican Museum of Etruscan antiquities. Fig. 188 represents another specimen of Etruscan gold filigree work with a circle and Swastika. It is a "bulla," an ornament said to indicate the rank of the wearer among the Etruscan people. It is decorated with a circle and Swastika inside. The figure is taken from "L'Art pour Tous," and is reproduced by Waring.

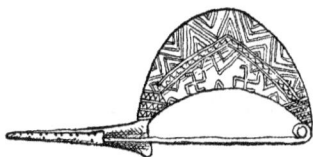

Fig. 187.

GOLD FIBULA WITH SWASTIKAS (LEFT).

Etruscan Museum, Vatican.

Catalogue of the Etruscan Museum, part 1, pl. 26, fig. 6.

⅓ natural size.

Fig. 188.

ETRUSCAN GOLD BULLA WITH SWASTIKA ON BOTTOM.

Waring, "Ceramic Art in Remote Ages," pl. 42, fig. 4 a.

An ornamental Swastika (fig. 189) is found on a silver bowl from Cervetri (Cære), Etruria. It is furnished by Grifi, and reproduced by Waring. This specimen is to be remarked as having a small outward flourish from the extreme end of each arm, somewhat similar to that made by the Jains (fig. 33), or on the "Tablet of honor" of Chinese porcelain (fig. 31). Fig. 190 shows an Etruscan bronze fibula with two Swastikas and two Maltese crosses in the pin shield. It is in the Museum of Copenhagen, and is taken from the report of the Congrés Internationale d'Anthropologie et d'Archæologie Préhistorique, Copenhagen, 1875, page 486. This specimen, by its rays or crotchets around the junction of the pin with the shield, furnishes the basis of the argument by Goblet d'Alviella[1] that the Swastika was evolved from the circle and was a symbol of the sun or sun-god. (See p. 785.)

Fig. 189.

ORNAMENTAL SWASTIKA ON ETRUSCAN SILVER BOWL.

Cervetri (Cære), Etruria.

Waring, "Ceramic Art in Remote Ages," pl. 41, fig. 13.

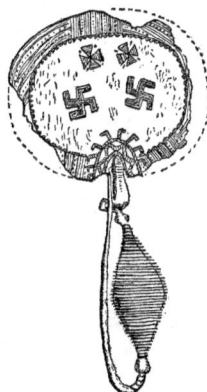

Fig. 190.

BRONZE FIBULA WITH TWO SWASTIKAS AND SUPPOSED RAYS OF SUN.[2]

Etruria.

Copenhagen Museum.

Goblet d'Alviella, fig. 19 a, De Mortillet, "Musée Préhistorique," fig. 1263.

¼ natural size.

Bologna was the site of the Roman city Bononia, and is supposed to have been that of Etruscan Felsina. Its Etruscan cemetery is extensive. Different names have been given to the excavations, sometimes from the owner of the land and at other times from the names of excavators. The first cemetery opened was called Villanova. The culture was different from that of the other parts of Etruria. By some it is believed to be older, by others younger, than the rest of Etruria. The Swastika is found throughout the entire

[1] "La Migration des Symboles," p. 67.
[2] See p. 786.

Villanova epoch. Fig. 191 shows a pottery vase from the excavation Arnoaldi. It is peculiar in shape and decoration, but is typical of that epoch. The decoration was by stamps in the clay (intaglio) of a given subject repeated in the narrow bands around the body of the vase. Two of these bands were of small Swastikas with the ends all turned to the right. Fig. 192 shows a fragment of pottery from the Felsina necropolis, Bologna, ornamented with a row of Swastikas stamped into the clay in a manner peculiar to the locality.

Fig. 191.

POTTERY URN ORNAMENTED WITH SUCCESSIVE BANDS IN INTAGLIO, TWO OF WHICH ARE COMPOSED OF SWASTIKAS.

Necropolis Arnoaldi, Bologna.

Museum of Bologna.

Gozzadini, "Scavi Archæologici," etc., pl. 4, fig. 8.

Fig. 193 shows the end view of one of the bobbins from Bologna, Italy, in the possession of Count Gozzadini by whom it was collected. The decoration on the end, as shown by the figure, is the Swastika. The main arms are made up of three parallel lines, which intersect each other at right angles, and which all turn to the right at right angles. The lines are not incised, as is usual, but, like much of the decoration belonging to this culture, are made by little points consecutively placed, so as to give the appearance of a continuous line.

Swastikas turning both ways are on one or both extremities of many terra-cotta cylinders found in the terramare at Coazze, province of Verona, deposited in the National (Kircheriano) Museum at Rome. (See figs. 380 and 381 for similar bobbins.)

Fig. 192.

FRAGMENT OF POTTERY WITH ROW OF SWASTIKAS IN INTAGLIO.

Necropole Felsinea, Italy.

Museo Bologna.

Gozzadini, "Due Sepolcri," etc., p. 7.

⅓ natural size.

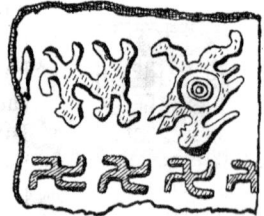

Fig. 193.

SWASTIKA SIGN ON CLAY BOBBIN.

Type Villanova, Bologna.

De Mortillet, "Musée Préhistorique," fig. 1239.

The museum at Este, Italy, contains an elegant pottery vase of large dimensions, represented in fig. 194, the decoration of which is the Greek fret around the neck and the Swastika around the body, done with small nail heads or similar disks inserted in the clay in the forms indicated. This association of the Swastika and the Greek fret on the same object is satisfactory evidence of their contemporaneous existence, and is thus far evidence that the one was not derived from the other, especially as the authorities who claim this derivation are at variance as to which was parent and which, child. (See fig. 133.)

A Swastika of the curious half-spiral form turned to the left, such as has been found in Scandinavia and also among the Pueblo Indians of the United States, is in the museum at Este.

When in the early centuries of the Christian era the Huns made their irruption into Europe, they apparently possessed a knowledge of the Swastika. They settled in certain towns of northern Italy, drove off the inhabitants, and occupied the territory for themselves. On the death of Attila and the repulse of the Huns and their general return to their native country, many small tribes remained and gradually became assimilated with the population. They have remained in northern Italy under the title of Longobards. In this Longobardian civilization or barbarism, whichever we may call it, and in their style of architecture and ornament, the Swastika found a prominent place, and is spoken of as Longobardian.

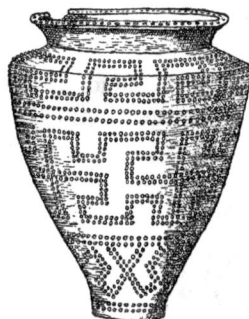

Fig. 194.
POTTERY VASE ORNAMENTED WITH BRONZE NAIL HEADS IN FORM OF SWASTIKA.
Este, Italy.
Matériaux pour l'Histoire Primitive et Naturelle de l'Homme, 1884, p. 14.

It is needless to multiply citations of the Swastika in Roman and Christian times. It would would appear as though the sign had descended from the Etruscans and Samnites along the coast and had continued in use during Roman times. Schliemann says[1] that it is found frequently in the wall paintings at Pompeii; even more than a hundred times in a house in the recently excavated street of Vesuvius. It may have contested with the Latin cross for the honor of being the Christian cross, for we know that the St. Andrew's cross in connection with the Greek letter P (fig. 6) did so, and for a long time stood as the monogram of Christ and was the Labarum of Constantine. All three of these are on the base of the Archiepiscopal chair in the cathedral at Milan.[2]

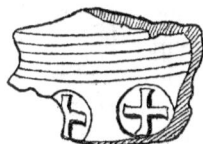

Fig. 195.
FRAGMENT OF POTTERY WITH SWASTIKA STAMPED IN RELIEF.

Swiss lake dwellings.—Figs. 195 and 196 are interesting as giving an insight into the method of making the sign of the Swastika. Fig. 195 shows a fragment of pottery bearing a stamped intaglio Swastika (right), while fig. 196 represents the stamp, also in pottery, with which the imprint was made. They are figured by Keller,[3] and are described on page 339, and by Chantre.[4]

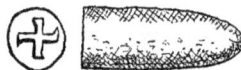

Fig. 196.
STAMP FOR MAKING SWASTIKA SIGN ON POTTERY.
Swiss lake dwelling of Bourget, Savoy.
Musée de Chambéry.
Chantre, "Age du Bronze," figs. 53, 55, and Keller, "Lake Dwellings of Europe," pl. 161, fig. 3.

They were found in the Swiss lake dwelling of Bourget (Savoy) by the Duc de Chaulnes, and are credited to his Museum of Chambéry.

[1] "Ilios," p. 352.
[2] There are bronze hatchets from Italy, with Swastikas in intaglio and in relief, in Musée St. Germain. De Mortillet, "Musée Préhistorique," figs. 1153, 1154.
[3] "Lake Dwellings," pl. 161, figs. 3, 4.
[4] "Age du Bronze," pt. 2, figs. 53–55, p. 195.

Germany and Austria.—Fig. 197 represents a fragment of a ceinture of thin bronze of the Halstattien epoch of the Bronze Age from a tumulus in Alsace. It is made after the style common to that period; the work is repoussé and the design is laid off by diagonal lines which divide the field into lozenges, wherein the Swastika is represented in various forms, some turned

Fig. 197.

FRAGMENT OF CEINTURE FROM A TUMULUS IN ALSACE.
Thin bronze repoussé with Swastikas of various kinds.
Bronze Age, Halstattien epoch.
De Mortillet, "Musée Préhistorique," fig. 1255.

square to the right, others to the left, while one is in spiral and is turned to the left. Other forms of the cross also appear with dots in or about the corners, which Burnouf associates with the myth of Agni and fire making, and which Zmigrodzki calls the *Croix swasticale.* This specimen is in the collection Nessel at Haguenau. Another ceinture was found at the same place and is displayed with it. It bears representations of the cross of different forms, one of which might be a Swastika with dotted cross lines, with the arms

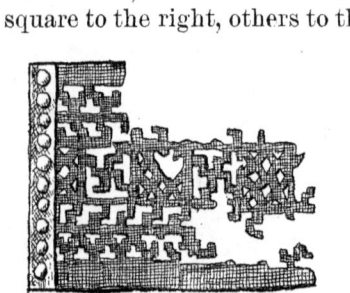

Fig. 198.

FRAGMENT OF A CEINTURE FROM THE TUMULUS OF METZSTETTEN, WÜRTEMBERG.
Thin bronze open work with intricate Swastikas.
Halstattien epoch.
De Mortillet, "Musée Préhistorique," fig. 1257, and Chantre, "Le Caucase," II, p. 50, fig. 25.

Fig. 199.

BRONZE FIBULA, THE BODY OF WHICH FORMS A SWASTIKA.
Museum of Mayence.
De Mortillet, "Musée Préhistorique," fig. 1266.

turned spirally to the left. Fig. 198 represents another fragment of a bronze ceinture from the same country and belonging to the same epoch. It is from the tumulus of Metzstetten, Würtemberg, and is in the Museum of Stuttgart. It is not repoussé, but is cut in openwork of intricate pattern in which the Swastika is the principal motif. A bronze fibula (fig. 199) is in the museum at Mayence, the body of which has the form of the normal Swastika. The arms are turned to the right and the lower one is broken off. The hinge for the pin was attached at one side or arm of the Swastika and the retaining clasp for the point at the other. Fig. 200 represents a prehistoric sepulchral urn

Fig. 200.

SEPULCHRAL URN WITH SWASTIKA.
North Germany.
Waring, "Ceramic Art in Remote Ages," pl. 7, fig. 94.

with a large Swastika, the arms being indicated by three parallel lines, after the same manner as the Swastika on the clay bobbin from

Bologna (fig. 193). It is reported by Lisch and Schröter, though the locality is not given. It is figured by Waring. The form, appearance, and decoration are of the type Villanova, thus identifying it with northern Italy.

The Swastika sign is on one of the three pottery vases found on Bishops Island, near Königswalde, on the right bank of the Oder, and on a vase from Reichersdorf, near Guben;[1] on a vase in the county of Lipto, Hungary,[2] and on pottery from the Cavern of Barathegy, Hungary.[3] Fig. 201 represents a spearhead of iron from Brandenburg, North Germany. It bears the mark of the Swastika with the ends turned to the left, all being at right angles, the ends ornamented with three dots recalling Zmigrodzki's *Croix swasticale* (figs. 12 and 13). By the side of this Swastika is a triskelion, or three-armed ogee sign, with its ends also decorated with the same three dots.

What relation there is between all these marks or signs and others similar to them, but separated by great distances of both time and space, it would be mere speculation to divine.

M. E. Chantre reports his investigations in certain Halstattien cemeteries in Italy and Austria.[4] At San Margarethen, on the road between Rudolfswerth and Kronau, Bavaria, he encountered a group of tumuli. Many objects of the "bel age du bronze" were found; among others, a bronze pin (fig. 202) with a short stem, but large, square, flat head, was found, with a normal Swastika engraved with small dots, pointillé, such as has been seen in Italy, Austria, and Armenia.

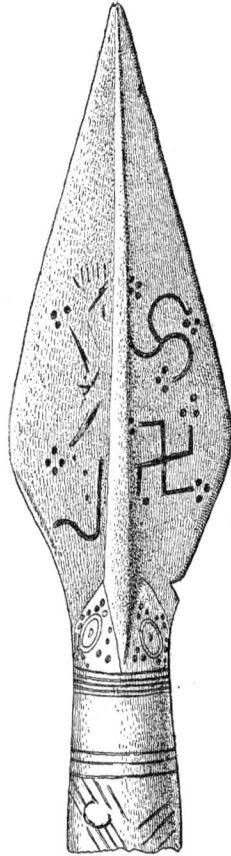

Fig. 201.

SPEARHEAD WITH SWASTIKA (CROIX SWASTICALE) AND TRISKELION.

Brandenburg, Germany.

Waring, "Ceramic Art in Remote Ages," pl. 44, fig. 21, and " Viking Age,' I, fig. 336 .

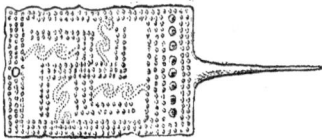

Fig. 202.

BRONZE PIN WITH SWASTIKA, POINTILLÉ, FROM MOUND IN BAVARIA.

Chantre, Matériaux pour l'Histoire Primitive et Naturelle de l'Homme, 1884, pp. 14, 120.

Belgium.—The Museum of Namur, Belgium, possesses a small object of bone, both points of which have

---

[1] Zeitschrift für Ethnographie, Berlin, 1871 and 1876.

[2] Coll. Majlath Bela; Hampel, "Antiquités Préhistoriques de la Hongrie;" Erztergom, 1877, pl. 20, No. 3.

[3] Hampel, "Catalogue de l'Exposition des Musées des Provinces," Budapest, 1876, p. 17; Schliemann, "Ilios," p. 352.

[4] Matériaux pour l'Histoire Primitive et Naturelle de l'Homme, 1884, pp. 14, 120.

been broken; its use is somewhat indeterminable, but it is believed by the curator of that museum and others to have been an arrowhead or spearhead. In form it belongs to Class A of stemmed implements, is lozenge-shaped, without shoulder or barb. It is a little more than two inches long, five-eighths of an inch wide, is flat and thin. On one side it bears two oblique or St. Andrew's crosses scratched in the bone; on the other, a figure resembling the Swastika. It is not the normal Swastika, but a variation therefrom. It is a cross about three-eighths of an inch square. The main stem lines cross each other at right angles; the ends of each of these arms are joined by two incised lines, which gives it the appearance of two turns to the right, but the junction is not well made, for the lines of the cross extend in every case slightly farther than the bent end. The variation from the normal Swastika consists of the variation produced by this second line. This object was lately found by M. Dupont, of Brussels, in the prehistoric cavern of Sinsin, near Namur. Most, or many, of these caverns belong to Paleolithic times, and one, the Grotte de Spy, has furnished the most celebrated specimens of the skeletons of Paleolithic man. But the cavern of Sinsin was determined, from the objects found therein, to belong to the Bronze Age.

Scandinavia.—The evidences of prehistoric culture have great resemblance throughout Denmark, Sweden, and Norway; so it is believed that during the prehistoric ages their peoples had the same culture, and the countries have been classed together as Scandinavia.

A bronze sword is reported by Mr. George Stephens [1] as having been found at Sæbo, Norway, with runes and a Swastika inlaid with silver. This specimen (fig. 203) was the subject of discussion before the Inter

TH   U   M   THOR   H   O

Fig. 203.

RUNIC INSCRIPTION CONTAINING A SWASTIKA.

Inlaid with silver on a bronze sword.

Saebo, Norway.

national Congress of Anthropology and Prehistoric Archæology,[2] at Budapest, 1876. Its runes were translated by Stephens, and being read from right to left, "OH THURMUTH," or "owns me Thurmuth." But on the same page he gives another sign for Thu and renders ⊬ as Odin or (W)oden. In the discussion before the congress it seems to have been agreed that the sign ⊬ stood for "blessing," "good luck," or some beneficent charm or benediction. A spearhead has been for

---

[1] "Old Northern Runic Monuments," pt. 3, p. 407.

[2] Proceedings of the Eighth Session, I, pp. 457–460.

years displayed in the museum at Torcello, near Venice, Italy, with a Swastika sign (fig. 204 a) prominent as an engraved sign.[1] Associated with it, but not a part of it, was an inscription (fig. 204 b), which has always been attributed to the Etrus-
cans. Mr. I. Undset, an archæologist in the museum of Chris-
tiania, made an ex-
tended visit through Italy in 1883, and on seeing this spearhead

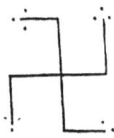

Fig. 204a.
SWASTIKA WITH DOTS.
Torcello, Italy.

AE   ING   N   E   TH   O

Fig. 204b
RUNIC INSCRIPTION ON SPEARHEAD.
Torcello, Italy.
Du Chaillu, "Viking Age," I, fig. 335.

recognized the inscription as runic and belonging to Scandinavia. The arms of the Swastika turned to the left, and the ends were finished with three dots of the same style as those described employed in the *Croix swasticale* (fig. 12). Figs. 205 and 206 represent articles of dress or toilet, and bear the Swastika. The first shows a red-ding comb, the Swastika on which turns to the right. It was probably of bone or horn, as are those of modern times. Fig. 206 shows a brooch, the interior decora-tion of which is a combination of Swas-tikas more or less interlaced. It is of bronze and was used as a dress ornament. Fig. 207 shows a large brooch, the bodies and bar of which are almost covered with the tetraskelion style of Swastika. There are six of the four-armed Swas-tikas, four of which turn to the left and two to the right. Another is a triskelion, the arms of which turn to the right.

Fig. 205.
REDDING COMB WITH SWASTIKA.
Scandinavia.

Fig. 206.
BRONZE BROOCH OR FIBULA WITH COMBINATION OF SWASTIKAS.
Scandinavia.

In Scandinavia more than in other countries the Swastika took the form of a rectangular body with arms projecting from each corner and bending in a spiral form, sometimes to the right, sometimes to the left.

---

[1] Du Chaillu, "Viking Age," I, fig. 335.

These are found more frequently on fibulæ or brooches and on swords and scabbards. In fig. 208 is shown a placque for a ceinture or belt, with a buckle to receive the thong. It contains two ogee Swastikas (tetraskelions). In this and fig. 207 the border and accessory decoration consist largely of ogee curves, which, here represented separate, would, if placed together as a cross, form the same style of Swastika as those mentioned. Figs. 209 and 210 show sword scabbards, with Swastikas turned both ways. Fig. 211 shows two triskelions. Fig. 212 represents a gold brooch from a grave at Fyen, reported by Worsaae and figured by Waring.[1]

Fig. 207.

BRONZE BROOCH WITH SWAS-
TIKAS.

Tetraskelions (right and left),
triskelion (left).
Scandinavia.

The brooch with ogee Swastika bears internal evidence of Scandinavian workmanship. There are other Swastikas of the same general form and style in distant localities, and this specimen serves to emphasize the extent of possible communication between distant peoples in prehistoric times. Fig. 213 represents a piece of horse-gear of bronze, silver plated and ornamented with Swastikas.

Fig. 208.

PLACQUE FOR CEINTURE, WITH
BUCKLE.

Two ogee Swastikas (tetraskelions).

Two of these are normal, the ends bent at right angles to the left, while the other is fancifully made, the only specimen yet found of that pattern.[2] It is not seen that these fanciful additions serve any purpose other than decoration. They do not appear to have changed the symbolic meaning of the Swastika. Fig. 214 represents

Fig. 209.

SCANDINAVIAN SWORD SCAB-
BARD.

Two ogee Swastikas (tetraskelions), right and left.

Fig. 210.

SCANDINAVIAN
SWORD SCAB-
BARD.

Ogee Swastika.

Fig. 211.

SCANDINAVIAN SWORD
SCABBARD.

Two triskelions, right
and left.

a sword scabbard belonging to the Vimose find, with a normal Swastika. Ludwig Müller reproduces a Swastika cross from a runic stone

---

[1] "Ceramic Art in Remote Ages," pl. 43, fig. 11; "Viking Age," II, fig. 1311; Englehardt, "L'Ancien Age de Fer," fig. 28.

[2] Du Chaillu, "Viking Age," I, fig. 379.

in Sweden. In an ancient church in Denmark, the baptismal font is decorated with Swastikas, showing its use in early Christian times. (See p. 878 for continuation of Swastika on Scandinavian or Danish gold bracteates.)

Mr. Paul du Chaillu, in his "Viking Age," mentions many specimens of Scandinavian and Norse antiquities bearing Swastika marks of divers styles: Bronze vessels (vol. 1, p. 100, note 1); iron spear point with runes and Swastika inlaid with silver, discovered in a tumulus with burnt bones, Muncheburg, fig. 336; another of the same, Volhynia, Russia, fig. 337; pottery vessel containing burnt bones, pointed iron knife, bronze needle, and melted glass beads, Bornholm, fig. 210; iron spearhead, Vimose bog find, (p. 207); border of finely woven silk cloth with gold and silver threads, from a mound (vol. 2, p. 289, fig. 1150).

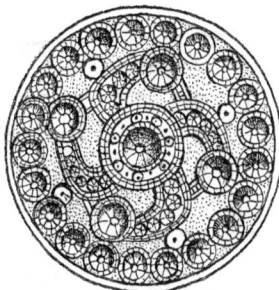

Fig. 212.

GOLD BROOCH WITH OGEE SWASTIKA.

Island of Fyen.

Waring, " Ceramic Art in Remote Ages," pl. 43, fig. 11.

Scotland and Ireland.—Specimens of the Swastika have been found on the Ogam stones in Scotland and Ireland (p. 797). In the churchyard of Aglish, county Kerry, Ireland, stand two stones bearing Ogam inscriptions. At the top of one is an ancient Celtic cross inclosed in a circle similar to fig. 7; immediately under it are two Swastika marks of four arms crossing at right angles, each arm bent to the right also at right angles. On two corners of the stone are inscriptions of the usual Ogam characters. The translation may be given, but seems to be unimportant and without apparent bearing upon this question. They are somewhat obliterated and their reading difficult. So far as made out, they are as follows: Maqimaqa and Apiloggo.

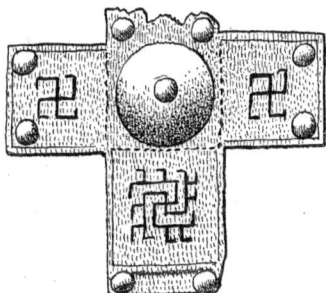

Fig. 213.

SCANDINAVIAN HORSE-GEAR.

Silver plated on bronze.

Waring, " Ceramic Art in Remote Ages," pl. 44, fig. 16 ; Du Chaillu, " Viking Age," i, fig. 379.

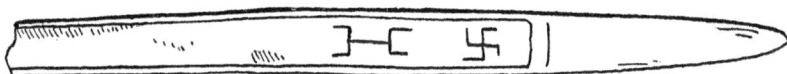

Fig. 214.

SCANDINAVIAN SWORD SCABBARD WITH NORMAL SWASTIKA.

Vimose bog find.

In Scotland, the Newton stone, in the grounds of the Newton House, bears an Ogam inscription, the meaning of which has no bearing upon the subject. But on the upper part of one of its faces appears an inscription, boldly and deeply incised, of forty-four characters arranged horizontally in six lines. These are of so remarkable a type as to have

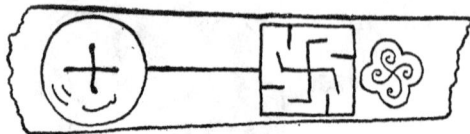

Fig. 215.

SCULPTURED STONE.

Greek cross in circle, normal Swastika in square, and ogee Swastika in quatrefoil.

Ireland.

puzzled every philologist and paleographer who has attempted their decipherment. The late Alexander Thomson, esq., of Banchory, Scotland, circulated a photograph and description of this monument among antiquarians with a request for their decipherment of it. Various readings have been given by the learned gentlemen, who have reported it to be Hebrew, Phenician, Greek, Latin, Aryan, Irish, and Anglo Saxon respectively. Brash[1] gives his opinion that the inscription is in debased Roman letters of a type frequently found in ancient

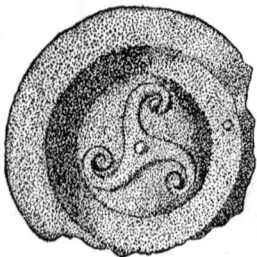

Fig. 216.

FRAGMENT OF THIN BRONZE REPOUSSÉ.

Ogee Swastika.

Ireland.

Munro, "Lake Dwellings of Europe," pl. 124, figs. 20–22.

inscriptions, its peculiarities being much influenced by the hardness of the stone at the time of cutting and of the subsequent weather wear of ages. The interest of this monument to us is that the third character in the fourth line is a Swastika. It is indifferently made, the lines do not cross at right angles, two of the ends are curved, and the two others bent at a wider than right angle. There are four characters in the line closely following each other. (See p. 797.)

Fig. 217.

FRAGMENT OF THIN BRONZE.

Triskelion.

Ireland.

Munro, "Lake Dwellings of Europe," p. 384, pl. 124, figs. 20–22.

The Logie stone, in Aberdeenshire, Scotland, bearing Ogam characters, contains a figure or mark reported by George M. Atkinson as a Swastika.[2]

On the Celtic crosses of Scotland certain marks appear which are elsewhere found associated with Swastika,

Fig. 218.

BRONZE PIN WITH SMALL NORMAL SWASTIKA ON HEAD.

Crannog of Lochlee, Tarbolton, Scotland.

Munro, "Lake Dwellings of Europe," p. 417.

and consequently have some relation therewith. The "Annam Stone" bears the mark of a Swastika (left) within three concentric circles, around the outside of which is a circle of dots.[3]

---

[1] "Ogam Inscribed Monuments," p. 359, pl. xlix.

[2] Ibid., p. 358, pl. xlviii.

[3] Greg, Archæologia, XLVIII, pt. 2, pl. 19, fig. 27.

Ludwig Müller reports the Swastika in Scotland and Ireland on Christian tombs, associated with Latin crosses.[1]

A sculptured stone in Ireland (fig. 215) shows on the face three varieties of the cross, a Greek cross in a circle, a Swastika with square ends turned to the right, within a rectangle, and an ogee (tetraskelion) turned to the right, inclosed in a quatrefoil.[2]

An Irish bowl showed a Swastika thus ⅃. Dr. R. Munro[3] reports from the Crannog of Lesnacroghera country, Antrim, Ireland, two pieces or disks of thin bronze, repoussés (fig. 216), bearing the sign of the Swastika and having the four arms of the spirals turned to the left. The similarity of this figure with those shown on the shields of the Pima Indians of New Mexico and Arizona (figs. 257 and 258) is to be remarked. Fig. 217 shows a triskelion of symmetric spirals turned to the right. In the Crannog of Lochlee, near Tarbolton, a bronze pin was found (fig. 218), the head of which was inclosed in a ring. On one side of the head was engraved a Greek cross, on the other was a normal Swastika turned to the right. The same crannog furnished a piece of ash wood five inches square, which had been preserved, as were all the other objects, by the peat, on which was carved a triskelion (fig. 219) after the form and style of those on the Missouri mound pottery.

Fig. 219.

CARVED TRISKELION FOUND ON FRAGMENT OF ASH WOOD.

Crannog of Lochlee, Tarbolton, Scotland.

Munro, "Lake Dwellings of Europe," p. 415.

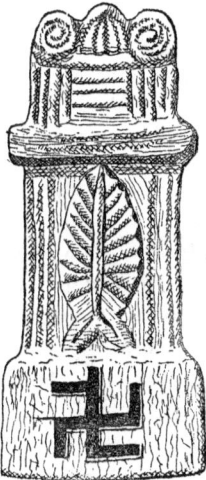

Fig. 220.

STONE ALTAR WITH SWASTIKA ON PEDESTAL.

France.

Museum of Toulouse.

De Mortillet, "Musée Préhistorique," fig. 1267.

GALLO-ROMAN PERIOD.

France.—The employment of the Swastika in France did not cease with the Bronze or Iron ages, but continued into the occupation of Gaul by the Romans.

Fig. 220 represents a stone altar erected in the south of France among the Pyrenees about the time of the advent of the Romans. It has a Swastika engraved on its pedestal. The upper arm has been carried beyond the body of the sign, whether by intention is not

[1] "La Migration des Symboles," p. 49.

[2] Zmigrodzki "Zur Geschichte der Suastika," taf. 6, fig. 248.

[3] "Lake Dwellings of Europe," p. 384, pl. 124, figs. 20–22.

apparent. Fig. 221 represents a pottery bottle with another specimen of Swastika belonging to the same (Gallo-Roman) epoch, but coming from the extreme north of Gaul, the neighborhood of Rouen. It is to be remarked that the ends of this Swastika give the outward curve or flourish similar to that noticed by Dr. Schlie-mann on the spindle-whorl of Troy, and is yet employed in making the Jain Swastika (fig. 33).

M. Alexander Bertrand[1] speaks of the discovery at Velaux, in the department of Bouches-du-Rhône, of the headless statue of a crouching or squatting guard which has a row of Swas-tikas across his breast, while beneath is a range of crosses, Greek or Latin. The newest examples of the Swastika belonging to this epoch have been found at Estinnes, Hainaut, and at Anthée, Namur, Belgium, on pieces of Roman tile; also on a tombstone in the Roman or Belgo-Roman cemetery of Juslenville near Pepinster.[2] This is a Pagan tomb, as evidenced by the inscriptions commenced "D. M." (*Diis Manibus*).[3]

Fig. 221.

POTTERY BOTTLE OF DARK GRAY WITH SWASTIKA AND DECORA-TION IN WHITE BARBOTINE.

Gallo-Roman Epoch.

Museum of Rouen.

De Mortillet, "Musée Préhistorique," fig. 1246.

ANGLO-SAXON PERIOD.

Britain.—Greg reports[4] a silver disk 1½ inches in diameter, with a triskelion made by punched dots, in the same style as the pin heads from Armenia (figs. 35 and 36). This was from grave 95 in an Anglo-Saxon cemetery at Sleafors, England, excavated by George W. Thomas and sold at Boston; bought by A. W. Franks and given to the British Museum. Grave 143 had a large cruciform fibula of bronze, partly gilt, similar to those from Scandinavia, with a Swastika on the central ornament thus ⨂. The slight curve or flourish on the outer end of the bent arm of this specimen resembles the Jain Swastika (fig. 33), though this bends to the left, while the Jain Swastikas bend to the right. Fig. 222 shows an Anglo-Saxon bronze gilt fibula with a peculiar form of Swastika leaving a square with dot and circle in its center. It was found in Long Wittenham, Berkshire, was reported in Archæologia,[6] and is figured

Fig. 222.

ANGLO-SAXON BRONZE GILT FIBULA.[5]

Simulation of Swastika.

Long Wittenham, Berk-shire, England.

[1] "L'Autel de Saintes et les triades gauloises," Revue Archæol., 1880, XXXIX, p. 343.
[5] Institut Archæologique Liégeois, X, 1870, p. 106, pl. 13.
[2] "La Migration des Symboles," p. 47, fig. 13.
[4] Archæologia, L, pt. 2, p. 406, pl. 23, fig. 7.
[5] See fig. 238.
[6] Archæologia, XXXI.

by Waring.[1] A figure having great similarity to this, even in its peculiarities and called a Swastika, was found on a shell in Toco Mound, Tennessee (fig. 238). Fig. 223 represents an Anglo-Saxon urn from Shropham, Norfolk. Its decorations consist of isolated figures like crosses, etc., arranged in horizontal bands around the vessel, and separated by moldings. The lower row consists of Swastikas of small size stamped into the clay and arranged in isolated squares. There are twenty Swastikas in the band; though they all turn to the right, they are not repetitions. They were made by hand and not with the stamp. They are white on a blackish ground. The original, which is in the British Museum, is cited by Kemble and figured by Waring.[2]

Fig. 223.

POTTERY URN.

Band of twenty hand-made Swastikas. white, on blackish ground.

Shropham, Norfolk, England.

British Museum.

Waring, "Ceramic Art in Remote Ages," pl. 3, fig. 50.

THE SWASTIKA ON ANCIENT COINS.

There has been much ink and imagination used, most of which has been wasted, in the discussion of this branch of this subject. The opinion has been expressed by many persons that the triskelion which formed the armorial emblem of the island of Sicily, and also of the Isle of Man, is but an evolution from or modification of the Swastika. In the judgment of the author this is based rather upon the similarity of the designs than upon any likeness in their origin and history. The acceptance by modern writers of this theory as a fact is only justified from its long-continued repetition.

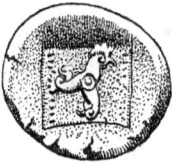

Fig. 224.[3]

LYCIAN COIN.

Triskelion with three arms representing cocks' heads and necks.

Triskelion, Lycia.—The triskelion on ancient coins first appears on the coins of Lycia, in Asia Minor, about B. C. 480. It was adopted for Sicily by Agathocles, B. C. 317 to 307. The coins of Lycia were first three cocks' heads and necks joined together equidistant in the center of the field, as shown in fig. 224, while figs. 225 and 226 bear a center dot and circle. This forms a hub and axle. Out of this hub spring three arms or rays, practically equidistant, the outer ends being bent to the left. They increase in size as they progress

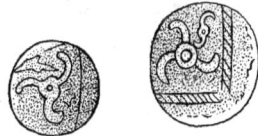

Figs. 225 and 226.[3]

LYCIAN COINS.

Triskelions with central dots and circles.

Waring, "Ceramic Art in Remote Ages," pl. 42, figs. 12, 13.

---

[1] "Ceramic Art in Remote Ages," pl. 43, fig. 10.

[2] Ibid., pl. 3, fig. 50.

[3] See p. 787.

outward and are largest at the outer ends. In fig. 226 there is a mint mark or counter mark of the same design as the triskelion, except that it has but two arms or rays (diskelion).

Perrot and Chipiez,[1] speaking of Lycia, say:

> The device of many of her coins is the "triskelis" or so-called "triquetra" (literally, three-cornered, triangular), a name derived from three serpents' heads, which usually figure in the field, much after the fashion of those supporting the famous tripod at Delphi,[2] consecrated by the Greeks to Apollo after the battle of Platæa. The number of heads is not constant, some coins having as many as four, "tetraskelis," while others have but two, "diskelis."[3]

The Greeks connected the symbol with the cult of Apollo, which they represented as very popular and of hoary antiquity in Lycia. The three-rayed design appears to have gained the victory over the others, and came into commoner use. It is found on Assyrian coins, and also as a countermark on coins of Alexander, B. C. 333 to 323. A comparison of these designs with the Swastika will, it is believed, show their dissimilarity, and the non-existence of relationship. In the Lycian designs, whether with two, three, or four rays, there is a central hub out of which the spokes spring. In the center of the hub is the small circle and dot which might represent the axle on which the machine revolved. In fact, the Lycian design is a fair representation of the modern screw propeller, and gives the idea of a whirling motion.

Compare these peculiarities with the Swastika. The Swastika is almost always square, is always a cross at right angles or near it, and whatever may become of the ends or arms of the cross, whether they be left straight, bent at right angles, or in a curve, it still gives the idea of a cross. There is no center except such as is made by the crossing of the two arms. There is not, as in these triskelions, a central hub. There is no dot or point around which the design or machine could be made to revolve, as in these Lycian triskelions; nothing of the central boss, cup, or nave, which forms what the Germans call the "Rad-Kreuz," wheel cross, as distinguished from the square cross.

In this regard Greg says:

> If R. Brown's lunar and Semitic or Asiatic origin of the triquetra, however, should be established, then the entire argument of the triquetra being derived from the fylfot, or vice versa, falls to the ground. * * * That the device arose out of the triskele and triquetra I do not think can be proved. It is clear the 卐 was a far older and more widely spread symbol than the triskele, as well as a more purely Aryan one.

Waring, explaining the tetraskelion (four-armed), declares it to have preceded the triskelion (three-armed), and he explains its meaning,[4] citing Sir Charles Fellows, as being a harpago, a grappling iron, a canting sign for Harpagus, who conquered Lycia for Cyrus, circa, 564 B. C.

---

[1] "History of Art in Phrygia, Lydia, Caria, and Lycia," p. 391.

[2] An unique cast of this tripod is in the U. S. National Museum, Department of Oriental Antiquities.

[3] The number of heads may have been regulated by the size of the coins in question, probably answering to different values.

[4] "Ceramic Art in Remote Ages," p. 85.

This, with the statement of Perrot and Chipiez (p. 872 of this paper), is a step in explanation of the adoption of the triskelion, and together they suggest strongly that it had no relation to the Swastika. At the date of the appearance of the triskelion on the Lycian coins the Swastika was well known throughout the Trojan peninsula and the Ægean Sea, and the difference between them was so well recognized that one could not possibly have been mistaken for the other.

Triskelion, Sicily.—N o w we pass to the consideration of the triskelion of Sicily. Fig. 227 represents a coin of Sicily. On the obverse the head of Persephone, on the

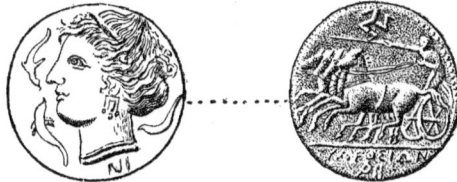

Fig. 227.

SICILIAN COIN WITH QUADRIGA AND TRISKELION.

British Museum.

Barclay Head, " Coins of the Ancients," etc., pl. 35, fig. 28.

reverse the quadriga, and above, the triskelion. Other specimens of the same kind, bearing the same triskelion, are seen in Barclay Head's work on the "Coinage of Syracuse" and his "Guide to the Ancient Coins in the British Museum." They belong to the early part of the reign of Agathocles, B. C. 317 to 310. In these specimens the triskelion is quite small; but as the coins belong to the period of the finest engraving and die-sinking of Greece, the representation, however minute, is capable of

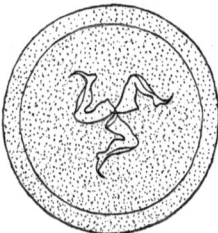

Fig. 228.

WARRIOR'S SHIELD.

From a Greek vase, representing Achilles and Hector.

Agrigentum, Sicily.

Waring, " Ceramic Art in Remote Ages," pl. 42, fig. 24.

decipherment. Fig. 228 is taken from the shield of a warrior on a Greek vase representing Achilles and Hector, in which the armorial emblem of Sicily, the triskelion, occupies the entire field,[1] and represents plainly that it is three human legs, conjoined at the thigh, bent sharply at the knee, with the foot and toes turned out. Some of these have been represented covered with mail armor and the foot and leg booted and spurred. It is evident that these are human legs, and so were not taken from the screw propeller of Lycia, while they have no possible relation to the crossed arms of the Swastika, and all this despite their similarity of appearance. This is rendered clearer by Waring,[2] where the armorial emblem on a warrior's shield is a single human leg, bent in the same manner, instead of three. Apropos of Swastikas on warriors' shields, reference is made to figs. 257 and 258, which represent two shields of Pima Indians, New Mexico, both of which have been in battle and both have the four-armed Swastika or tetraskelion. There is not in the Swastika, nor was there ever, any central part, any hub, any axis, any revolution. It is asserted that originally the triskelion of Sicily, pos-

---

[1] " Ceramic Art in Remote Ages," pl. 13, fig. 24.

Ibid., pl. 13, fig. 21.

sibly of Lycia, was a symbol of the sun, morning, midday, and afternoon, respectively. But this was purely theoretical and without other foundation than the imagination of man, and it accordingly gave way in due course. Pliny denies this theory and attributes the origin of the triskelion of Sicily to the triangular form of the island, ancient Trinacria, which consisted of three large capes equidistant from each other, pointing in their respective directions, the names of which were Pelorus, Pachynus, and Lilybæum. This statement, dating to so early a period, accounting for the triskelion emblem of Sicily, is much more reasonable and ought to receive greater credit than that of its devolution from the Swastika, which theory is of later date and has none of these corroborations in its favor. We should not forget in this argument that the Swastika in its normal form had been for a long time known in Greece and in the islands and countries about Sicily.

Among hundreds of patterns of the Swastika belonging to both hemispheres and to all ages, none of them have sought to represent anything else than just what they appear to be, plain marks or lines. There is no likeness between the plain lines of the Swastika and the bent form of the human leg, with the foot turned outward, incased in chain armor and armed with spurs.

Whenever or however the triskelion occurred, by whom it was invented, what it represented, how it comes to have been perpetuated, is all lost in antiquity and may never be known; but there does not seem to be any reason for believing it to have been an evolution from the Swastika.

Triskelion, Isle of Man.—The triskelion of Sicily is also the armorial emblem of the Isle of Man, and the same contention has been made for it, i. e., that it was a modification of the Swastika. But its migration direct from Sicily to the Isle of Man can be traced through the pages of history, and Mr. John Newton,[1] citing the Manx Note Book for January, 1886, has given this history at length, of which the following is a résumé:

Prior to the thirteenth century the Isle of Man was under dominion of the Norse Vikings, and its armorial emblems were theirs; usually a ship under full sail. Two charters of Harold, King of Man (1245, 1246 in the Cotton MSS.), bear seals with this device. Twenty years later, after the conquest of the island by, and its cession to, Alexander III of Scotland, A. D. 1266, the Norse emblems disappeared entirely, and are replaced by the symbol of the three legs covered with chain armor and without spurs. "It appears then," says Newton, "almost certain, though we possess no literary document recording the fact, that to Alexander III of Scotland is due the introduction of the ' Tre Cassyn' as the distinguishing arms of the Isle of Man." He then explains how this probably came about: Frederick II (A. D. 1197–1250), the Norman King of Sicily, married Isabella, the daughter of Henry III of England.

---

[1] Athenæum, No. 3385, September 10, 1892, p. 353.

A quarrel between the King of Sicily and the Pope led the latter to offer the crown to Henry III of England, who accepted it for his son Edmund (the Hunchback), who thereupon took the title of King of Sicily and quartered the Sicilian arms with the Royal arms of England. The negotiations between Henry and the Pope progressed for several years (1255 to 1259), when Henry, finding that he could no longer make it an excuse for raising money, allowed it to pass into the limbo of forgotten objects.

Alexander III of Scotland had married Margaret, the youngest daughter of Henry III, and thus was brother-in-law to Edmund as well as to Frederick. In 1256, and while these negotiations between Henry and the Pope concerning Sicily were in progress, Alexander visited, at London, his royal father-in-law, the King of England, and his royal brother-in-law, the King of Sicily, and was received with great honors. About that time Haco, the Norse king of the Isle of Man, was defeated by Alexander III of Scotland, and killed, soon after which event (1266) the Isle of Man was ceded to the latter. The Norse coat of arms disappeared from the escutcheon of the Isle of Man, and, being replaced by the three legs of Sicily, Mr. Newton inquires:

What more likely than that the King (Alexander III), when he struck the Norwegian flag, should replace it by one bearing the picturesque and striking device of Sicily, an island having so many points of resemblance with that of Man, and over which his sister ruled as Queen and her brother had been appointed as King?

However little we may know concerning the method of transfer of the coat of arms from Sicily to the Isle of Man, we are not left at all in doubt as to the fact of its accomplishment; and the triskelion of Sicily became then and has been ever since, and is now, the armorial emblem of the Isle of Man.

The Duke of Athol, the last proprietary of the Isle of Man, and who, in 1765, sold his rights to the Crown of England, still bears the arms of Man as the fifth quartering, "The three human legs in armor, conjoined at the upper part of the thigh and flexed in triangle, proper garnished," being a perpetuation of the triskelion or triquetrum of Sicily.[1]

The arms of the Isle of Man afford an excellent illustration of the migration of symbols as maintained in the work of Count Goblet d'Alviella; but the attempt made by others to show it to be an evolution from and migration of the Swastika is a failure.

Punch marks on Corinthian coins mistaken for Swastikas.—But is the Swastika really found on ancient coins? The use of precious metals as money dates to an unknown time in antiquity. Gold was used in early Bible times (1500 B. C.) among nearly every people as money, but it was by weight as a talent, and not as minted coin. The coinage of money began about 700 B. C. in Lydia. Lydia was a province on the western side of the peninsula of Asia Minor looking out toward Greece,

---

[1] Debrett's "Complete Peerage of the United Kingdom of Great Britain and Ireland."

while Lycia, its neighbor, was a province on the southern side looking toward the island of Rhodes. The Lydians began coinage by stamping with a punch each ingot or nugget of gold or silver, or a mixture of them called "Electrum." In the beginning these ingots were marked upon but one side, the reverse showing plainly the fiber of the anvil on which the ingot was laid when struck with the punch. But in a short time, it may have been two hundred years, this system was changed so as to use a die which would be reproduced on the coin when it was struck with a punch. The lion, bull, boar, dolphin, and many other figures were employed as designs for these dies. Athens used an owl; Corinth, Pegasus; Metapontine, a sheaf of wheat; Naples, a human-headed bull. The head and, occasionally, the entire form of the gods were employed. During almost the entire first period of nigh three hundred years the punch was used, and the punch marks show on the reverse side of the coins. These punch marks were as various as the dies for the obverse of the coins, but most of them took a variety of the square, as it would present the greatest surface of resistance to the punch. Even the triskelion of the Lycian coins is within an indented square (figs. 225 and 226). A series of these punch marks is given for demonstration on pl. 9. A favorite design was a square punch with a cross of two arms passing through the center, dividing the field into four quarters. Most of the punch marks on the coins of that period were of this kind. These punch marks and the method and machinery with which they were made are described in standard numismatic works.[1]

Fig. 229.

CORINTHIAN COINS.

Obverse and reverse.

Punch mark resembling Swastika.

It is believed by the author that the assertions as to the presence of the Swastika on these ancient coins is based upon an erroneous interpretation of these punch marks. Fig. 229 shows the obverse and reverse of a coin from Corinth. It belonged to the first half of the sixth century B. C. The obverse represents a Pegasus standing, while the reverse is a punch mark, said to have been a Swastika; but, examining closely, we will find there is no Swastika in this punch mark. The arms of the normal Swastika consist of straight lines crossing each other. In this case they do not cross. The design consists of four gammas, and each gamma is separated from its fellows, all forming together very nearly the same design as hundreds of other punch marks of the same period. If each outer arm of this mark is made slightly longer, the Swastika form disappears and the entire design resolves

---

[1] Snowden, "Mint Manual of Coins of all Nations," Introduction, pp. ix–xiv; Ackerman, "Roman Coins," pl. 14.

EXPLANATION OF PLATE 9.

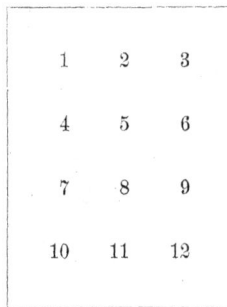

1	2	3
4	5	6
7	8	9
10	11	12

PUNCH MARKS ON REVERSE OF ANCIENT COINS.

Fig. 1. COIN OF LYDIA. Electrum. Oblong sinking between two squares. Babylonian stater. The earliest known coinage. Circa 700 B. C.

2. PHENICIAN HALF STATER. Electrum. Incuse square with cruciform ornament.

3. SILVER COIN OF TEOS. Incuse square. Circa 544 B. C.

4. SILVER COIN OF ACANTHUS. Incuse square.

5. SILVER COIN OF MENDE. Incuse triangles.

6. SILVER COIN OF TERONE. Incuse square.

7. COIN OF BISALTÆ.[1] Incuse square. Octadrachm.

8. SILVER COIN OF ORRESCII.[1] Incuse square. Octadrachm.

9. CORINTHIAN SILVER COIN. Incuse square divided into eight triangular compartments. The earliest coin of Corinth, dating B. C. 625 to 585.

10. SILVER COIN OF ABDERA. Incuse square.

11. SILVER COIN OF BYZANTIUM. Incuse square, granulated.

12. SILVER COIN OF THRASOS (THRACE). Incuse square.

---

[1] The Bisaltæ and Orrescii were Thracian tribes who dwelt in the valleys of the Strymon and the Angites, to the north of the Pangæan Range.

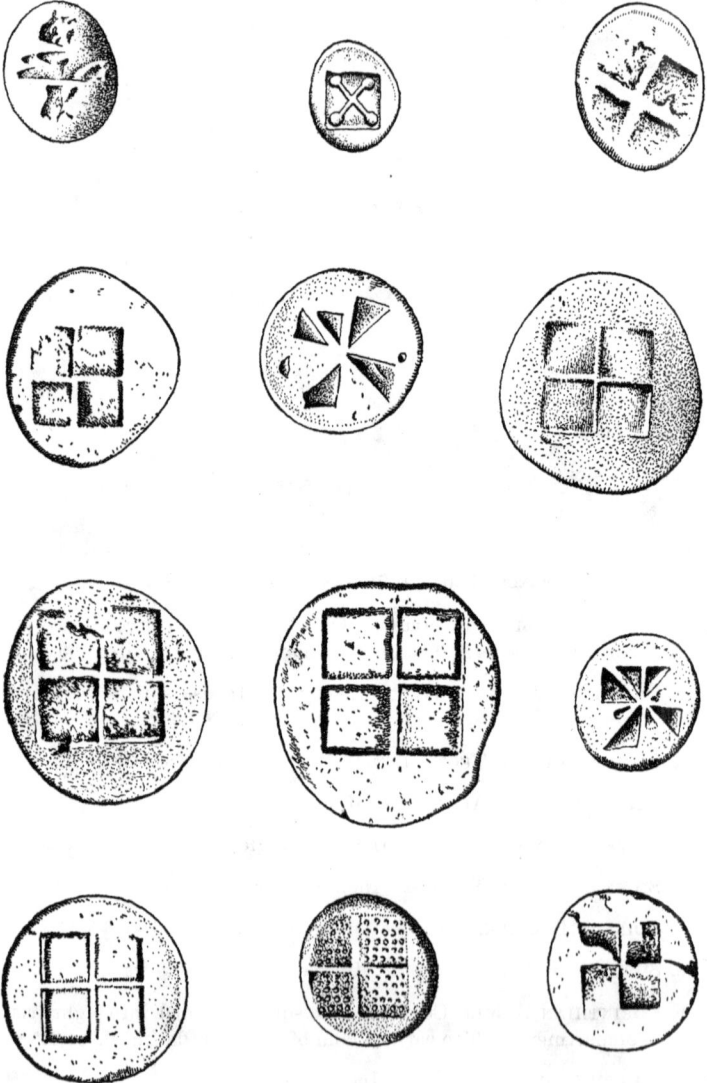

PUNCH MARKS ON REVERSE OF ANCIENT COINS.

itself into the square habitually employed for that purpose. If the punch mark on this Corinthian coin be a Swastika, it depends upon the failure to make the extreme end of the bent arm an eighth of an inch longer. This is too fine a point to be relied upon. If this punch mark had these arms lengthened an eighth of an inch, it would confessedly become a square.

Swastika on ancient Hindu coins.—It is not to be inferred from this opposition that the Swastika never appeared on ancient coins. It did appear, but seems to have been of a later date and to have belonged farther east among the Hindus. Fig. 230 shows an ancient (Hindu?) coin reported by Waring, who cites Cunningham as authority for its having been found at Ujain. The design consists of a cross with independent circles on the outer end of each of the four

Fig. 230.

ANCIENT HINDU COIN IN
THE FORM OF A CROSS
WITH A SWASTIKA ON
THE EXTREMITY OF
EACH ARM.[1]

Waring, "Ceramic Art in Remote Ages," pl. 41, fig. 19.

arms, the circles being large enough to intersect each other. The field of each of these circles bears a Swastika of normal form. Other coins are cited of the same style, with small center dots and concentric circles in the stead of the Swastika. What meaning the Swastika has here, beyond the possible one of being a lucky penny, is not suggested.

Other ancient Hindu coins bearing the Swastika (figs. 231–234) are attributed to Cunningham by Waring.[2] These are said by Waring to be Buddhist coins found at Behat near Scharaupur. Mr. E. Thomas, in his article on the "Earliest Indian Coinage,"[3] ascribes them to the

Fig. 231.   Fig. 232.   Fig. 233.   Fig. 234.

ANCIENT HINDU COINS WITH SWASTIKAS, NORMAL AND OGEE.

Waring, "Ceramic Art in Remote Ages," pl. 41, figs. 20–24.

reign of Krananda, a Buddhist Indian king contemporary with or prior to Alexander, about 330 B. C.

The coins of Krananda,[4] contemporary of Alexander the Great,[5] bear the Swastika mark, associated with the principal Buddhist marks, the trisula, the stupha, sacred tree, sacred cone, etc. Waring says[6] that according to Prinsep's "Engravings of Hindu Coins," the Swastika seems to disappear from them about 200 B. C., nor is it found on the

---

[1] See p. 788.

[2] "Ceramic Art in Remote Ages," pl. 41, figs. 20–23.

[3] Numismatic Chron. (new series), IV.

[4] "La Migration des Symboles," figs. 17, 123.

[5] Edward Thomas, Journ. Royal Asiatic Soc. (new series), I, p. 475.

[6] "Ceramic Art in Remote Ages," p. 83.

Indo-Bactrian, the Indo-Sassanian, or the later Hindu or subsequent Mohammedan, and he gives in a note the approximate dates of these dynasties: Early native Buddhist monarchs from about 500 B. C. to the conquest of Alexander, about 330 B. C.; the Indo-Bactrian or Greek successors of Alexander from about 300 to 126 B. C.; the Indo-Parthian or Scythic from about 126 B. C.; the second Hindu dynasty from about

Fig. 235.
ANCIENT COIN WITH SWASTIKA.
Gaza, Palestine.
Waring, "Ceramic Art in Remote Ages," pl. 42, fig. 6.

56 B. C.; the Indo-Sassanian from A. D. 200 to 636, and subsequent to that the Indo-Mohammedan from the eleventh to the close of the thirteenth century; the Afghan dynasty from A. D. 1290 to 1526, and the Mongol dynasty to the eighteenth century, when it was destroyed by Nadir Shah. (See p. 772.)

Swastika on coins in Mesembria and Gaza.—Mr. Percy Gardner, in his article, "Ares as a Sun-god,"[1] finds the Swastika on a coin of Mesembria in Thrace. He explains that "Mesembria is simply the Greek word for noon, midday ($\mu\varepsilon\sigma\eta\mu\beta\rho i\alpha$)." The coins of this city bear the inscription $ME\Sigma\text{⊥}$, which Greg[2] believes refers by a kind of pun to the name of the city, and so to noon, or the sun or solar light.

The answer to this is the same given throughout this paper, that it may be true, but there is no evidence in support of it. Max Müller[3] argues that this specimen is decisive of the meaning of the sign Swastika. Both these gentlemen place great stress upon the position which the Swastika held in the field relative to other objects, and so determine it to have represented the sun or sunlight; but all this seems *non sequitur*. A coin from Gaza, Palestine, ancient, but date not given, is attributed to R. Rochette, and by him to Munter (fig. 235). The Swastika sign is not perfect, only two arms of the cross being turned, and not all four.

Fig. 236.
GOLD BRACTEATE WITH JAIN SWASTIKA.
Denmark.
Waring, "Ceramic Art in Remote Ages," pl. 1, fig. 9.

Swastika on Danish gold bracteates.—Fig. 236 represents a Danish gold bracteate with a portrait head, two serpents, and a Swastika with the outer ends finished with a curve or flourish similar to that of the Jains (fig. 33).

There are other bracteates with the Swastika mark, which belong to the Scandinavian countries.[4] Some of them bear signs referring to Christian civilization, such as raising hands in prayer; and from a determination of the dates afforded by the coins and other objects the Swastika can be identified as having continued into the Christian era.

The coinage of the ancient world is not a prolific field for the dis-

[1] "Numismatic Chron.," pt. I, 1880. See p. 788 of this paper.
[2] Archæologia, XLVIII, pt. II, 1885, p. 306.
[3] Athenæum, August 20, 1892.
[4] "Viking Age," II, figs. 1307, 1309.

covery of the Swastika. Other specimens may possibly be found than those here given. This search is not intended to be exhaustive. Their negative information is, however, valuable. It shows, first, that some of the early stamps or designs on coins which have been claimed as Swastikas were naught but the usual punch marks; second, it shows a limited use of the Swastika on the coinage and that it came to an end in very early times. Numismatics afford great aid to archæology from the facility and certainty with which it fixes dates. Using the dates furnished by the coinage of antiquity, it is gravely to be questioned whether the prolific use of the Swastika in Asia Minor (of which we have such notable examples on specimens of pottery from the hill of Hissarlik, in Greece) did not terminate before coinage began, or before 480 B. C., when the period of finer engraving began, and it became the custom to employ on coins the figures of gods, of tutelary deities, and of sacred animals. Thus the use of the Swastika became relegated to objects of commoner use, or those having greater relation to superstition and folklore wherein the possible value of the Swastika as an amulet or sign with power to bring good luck could be better employed; or, as suggested by Mr. Greg, that the great gods which, according to him, had the Swastika for a symbol, fell into disrepute and it became changed to represent something else.

UNITED STATES OF AMERICA.

PRE-COLUMBIAN TIMES.

Fains Island and Toco Mounds, Tennessee.—That the Swastika found its way to the Western Hemisphere in prehistoric times can not be doubted. A specimen (fig. 237) was taken by Dr. Edward Palmer in the year 1881 from an ancient mound opened by him on Fains Island, 3 miles from Bainbridge, Jefferson County, Tenn. It is figured and described in the Third Annual Report of the Bureau of Ethnology,[1] as follows:

A shell ornament, on the convex surface of which a very curious ornamental design has been engraved. The design, inclosed by a circle, represents a cross such as would be formed by two rectangular tablets or slips slit longitudinally and interlaced at right angles to each other. The lines are neatly and deeply incised. The edge of the ornament has been broken away nearly all around.

The incised lines of this design (fig. 237) represent the Swastika turned to the left (though the description does not recognize it as such). It has small circles with dots in the center, a style of work that may become of peculiar value on further investigation, but not to be confounded with the dots or points in what M. Zmigrodzki calls the *Croix swasticale.* The mound from which this specimen came, and the objects associated with it, show its antiquity and its manufacture by the aborigines untainted by contact with the whites. The mound is on the

---

[1] Page 436, fig. 140.

east end of Fains Island. It was 10 feet in height and about 100 feet in circumference at the base. In the bed of clay 4 feet beneath the surface were found the remains of 32 human skeletons; of these, only 17 skulls could be preserved. There had been no regularity in placing the bodies.

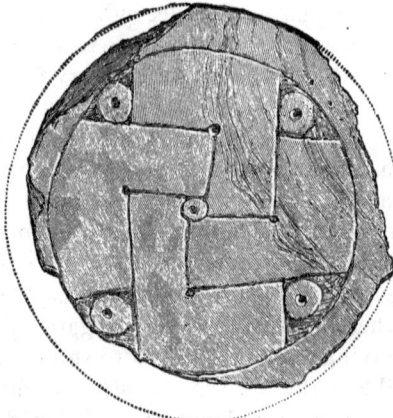

Fig. 237.

SHELL GORGET WITH ENGRAVED SWASTIKA, CIRCLES, AND DOTS.

Fains Island, Tennessee.

Cat. No. 62928 U. S. N. M.

The peculiar form of this Swastika is duplicated by a Runic Swastika in Sweden, cited by Ludwig Müller and by Count d'Alviella.[1]

The following objects were found in the mound on Fains Island associated with the Swastika shell (fig. 237) and described, and many of them figured:[2] A gorget of the same *Fulgur* shell (fig. 239); a second gorget of *Fulgur* shell with an engraved spider (fig. 278); a pottery vase with a figure of a frog; three rude axes from four to seven inches in length, of diorite and quartzite; a pierced tablet of slate; a disk of translucent quartz 1¾ inches in diameter and three-quarters of an inch in thickness; a mass of pottery, much of it in fragments, and a number of bone implements, including needles and paddle-shaped objects. The shell objects (in addition to the disks and gorgets mentioned) were pins made from the columellæ of Fulgur (*Busycon perversum?*) of the usual form and about four inches in length. There were also found shell beads, cylindrical in form, an inch in length and upward of an inch in diameter, with other beads of various sizes and shapes made from marine shells, and natural specimens of *Io spinosa, Unio probatus.*

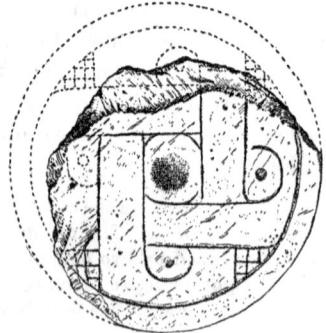

Fig. 238.

ENGRAVED SHELL WITH SWASTIKA, CIRCLES, AND DOTS.

Toco Mound, Monroe County, Tenn.

Cat. No. 115624, U. S. N. M.

The specimen represented in fig. 238 is a small shell from the Big Toco mound, Monroe County, Tenn., found by Mr. Emmert with skeleton No. 49 and is fig. 262, Twelfth Annual Report of the Bureau of Ethnology, 1890–91, page 383, although it is not described. This is a circular disk of *Fulgur*

---

[1] Proc. Royal Danish Acad. Sci., 5th ser., III, p. 94, fig. a; "La Migration des Symboles," p. 50, fig. 16.

[2] Third Ann. Rep. Bureau of Ethnology, 1881–82, p. 464 et seq., figs. 139–141.

PLATE 10.

ENGRAVED FULGUR (?) SHELL, RESEMBLING STATUE OF BUDDHA.

Toco Mound, Tennessee.

Cat. No. 115560, U. S. N. M.

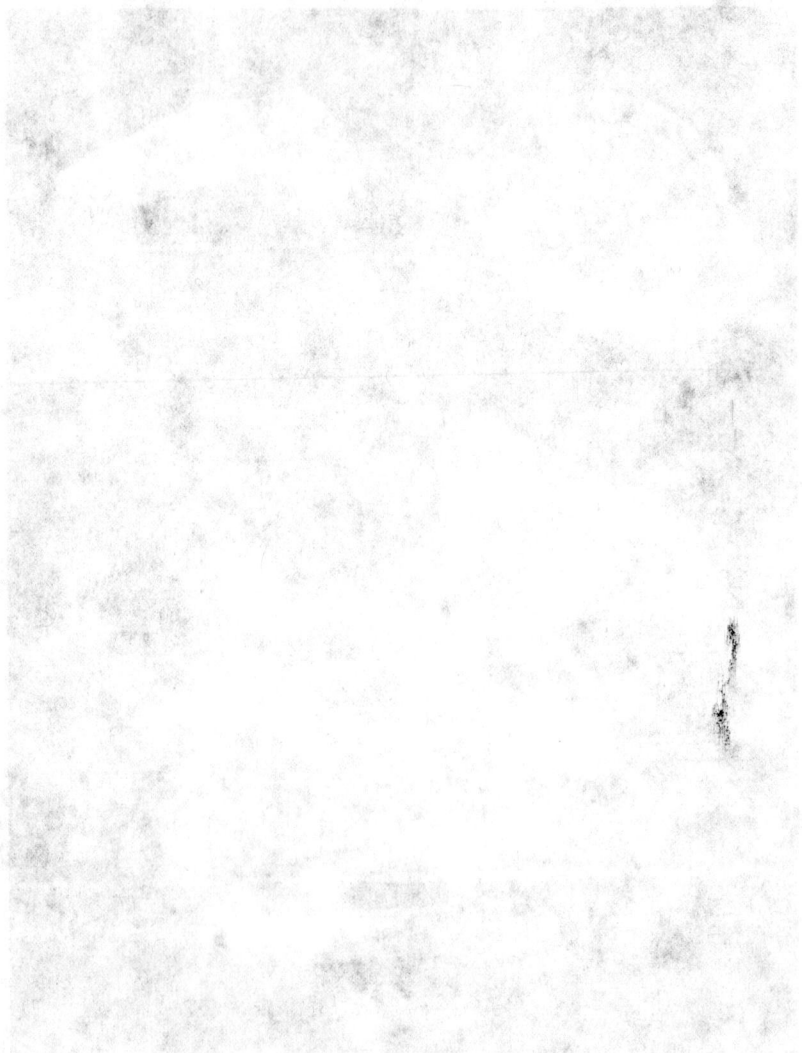

shell, much damaged around the edge, 1½ inches in diameter, on which has been engraved a Swastika. It has a small circle and a dot in the center, around which circle the arms of the Swastika are inter-laced. There are also circles and central dots at each turn of the four arms. The hatch work in the arc identifies this work with that of other crosses and a triskelion from the same general locality—figs. 302, 305, and 306, the former being part of the same find by Mr. Emmert. Fig. 222, a bronze gilt fibula from Berkshire, England, bears a Swastika of the same style as fig. 238 from Tennessee. The circles and central dots of fig. 238 have a similarity to Peruvian ornamenta-tion. The form and style, the broad arms, the circles and central dots, the lines of engravings, show such similarity of form and work as mark this specimen as a congener of the Swastika from Fains Island (fig. 237). The other objects found in the mound associated with this Swas-tika will be described farther on.

There can be no doubt of these figures being the genuine Swastika, and that they were of aboriginal workmanship. Their discovery immediately suggests investigation as to evidences of communication with the Eastern Hemisphere, and naturally the first question would be, Are there any evidences of Buddhism in the Western Hemisphere? When I found, a few days ago, the two before-described representa-tions of Swastikas, it was my belief that no reliable trace of Buddha or the Buddhist religion had ever been found among the aboriginal or prehistoric Americans. This statement was made, as almost all other statements concerning prehistoric man should be, with reserve, and subject to future discoveries, but without idea that a discovery of evi-dence on the subject was so near. In searching the U. S. National Museum for the objects described in the Second Annual Report of the Bureau of Ethnology under the title of "Art in Shell among the Ancient Americans," the writer discovered a neglected specimen of a mutilated and damaged shell (pl. 10), marked as shown on the back, found by Mr. Emmert, an employé of the Bureau of Ethnology, in the year 1882. Its original field number was 267, Professor Thomas's 6542, the Museum number 115562, and it was found in the Big Toco mound, Monroe County, Tenn. It is not figured nor mentioned in any of the Bureau reports. It is greatly to be regretted that this shell is so mutilated. In its present condition no one can say positively what it is, whether a statue of Buddha or not; but to all appearances it represents one of the Buddhist divinities. Its material, similar to the hundred others found in the neighborhood, shows it to have been indigenous, yet parts of its style are different from other aboriginal North American images. Atten-tion is called to the slim waist, the winged arms, the crossed legs, the long feet, breadth of toes, the many dots and circles shown over the body, with triple lines of garters or anklets. All these show a different dress from the ancient North American. The girdle about the waist, and the triangular dress which, with its decorations and arrangement of dots and circles, cover the lower part of the body, are to be remarked. While there are several specimens of aboriginal art from this part of the country which bear these peculiarities of costumes, positions, appearance, and manner of work, showing them to have been in use among a portion of the people, yet they are not part of the usual art products. There is a manifest difference between this and the ordinary statue of the Indian or of the mound builder of that neighborhood or epoch.

It is not claimed that this shell proves the migration of Buddhism from Asia, nor its presence among North American Indians. "One swallow does not make a summer." But this figure, taken in connection with the Swastika, presents a set of circumstances corresponding with that possibility which goes a long distance in forming circumstantial evidence in its favor.

M. Gustave d'Eichthal wrote a series of essays in the Revue Archæ-ologique, 1864–65, in which he collated the evidence and favored the theory of Buddhist influence in ancient America. Other writers have taken the same or similar views and have attributed all manner of foreign influence, like the Lost Tribes of Israel, etc., to the North American Indian,[1] but all these theories have properly had but slight influence in turning public opinion in their direction. Mr. V. R. Gandhi, in a recent letter to the author, says of this specimen (pl. 10):

While Swastika technically means the cross with the arms bent to the right, later on it came to signify anything which had the form of a cross; for instance, the posture in which a persons sits with his legs crossed is called the Swastika posture;[2] also when a person keeps his arms crosswise over his chest, or a woman covers her breast with her arms crossed, that particular attitude is called the Swastika attitude, which has no connection, however, with the symbolic meaning of the Swastika with four arms. The figure [pl. 10], a photograph of which you gave me the other day, has the same Swastika posture. In matters of concentration and meditation, Swastika posture is oftentimes prescribed, which is also called Sukhasana, meaning a posture of ease and comfort. In higher forms of concentration, the posture is changed from Sukhasana to Padmasana, the posture which is generally found in Jain and Buddhist images. The band around the waist, which goes from the navel lower on till it reaches the back part, has a peculiar significance in the Jain philosophy. The Shvetamber division of the Jain community have always this kind of band in their images. The object is twofold: The first is that the generative parts ought not to be visible; the second is that this band is considered a symbol of perfect chastity.

There can be no doubt of the authenticity of these objects, nor any suspicion against their having been found as stated in the labels attached. They are in the Museum collection, as are other specimens. They come unheralded and with their peculiar character unknown. They were obtained by excavations made by a competent and reliable investigator who had been engaged in mound exploration, a regular employé of the Bureau of Ethnology, under the direction of Prof.

[1] This theory was first announced by Antonio de Montezinos and published by MANASSEH ben ISRAEL in Amsterdam, 1636. In Leser Library, Phil., and Cohen Library, Balto. Catalogued by Dr. Cyrus Adler. First English Ed. by Moses Wall, London: 1651, republished by Dr. Grossmann, Am. Jews' Annual, 1889, p. 83.
[2] Max Müller and Ohnefalsch-Richter agree with this. See pp. 772, 773 of this paper.

Cyrus Thomas during several years, and always of good reputation and unblemished integrity. They come with other objects, labeled in the same way and forming one of a series of numbers among thousands. Its resemblance to Buddhist statues was apparently undiscovered or unrecognized, at least unmentioned, by all those having charge of it, and in its mutilated condition it was laid away among a score of other specimens of insufficient value to justify notice or publication, and is now brought to light through accident, no one having charge of it recognizing it as being different from any other of the half hundred engraved shells theretofore described. The excavation of Toco mound is described by Professor Thomas in the Twelfth Annual Report of the Bureau of Ethnology, pages 379–384.

We can now be governed only by the record as to the objects associated with this shell (pl. 10), which shows it to have been found with skeleton No. 8, in Big Toco mound, Monroe County, Tenn., while the Swastika of figure 238 was found with skeleton No. 49. Toco mound contained fifty-two skeletons, or, rather, it contained buried objects reported as from that many skeletons. Those reported as with skeleton No. 8 were, in addition to this gorget: One polished stone hatchet, one stone pipe, and one bowl with scalloped rim. Toco mound seems to have been exceedingly rich, having furnished 198 objects of considerable importance. Association of discovered objects is one of the important means of furnishing evidence in prehistoric archæology. It is deemed of sufficient importance in the present case to note objects from Toco mound associated with the Buddha statue. They are given in list form, segregated by skeletons:

Skeleton No.

4. Two polished stone hatchets, one discoidal stone.
5. One polished stone hatchet.
7. Two large seashells.
8. One stone pipe, one polished stone hatchet, one ornamented shell gorget (the Buddha statue, pl. 10), one ornamented bowl, with scalloped rim.
9. Two polished stone hatchets.
12. A lot of small shell beads.
13. Four bone implements (one ornamented), one stone pipe, two shell gorgets (one ornamented), one bear tooth.
17. One polished stone hatchet.
18. Two polished stone hatchets, one stone pipe, one boat-shaped bowl (ornamented), one shell gorget (ornamented), one shell mask, one shell pin, one shell gorget, one bear tooth, lot of shell beads.
22. Two polished stone chisels, one stone disk.
24. One polished stone hatchet.
26. Two polished stone hatchets, one waterworn stone, two hammer stones.
27. One polished stone hatchet.
28. Two polished stone hatchets, one ornamented bowl.
31. One polished stone hatchet, one polished stone chisel.
33. Two polished stone hatchets, one two-eared pot, one small shell gorget, three shell pins, fragments of pottery.
34. Three polished stone hatchets.
36. One discoidal stone.

Skeleton No.

37. One polished stone chisel, one stone pipe, one shell mask (ornamented).
41. One polished stone hatchet, one stone pipe, pottery vase with ears (ornamented), one shell mask, one shell pin, four arrowheads (two with serrated edges), two stone perforators.
43. Lot of shell beads.
49. One polished stone hatchet, one spade-shaped stone ornament (perforated), one spear-head, one stone pipe, one pottery bowl with two handles, two shell masks (ornamented), twenty-seven bone needles, two beaver teeth, one bone implement (raccoon), piece of mica, lot of red paint, two shell gorgets (one ornamented with Swastika, fig. 238), thirty-six arrow-heads, lot of flint chips, fragment of animal jaw and bones, lot of large shells, one image pot.
51. One shell pin, one shell mask, one arrow-head, two small shell beads.
52. One shell mask, one shell gorget, one shell ornament.

These objects are now in the U. S. National Museum and in my department. The list is taken from the official catalogue, and they number from 115505 to 115684. I have had the opportunity of comparing the objects with this description and find their general agreement. Dr. Palmer, the finder, was an employé of the Bureau of Ethnology, is a man of the highest character, of great zeal as an archæologist and naturalist, and has been for many years, and is now, in the employ of the Bureau or Museum, always with satisfaction and confidence. Mr. Emmert was also an employé of the Bureau for many years, and equally reliable.

The specimens of shell in this and several other mounds, some of which are herein figured, were in an advanced stage of decay, pitted, discolored, and crumbling, requiring to be handled with the utmost care to prevent disintegration. They were dried by the collector, immersed in a weak solution of glue, and forwarded immediately (in 1885), with other relics from the neighborhood, to the Bureau of Ethnology and National Museum at Washington, where they have remained ever since. There is not the slightest suspicion concerning the genuineness or antiquity of this specimen or of those bearing the Swastika as belonging to the mound-building epoch in the valley of the Tennessee.

Other figures of sufficient similarity to the Swastika have been found among the aborigines of North America to show that these do not stand alone; and there are also other human figures which show a style of work so similar and such resemblance in detail of design as to establish the practical identity of their art. One of these was a remarkable specimen of engraved shell found in the same mound, Fains Island, which contained the first Swastika (fig. 237). It is described in the Second Annual Report of the Bureau of Ethnology, page 301, under the name of McMahon's mound. It is a large polished Fulgur shell disk which, when entire, has been nearly 5 inches in diameter (fig. 239). A little more than one-third has crumbled away, and the remaining portion has been preserved only by careful handling and immediate immersion in a solution of glue. It had been engraved on the concave side. The design represents two human figures plumed and winged, armed with eagles' talons and engaged in mortal combat. The design apparently covered the entire shell, leaving no space for encircling lines. The two figures are in profile and face each other in a fierce onset. Of the right-hand figure, only the body, one arm, and one leg remain. The left-hand figure is almost complete. The outline of the face, one arm, and one foot is all that is affected. The right hand is raised above the head in the act of brandishing a long knife pointed at both ends. The other combatant, clutching in his right hand a savage-looking

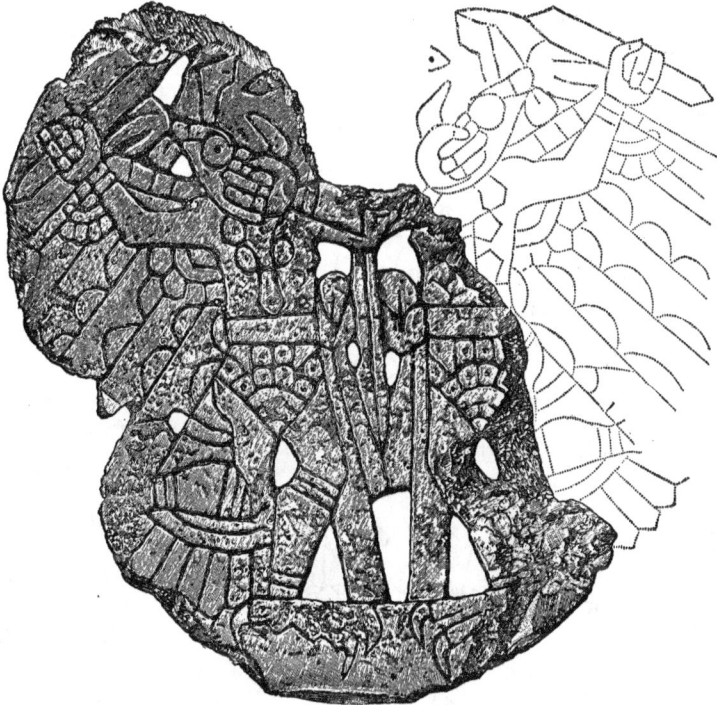

Fig. 239.

SHELL GORGET.

Two fighting figures with triangular breech-clout, garters and anklets, and dots and circles.

Fains Island, Tennessee.

Third Annual Report of the Bureau of Ethnology, p. 452, fig. 128.

Cat. No. 62930, U. S. N. M.

blade with its point curved, seems delivering a blow in the face of his antagonist. Of the visible portions of the figures, the hands are vigorously drawn, the thumbs press down upon the outside of the forefingers in a natural effort to tighten the grasp. The body, arms, and legs are well defined and in proper proportion, the joints are correctly placed, the left knee is bent forward, and the foot planted firmly on the ground, while the right is thrown gracefully back against the rim at the left, and the legs terminate in well-drawn eagles' feet armed with curved talons.   The head is decorated with a single plume which springs from a circular ornament placed over the ear; an angular figure extends forward from the base of this plume, and probably represents what is left of the headdress proper.   In front of this—on the very edge of the crumbling shell—is one-half of the lozenge-shaped eye, the dot representing the pupil being almost obliterated. The ankles and legs just below the knee and the wrists each have three lines representing bracelets or anklets. It is uncertain whether the leg is covered or naked; but between the waistband and the leggings, over the abdomen, is represented on both figures a highly decorated triangular garment, or, possibly coat of mail, to which particular attention is called.[1] In the center, at the top, just under the waistband, are four circles with dots in the center arranged in a square; outside of this, still at the top, are two triangular pieces, and outside of them are two more circles and dots; while the lower part of the triangle, with certain decorations of incised lines, completes the garment. This decoration is the same on both figures, and corresponds exactly with the Buddha figure. An ornament is suspended on the breast which shows three more of the circles and dots. The earring is still another. The right-hand figure, so far as it can be seen, is a duplicate of the left, and in the drawing it has, where destroyed, been indicated by dotted lines.   It is remarkable that the peculiar clothing or decoration of these two figures should be almost an exact reproduction of the Buddha figure (pl. 10).   Another

Fig. 240.

COPPER PLATE.

Entowah Mound, Georgia.

Fifth Annual Report of the Bureau of Ethnology, fig. 42.

Cat. No. 91113, U. S. N. M.

---

[1] Cf. Ghandi, p. 882, of this paper.

interesting feature of the design is the highly conventionalized wing which fills the space beneath the uplifted arm. This wing is unlike the usual specimens of aboriginal art which have been found in such profusion in that neighborhood. But it is again remarkable that this conventionalized wing and the bracelets, anklets, and garters should correspond in all their peculiarities of construction and design with the

Fig. 241.
COPPER PLATE.
Repoussé work.
Entowah Mound, Georgia.
Cat. No. 91117, U. S. N. M.

wings on the copper and shell figures from the Etowah mound, Georgia (figs. 240, 241, and 242)[1]. Behind the left-hand figure is an ornament resembling the spreading tail of an eagle which, with its feather arrangement and the detail of their mechanism, correspond to a high degree with the eagle effigies in repoussé copper (fig. 243) from the mound in

[1] Fifth Ann. Rep. Bureau of Ethnology, 1883–84, pp. 96–106, figs. 42, 43, 45.

Union County, Ill., shown in the Fifth Annual Report of the Bureau of Ethnology (p. 105) and in the Twelfth Annual Report (p. 309).

Hopewell Mound, Chillicothe, Ross County, Ohio.—A later discovery of the Swastika belonging to the same period and the same general locality—that is, to the Ohio Valley—was that of Prof. Warren K. Moorehead, in the fall and winter of 1891–92, in his excavations of the Hopewell mound, seven miles northwest of Chillicothe, Ross County, Ohio.[1] The locality of this mound is well shown in Squier and Davis's work on the "Monuments of the Mississippi Valley" (pl. 10, p. 26), under the name of "Clark's Works," here reproduced as pl. 11. It is the large irregular unnumbered triple mound just within the arc of the circle shown in the center of the plan. The excavation contemplated the destruction of the mound by cutting it down to the surrounding level and scattering the earth of which it was made over the surface; and this was done. Preparatory to this, a survey and ground plan was made (pl. 12). I assisted at this survey and can vouch for the general correctness. The mound was surrounded by parallel lines laid out at right angles and marked by stakes 50 feet apart. The mound was found to be 530 feet long and 250 feet wide. Squier and Davis reported

Fig. 242.

ENGRAVED SHELL.

Triangular breech-clout with dots and circles.

Entowah Mound, Georgia.

Cat. No. 91443, U. S. N. M.

its height at 32 feet, but the excavation of the trenches required but 18 and 16 feet to the original surface on which the mound was built. It was too large to be cut down as a whole, and for convenience it was decided by Mr. Moorehead to cut it down in trenches, commencing on the northeast. Nothing was found until, in opening trench 3, about five feet above the base of the mound, they struck a mass of thin worked copper objects, laid flat one atop the other, in a rectangular space, say three by four feet square. These objects are unique in American prehistoric archæology. Some of them bore a resemblance in form to the scalloped mica pieces found by Squier and Davis, and described by them in

[1] These explorations were made for the Department of Ethnology at the World's Columbian Exposition, Chicago, 1893.

PLAN OF NORTH FORK (HOPEWELL) WORKS.

Ross County, Ohio.

Smithsonian Contributions to Knowledge, Vol. I, Pl. X.

PLATE 12.

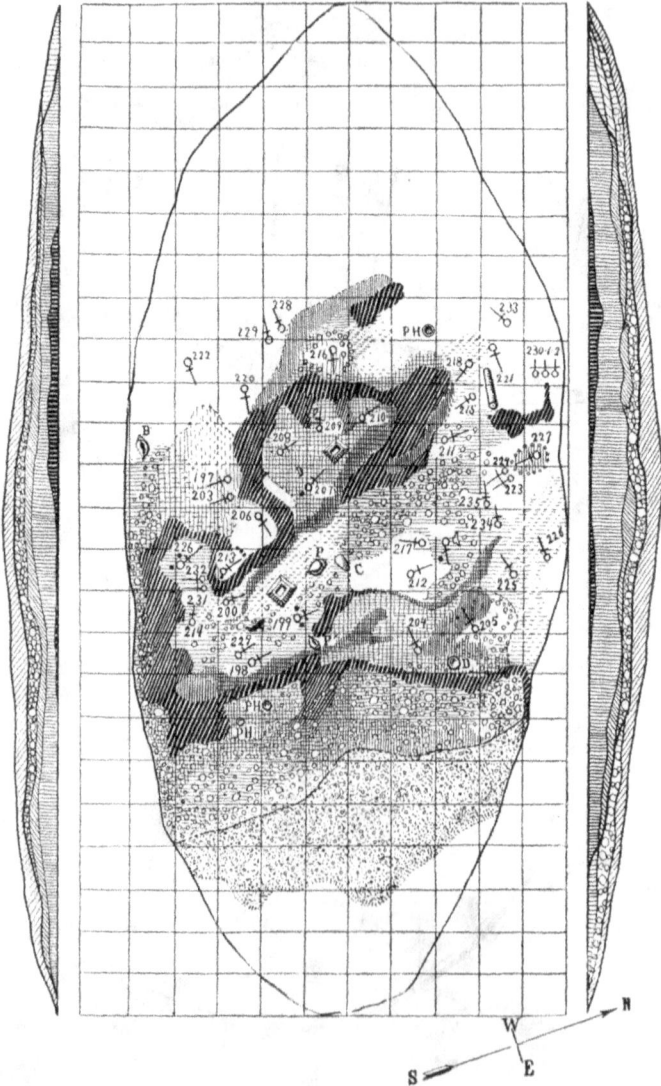

PLAN OF HOPEWELL MOUND, IN WHICH ABORIGINAL COPPER SWASTIKAS WERE FOUND.

Ross County, Ohio.

Moorehead, "Primitive Man in Ohio," Pl. xxxiv.

their "Ancient Monuments of the Mississippi Valley" (p. 240), and also those of the same material found by Professor Putnam in the Turner group of mounds in the valley of the Little Miami. They had been apparently laid between two layers of bark, whether for preservation or mere convenience of deposit, can only be guessed.

The following list of objects is given, to the end that the reader may see what was associated with these newly found copper Swastikas: Five Swastika crosses (fig. 244); a long mass of copper covered with wood on one side and with squares and five similar designs traceable on the reverse; smaller mass

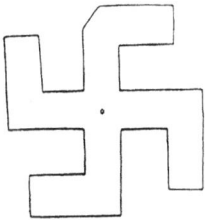

Fig. 243.
COPPER PLATE SHOWING FIGURE OF EAGLE.
Repoussé work.
Union County, Ill.
Cat. No. 91507, U. S. N. M.

Fig. 244.
SWASTIKA CROSS OF THIN COPPER.
Hopewell Mound, Ross County, Ohio.
¼ natural size.

of copper; eighteen single copper rings; a number of double copper rings, one set of three and one set of two; five pan lids or hat-shaped rings; ten circular disks with holes in center, represented in fig. 245, originally placed in a pile and now oxidized together; also large circular, stencil-like ornaments, one (fig. 246) 7½ inches in diameter; another (fig. 247) somewhat in the shape of a St. Andrew's cross, the extreme length over the arms being 8¾ inches.

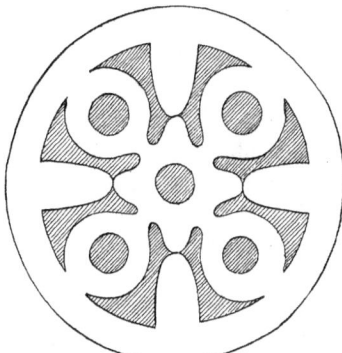

Fig. 245.
FLAT RING OF THIN COPPER.
Hopewell Mound, Ross County, Ohio.
⅓ natural size.

Fig. 246.
STENCIL ORNAMENT OF THIN COPPER.
Hopewell Mound, Ross County, Ohio.
⅛ natural size.

About five feet below the deposit of sheet copper and 10 or 12 feet to the west, two skeletons lay together. They were covered with copper plates and fragments, copper hatchets, and pearl beads, shown in the list below, laid in rectangular form about seven feet in length and five feet in width, and so close as to frequently overlap.

There were also found sixty-six copper hatchets, ranging from $1\frac{1}{2}$ to $22\frac{1}{2}$ inches in length; twenty-three copper plates and fragments; one copper eagle; eleven semicircles, bars, etc.; two spool-shaped objects; four comb-shaped effigies; one wheel with peculiar circles and bars of copper; three long plates of copper; pearl and shell beads and teeth; a lot of extra fine pearls; a lot of wood, beads, and an unknown metal; a lot of bones; a human jaw, very large; a fragmentary fish resembling a sucker (fig. 248);

Fig. 247.
STENCIL ORNAMENT OF THIN COPPER.
Hopewell Mound, Ross County, Ohio.
¾ natural size.

one stool of copper with two legs; broken copper plates; one broken shell; bear and panther tusks; mica plates; forty fragmentary and entire copper stencils of squares, circles, diamonds, hearts, etc.; copper objects, saw-shaped;

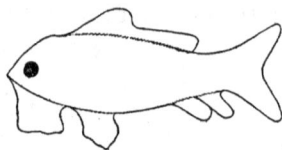

Fig. 248.
FISH ORNAMENT OF THIN COPPER.
Hopewell Mound, Ross County, Ohio.
⅙ natural size.

twenty ceremonial objects, rusted or oxidized copper; two diamond-shaped stencils, copper (fig. 249); four peculiar spool-shaped copper ornaments, perforated, showing repoussé work (fig. 250).

I made sketches of two or three of the bone carvings, for the purpose of showing the art of the people who constructed this monument, so that by comparison with that of other known peoples some knowledge may be obtained, or theory advanced, concerning the race or tribe to which they belonged and the epoch in which they lived. Fig. 251 shows an exquisite bone carving of a paroquet which belongs much farther south and not found in that locality in modern times. The design shown in fig. 252 suggests

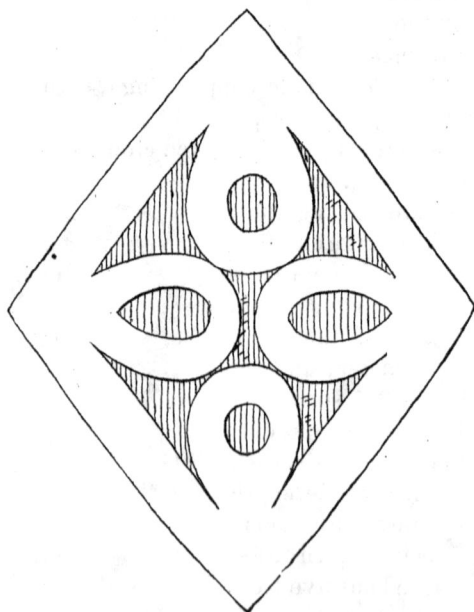

Fig. 249.
LOZENGE-SHAPED STENCIL OF THIN COPPER,
Hopewell Mound, Ross County, Ohio.
¾ natural size.

a Mississippi Kite, but the zoologists of the Museum, while unable to determine with exactitude its intended representation, chiefly from the mutilated condition of the fragment, report it more likely to be the

PLATE 13.

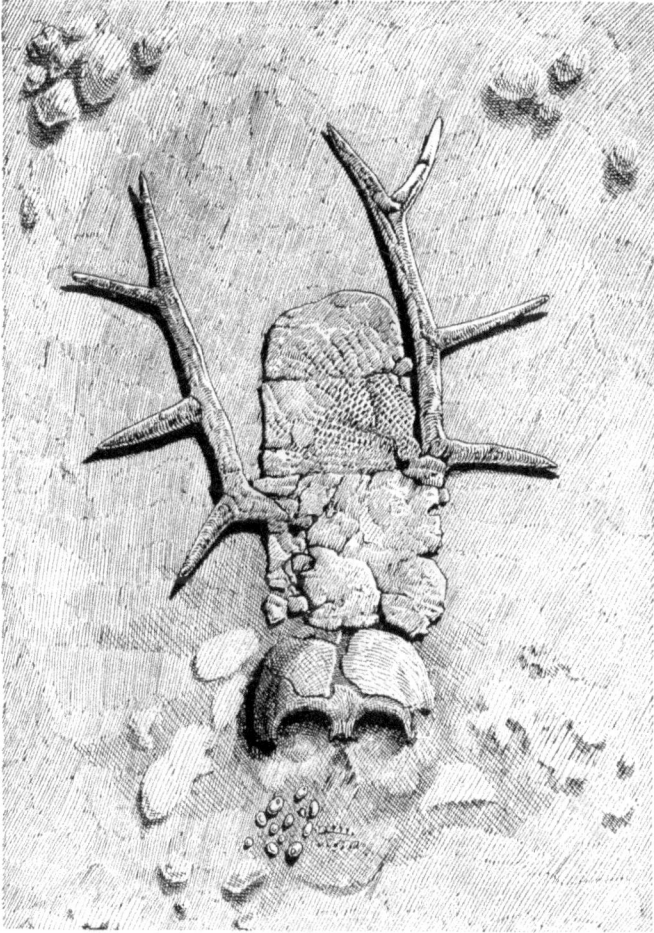

HUMAN SKULL WITH COPPER-COVERED HORNS.

Hopewell Mound, Ross County, Ohio.

Moorehead, " Primitive Man in Ohio," frontispiece.

PREHISTORIC ALTAR.

Hopewell Mound, Ross County, Ohio.

Found near the copper Swastika shown in fig. 244.

Moorehead, "Primitive Man in Ohio", Fig. XXXVII. Cat. No. 148662, U. S. N. M.

head of the "leather-back" turtle. Fig. 253 probably represents an otter with a fish in his mouth.

In trench No. 3, 15 skeletons (numbered 264 to 278, inclusive), were found on the base line, all extended. Objects of coal, bone, shell, or stone, had been placed with nearly all of them. Nos. 265 and 266 were laid on blocks of burnt earth 3 inches higher than the base of the mound. One of the skeletons in this mound (No. 248) is shown in pl. 13. It was a most remarkable specimen, and forms the frontispiece of Prof. W. K. Moorehead's volume "Primitive Man in Ohio," where it is described (p. 195) as follows:

At his head were imitation elk horns, neatly made of wood and covered with sheet copper rolled into cylindrical forms over the prongs. The antlers were 22 inches

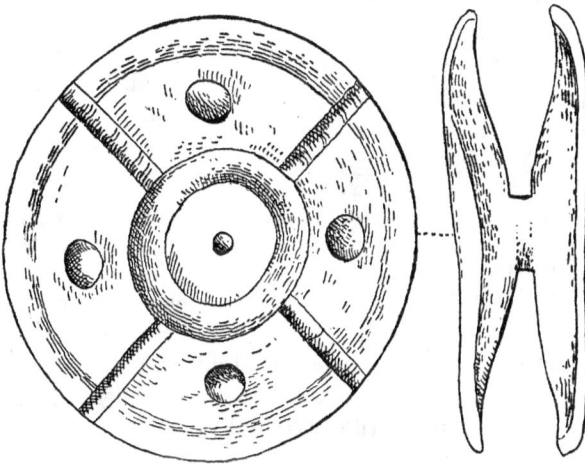

Fig. 250.
SPOOL-SHAPED OBJECT OF COPPER.
Repoussé and intaglio decoration.
Hopewell Mound, Ross County, Ohio.
Natural size.

high and 19 inches across from prong to prong. They fitted into a crown of copper bent to fit the head from occipital to upper jaw. Copper plates were upon the breast and stomach, also on the back. The copper preserved the bones and a few of the sinews. It also preserved traces of cloth similar to coffee sacking in texture, interwoven among the threads of which were 900 beautiful pearl beads, bear teeth split and cut, and hundreds of other beads, both pearl and shell. Copper spool-shaped objects and other implements covered the remains. A pipe of granite and a spearhead of agate were near the right shoulder. The pipe was of very fine workmanship and highly polished.

While digging out skeletons 280 to 284, Professor Moorehead says they touched the edge of an altar (pl. 14). It was on the base line and 15 feet north of the copper find before described. On the 5th of January, 1892, the altar was uncovered, and the earth, charcoal, and objects within it put into five soap boxes and transported to headquarters, where the material was assorted in my presence and with my aid. The mass on the altar had been charred throughout. It contained, in part, mica ornaments, beads, spool-shaped objects, whale, bear, and panther teeth, flint knives, carved effigies of bone and stone, some of which were broken, while others were whole. There were stone tablets, slate orna-

Fig. 251.

FRAGMENT OF ENGRAVED BONE REPRESENTING A PAROQUET.
Hopewell Mound, Ross County, Ohio.
Natural size.

ments, copper balls, fragments of cloth, rings of chlorite, quartz crystals perforated and grooved, and a few pieces of flint and obsidian, with several thousand pearls drilled for suspension. These objects were heaped in the cavity of the altar without any regularity. All were affected by heat, the copper being fused in many cases. The teeth and tusks were charred, split, and calcined. There were no ashes. All the fuel was charcoal, and from the appearance of the débris, es-

pecially the wood, earth, and bone, one might suppose that after the fire had started it had not been allowed to burn to ashes as if in the open air, but had been covered with earth, and so had smoldered out as in a charcoal pit.

Evidence was found of an extended commerce with distant localities, so that if the Swastika existed in America it might be expected here. The principal objects were as follows: A number of large seashells (*Fulgur*) native to the southern Atlantic Coast 600 miles distant, many of them carved; several thousand pieces of mica from the mountains of Virginia or North Carolina, 200 or more miles distant; a thousand large blades of beautifully chipped objects in obsidian, which could not have been found nearer than the Rocky Mountains, 1,000 or 1,200 miles distant; four hundred pieces of wrought copper, believed to be from the Lake Superior region, 150

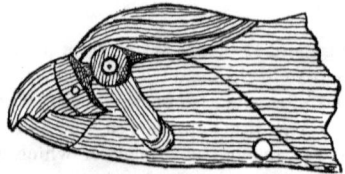

Fig. 252.

FRAGMENT OF ENGRAVED BONE PROBABLY REP-
RESENTING A MISSISSIPPI KITE OR LEATHER-
BACK TURTLE.
Hopewell Mound, Ross County, Ohio.
Natural size.

miles distant; fifty-three skeletons, the copper headdress (pl. 13) made in semblance of elk horns, 16 inches high, and other wonderful things. Those not described have no relation to the Swastika.

These objects were all prehistoric. None of them bore the slightest evidence of contact with white civilization. The commoner objects would compare favorably with those found in other mounds by the same and other investigators. Much of it may be undetermined. It is strange to find so many objects brought such long distances, and we may not be able to explain the problem presented; but there is no authority for injecting any modern or European influence into it. By what people were these made? In what epoch? For what purpose? What did they represent? How did this ancient, curious, and widespread sign, a recognized symbol of religion of the Orient, find its way to the bot-

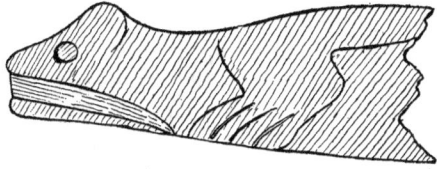

Fig. 253.
FRAGMENT OF ENGRAVED BONE PROBABLY REPRESENTING AN OTTER WITH A FISH IN ITS MOUTH.
Natural size.

Fig. 254.
WATER JUG WITH FIGURE OF SWASTIKA.
Decoration, red on yellow ground.
Poinsett County, Ark.
Cat. No. 91230, U. S. N. M.

tom of one of the mounds of antiquity in the Scioto Valley? These are questions easy to ask but difficult to answer. They form some of the riddles of the science of prehistoric anthropology.

Mounds in Arkansas.—A water jug in the collection of the U. S. National Museum (fig. 254) was obtained in 1883 by P. W. Norris, of the Bureau of Ethnology, from a mound in Poinsett County, Ark. It is of yellow ground, natural color of clay, and decorated with light red paint. The paint is represented in the cut by the darkened surfaces. The four quarters of the jug are decorated alike, one side of which is shown in the cut. The center of the design is the Swastika with the arm crossing at right angles, the ends turned to the right, the effect being produced by an enlargement on the right side of each arm until they all join the circle. A similar water jug with a Swastika mark of the same type as the foregoing decorates Major Powell's desk in the Bureau of Ethnology.

Marquis Nadaillac[1] describes and figures a grooved ax from Pemberton, N. J., on which some persons have recognized a Swastika, but which the Marquis doubts, while Dr. Abbott[2] denounces the inscription as a fraud.

NORTH AMERICAN INDIANS.

The Kansas.—The Rev. J. Owen Dorsey[3] describes the mourning customs of the Kansas Indians. In the course of his description he tells of a council of ceremony held among these Indians to decide if they should go on the warpath. Certain sacred songs were sung which had been arranged according to a chart, which Mr. Dorsey introduces as pl. 20, page 676. The outside edge of this chart bore twenty-seven

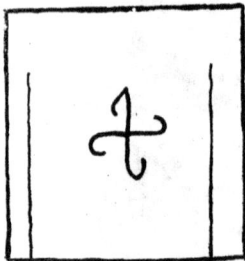

Fig. 255.

KANSA INDIAN WAR CHART.

Swastika sign for winds and wind songs.

J. Owen Dorsey, American Naturalist, July, 1885, p. 670.

ideographs, which suggest or determine the song or speech required. No. 1 was the sacred pipe; No. 2, the maker of all songs; No. 3, song of another old man who gives success to the hunters; No. 4 (fig. 255 in the present paper) is the Swastika sign, consisting of two ogee lines intersecting each other, the ends curved to the left. Of it, Mr. Dorsey says only the following:

Fig. 4. Tadje wayun, wind songs. The winds are deities; they are Bazanta (at the pines), the east wind; Ak'a, the south wind; A'k'a jiñga or A'k'uya, the west wind; and Hnia (toward the cold), the north wind. The warriors used to remove the hearts of slain foes, putting them in the fire as a sacrifice to the winds.

In the Eleventh Annual Report of the Bureau of Ethnology (p. 525) Mr. Dorsey repeats this statement concerning the names of the winds, and shows how, in their invocations, the Kansas began with the east wind and went around to the right in the order here given. His fig. 195 illustrates this, but the cross has straight arms. In response to my personal inquiry, Mr. Dorsey says the war chart[4] was drawn for him, with the Swastika as represented, by Pahanle-gaqle, the war captain,

---

[1] "Prehistoric America," p. 22, note 24, fig. 9.
[2] "Primitive Industry," p. 32.
[3] American Naturalist, XIX, July, 1885, p. 670.
[4] Ibid., pl. 20.

CEREMONIAL BEAD NECKLACE WITH SWASTIKA ORNAMENTATION.

Sac Indians, Cook County (Kansas) Reservation.

who had official charge of it and who copied it from one he had inherited from his father and his "father's fathers"; and Mr. Dorsey assured me that there can be no mistake or misapprehension about this Indian's intention to make the sign as there represented. Asked if the sign was common and to be seen in other cases or places, Mr. Dorsey replied that the Osage have a similar chart with the same and many other signs or pictographs—over a hundred—but except these, he knows of no similar signs. They are not in common use, but the chart and all it contains are sacred objects, the property of the two Kansas gentes, Black Eagle and Chicken Hawk, and not to be talked of nor shown outside of the gentes of the council lodge.[1]

The Sac Indians.—Miss Mary A. Owen, of St. Joseph, Mo., sending some specimens of beadwork of the Indians (pl. 15) from the Kansas Reservation, two of which were garters and the third a necklace 13 inches long and 1 inch wide, in which the Swastikas represented are an inch square, writes, February 2, 1895, as follows:

The Indians call it [the Swastika] the "luck," or "good luck." It is used in necklaces and garters by the sun worshippers among the Kickapoos, Sacs, Pottawatomies, Iowas, and (I have been told) by the Winnebagoes. I have never seen it on a Winnebago. The women use the real Swastika and the Greek key pattern, in the silk patchwork of which they make sashes and skirt trimmings. As for their thinking it an emblem of fire or deity, I do not believe they entertain any such ideas, as some Swastika hunters have suggested to me. They call it "luck," and say it is the same thing as two other patterns which I send in the mail with this. They say they "always" made that pattern. They must have made it for a long time, for you can not get such beads as compose it, in the stores of a city or in the supplies of the traders who import French beads for the red folk. Another thing. Beadwork is very strong, and this is beginning to look tattered, a sure sign that it has seen long service.

These sun worshippers—or, if you please, Swastika wearers—believe in the Great Spirit, who lives in the sun, who creates all things, and is the source of all power and beneficence. The ancestors are a sort of company of animal saints, who intercede for the people. There are many malicious little demons who thwart the ancestors and lead away the people at times and fill them with diseases, but no head devil. Black Wolf and certain ghosts of the unburied are the worst. Everybody has a secret fetish or "medicine," besides such general "lucks" as Swastikas, bear skins, and otter and squirrel tails.

Of the other cult of the peoples I have mentioned, those who worship the sun as the deity and not the habitation, I know nothing. They are secret, suspicious, and gloomy, and do not wear the "luck." I have never seen old people wear the "luck."

Now, I have told you all I know, except that it [the Swastika] used in ancient times to be made in quill embroidery on herb bags.

Miss Owen spoke of other garters with Swastikas on them, but she said they were sacred, were used only during certain ceremonies, and she knew not if she could be able to get or even see them. During the prolongation of the preparation of this paper she wrote two or three times, telling of the promises made to her by the two Sac women who were the owners of these sacred garters, and how each time they

---

[1] This was the last time I ever saw Mr. Dorsey. He died within a month, beloved and regretted by all who knew him.

had failed. Yet she did not give up hope. Accordingly, in the winter
of 1896, the little box containing the sacred garters arrived. Miss
Owen says the husbands of these two Sac women are Pottawatomies
on the Cook County (Kans.) Reservation. They are sun worshippers.
These garters have been sketched and figured in pl. 16.

The Pueblos.—The Pueblo country in Colorado, Utah, New Mexico,
and Arizona, as is well known, is inhabited by various tribes of Indians
speaking different languages, separated from one another and from all
other tribes by differences of language, customs, and habit, but somewhat akin to each other in culture, and many things different from
other tribes are peculiar to them. These have been called the "Pueblo
Indians" because they live in pueblos or towns. Their present country
includes the regions of the ancient cliff dwellers, of whom they are
supposed to be the descendants. In those manifestations of culture
wherein they are peculiar and different from other
tribes they have come to be considered something
superior. Any search for the Swastika in America
which omitted these Indians would be fatally
defective, and so here it is found. Without spec-
ulating how the knowledge of the Swastika came
to them, whether by independent invention or
brought from distant lands, it will be enough to
show its knowledge among and its use by the
peoples of this country.

In the Annual Report of the Bureau of Ethnology for the year 1880–81 (p. 394, fig. 562) is

Fig. 256.

DANCE RATTLE MADE OF A
SMALL GOURD DECORATED
IN BLACK, WHITE, AND RED.
Ogee Swastika on each side.
Second Annual Report of the Bureau
of Ethnology, fig. 526.
Cat. No. 42042, U. S. N. M.

described a dance rattle made from a small gourd,
ornamented in black, white, and red (fig. 256).
The gourd has a Swastika on each side, with the
ends bent, not square, but ogee (the tetraskelion).
The U. S. National Museum possesses a large
number of these dance rattles with Swastikas on

their sides, obtained from the Pueblo Indians of New Mexico and Arizona. Some of them have the natural neck for a handle, as shown in
the cut; others are without neck, and have a wooden stick inserted
and passed through for a handle. Beans, pebbles, or similar objects
are inside, and the shaking of the machine makes a rattling noise which
marks time for the dance.

The Museum possesses a large series of pottery from the various
pueblos of the Southwest; these are of the painted and decorated
kind common to that civilization and country. Some of these pieces
bear the Swastika mark; occasionally it is found outside, occasionally inside. It is more frequently of the ogee form, similar to that on
the rattle from the same country (fig. 256). The larger proportion of
these specimens comes from the pueblos of Santa Clara and St. Ildefonso.

PLATE 16.

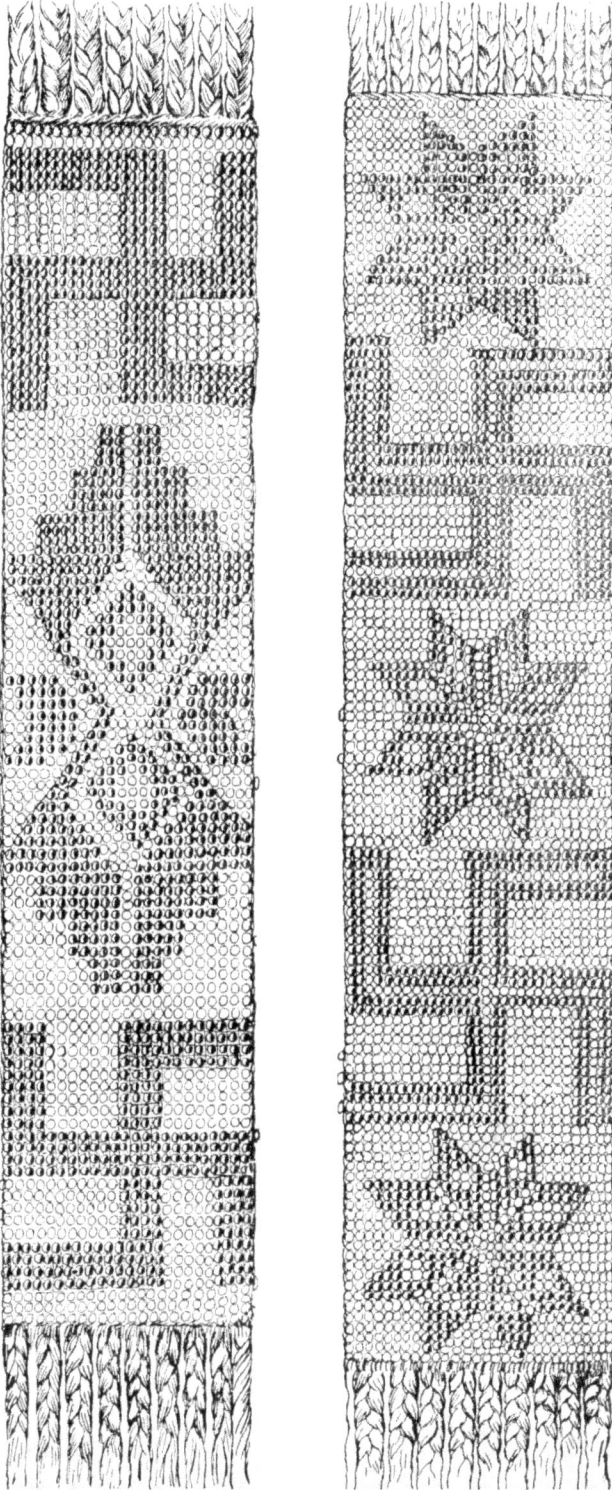

CEREMONIAL BEAD GARTERS WITH SWASTIKAS.

Sac Indians, Cook County (Kansas) Reservation.

Dr. Schliemann reports:[1]

We also see a Swastika (turned to the left) scratched on two terra cotta bowls of the Pueblo Indians of New Mexico, preserved in the ethnological section of the Royal Museum at Berlin.

G. Nordenskiöld,[2] in the report of his excavations among the ruined pueblos of the Mesa Verde, made in southwestern Colorada during the summer of 1891, tells of the finding of numerous specimens of the Swastika. In pl. 23, fig. 1, he represents a large, shallow bowl in the refuse heap at the "Step House." It was 50 centimeters in diameter, of rough execution, gray in color, and different in form and design from other vessels from the cliff houses. The Swastika sign (to the right) was in its center, and made by lines of small dots. His pl. 27, fig. 6, represents a bowl found in a grave (g on the plan) at "Step House." Its decoration inside was of the usual type, but the only decoration on the outside consisted of a Swastika, with arms crossing at right angles and ends bent at the right, similar to fig. 9. His pl. 18, fig. 1, represented a large bowl found in Mug House. Its decoration consisted in part of a Swastika similar in form and style to the Etruscan gold "bulla," fig. 188 in this paper. Certain specimens of pottery from the pueblos of Santa Clara and St. Ildefonso, deposited in the U. S. National Museum (Department of Ethnology), bear Swastika marks, chiefly of the ogee form.[3]

The Navajoes.—Dr. Washington Matthews, U. S. A., than whom no one has done better, more original, nor more accurate anthropologic work in America, whether historic or prehistoric, has kindly referred me to his memoir in the Fifth Annual Report of the Bureau of Ethnology, comprising 82 pages, with 9 plates and 9 figures, entitled "The Mountain Chant; a Navajo ceremony." It is descriptive of one of a number of ceremonies practiced by the shamans or medicine men of the Navajo Indians, New Mexico. The ceremony is public, although it takes place during the night. It lasts for nine days and is called by the Indians "*dsilyídje qaçàl*"—literally, "chant toward (a place) within the mountains." The word "*dsilyi*" may allude to mountains in general, to the Carrizo Mountains in particular, to the place in the mountains where the prophet (originator of these ceremonies) dwelt, or to his name, or to all of these combined. "*Qaçàl*" means a sacred song or a collection of sacred songs. Dr. Matthews describes at length the myth which is the foundation of this ceremony, which must be read to be appreciated, but may be summarized thus: An Indian family, consisting of father, mother, two sons, and two daughters, dwelt in ancient times near the Carrizo Mountains. They lived by hunting and trapping; but the

---

[1] "Troja," p. 123.

[2] "The Cliff Dwellers of the Mesa Verde, Southwestern Colorado," P. A. Norstedt & Son, Chicago, 1893.

[3] From letter of Mr. Walter Hough, Winslow, Ariz. " I send you two pieces of pottery [bearing many ogee Swastikas] from the ruins near here formerly inhabited by the Moki. Many of the bowls which we have found in this ruin had the Swastika as a major *motif* in the decoration."

See also The Archæologist, III, No. 7, p. 248.

place was desert, game scarce, and they moved up the river farther
into the mountains. The father made incantations to enable his two
sons to capture and kill game; he sent them hunting each day, direct-
ing them to go to the east, west, or north, but with the injunction not
to the south. The elder son disobeyed this injunction, went to the
south, was captured by a war party of Utes and taken to their home
far to the south. He escaped by the aid of *Yàybichy* (*Qastcèëlçi*) and
divers supernatural beings. His adventures in returning home form
the body of the ceremony wherein these adventures are, in some degree,
reproduced. Extensive preparations are made for the performance of
the ceremony. Lodges are built and corrals made for the use of the
performers and the convenience of their audience. The fête being
organized, stories are told, speeches made, and sacred songs are sung
(the latter are given by Dr. Matthews as "songs of sequence," because
they must be sung in a progressive series on four certain days of the
ceremony). Mythological charts of dry sand of divers colors are made
on the earth within the corrals after the manner of the Navajo and
Pueblo Indians. These dry sand paintings are made after a given
formula and intended to be repeated from year to year, although no
copy is preserved, the artists depending only upon the memory of their
shaman. One of these pictures or charts represents the fugitive's
escape from the Utes, his captors, down a precipice into a den or cave
in which burnt a fire "on which was no wood." Four pebbles lay on
the ground together—a black pebble in the east, a blue one in the
south, a yellow one in the west, and a white one in the north. From
these flames issued. Around the fire lay four bears, colored and placed
to correspond with the pebbles. When the strangers (Qastcèëlçi and
the Navajo) approached the fire the bears asked them for tobacco, and
when they replied they had none, the bears became angry and thrice
more demanded it. When the Navajo fled from the Ute camp, he had
furtively helped himself from one of the four bags of tobacco which the
council was using. These, with a pipe, he had tied up in his skin robe;
so when the fourth demand was made he filled the pipe and lighted it
at the fire. He handed the pipe to the black bear, who, taking but one
whiff, passed it to the blue bear and immediately fell senseless. The
blue bear took two whiffs and passed the pipe, when he too fell over
unconscious. The yellow bear succumbed after the third whiff, and
the white bear in the north after the fourth whiff. Now the Navajo
knocked the ashes and tobacco out of his pipe and rubbed the latter
on the feet, legs, abdomen, chest, shoulders, forehead, and mouth of
each of the bears in turn, and they were at once resuscitated. He
replaced the pipe in the corner of his robe. When the bears recovered,
they assigned to the Navajo a place on the east side of the fire where
he might lie all night, and they brought out their stores of corn meal,
tciltcin, and other berries, offering them to him to eat; but Qastcèëlçi
warned him not to touch the food, and disappeared. So, hungry as he
was, the Indian lay down supperless to sleep. When he awoke in the

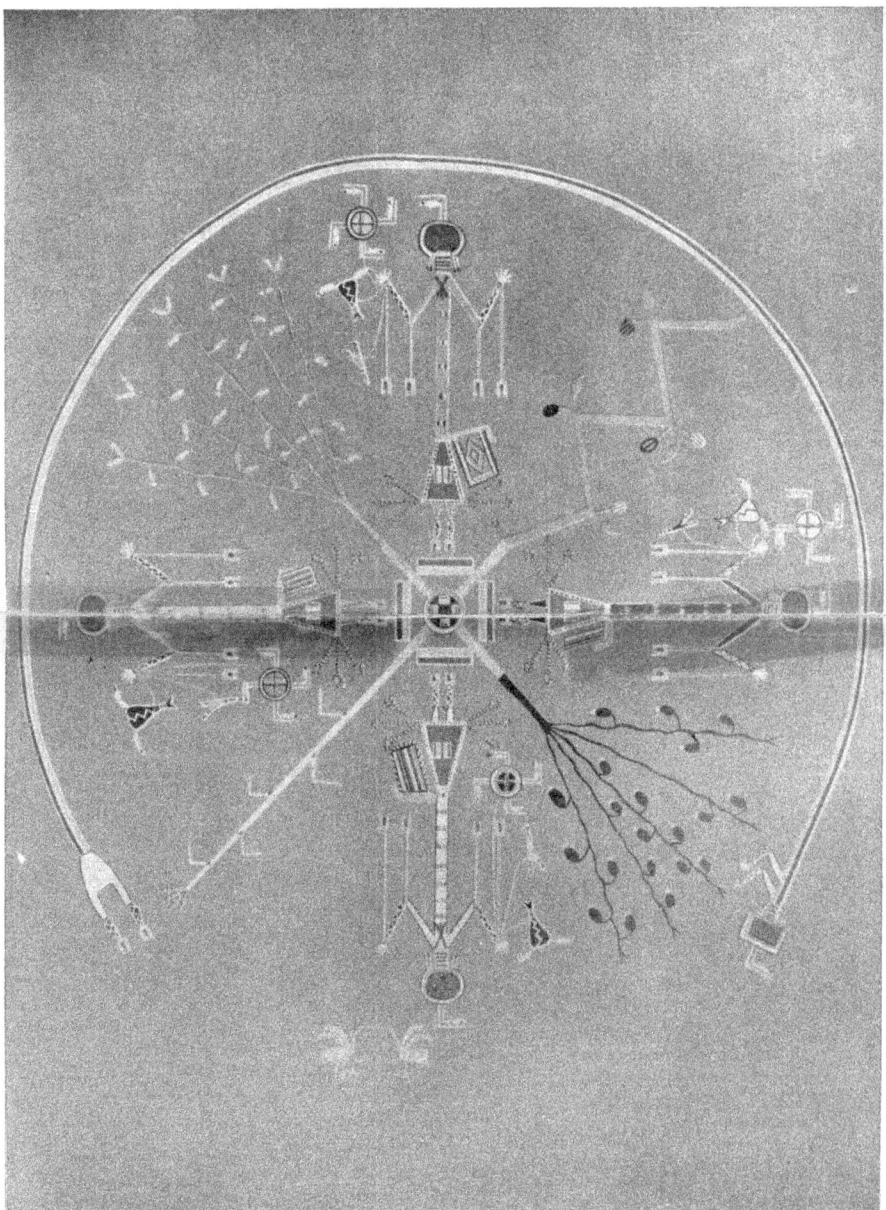

NAVAJO DRY PAINTING CONTAINING SWASTIKAS.

Dr. Washington Matthews, "The Mountain Chant: A Navajo Ceremony," Fifth Annual Report of the Bureau of Ethnology 1883-84, Pl. XVII.

PLATE 17.

morning, the bears again offered food, which he again declined, saying he was not hungry. Then they showed him how to make the bear *kethàwns*, or sticks, to be sacrificed to the bear gods, and they drew from one corner of the cave a great sheet of cloud, which they unrolled, and on it were painted the forms of the "yays" of the cultivated plants.

In Dr. Matthews's memoir (marked third, but described on p. 447 as the second picture), is a representation of the painting which the prophet was believed to have seen at the home of the bears in the Carrizo Mountains. This is here reproduced as pl. 17. In the center of the figure is a bowl of water covered with black powder; the edge of the bowl is garnished with sunbeams, while outside of it and forming a rectangle are the four *ca'bitlol* of sunbeam rafts on which seem to stand four gods, or "yays," with the plants under their special protection, which are painted the same color as the gods to which they belong. These plants are represented on their left hand, the hand being open and extended toward them. The body of the eastern god is white, so is the stalk of corn at his left in the southeast; the body of the southern god is blue, so is the beanstalk beside him in the southwest; the body of the western god is yellow, so is his pumpkin vine in the northwest; the body of the north god is black, so is the tobacco plant in the northeast. Each of the sacred plants grows from five white roots in the central waters and spreads outward to the periphery of the picture. The figures of the gods form a cross, the arms of which are directed to the four cardinal points; the plants form another cross, having a common center with the first, the arms extending to the intermediate points of the compass. The gods are shaped alike, but colored differently; they lie with their feet to the center and heads extended outward, one to each of the four cardinal points of the compass, the faces look forward, the arms half extended on either side, the hands raised to a level with the shoulders. They wear around their loins skirts of red sunlight adorned with sunbeams. They have ear pendants, bracelets, and armlets, blue and red, representing turquoise and coral, the prehistoric and emblematic jewels of the Navajo Indians. Their forearms and legs are black, showing in each a zigzag mark representing lightning on the black rain clouds. In the north god these colors are, for artistic reasons, reversed. The gods have, respectively, a rattle, a charm, and a basket, each attached to his right hand by strings. This basket, represented by concentric lines with a Greek cross in the center, all of the proper color corresponding with the god to whom each belongs, has extending from each of its quarters, arranged perpendicularly at right angles to each other, in the form of a cross, four white plumes of equal length, which at equal distances from the center are bent, all to the left, and all of the same length. Thus are formed in this chart four specimens of the Swastika, with the cross and circle at the intersection of the arms. The plumes have a small black spot at the tip end of each.

Dr. Matthews informs me that he has no knowledge of any peculiar meaning attributed by these Indians to this Swastika symbol, and we

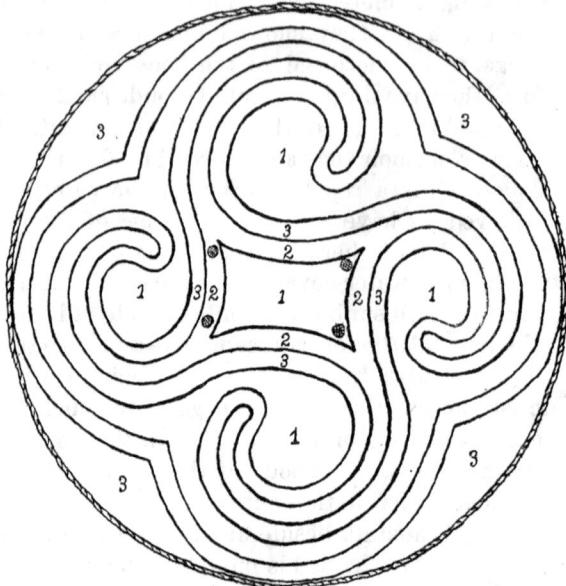

Fig. 257.

WAR SHIELD USED BY THE PIMA INDIANS.

Ogee Swastika (tetraskelion) in three colors: (1) blue, (2) red, (3) white.

Cat. No. 27829, U. S. N. M.

Fig. 258.

WAR SHIELD WITH OGEE SWASTIKA IN CENTER.

Pima Indians.

The hole near the lower arm of the Swastika was made by an arrow.

Property of Mr. F. W. Hodge.

know not whether it is intended as a religious symbol, a charm of bless-ing, or good luck, or whether it is only an ornament. We do not know whether it has any hidden, mysterious, or symbolic meaning; but there it is, a prehistoric or Oriental Swastika in all its purity and simplicity, appearing in one of the mystic ceremonies of the aborigines in the great American desert in the interior of the North American Continent.

The Pimas.—The U. S. National Museum possesses a shield (Cat. No. 27829) of bull hide, made by the Pima Indians. It is about 20 inches in diameter, and bears upon its face an ogee Swastika (tetraskelion), the ends bent to the right. The body and each arm is divided longitudi-nally into three stripes or bands indicated by colors, blue, red, and white, arranged alternately. The exterior part of the shield has a white ground, while the interior or center has a blue ground. This shield (fig. 257) is almost an exact reproduction of the Swastika from Mycenæ (fig. 161), from Ireland (fig. 216), and from Scandinavia (figs. 209 and 210). Fig. 258 shows another Pima shield of the same type. Its Swastika is, however, painted with a single color or possibly a mixture of two, red and white. It is ogee, and the ends bend to the left. This shield is the property of Mr. F. W. Hodge, of the Bureau of Ethnology. He obtained it from a Pima Indian in Arizona, who assured him that the hole at the end of the lower arm of the Swastika was made by an arrow shot at him by an Indian enemy.

COLONIAL PATCHWORK.

In Scribner's Magazine for September, 1894, under the title of "Tap-estry in the New World," one of our popular writers has described, with many illustrations, the bedquilt patterns of our grandmothers' time. One of these she interprets as the Swastika. This is, however, believed to be forced. The pattern in question is made of patches in the form of rhomboids and right-angled triangles sewed and grouped somewhat in the form of the Swastika (fig. 259). It is an in-vented combination of patch-work which formed a new pat-tern, and while it bears a slight resemblance to the Swastika, lacks its essential elements. It was not a symbol, and rep-resents no idea beyond that of a pretty pattern. It stood

Fig. 259.

COLONIAL PATCHWORK WITH FIGURES RESEMBLING SWASTIKAS.

Scribner's Magazine, September, 1894.

for nothing sacred, nor for benediction, blessing, nor good luck. It was but an ornamental pattern which fortuitously had the resem-blance of Swastika. It was not even in the form of a cross. The difference between it and the Swastika is about the same there would be between the idle and thoughtless boy who sporadically draws the cross on his slate, meaning nothing by it, or at most only to make an ornament, and the devout Christian who makes the same sign on entering the church, or the Indian who thus represents the four winds of heaven. He who made the Swastika recognizes an occult power for good and against evil, and he thereby invokes the power to secure prosperity. She who made the quilt pattern apparently knew nothing of the old-time Swastika, and was not endeavoring to reproduce it or anything like it. She only sought to make such an arrangement of rhomboidal and triangular quilt patches as would produce a new ornamental pattern.

CENTRAL AMERICA.

NICARAGUA.

The specimen shown in fig. 260 (Cat. No. 23726, U.S.N.M.) is a fragment, the foot of a large stone metate from Zapatero, Granada, Nicaragua. The metate was chiseled or pecked out of the solid. A sunken panel is surrounded by moldings, in the center of which appears, from its outline, also by raised moldings, a figure, the outline of which is a Greek cross, but whose exterior is a Swastika. Its form as such is

Fig. 260.

FRAGMENT OF THE FOOT OF A STONE METATE WITH FIGURE OF SWASTIKA.

Nicaragua.

Cat. No. 23726, U. S. N. M.

perfect, except that one bent arm is separated from its stem by a shallow groove.

"The Cross, Ancient and Modern," by W. W. Blake, shows, in its fig. 57, a Swastika pure and simple, and is cited by its author as representing a cross found by Squier in Central America. The Mexican enthusiast, Orozco y Perra, claims at first glance that it shows Buddhist origin, but I have not been able as yet to verify the quotation.

YUCATAN.

Dr. Schliemann reports, in the Ethnological Museum at Berlin, a pottery bowl from Yucatan ornamented with a Swastika, the two main arms crossing at right angles, and he adds,[1] citing Le Plongeon, "Fouilles au Yucatan," that "during the last excavations in Yucatan this sign was found several times on ancient pottery."

Le Plongeon discovered a fragment of a stone slab in the ancient Maya city of Mayapan, of which he published a description in the Pro-

---

[1] "Troja," p. 122.

ceedings of the American Antiquarian Society. It contains an ogee Swastika (tetraskelion), with ends curved to the left and an inverted U with a wheel (fig. 261). Le Plongeon believed it to be an Egyptian inscription, which he translated thus: The character, inverted U, stood for *Ch* or *K;* the wheel for the sun, *Aa* or *Ra*, and the Swastika for *Ch* or *K*, making the whole to be *Chach* or *Kak*, which, he says, is the word *fire* in the Maya language.[1]

COSTA RICA.

A fragment of a metate (Cat. No. 9693, U. S. N. M.) found on Lempa River, Costa Rica, by Capt. J. M. Dow, has on its bottom a Swastika similar to that on the metate from Nicaragua. Specimen No. 59182, U. S. M. N., is a fragment of a pottery vase from Las Huacas, Costa Rica, collected by Dr. J. F. Bransford. It is

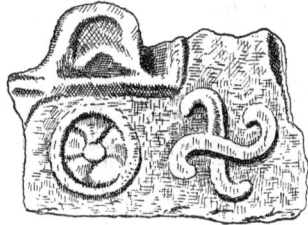

Fig. 261.

FRAGMENT OF STONE SLAB FROM THE
ANCIENT MAYA CITY OF MAYAPAN.

Ogee Swastika (tetraskelion).

Proceedings of the American Antiquarian Society,
April 21, 1881.

natural maroon body color, decorated with black paint. A band two inches wide is around the belly of the vase divided into panels of solid black alternated with fanciful geometric figures, crosses, circles, etc. One of these panels contains a partial Swastika figure. The two main arms cross at right angles in Greek form. It is a partial Swastika in that, while the two perpendicular arms bend at right angles, turning six times to the right; the two horizontal arms are solid black in color, as though the lines and spaces had run together.

SOUTH AMERICA.

BRAZIL.

The leaden idol (fig. 125) (Artemis Nana[2] of Chaldea, Sayce; statuettes of the Cyclades, Lenormant) found by Dr. Schliemann in the third, the burnt city of Hissarlik, Troy, was described (p. 829) with its Swastika on the triangular shield covering the pudendum, with the statement that it would be recalled in the chapter on Brazil.

The aboriginal women of Brazil wore a triangular shield or plaque over their private parts. These shields are made of terra cotta, quite thin, the edges rounded, and the whole piece rubbed smooth and polished. It is supported in place by cords around the body, which are attached by small holes in each angle of the triangle. The U. S. National Museum possesses several of these plaques from Brazil, and several were shown at the Chicago Exposition.

---

[1] The presence of the Swastika is the only purpose of this citation. The correctness of the translation is not involved and is not vouched for.

[2] Equivalent to Istar of Assyria and Babylon, Astarte of Phenicia, to the Greek Aphrodite, and the Roman Venus.

The consideration of the leaden idol of Hissarlik, with a Swastika, as though for good luck, recalled to the author similar plaques in his department from Brazil. Some are of common yellow ware, others were finer, were colored red and rubbed smooth and hard, but were without decoration. The specimen shown in pl. 18 (upper figure) was from Marajo, Brazil, collected by Mr. E. M. Brigham. It is of light gray, slip washed, and decorated with pale red or yellow paint in bands, lines, parallels, geometric figures. The specimen shown in the lower figure of the same plate, from the Caneotires River, Brazil, was collected by Prof. J. B. Steere. The body color, clay, and the decoration paint are much the same as the former. The ornamentation is principally by two light lines laid parallel and close so as to form a single line, and is of the same geometric character as the incised decoration ornament on other pieces from Marajo Island. Midway from top to bottom, near the outside edges, are two Swastikas. They are about five-eighths of an inch in size, are turned at right angles, one to the right and the other to the left. These may have been a charm signifying good fortune in bearing children. (See pp. 830–832.)

These specimens were submitted by the author to the Brazilian minister, Señor Mendonça, himself an archæologist and philologist of no small capacity, who recognized these objects as in use in ancient times among the aborigines of his country. The name by which they are known in the aboriginal language is *Tambeao* or *Tamatiatang*, according to the dialects of different provinces. The later dialect name for apron is reported as *tunga*, and the minister makes two remarks having a possible bearing on the migration of the race: (1) The similarity of *tunga* with the last syllable of the longer word, *atang*, and (2) that *tunga* is essentially an African word from the west coast. Whether this piece of dress so thoroughly savage, with a possible ceremonial meaning relating to sex or condition, with its wonderful similarity of names, might not have migrated in time of antiquity from the west coast of Africa to the promontory of Brazil on the east coast of America where the passage is narrowest, is one of those conundrums which the prehistoric anthropologist is constantly encountering and which he is usually unable to solve.

The purpose of these objects, beyond covering the private parts of the female sex, is not known. They may have been ceremonial, relating, under certain circumstances, to particular conditions of the sex, or they may have been only variations of the somewhat similar covers used by the male aborigine. They bear some resemblance to the *Ceintures de Chasteté*, specimens of which are privately shown at the Musée de Cluny at Paris. These are said to have been invented by Françoise de Carara, viguier imperial (provost) of Padua, Italy, near the end of the fourteenth century. He applied it to all the women of his seraglio. He was beheaded A. D. 1405, by a decree of the Senate of Venice, for his many acts of cruelty. The palace of St. Mark contained for a long time a box or case of these ceintures with their locks

FOLIUM VITUS ("FIG LEAVES").
Terra-cotta covers, "tunga."
Aborigines of Brazil.

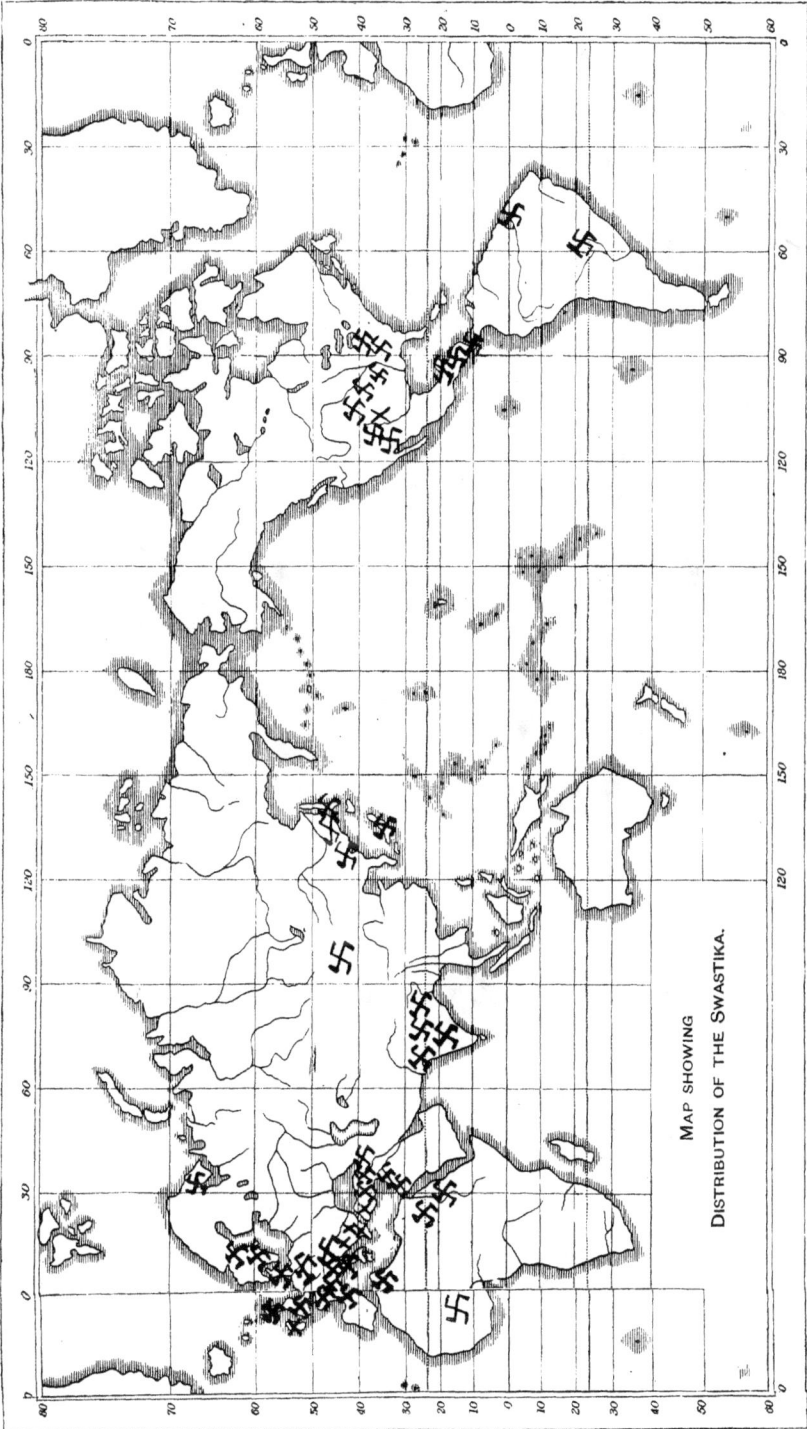

MAP SHOWING
DISTRIBUTION OF THE SWASTIKA.

attached, which were represented as *des pieces de conviction* of this monster.[1] Voltaire describes his hero "*qui tient sous la clef, la vertu de sa femme.*"

PARAGUAY.

Dr. Schliemann reports that a traveler of the Berlin Ethnological Museum obtained a pumpkin bottle from the tribe of Lenguas in Paraguay which bore the imprint of the Swastika scratched upon its surface, and that he had recently sent it to the Royal Museum at Berlin.

III.—FORMS ALLIED TO THE SWASTIKA.

MEANDERS, OGEES, AND SPIRALS, BENT TO THE LEFT AS WELL AS TO THE RIGHT.

There are certain forms related to the normal Swastika and greatly resembling it—meanders, ogees, the triskelion, tetraskelion, and five and six armed spirals or volutes. This has been mentioned above (page 768), and some of the varieties are shown in fig. 13. These related forms have been found in considerable numbers in America, and this investigation would be incomplete if they were omitted. It has been argued (p. 839) that the Swastika was not evolved from the meander, and this need not be reargued.

The cross with the arms bent or twisted in a spiral is one of these related forms. It is certain that in ancient, if not prehistoric, times the cross with extended spiral arms was frequently employed. This form appeared in intimate association with the square Swastikas which were turned indifferently to the right and left. This association of different yet related forms was so inti-

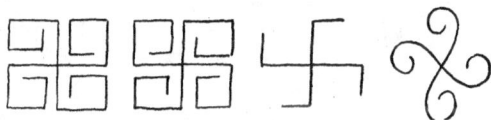

Fig. 262.

DIFFERENT FORMS OF SWASTIKA FOR COMPARISON.

mate, and they were used so indiscriminately as to justify the contention that the maker or designer recognized or admitted no perceptible or substantial difference between the square and spiral forms, whether they turned to the right or left, or whether they made a single or many turns, and that he classed them as the same sign or its equivalent. A Greek vase (fig. 174) shows five Swastikas, four of which are of different form (fig. 262). Curiously enough, the design of this Greek vase is painted maroon on a yellow ground, the style generally adopted in the vases from the mounds of Missouri and Arkansas, which mostly represent the spiral Swastika.

In Ireland a standing stone (fig. 215) has two forms of Swastika side by side. In one the arms are bent square at the corners, the other has curved or spiral arms, both turned to the right. These examples are so numerous that they would seem convincing in the absence of any other evidence (figs. 166 to 176).

[1] Cited in "Misson Voyage d'Italie," tome 1, p. 217; Dulaure, "Histoire des Differens Cultes," II; Brantôme, "Dames Galantes"; Rabelais, "Pantagruel," 3, chap. 35,

ABORIGINAL AMERICAN ENGRAVINGS AND PAINTINGS.

These allied forms of Swastika appear on prehistoric objects from mounds and Indian graves in different parts of the country and in times of high antiquity as well as among modern tribes. This paper contains the results of the investigations in this direction.

DESIGNS ON SHELL.

The Department of Prehistoric Anthropology in the U. S. National Museum, contains a considerable number of large shells of aboriginal

Fig. 263.
SHELL GORGET.
Cross, circle, sun's rays(?), and heads of four ivory-billed woodpeckers(?) arranged to form a Swastika.
Mississippi.

workmanship. The shell most employed was that of the genus *Fulgur*, a marine shell found on the coast from Florida to the capes. The *Unio* was employed, as well as others. These marine shells were transported long distances inland. They have been found in mounds and Indian graves a thousand miles from their original habitat. They served as utensils as well as ornaments. In many specimens the whorl was cut out, the shells otherwise left entire, and they served as vessels for holding or carrying liquids. When intended for ornaments, they were cut into the desired form and engraved with the design; if to be used as gorgets, holes were drilled for suspension. Frequently they were smoothed on the outside and the design engraved thereon. The preference of the aborigines for the *Fulgur* shell may have been by reason of its larger size. Among the patterns employed for the decoration of

Figs. 264.

SHELL GORGET FROM TENNESSEE.

Square figure with ornamental corners and heads of ivory-billed woodpecker arranged to form a figure resembling the Swastika.

these shells, the Swastika, in the form of spirals, volutes, or otherwise, appeared, although many others, such as the rattlesnake, birds, spiders,

Fig. 265.

SHELL GORGET FROM TENNESSEE.

Square figure with ornamental corners and heads of ivory-billed woodpecker arranged to form a figure resembling the Swastika.

and human masks were employed. No detailed description of the patterns of this shellwork will be attempted, because figures will be required to give the needed information for the interpretation of the Swastika. Many of the cuts and some of the descriptions are taken from the annual reports of the Bureau of Ethnology and, so far as relates to shell, mostly from Mr. Holmes's paper on "Art in Shell of the Ancient Americans." I desire to express my thanks for all cuts obtained from the Bureau publications.

Ivory-billed woodpecker.—A series of gorgets in shell have been found ornamented with designs resembling the Swastika, which should be noticed. They combine the square and the cross, while the head and bill of the bird form the *gamma* indicative of the Swastika. Fig. 263, taken from the Second Annual Report of the Bureau of Ethnology, 1880–81 (pl. 58), shows one of these shell gorgets from Mississippi, which "was, in all probability, obtained from one of the multitude of ancient sepulchres that abound in the State of Mississippi." The design is engraved on the convex side, the perforations are placed near the margin, and show much wear by the cord of suspension. In the center is a nearly symmetrical Greek cross inclosed in a circle of $1\frac{1}{4}$ inches. The spaces between the arms are emblazoned with radiating lines. Outside this circle are twelve small pointed or pyramidal rays. A square framework of four continuous parallel lines looped at the corners incloses this symbol; projecting from the center of each side of this square, opposite the arms of the cross, are four heads of birds representing the ivory-billed woodpecker, the heron, or the swan. The long, slender, and straight mandibles give the Swastika form to the object. Mr. Holmes says (p. 282) that he has been able to find six of these specimens, all of the type described, varying only in detail, workmanship, and finish.

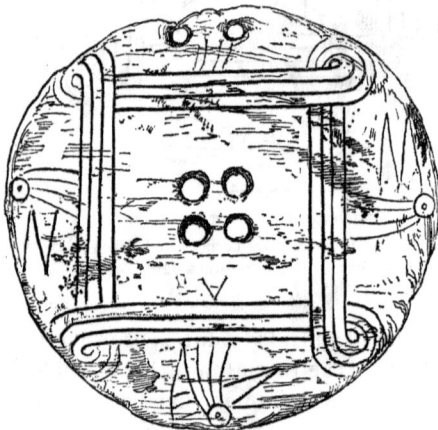

Fig. 266.

SHELL GORGET FROM TENNESSEE.

Square figure with ornamental corners and heads of ivory-billed woodpecker arranged to form a figure resembling the Swastika.

Figs. 264, 265, and 266,[1] represent three of these shell gorgets. The first was obtained by Professor Putnam from a stone grave, Cumberland River, Tennessee. It is about $2\frac{1}{2}$ inches in diameter and, like the former, it has a Greek cross in the center. The second was obtained by Mr. Cross from a stone grave near Nashville, Tenn. The third is from a stone grave near Oldtown, Tenn. All these have been drilled for suspension and are much worn.

The triskele, triskelion, or triquetrum.—These are Greek and Latin terms for the spiral volute with three branches or arms. The coins of Lycia were in this form, made originally by the junction of three cocks' heads and necks. The armorial bearings of the island of Sicily, in ancient times, consisted of three human legs joined at the thigh and flexed, sometimes booted and spurred (p. 873).

Aboriginal shell gorgets have been found in the mounds of Tennessee and the adjoining country, which were engraved with this design, though always in spiral form. There seems to have been no distinction

---

[1] Second Ann. Rep. Bureau of Ethnology, p. 59.

in the direction of the volutes, they turning indifferently to the right or to the left. Because of their possible relation to the Swastika it has been deemed proper to introduce them.

Fig. 267 [1] shows a *Fulgur* shell specimen obtained by Major Powell from a mound near Nashville, Tenn. It was found near the head of a skeleton. Its substance is well preserved; the surface was once highly polished, but now is pitted by erosion and discolored by age. The design is engraved on the concave surface as usual, and the lines are

Fig. 267.

SCALLOPED SHELL DISK (FULGUR) FROM A MOUND NEAR NASHVILLE, TENN.

Three spiral volutes (triskelion).

accurately drawn and clearly cut. The central circle is three-eighths of an inch in diameter and is surrounded by a zone one-half an inch in width, which contains a triskelion or triquetrum of three voluted lines beginning near the center of the shell on the circumference of the inner circle of three small equidistant perforations, and sweeping outward spirally to the left as shown in the figure, making upward of half a revolution. These lines are somewhat wider and more deeply engraved than

---

[1] Second Ann. Rep. Bureau of Ethnology, 1880–81, p. 273, pl. 54.

the other lines of the design. In some specimens they are so deeply cut
as to penetrate the disk, producing crescent-shaped perforations. Two
medium-sized perforations for suspension have been made near the
inner margin of one of the bosses next the dotted zone; these show
abrasion by the cord of suspension. These perforations, as well as the
three near the center, have been bored mainly from the convex side of
the disk.

Fig. 268 [1] represents a well-preserved disk with four volute arms forming the tetraskelion, and thus allied to the Swastika. The volutes (to

Fig. 268.

SCALLOPED SHELL DISK FROM A MOUND NEAR NASHVILLE TENN.

Circles and dots and four spiral volutes (tetraskelion).

the right) are deeply cut and for about one-third their length penetrate the shell, producing four crescent-shaped perforations which show
on the opposite side. This specimen is from a stone grave near Nashville, Tenn., and the original is in the Peabody Museum. Fig. 269 [2]
shows a specimen from the Brakebill mound, near Knoxville, Tenn. It
has a dot in the center, with a circle five-eighths of an inch in diameter. There are four volute arms which start from the opposite sides of

[1] Second Ann. Rep. Bureau of Ethnology, 1880–81, pl. 55, fig. 1.
[2] Ibid., pl. 55, fig. 2.

Fig. 269.

SHELL DISK FROM BRAKEBILL MOUND, NEAR KNOXVILLE, TENN.

Dot and circle in center and ogee Swastika (tetraskelion) marked but not completed.

Figs. 270 and 271.

ENGRAVED SHELL DISK.

Obverse and reverse.

Three-armed volute (triskelion).

this circle, and in their spiral form extend to the right across the field, increasing in size as they approach the periphery. This is an interesting specimen of the tetraskelion or spiral Swastika, in that it is unfinished, the outline having been cut in the shell sufficient to indicate the form, but not perfected. Figs. 270 and 271 show obverse and reverse sides of the same shell. It comes from one of the stone graves of Tennessee, and is thus described by Dr. Joseph Jones, of New Orleans,[1] as a specimen of the deposit and original condition of these objects:

Fig. 272.
ENGRAVED SHELL DISK.
Tennessee.
Three-armed volute (triskelion).

In a carefully constructed stone sarcophagus in which the face of the skeleton was looking toward the setting sun, a beautiful shell ornament was found resting upon the breastbone of the skeleton. This shell ornament is 4.4 inches in diameter, and it is ornamented on its concave surface with a small circle in the center and four concentric bands, differently figured, in relief. The first band is filled up by a triple volute; the second is plain, while the third is dotted and has nine small round bosses carved at unequal distances upon it. The outer band is made up of fourteen small elliptical bosses, the outer edges of which give to the object a scalloped rim. This ornament, on its concave figured surface, has been covered with red paint, much of which is still visible. The convex smooth surface is highly polished and plain, with the exception of the three concentric marks. The material out of which it is formed was evidently derived from a large flat seashell. * * * The form of the circles or "suns" carved upon the concave surface is similar to that of the paintings on the high rocky cliffs on the banks of the Cumberland and Harpeth rivers. * * * This ornament when found lay upon the breastbone with the concave surface uppermost, as if it had been worn in this position suspended around the neck, as the two holes for the thong

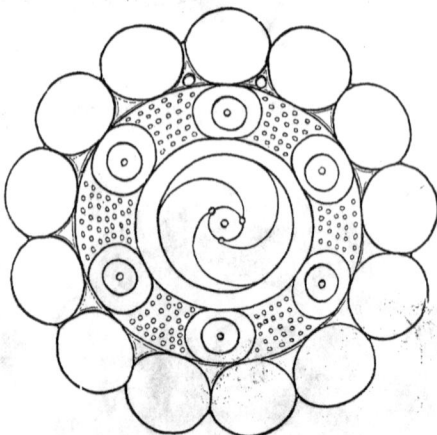

Fig. 273.
ENGRAVED SHELL DISK.
Tennessee.
Three-armed volute (triskelion).

or string were in that portion of the border which pointed directly to the chin or central portion of the jaw of the skeleton. The marks of the thong by which it was suspended are manifest upon both the anterior and posterior surfaces, and, in addition to this, the paint is worn off from the circular space bounded below by the two holes.

[1] Second Ann. Rep. Bureau of Ethnology, 1880–81, p. 276, pl. 56, figs. 1, 2.

Fig. 271 represents the back or convex side of the disk shown in fig. 270. The long curved lines indicate the laminations of the shell, and the three crescent-shaped figures near the center are perforations resulting from the deep engraving of the three lines of the volute on the concave side. The stone grave in which this ornament was found occupied the summit of a mound on the banks of the Cumberland River, opposite Nashville, Tenn.

Figs. 272, 273, and 274 are other representations of shell carved in spirals, and may have greater or less relation to the Swastika.[1] They are inserted for comparison and without any expression of opinion. They are drawn in outline, and the spiral form is thus more easily seen.

Mr. Holmes[2] makes some observations upon these designs and gives his theory concerning their use:

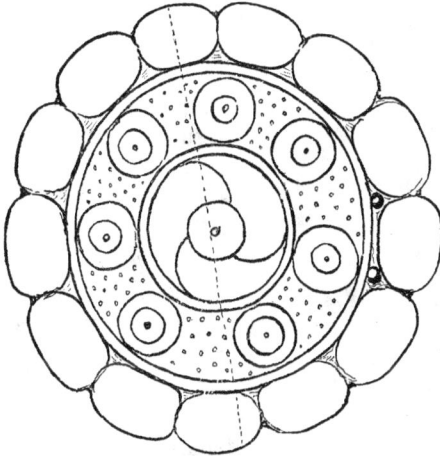

Fig. 274.
ENGRAVED SHELL DISK.
Tennessee.
Three-armed volute (triskelion).

I do not assume to interpret these designs; they are not to be interpreted. All I desire is to elevate these works from the category of trinkets to what I believe is their rightful place—the serious art of a people with great capacity for loftier works. What the gorgets themselves were, or of what particular value to their possessor, aside from simple ornaments, must be, in a measure, a matter of conjecture. They were hardly less than the totems of clans, the insignia of rulers, or the potent charms of the priesthood.

The spider.—The spider was represented on the shell gorgets. Figs. 275 to 278[3] present four of these gorgets, of which figs. 275 to 277 display the Greek cross in the center, surrounded by two concentric incised lines forming a circle which is the body of a spider. Fig. 276 shows the same spider and circle, and inside of it a cross much resem-

Fig. 275.
ENGRAVED SHELL GORGET.
Figure representing a spider; circles and Greek crosses.

---

[1] Op. cit., p. 276, pl. 56, figs. 3, 5, 6.

[2] Op. cit., p. 281.

[3] Second Ann. Rep. Bureau of Ethnology, 1880–81, pl. 61.

bling the Swastika, in that the arms are turned at their extremities to the right and form, in an inchoate manner, the gamma.   Fig. 278 represents the shell with the spider, and, though it contains no cross nor semblance of the Swastika, derives its value from having been taken from the same mound on Fains Island, Tennessee, as was the true Swastika. (See fig. 237.)

The rattlesnake.—The rattlesnake was a favorite design on these gorgets, affording, as it did, an opportunity for the aborigines to make a display of elegance of design, and of accuracy and fineness in execution.   Fig. 279 is a specimen in which the snake is represented coiled, the head in the center, the mouth V-shaped in strong lines, the body in volute fashion; on the

Fig. 276.
ENGRAVED SHELL GORGET.

outside of the circle the tail is shown by its rattle. This specimen is represented three-fourths size, and comes from McMahon mound, Tennessee. Four others of similar design are also from Tennessee and the adjoining States, but the locality is more restricted than is the case with other shell disk ornaments.

The human face and form.—These were also carved and wrought upon shells in the same general locality. The engraving is always on the convex side of the shell which has been reduced to a pear-shaped form.[1]

Fig. 277.
ENGRAVED SHELL GORGET.

[1] Second Ann. Rep. Bureau of Ethnology, pls. 69–73.

Fig. 278.
ENGRAVED SHELL GORGET.
Fains Island, Tennessee.

Fig. 279.
ENGRAVED SHELL GORGET REPRESENTING A RATTLESNAKE.
McMahon Mound, Tennessee.
Second Annual Report of the Bureau of Ethnology, pl. LXIII.

These human faces and forms (figs. 280–288), as well as the others, belong to the mound builders, and are found with their remains in the mounds. The figures are inserted, as is the rattlesnake, for compari-

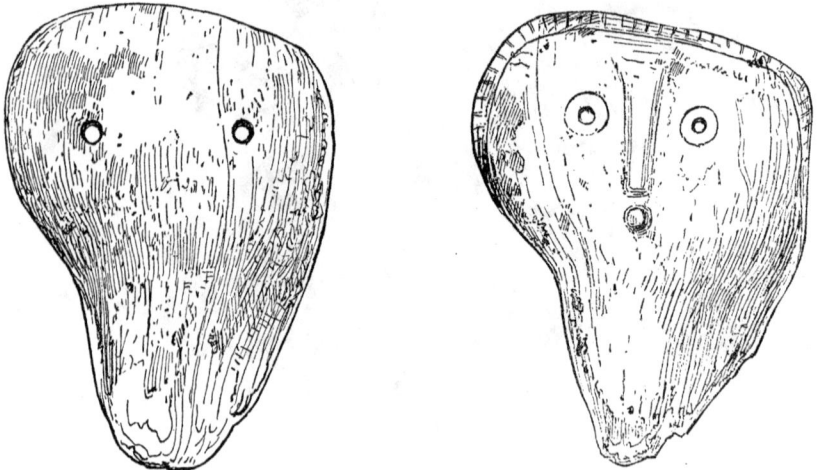

Figs. 280 and 281.
ENGRAVED SHELLS WITH REPRESENTATIONS OF THE HUMAN FACE.
McMahon Mound, Tennessee.
Second Annual Report of the Bureau of Ethnology, pl. LXIX.

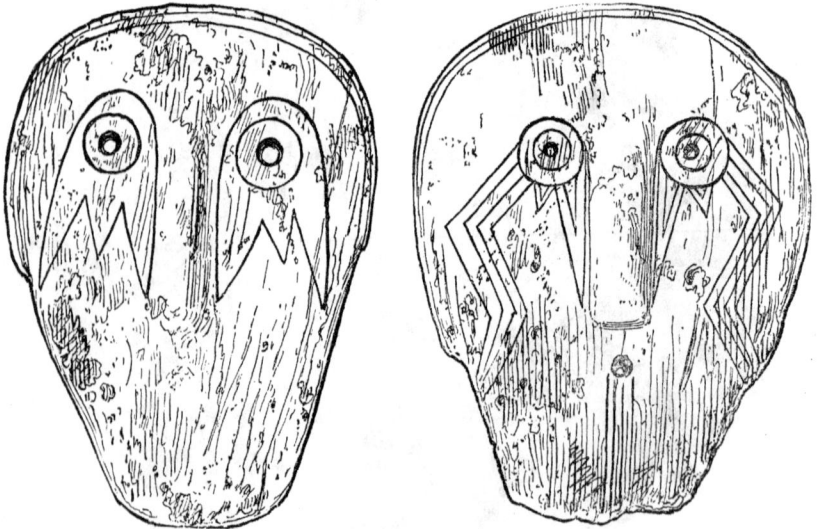

Figs. 282 and 283.
ENGRAVED SHELLS WITH REPRESENTATIONS OF THE HUMAN FACE.
Tennessee.
Second Annual Report of the Bureau of Ethnology, pl. LXIX.

son with the shell designs and work shown in the Buddha figure (pl. 10) and its associates. Slight inspection will show two styles, differing materially. To decide which was foreign and which domestic,

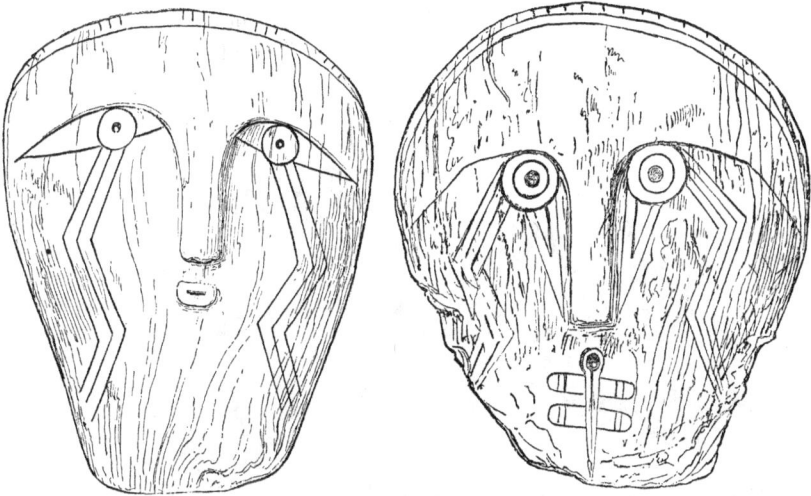

Figs. 284 and 285.
ENGRAVED SHELLS WITH REPRESENTATIONS OF THE HUMAN FACE.
Virginia
Second Annual Report of the Bureau of Ethnology, pl. LXIX.

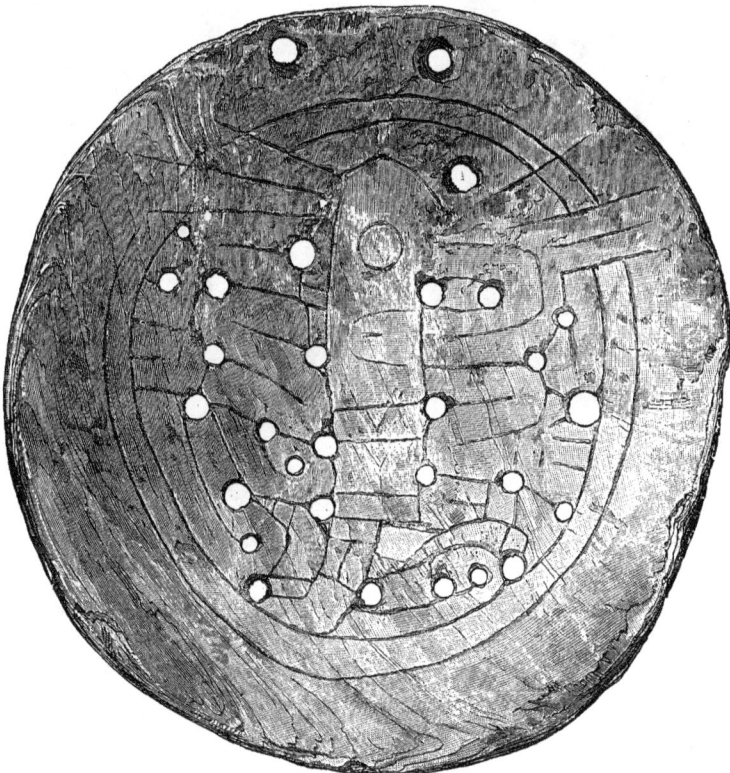

Fig. 286.
ENGRAVED SHELL WITH REPRESENTATION OF A HUMAN FIGURE
McMahon Mound, Tennessee.
Second Annual Report of the Bureau of Ethnology, pl. LXXI.

which was imported and which indigenous, would be to decide the entire question of migration, and if done off-hand, would be presumptuous. To make a satisfactory decision will require a marshaling and consideration of evidence which belongs to the future.   The specimens shown

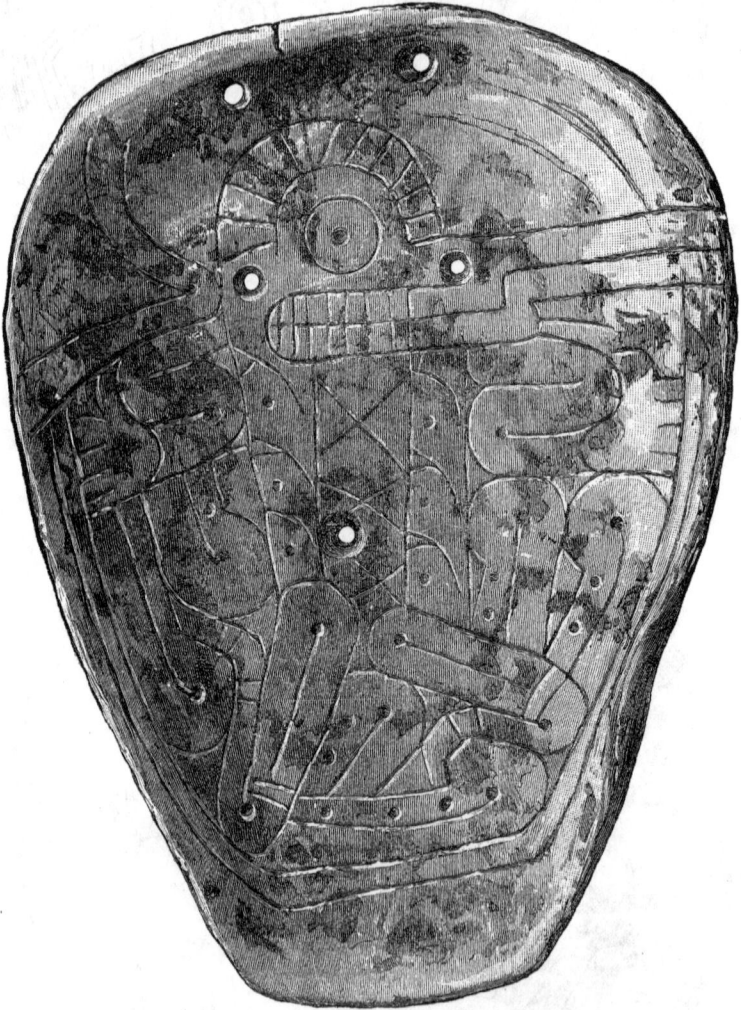

Fig. 287.
ENGRAVED SHELL WITH REPRESENTATION OF A HUMAN FIGURE.
Tennessee.
Second Annual Report of the Bureau of Ethnology, pl. LXXII.

in figs. 280 to 285 are from Tennessee and Virginia.   They are all masks, bearing representations of the human face.   The first two are from the McMahon mound, Tennessee; that in fig. 282 from Brakebill mound, Tennessee, and that represented in fig. 283 from Lick Creek mound, Tennessee.   The shell shown in fig. 284 is from Aquia Creek, Virginia,

and that in fig. 285 is from a mound in Ely County, Va. The workmanship on these has no resemblance to that on the Buddha figure
(pl. 10), nor does its style compare in any manner therewith.

On the contrary, figs. 286 to 288, representing sketches (unfinished) of
the human figure, from mounds in Tennessee and Missouri, have some
resemblance in style of work, though not in design, to that of the
Buddha and Swastika figures. The first step in execution, after the
drawing by incised lines, seems to have been to drill holes through

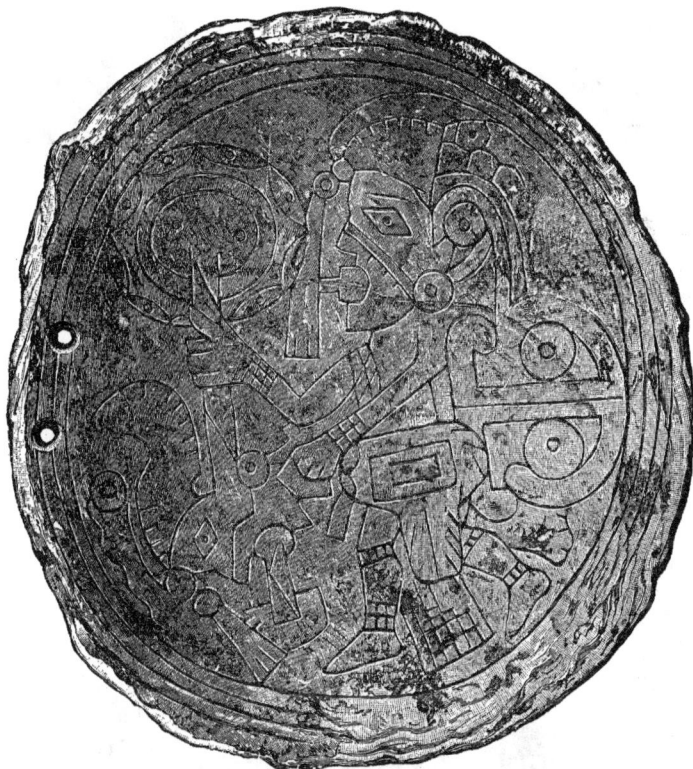

Fig. 288.
ENGRAVED SHELL GORGET WITH REPRESENTATION OF A HUMAN FIGURE.
Missouri.
Second Annual Report of the Bureau of Ethnology, pl. LXXIII.

the shell at each corner and intersection. The work on the specimen
shown in fig. 286 has progressed further than that on the specimens
shown in figs. 287 and 288. It has twenty-eight holes drilled, all at
corners or intersections. This is similar to the procedure in the Buddha
statue (pl. 10). In fig. 287 the holes have not been drilled, but each
member of the figure has been marked out and indicated by dots in the
center, and circles or half circles incised around them in precisely the
same manner as in both Swastikas (figs. 237 and 238), while fig. 288
continues the resemblance in style of drawing. It has the same peculiar

garters or bracelets as the Buddha, the hand is the same as in the
fighting figures (fig. 239), and the implement he holds resembles closely
those in the copper figures (figs. 240 and 241).

DESIGNS ON POTTERY.

Spiral-volute designs resembling the Swastika in general effect are
found on aboriginal mound pottery from the Mississippi Valley. The
Fourth Annual Report of the Bureau of Ethnology, 1882–83,[1] shows

Fig. 289.
POTTERY VSSSEL.
Four-armed volute, ogee Swastika (tetraske-
lion).
Arkansas.
⅓ natural size.

Fig. 290.
POTTERY VESSEL.
Four volutes resembling Swastika.
Pecan Point, Ark.
⅓ natural size.

many of these. Fig. 289 represents a teapot-shaped vessel from Arkansas, on the side of which, in incised lines, is shown the small
circle which we saw on the shell disks, and springing from the four
opposite sides are three incised lines, twisting spirally to the right,
forming the four
volutes of the Swas-
tika (tetraskelion)
and covering the en-
tire side of the ves-
sel. The same spiral
form of the Swas-
tika is given in fig.
290, a vessel of ec-
centric shape from
Pecan Point, Ark.
The decoration is in
the form of two lines
crossing each other
and each arm then
twisting to the

Fig. 291.
POTTERY VESSEL MADE IN THE FORM OF AN ANIMAL.
Spiral volutes, nine arms.
Pecan Point, Ark.
⅓ natural size.

right, forming volutes, the incised lines of which, though drawn close

---

[1] Figs. 402, 413, 415, 416.

together and at equal distances, gradually expand until the ornament covers the entire side of the vase. It is questionable whether this or any of its kindred were ever intended to represent either the Swastika or any other specific form of the cross. One evidence of this is that these ornaments shade off indefinitely until they arrive at a form which was surely not intended to represent any form of the cross, whether Swastika or not. The line of separation is not now suggested by the author. An elaboration of the preceding forms, both of the vessel and its ornamentation, is shown by the vessel represented in fig. 291, which is fashioned to represent some grotesque beast with horns, expanding nostrils, and grinning mouth, yet which might serve as a teapot as well as the former two vessels.

Fig. 292.

POTTERY BOWL ORNAMENTED WITH MANY-ARMED VOLUTES.

Arkansas.

½ natural size.

The decoration upon its side has six incised lines crossing each other in the center and expanding in volutes until they cover the entire side of the vessel, as in the other specimens. Fig. 292 shows a pot from Arkansas. Its body is decorated with incised lines arranged in much the same form as fig. 291, except that the lines make no attempt to form a cross. There are nine arms which spring from the central point and twist spirally about as volutes until they cover the field, which is one-third the body of the bowl. Two other designs of the same kind complete the circuit of the pot and form the decoration all around. Fig. 293[1] represents these volutes in incised lines of considerable fineness, close together, and in great numbers, forming a decoration on each of the sides of the vase, separated by three nearly perpendicular lines.

Fig. 293.

POTTERY VASE ORNAMENTED WITH VOLUTES.

Arkansas.

---

[1] Third Ann. Rep. Bureau of Ethnology, fig. 157.

The spiral Swastika form appears painted upon the pottery from Arkansas. The specimen shown in fig. 294[1] is a tripod bottle. The decoration upon the side of the body consists of two lines forming the cross, and the four arms expand in volutes until the ornament covers one-third of the vessel, which, with the other two similar ornaments, extend around the circumference. This decoration is painted in red and white colors on a gray or yellowish ground. Fig. 295 shows a bowl from mound No. 2, Thorn's farm, Taylor Shanty group, Mark Tree,

Fig. 294.
TRIPOD POTTERY VASE.
Four-armed volutes making spiral Swastika.
Arkansas.
⅓ natural size.

Poinsett County, Ark. It is ten inches wide and six inches high. The clay of which it is made forms the body color—light gray. It has been painted red or maroon on the outside without any decoration, while on the inside is painted with the same color a five-armed cross, spirally arranged in volutes turning to the right. The center of the cross is at the bottom of the bowl, and the painted spiral lines extend over the bottom and up the sides to the rim of the bowl, the interior being

---

[1] Fourth Ann. Rep. Bureau of Ethnology, 1882–83, fig. 442.

entirely covered with the design. Another example of the same style
of decoration is seen on the upper surface of an ancient vase from the
province of Cibola.[1]

The specimen shown in fig. 296 is from the mound at Arkansas Post,
in the county and State of Arkansas.[2] It represents a vase of black
ware, painted a yellowish ground, with a red spiral scroll. Its diam-

Fig. 295.
POTTERY BOWL WITH FIVE-ARMED SPIRAL SWASTIKA ON THE BOTTOM.
Poinsett County, Ark.
Cat. No. 114035, U. S. N. M.

eter is 5½ inches. These spiral figures are not uncommon in the
localities heretofore indicated as showing the normal Swastika. Figs.
297 and 298[3] show parallel incised lines of the same style as those

[1] Fourth Ann. Rep. Bureau of Ethnology, 1882–83, p. 343, fig. 331.
[2] Third Ann. Rep. Bureau of Ethnology, 1881–82, fig. 165.
[3] Ibid., pp. 502, 503, figs. 186, 189.

forming the square in the bird gorgets already noted (figs. 263–267). Fig. 297 shows a bowl nine inches in diameter; its rim is ornamented with the head and tail of a conventional bird, which probably served as handles. On the outside, just below the rim, are the four incised parallel lines mentioned. In the center of the side is represented a rolling under or twisting of the lines, as though it represented a ribbon. There are three on each quarter of the bowl, that next the head being plain. Fig. 298 represents a bottle 6½ inches in diameter, with parallel incised lines, three in number, with the same twisting or folding of the ribbon-like decora-

Fig. 296.
VESSEL OF BLACK WARE.
Spiral scroll.
Arkansas.

tion. This twists to the left, while that of fig. 297 twists in the opposite direction. Both specimens are from the vicinity of Charleston, Mo.

DESIGNS ON BASKETRY.

The volute form is particularly adapted to the decoration of basketry, of which fig. 299 is a

Fig. 297.
BIRD-SHAPED POTTERY BOWL.
Three parallel incised lines with ribbon fold.
Charleston, Mo.

specimen. These motifs were favorites with the Pueblo Indians of New Mexico and Arizona.

Fig. 298.
POTTERY BOWL.
Three parallel incised lines with ribbon fold.
Charleston, Mo.

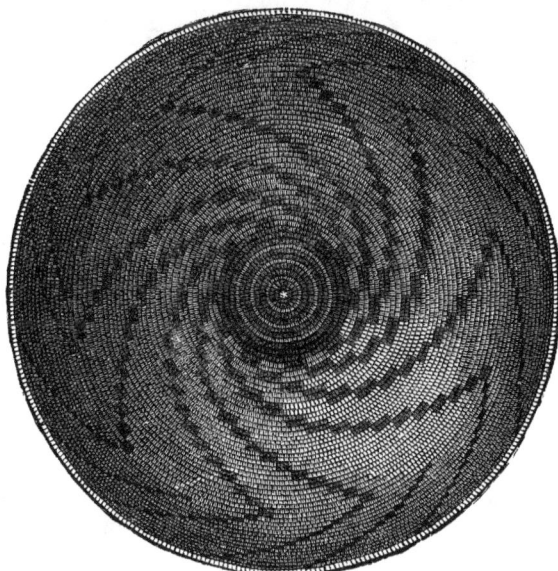

Fig. 299.
BASKETWORK WITH MANY-ARMED VOLUTES.
Fourth Annual Report of the Bureau of Ethnology, fig. 485.

IV.—THE CROSS AMONG THE AMERICAN INDIANS.

DIFFERENT FORMS.

The foregoing specimens are sufficient evidence of the existence of the Swastika among the aboriginal North Americans during the mound-building period, and although there may be other specimens of the Swastika to be reported, yet we might properly continue this investigation for the purpose of determining if there be any related forms of the cross among the same peoples. This is done without any argument

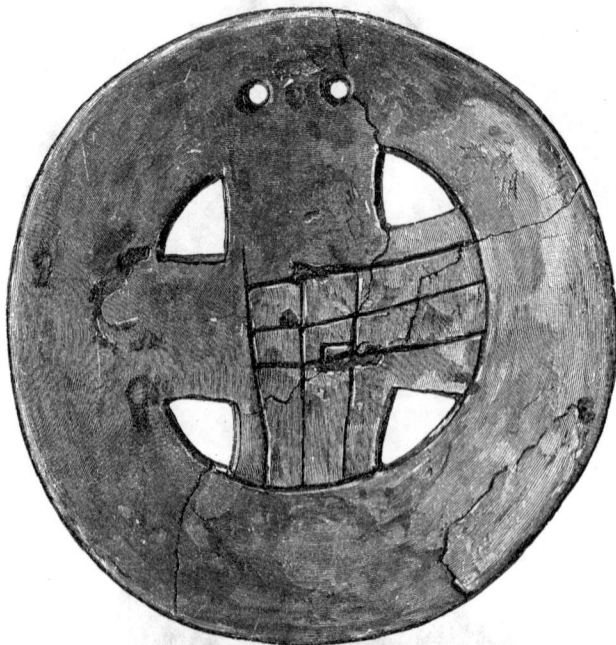

Fig. 300.
ENGRAVED SHELL GORGET.
Greek cross with incised lines resembling a Swastika.
Union County, Ill.

as to the use of these designs beyond that attributed to them. The illustrations and descriptions are mainly collected from objects in and reports of the U. S. National Museum and the Bureau of Ethnology.

THE CROSS ON OBJECTS OF SHELL AND COPPER.

The shell gorget presented in fig. 300 belongs to the collection of Mr. F. M. Perrine, and was obtained from a mound in Union County, Ill. It is a little more than three inches in diameter and has been ground to a uniform thickness of about one-twelfth of an inch. The surfaces are smooth and the margin carefully rounded and polished.

Near the upper edge are two perforations, both well worn with cord-marks indicating suspension. The cross in the center of the concave face of the disk is quite simple and is made by four triangular perforations which separate the arms. The face of the cross is ornamented with six carelessly drawn incised lines interlacing in the center as shown in the figure, three extending along the arm to the right and three passing down the lower arm to the inclosing line. Nothing has been learned of the character of the interments with which this speci-

Fig. 301.
ENGRAVED SHELL GORGET.
Greek cross.
Charleston, Mo.
Second Annual Report of the Bureau of Ethnology, pl. LI, fig. 2.

men was associated.[1] The incised lines of the specimen indicate the possible intention of the artist to make the Swastika. The design is evidently a cross and apparently unfinished.

The National Museum possesses a large shell cross (fig. 301) which, while quite plain as a cross, has been much damaged, the rim that formerly encircled it, as in the foregoing figure, having been broken away and lost. The perforations are still in evidence. The specimen

[1] Second Ann. Rep. Bureau of Ethnology, 1880–81, p. 271, pl. 51, fig. 1.

is much decayed and came to the National Museum with a skull from a grave at Charleston, Mo.; beyond this there is no record. The specimen shown in fig. 302 is quoted as a "typical example of the cross of the mound-builder." It was obtained from a mound on Lick Creek, Tennessee, and is in the Peabody Museum, Cambridge, Mass. While an elaborate description is given of it and figures are mentioned as "devices probably significant," and "elementary or unfinished," and more of the same, yet nowhere is suggested any relationship to the Swastika, nor even the possibility of its existence in America.

Fig. 302.

SHELL GORGET WITH ENGRAVING OF GREEK CROSS AND INCHOATE SWASTIKA.

Second Annual Report of the Bureau of Ethnology, pl. LII, fig. 3.

A large copper disk from an Ohio mound is represented in fig. 303. It is in the Natural History Museum of New York. It is eight inches in diameter, is very thin, and had suffered greatly from corrosion. A symmetrical cross, the arms of which are five inches in length, has been cut out of the center. Two concentric lines have been impressed in the plate, one near the margin and the other touching the ends of the cross. Fig. 304 shows a shell gorget from a mound on Lick Creek, Tennessee. It is much corroded and broken, yet it shows the cross plainly. There are sundry pits or dots made irregularly over the surface, some of which have perforated the shell. Pl. 19 represents a recapitulation of specimens of crosses, thirteen in number, "most of

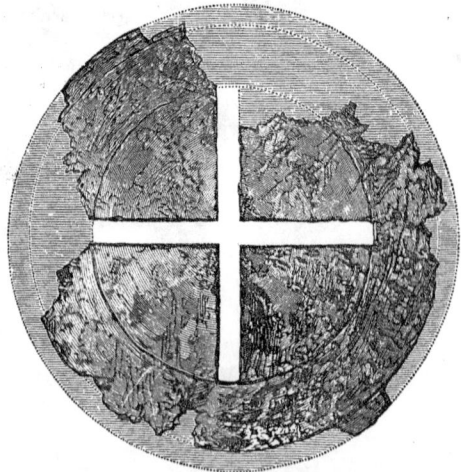

Fig. 303.

FRAGMENT OF COPPER DISK WITH GREEK CROSS IN INNER CIRCLE.

Ohio.

American Museum of Natural History, New York City.

Second Annual Report of the Bureau of Ethnology, pl. LII, fig. 4.

which have been obtained from the mounds or from ancient graves within the district occupied by the mound-builders. Eight are engraved upon shell gorgets, one is cut in stone, three are painted upon pottery,

EXPLANATION OF PLATE 19.

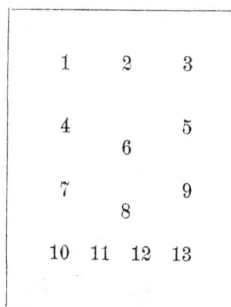

1	2	3	
4			5
	6		
7			9
	8		
10	11	12	13

VARIOUS FORMS OF CROSSES IN USE AMONG NORTH AMERICAN INDIANS, FROM GREEK CROSS
TO SWASTIKA.

Fig. 1. GREEK CROSS.

2. GREEK CROSS.

3. CROSS ON COPPER.

4. CROSS ON SHELL.

5. GREEK CROSS.

6. GREEK CROSS.

7. LATIN CROSS (Copper).

Fig. 8. GREEK CROSS.

9. LATIN CROSS (Copper).

10. SWASTIKA ON SHELL.

11. SWASTIKA ON SHELL.

12. SWASTIKA ON POTTERY.

13. SWASTIKA ON POTTERY.

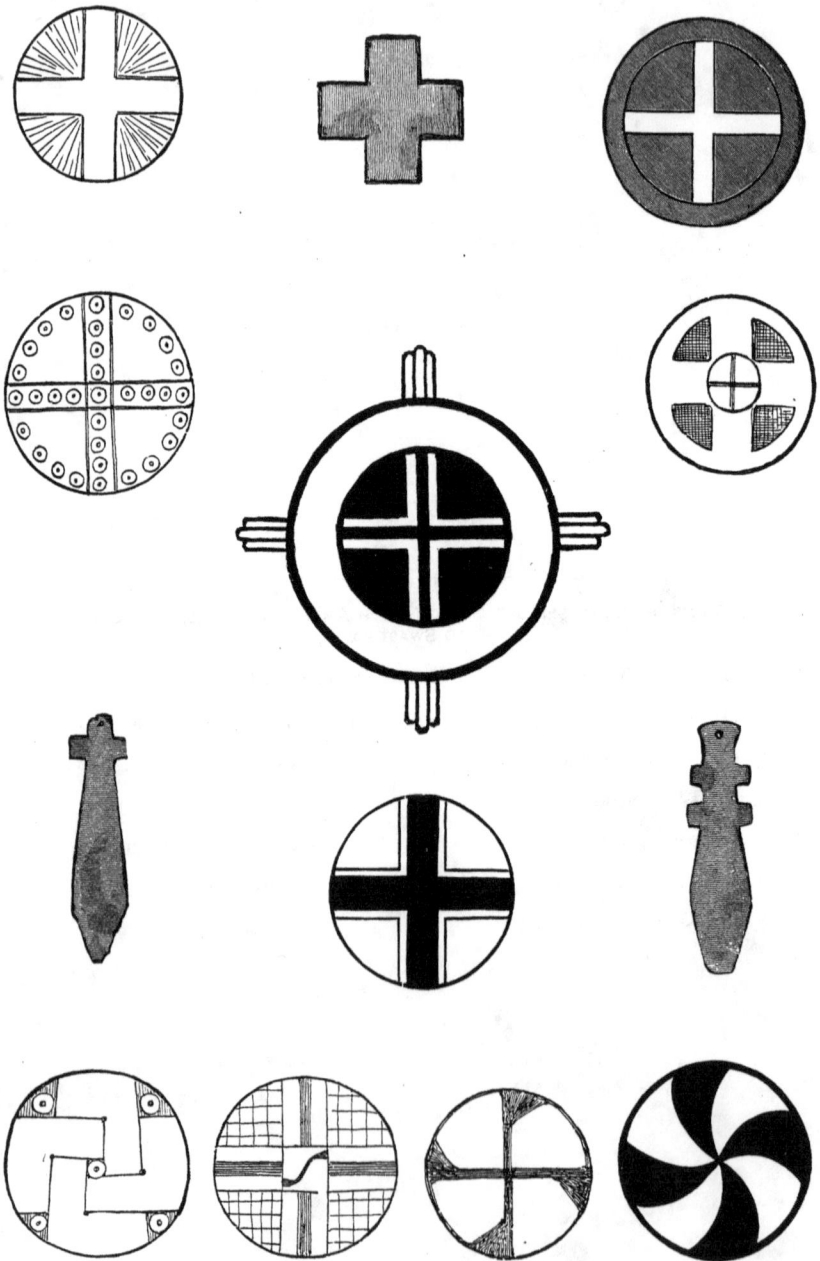

VARIOUS FORMS OF CROSSES IN USE AMONG NORTH AMERICAN INDIANS, FROM GREEK CROSS TO SWASTIKA.

Second Annual Report of the Bureau of Ethnology, 1880–81, Pl. LIII.

and four are executed upon copper. With two exceptions, they are inclosed in circles, and hence are symmetrical Greek crosses, the ends being rounded to conform to a circle."[1] Figs. 7 and 9 of pl. 19 represent forms of the Latin cross, and are modern, having doubtless been introduced by European priests. Figs. 10 to 13 are representatives of the Swastika in some of its forms.

The U. S. National Museum possesses a small shell ornament (fig. 305) in the form of a cross, from Lenoir's burial place, Fort Defiance, Caldwell County, N. C., collected by Dr. Spainhour and Mr. Rogan, the latter being an employé of the Bureau of Ethnology. It is in the form of a Greek cross, the four arms crossing at right angles and being of equal length. The arms are of the plain shell,

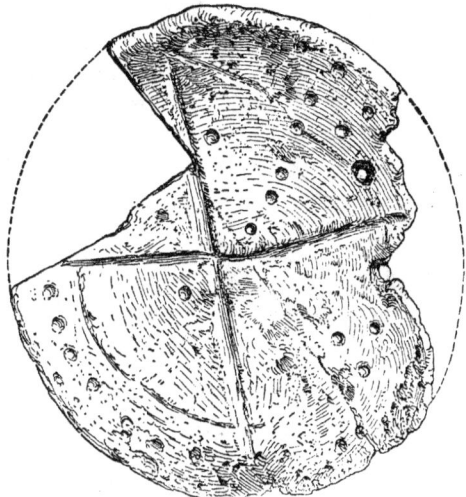

Fig. 304.
ENGRAVED SHELL DISK GORGET.
Rude cross with many dots.
Lick Creek, Tenn.
Second Annual Report of the Bureau of Ethnology, pl. 52, fig. 2.

while they are brought to view by the field being cross-hatched. The specimen has, unfortunately, been broken, and being fragile has been secured in a bed of plaster.

This and the foregoing specimens have been introduced into this paper that the facts of their existence may be presented for consideration, and to aid in the determination whether the cross had any peculiar or particular meaning. The questions involuntarily arise, Was it a symbol with a hidden meaning, religious or otherwise; was it the

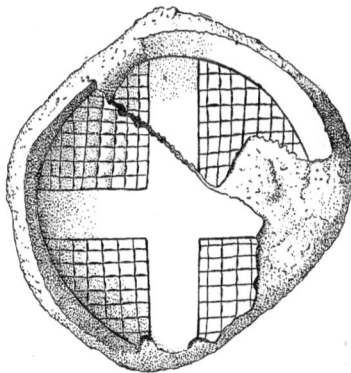

Fig. 305.
ENGRAVED SHELL WITH FIGURE OF GREEK CROSS.
Caldwell County, N. C.
Cat. No. 33169, U. S. N. M.

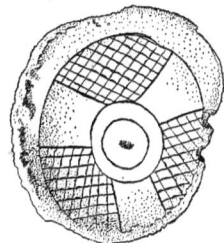

Fig. 306.
ENGRAVED SHELL WITH THREE-ARMED CROSS (TRISKELION).
Lick Creek, Tenn.
Cat. No. 83170, U. S. N. M.

totem of a clan, the insignia of a ruler, the charm of a priesthood, or did it, with all the associated shell engravings, belong to the category of trinkets? These questions may be partially answered in the section on the meanings given to the cross by the North American Indians (p. 933).

There is also introduced, as bearing on the question, another shell ornament (fig. 306), the style, design, and workmanship of which has such resemblance to the foregoing that if they had not been (as they were) found together we would be compelled to admit their identity of origin, yet the latter specimen has but three arms instead of four. This might take it out of the category of crosses as a symbol of any religion of which we have knowledge.

Fig. 307.
DRILLED AND ENGRAVED SHELL OR "RUNTEE."
Dotted Greek cross and circle.
Arizona.

Many of the art objects in shell heretofore cited were more or less closely associated; they came from the same neighborhood and were the results of the same excavations, conducted by the same excavators. In determining the culture status of their makers, they must be taken together.

Fig. 308.
DRILLED AND ENGRAVED SHELL OR "RUNTEE."
Dots and rings forming circle and Greek cross.
Ohio.

When we consider the variety of the designs which were apparently without meaning except for ornamentation, like the circles, meanders, zigzags, chevrons, herringbones, ogees, frets, etc., and the representations of animals such as were used to decorate the pipes of the aborigines, not alone the bear, wolf, eagle, and others which might be a totem and represent a given clan, but others which, according to our knowledge and imagination, have never served for such a purpose, as the man-

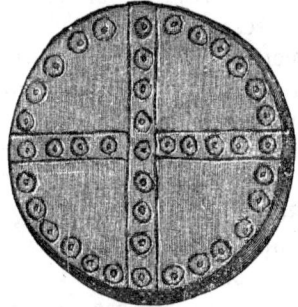

Fig. 309.
DRILLED AND ENGRAVED SHELL OR "RUNTEE."
Dots and rings forming circle and Greek cross.
New York.

atee, beaver, wildcat, heron, finch, sparrow, crow, raven, cormorant, duck, toucan, goose, turkey, buzzard, cardinal, parroquet, conies, lizard; when we further consider that the cross, whether Greek, Latin, or Swastika form, is utterly unlike any known or possible totem of clan, insignia of ruler, or potent charm of priesthood; when we consider these things, why should we feel ourselves compelled to accept these signs as symbols of a hidden meaning, simply because religious sects in different parts of the world and at different epochs of history have chosen them or some of them to represent their peculiar religious ideas? This question covers much space in geography and in time, as well as on paper. It is not answered here, because no answer can be given which would be accepted as satisfactory, but it may serve as a track or indication along which students and thinkers might pursue their investigations.

The U. S. National Museum possesses a necklace consisting of three shell ornaments, interspersed at regular intervals with about fifty small porcelain beads (fig. 307).[1] It was obtained by Capt. George M. Whipple from the Indians of New Mexico. These shell ornaments are similar to objects described by Beverly in his work on the "History of Virginia," page 145, as "runtees" and "made of the conch shell; only the shape is flat as a cheese and drilled edgewise." It is to be remarked that on its face as well as on figs. 308 and 309[1] appears a cross of the Greek form indicated by these peculiar indentations or drillings inclosed in a small circle. The specimen shown in fig. 308 is from an ancient grave in Upper Sandusky, Ohio, and that shown in fig. 309 from an Indian cemetery at Onondaga, N.Y. Similar specimens have been found in the same localities.

Fig. 310.
POTTERY JAR WITH CROSSES, ENCIRCLING RAYS AND SCALLOPS.
Third Annual Report of the Bureau of Ethnology, fig. 188.

THE CROSS ON POTTERY.

Fig. 310 shows a small globular cup of dark ware from the vicinity of Charleston, Mo.; height, $2\frac{1}{2}$ inches; width, $3\frac{1}{2}$ inches. It has four large nodes or projections, and between them, painted red, are four ornamental circles, the outside one of which is scalloped or rayed, while the inside one bears the figure of a Greek cross. The specimen shown in fig. 311 (Cat. No. 47197, U.S.N.M.) is a medium-sized decorated olla with scalloped margin, from New Mexico, collected by Colonel Stevenson. It has two crosses—one Greek, the other Maltese—both inclosed in circles and forming centers of an elaborate, fanciful, shield-like decoration. In fig. 312 (Cat. No. 39518, U.S.N.M.) is shown a Cochiti painted water vessel, same collection, showing a Maltese cross.

Dozens of other specimens are in the collections of the U. S. National Museum which would serve to illustrate the extended and extensive

---

[1] Schoolcraft, "History of the Indian Tribes," III, pl. 25; Second Ann. Rep. Bureau of Ethnology, 1880–81, pl. 36.

Fig. 311.

OLLA DECORATED WITH GREEK AND MALTESE CROSSES.

Second Annual Report of the Bureau of Ethnology, fig. 708.

Fig. 312.

POTTERY WATER VESSEL.

Maltese cross.

Second Annual Report of the Bureau of Ethnology, fig. 642.

PLATE 20.

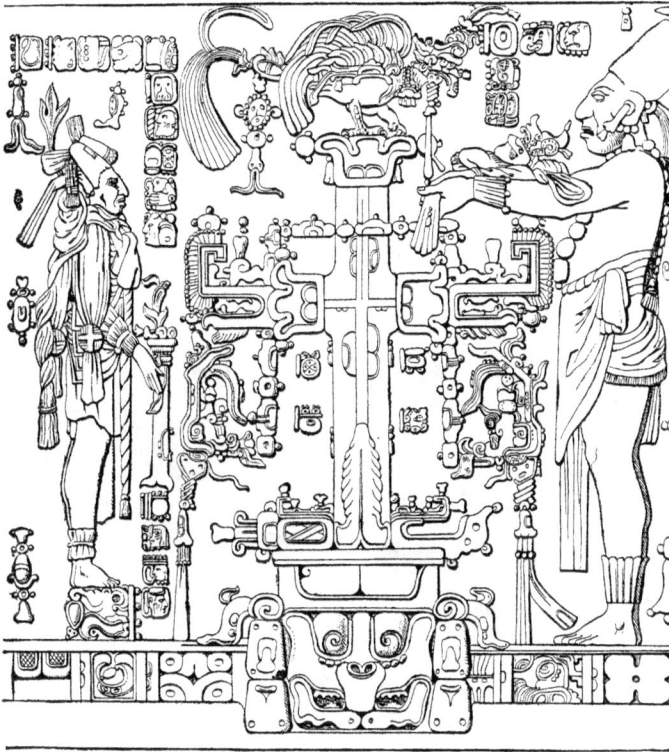

PALENQUE CROSS, FOLIATED.
Smithsonian Contributions to Knowledge, Vol. xxii, fig. 7.

use of the cross in great variety of forms, so that no argument as to either the meaning or the extent of the cross can be based on the supposition that these are the only specimens. Fig. 313 (Cat. No. 132975, U.S.N.M.) shows a vase from Mexico, about 8 inches high, of fine red ware, highly polished, with an elaborate decoration. Its interest here is the Maltese cross represented on each side, with a point and concentric circles, from the outside of which are projecting rays. This may be the symbol of the sun, and if so, is shown in connection with the cross. This style of cross, with or without the sun symbol, is found in great numbers in Mexico—as, for example, the great cross, pl. 20, from the temple at Palenque.[1]

SYMBOLIC MEANINGS OF THE CROSS.

It would be an excellent thing to dissect and analyze the Swastika material we have found; to generalize and deduce from it a possible theory as to the origin, spread, and meaning of the Swastika and its related forms, and endeavor, by examination of its associated works, to discover if these were religious symbols or charms or mere decorations; and, following this, determine if possible whether the spread of these objects, whatever their meaning, was the result of migration, contact, or communication. Were they the result of similar, but independent, operations of the human mind, or were they but duplicate inventions, the result of parallelism in human thought? This investigation must necessarily be theoretical and speculative. The most that the author proposes is to suggest probabilities and point the way for further investigation. He may theorize

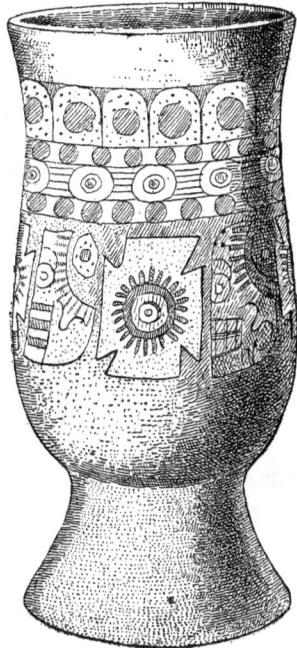

Fig. 313.

POTTERY VASE FINELY DECORATED IN RED AND WHITE GLAZE.

Maltese cross with sun symbol (?).

Cat. No. 132975, U. S. N. M.

and speculate, but recognizes what many persons seem not able to do—that speculation and theory are not to be substituted for cold facts. He may do no more than propound questions from which other men, by study, experience, philosophy, or psychology, may possibly evolve some general principle, or a theory pointing to a general principle, concerning the mode of extension and spread of culture among separate and independent peoples. When the facts shall have been gathered, marshaled, arranged side by side, and each aggregation of facts shall have been weighed, *pro* and *con*, and its fair value given "without

---

[1] Smithsonian Contributions to Knowledge, p. 33, pl. 14, fig. 7.

prejudice or preconceived opinion," then will be time enough to announce the final conclusion, and even then not dogmatically, but tentatively and subject to future discoveries.

Throughout this paper the author has sought but little more than to prepare material on the Swastika which can be utilized by those who come after him in the determination of the difficult and abstruse problems presented.

It is rare in the study of archæology and, indeed, in any science, that a person is able to assert a negative and say what does not exist. The present investigations are rendered much more comprehensive by the appearance of the extensive and valuable work of Col. Garrick Mallery in the Tenth Annual Report of the Bureau of Ethnology, on the subject of "Picture Writing of the American Indians." It is a work of about 800 pages, with 1,300 illustrations, and is the result of many years of laborious study. It purports to be a history, more or less complete, of the picture writing, signs, symbols, totems, marks, and messages of the American Indian, whether pictographs or petroglyphs. A large portion of his work is devoted to ideography, conventional signs, syllabaries and alphabets, homorophs and symmorophs, and their respective means of interpretation. Among these he deals, not specifically with the Swastika, but in general terms with the cross. Therefore, by looking at Colonel Mallery's work upon this chapter (p. 724), one is able to say negatively what has not been found.

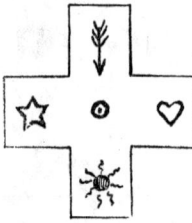

Fig. 314.

GREEK CROSS REPRESENTING WINDS FROM CARDINAL POINTS.

Dakota Indians.

Tenth Annual Report of the Bureau of Ethnology, fig. 1255.

Apropos of the meanings of the cross among the North American Indians Count Goblet d'Alviella says:[1]

> It is nevertheless incontestable that the pre-Columbian cross of America is a "*rose des vents*," representing the four directions whence comes the rain, or the cardinal points of the compass, etc., etc.

Colonel Mallery's volume shows that it meant many other things as well.

The four winds.—The Greek cross is the form found by Colonel Mallery to be most common among the North American aborigines, possibly because it is the simplest. In this the four arms are equal in length, and the sign placed upright so that it stands on one foot and not on two, as does the St. Andrew's cross. The Greek cross (fig. 314) represents, among the Dakotas, the four winds issuing out of the four caverns in which souls of men existed before the incarnation of the human body. All the medicine men—that is, conjurors and magicians—recollect their previous dreamy life in these places, and the instructions then received from the gods, demons, and sages; they recollect and describe their preexistent life, but only dream and speculate as to the future life beyond the grave. The top of the cross is the cold,

---

[1] "La Migration des Symboles," p. 18.

all-conquering giant, the North Wind, most powerful of all. It is worn on the body nearest the head, the seat of intelligence and conquering devices. The left arm covers the heart; it is the East Wind, coming from the seat of life and love. The foot is the melting, burning South

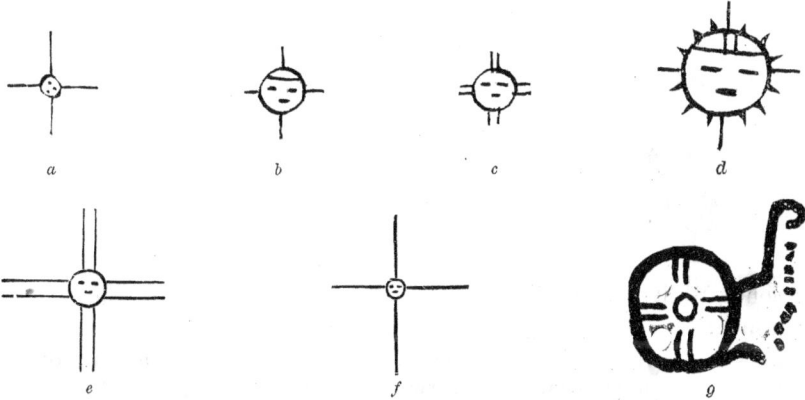

Fig. 315.

THE CROSS IN CONNECTION WITH THE CIRCLE.

Sun symbols(?).

Tenth Annual Report of the Bureau of Ethnology, figs. 1118, 1120, 1126.

Wind, indicating, as it is worn, the seat of fiery passion. The right arm is the gentle West Wind, blowing from the spirit land, covering the lungs, from which the breath at last goes out gently, but into unknown night. The center of the cross is the earth and man, moved by the conflicting influences of gods and winds.

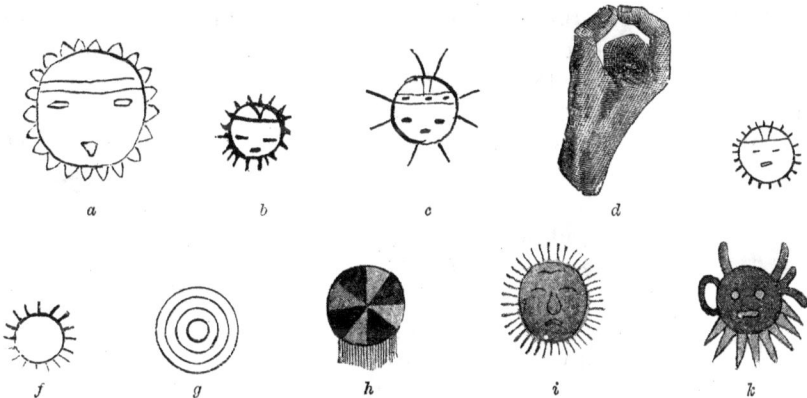

Fig. 316.

FIGURES OF CIRCLES AND RAYS PROBABLY REPRESENTING SUN SYMBOLS.

Tenth Annual Report of the Bureau of Ethnology, figs. 1118-1121, 1123.

Rev. John McLain, in his work on the "Blackfoot Sun-dance," says:

On the sacred pole of the sun lodge of the Blood Indian is a bundle of small brushwood taken from the birch tree, which is placed in the form of a cross. This was an ancient symbol evidently referring to the four winds.

Sun and star symbols.—Great speculation has been made, both in Europe and America, over the relation between the Swastika and the sun, because the two signs have been associated by primitive peoples.

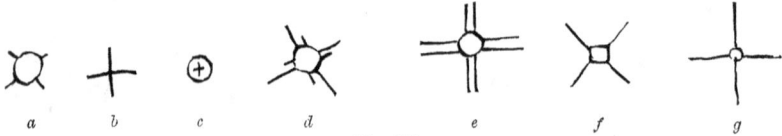

Fig. 317.

FIGURES OF CROSSES AND CIRCLES REPRESENTING STAR SYMBOLS.

Oakley Springs, Ariz.

Tenth Annual Report of the Bureau of Ethnology, fig. 1129.

Colonel Mallery gives the Indian signs for the sun, stars, and light.[1] These have been segregated, and it will be seen that the cross and circle are used indiscriminately for one and the other, and the fact of the two being found associated is no evidence of relationship in religious ideas (figs. 315–319).

Fig. 318.

STAR SYMBOL.

Circle and rays without cross.

Oakley Springs, Ariz.

Tenth Annual Report of the Bureau of Ethnology, fig. 1129.

Dwellings.—Among the Hidatsa, the cross and the circle represent neither the sun nor any religious ideas, but merely lodges, houses, or dwellings. The crosses in fig. 319 represent Dakota lodges; the small circles signify earth lodges, the points representing the supporting poles. Buildings erected by civilized people were represented by small rectangular figures, while the circles with dots in a square represent earth lodges, the home of the Hidatsa.

Dragon fly (Susbeca).—Among some of the Indian tribes, the Dakotas among others, the Latin cross is found, i. e., upright with three members of equal length, and the fourth, the foot, much longer. The use of this symbol antedates the discovery of America, and is carried back in tradition and myth. This sign signifies the mosquito hawk or the dragon fly (fig. 320). It is called in that language the "Susbeca," and is a supernatural being gifted with speech, warning man of danger, approaching his ear silently and at right angles, saying, "Tci," "tci," "tci," an interjection equivalent to "Look out!" "You are surely going to destruction!" "Look out!" "Tci," "tci," "tci!" The adoption of the dragon fly as a mysterious and

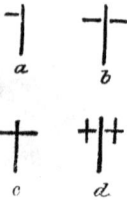

Fig. 319.

FIGURES OF CROSSES, CIRCLES, AND SQUARES REPRESENTING LODGES

Dakota Indians.

Tenth Annual Report of the Bureau of Ethnology, fig. 1203.

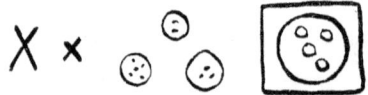

Fig. 320.

LATIN CROSSES REPRESENTING THE DRAGON FLY.

Dakota Indians.

---

[1] Tenth Ann. Rep. Bureau of Ethnology, 1888–89, figs. 1118–1129.

supernatural being is on account of its sudden appearance in numbers. In the still of the evening, when the shades of darkness come, then is heard in the meadows a sound as of crickets or frogs, but indistinct and prolonged; on the morrow the Susbeca will be hovering over it. It is the sound of their coming, but whence no one knows. The cross not only represents the shape of the insect, but also the angle of its approach. It is variously drawn, but usually as in fig. 320 *a* or *b*, and, in painting or embroidery. *c*, and sometimes *d*.

Fig. 321 is described in Keam's MS. as follows:

Fig. 321.

DOUBLE CROSS OF SIX ARMS REPRESENTING THE DRAGON FLY.

Moki Indians, Arizona.

Tenth Annual Report of the Bureau of Ethnology, fig. 1165.

This is a conventional design of dragon flies, and is often found among rock etchings throughout the plateau [Arizona]. The dragon flies have always been held in great veneration by the Mokis and their ancestors, as they have been often sent by Oman to reopen springs which Muingwa had destroyed and to confer other benefits upon the people.

This form of the figure, with little vertical lines added to the transverse lines, connects the Batolatci with the Ho-bo-bo emblems. The youth who was sacrificed and translated by Ho-bo-bo reappeared a long time afterwards, during a season of great drought, in the form of a gigantic dragon fly, who led the rain clouds over the lands of Ho-pi-tu, bringing plenteous rains.

Fig. 322

FIGURES OF CROSSES AS USED BY THE ESKIMO TO REPRESENT FLOCKS OF BIRDS.

Tenth Annual Report of the Bureau of Ethnology, fig. 1228.

Cat. Nos. 44211 and 45020, U. S. N. M.

Midē' or Shamans.—Colonel Mallery (or Dr. Hoffman) tells us (p. 726) that among the Ojibways of northern Minnesota the cross is one of the sacred symbols of the Society of Midē' or Shamans and has special reference to the fourth degree. The building in which the initiation is carried on has its opening toward the four cardinal points. The cross is made of saplings, the upright poles approaching the height of four to six feet, the transverse arms being somewhat shorter, each being of the same length as the top; the upper parts are painted white or besmeared with white clay, over which are spread small spots of red, the latter suggesting the sacred shell of Midē', the symbol of the order. The lower arm of the pole is square, the side toward the east being painted white to denote the source of light and warmth; the face on the south is green, denoting the source of the thunder bird which brings the rains and vegetation; the surface

Fig. 323.

PETROGLYPH FROM TULARE VALLEY, CALIFORNIA.

Large white Greek cross.

Tenth Annual Report of the Bureau of Ethnology, fig. 1229.

toward the west is covered with vermilion, relating to the land of the setting sun, the abode of the dead; the north is painted black, as the direction from which comes affliction, cold, and hunger.

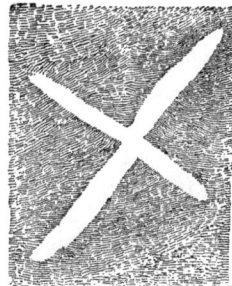

Flocks of birds.—Groups of small crosses on the sides of Eskimo bow drills represent flocks of birds (Cat. Nos. 45020 and 44211, U.S.N.M.). They are reproduced in fig. 322. Colonel Mallery's fig. 28, page 67, represents a cross copied from the Najowe Valley group of colored pictographs, 40 miles west of Santa Barbara, Santa Barbara County, Cal.

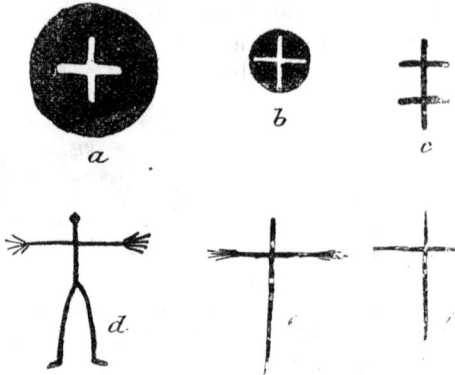

Fig. 324.

PETROGLYPHS FROM OWENS VALLEY, CALIFORNIA.

(a, b) Greek crosses, (c) double Latin cross, (d–f) Latin crosses representing human figures.

Tenth Annual Report of the Bureau of Ethnology, fig. 1230.

The cross measured 20 inches in length, the interior being painted black while the border is of a dark red tint. This design, as well as others in close connection, is painted on the walls of a shallow cave or rock shelter in the limestone formation. Fourteen miles west of Santa Barbara, on the summit of the Santa Ynez Mountains, is a cavern having a large opening west and north, in which are crosses of the Greek type, the interior portion being painted a dull earthy red, while the outside line is a faded-black tint. The cross measures nearly a foot in extent. At the Tulare Indian Agency, Cal., is an immense bowlder of granite. It has been split, and one of the lower quarters has been moved sufficiently to leave a passageway six feet wide and nearly ten feet high. The interior walls are well covered with large painted figures, while upon the ceilings are numerous forms of animals, birds, and insects. Among this latter group is a white cross about 18 inches in length (fig. 323), presenting a unique appearance, for the reason that it is the only petroglyph in that region to which the white coloring matter has been applied.

An interesting example of rock sculpturing in groups is in Owens Valley, south of Benton, Cal. Among them are various forms of crosses, and circles containing crosses of simple and complex types. The most interesting in this connection are the groups in fig. 324, a and b. The larger one, a, occurs upon a large bowlder of tracite 16 miles south of Benton, at the "Chalk grave." The circle is a depression about one inch in depth, the cross being in high relief. The small cross b, found three miles north from this is almost identical, the arms of the cross, however, extending to the rim of the circle. In this locality occurs also the cross, c, same figure, and some examples having more than two cross arms.

Fig. 325.

CROSS IN ZIGZAG LINES REPRESENTING THE HUMAN FORM.

Navajo Indians.

Human forms.—Other simple crosses represent the human form.

Some of these are engraved or cut on the rocks of Owens Valley and are similar to those above described (fig. 324), but they have been eroded, so that beyond the mere cross they show slight relation to the human body (fig. 324, d, e, f). Col. James Stevenson, describing the Hasjelti ceremony of the Navajoes,[1] shows the form of a man drawn in the sand (fig. 325). Describing the character shown in fig. 326, Keam says: "The figure represents a woman. The breath is displayed in the interior."[2]

Fig. 326.
MALTESE CROSS(?)
REPRESENTING A
WOMAN.
The figure in the
center is in-
tended to indi-
cate the breath.

Maidenhood.—Concerning fig. 327 Keam, in his manuscript, says the Maltese cross was the emblem of a virgin, and is still so recognized by the Moki. It is a conventional development of the common emblem of maidenhood, wherein the maidens wear their hair arranged as in a disk three or four inches in diameter on each side of the head (fig. 327 b). This discoidal arrangement of the hair is typical of the emblem of fructification worn by the virgin in the Muingwa festival. Sometimes the hair, instead of being worn in the complete discoidal form, is dressed upon two curving twigs, and presents the form of two semicircles upon each side of the head. The partition of these is sometimes horizontal, sometimes vertical. The combination of these styles (fig. 327a and b) present the forms from which the Maltese cross was conventionalized.[3]

a   b
Fig. 327.

MALTESE AND SAINT ANDREW'S
CROSSES.

Emblems of maidenhood.
Moki Indians.

Shaman's spirit.—Among the Kiatéxamut and Innuit tribes, a cross placed on the head, as in fig. 328, signified a shaman's evil spirit or demon. This is an imaginary being under the control of the shaman to execute his wishes.[4]

Divers significations.—The figure of the cross among the North American Indians, says Colonel Mallery,[5] has many differing sig-

Fig. 328.
CROSS WITH
BIFURCATED
FOOT.
Used by the
Innuits to
represent a
shaman or
evil spirit.

nifications. It appears "as the tribal sign for Cheyenne" (p. 383); "as Dakota lodges" (p. 582); "as a symbol for trade or exchange" (p. 613); "as a conventional sign for prisoners" (p. 227); "for personal exploits while elsewhere it is used in simple enumeration" (p. 348). Although this device is used for a variety of meanings when it is employed ceremonially or in elaborate pictographs of the Indians both of North and South America, it represents the four winds. This view long ago was suggested as being the signification of many Mexican crosses, and it is

---

[1] Eighth Ann. Rep. Bureau of Ethnology, p. 283.
[2] Tenth Ann. Rep. Bureau of Ethnology, 1888–89, fig. 1165.
[3] Ibid., fig. 1232.
[4] Ibid., fig. 1231.
[5] Ibid., p. 729.

sustained by Prof. Cyrus Thomas in his "Notes on Mayan Mexican Manuscript,"[1] where strong confirmatory evidence is produced by the arms of the crosses having the appearance of conventionalized wings similar to some representations of the thunder bird of the northern tribes; yet the same author, in his paper on the study of the "Troano Manuscript,"[2] gives fig. 329 as a symbol for wood. thus further showing the manifold concepts attached to the general form of the cross. Bandelier thinks that the cross so frequently used by the aborigines of Mexico and Central America were merely ornaments and not objects of worship, while the so-called crucifixes, like that on the Palenque tablet, were only the symbol of the "new fire," or the close of the period of fifty-two years. He believes them to be representations of the fire drills more or less ornamented. Zamacois[3] says that the cross was used in the religion of various tribes of the peninsula of Yucatan, and that it represented the god of rain.

Fig. 329.

ST. ANDREW'S CROSSES, USED AS A SYMBOL FOR WOOD.

Tenth Annual Report of the Bureau of Ethnology, fig. 1233.

It is a favorite theory with Major Powell, Director of the Bureau of Ethnology, that the cross was an original invention of the North American Indian, possibly a sign common to all savages; that it represented, first, the four cardinal points, north, south, east, and west; and afterwards by accretion, seven points, north, south, east, west, zenith, nadir, and here.

Capt. John G. Bourke, in his paper on the "Medicine Men of the Apache"[4] discourses on their symbolism of the cross. He says it is related to the cardinal points, to the four winds, and is painted by warriors on their moccasins when going through a strange district to keep them from getting on a wrong trail. He notes how he saw, in October, 1884, a procession of Apache men and women bearing two crosses, 4 feet 10 inches long, appropriately decorated "in honor of Guzanutli to induce her to send rain."

Dr. Brinton[5] tells of the rain maker of the Lenni Lenape who first drew on the earth the figure of a cross. Captain Bourke quotes from Father Le Clerq[6] as to the veneration in which the cross was held by the Gaspesian Indians, also from Herrara to the same effect. Professor Holmes[7] makes some pertinent observations with regard to the meanings of the cross given by the American Indians:

Some very ingenious theories have been elaborated in attempting to account for the cross among American symbols. Brinton believes that the great importance attached to the points of the compass—the four quarters of the heavens—by savage

[1] Second Ann. Rep. Bureau of Ethnology, p. 61.
[2] Contrib. North American Ethnology, v, p. 144.
[3] "Historia de Mexico," I, p. 238.
[4] Ninth Ann. Rep. Bureau of Ethnology, 1887–88, p. 479.
[5] "Myths of the New World," p. 96.
[6] "Gaspesi," London, 1691, pp. 170, 172, 199.
[7] Second Ann. Rep. Bureau of Ethnology, 1880–81, p. 270.

peoples, has given rise to the sign of the cross. With others, the cross is a phallic symbol derived, by some obscure process of evolution, from the veneration accorded to the procreative principle in nature. It is also frequently associated with sun worship, and is recognized as a symbol of the sun—the four arms being remaining rays after a gradual process of elimination. Whatever is finally determined in reference to the origin of the cross as a religious symbol in America will probably result from exhaustive study of the history, language, and art of the ancient peoples, combined with a thorough knowledge of the religious conceptions of modern tribes, and when these sources of information are all exhausted it is probable that the writer who asserts more than a probability will overreach his proofs. * * * A study of the de-

Fig. 330.

GRAPHIC DELINEATION OF ALLIGATOR.

From a vase of the lost color group.

Chiriqui.

Sixth Annual Report of the Bureau of Ethnology, fig. 257.

signs associated with the cross in these gorgets [figs. 302-304] is instructive, but does not lead to any definite result; in one case the cross is inscribed on the back of a great spider [figs. 275-278]; in another it is surrounded by a rectangular framework of lines, looped at the corners and guarded by four mysterious birds [figs. 263-266], while in others it is without attendant characters, but the workmanship is purely aboriginal. I have not seen a single example of engraving upon the shell that suggested a foreign hand, or a design, with the exception of this one [a cross], that could claim a European derivation. * * * Such delineations of the cross as we find embodied in ancient aboriginal art, represent only the final stages of its evolution, and it is not to be expected that its origin can be traced through them.

Continuing in his "Ancient Art in Chiriqui,"[1] presenting his " Series showing stages in the simplification of animal characters," and " derivation of the alligator," Professor Holmes elaborates the theory how the alligator was the original, and out of it, by evolution, grew the cross. His language and accompanying figures are quoted:

Fig. 331.

GRAPHIC DELINEATION OF ALLIGATOR.

From a vase of the lost color group.

Chiriqui.

Sixth Annual Report of the Bureau of Ethnology, fig. 258.

Of all the animal forms utilized by the Chiriquians, the alligator is the best suited to the purpose of this study, as it is presented most frequently and in the most varied forms. In figs. 257 and 258 [figs. 330 and 33 in the present paper] I reproduce drawings from the outer surface of a tripod bowl of the lost color group. Simple and formal as these figures are, the characteristic features of the creature—the sinuous body, the strong jaws, the upturned snout, the feet, and the scales—are forcibly expressed. It is not to be assumed that these examples represent the best delineative skill of the Chiriquian artist. The native painter must have executed very

---

[1] Sixth Ann. Rep. Bureau of Ethnology, p. 173 et seq., figs. 257-278.

much superior work upon the more usual delineating surfaces, such as bark and skins. The examples here shown have already experienced decided changes through the constraints of the ceramic art, but are the most graphic delineations preserved to us. They are free-hand products, executed by mere decorators, perhaps by women, who were servile copyists of the forms employed by those skilled in sacred art.

Fig. 332.

CONVENTIONAL FIGURE OF ALLIGATOR.

From a vessel of the lost color group.

Chiriqui.

Sixth Annual Report of the Bureau of Ethnology, fig. 259.

A third illustration from the same group of ware, given in fig. 259 [fig. 332 of the present paper] shows, in some respects, a higher degree of convention. * * *

I shall now call attention to some important individualized or well-defined agencies of convention.

First, and most potent, may be mentioned the enforced limits of the spaces to be decorated, which spaces take shape independently of the subject to be inserted. When the figures must occupy a narrow zone, they are elongated; when they must occupy a square, they are restricted longitudinally, and when they occupy a circle, they are of necessity coiled up. Fig. 265 [fig. 333 of the present paper] illustrates the effect produced by crowding the oblong figure into a short rectangular space. The head is turned back over the body and the tail is thrown down along the side of the space. In fig. 266 [fig. 334 of the present paper] the figure occupies a circle and is, in consequence, closely coiled up, giving the effect of a serpent rather than an alligator. * * *

I present five series of figures designed to illustrate the stages through which life forms pass in descending from the realistic to highly specialized conventional shapes. In the first

Fig. 333.

CONVENTIONAL FIGURE OF ALLIGATOR CROWDED INTO A SMALL GEOMETRICAL FIGURE.

Chiriqui.

Sixth Annual Report of the Bureau of Ethnology, fig. 265.

Fig. 334.

CONVENTIONAL FIGURE OF ALLIGATOR CROWDED INTO A CIRCLE.

Chiriqui.

Sixth Annual Report of the Bureau of Ethnology, fig. 266.

series (fig. 277) [fig. 335 of the present paper] we begin with *a*, a meager but graphic sketch of the alligator; the second figure, *b*, is hardly less characteristic, but is much simplified; in the third, *c*, we have still three leading features of the creature— the body line, the spots, and the stroke at the back of the head; and in the fourth, *d*, nothing remains but a compound yoke-like curve, standing for the body of the creature, and a single dot.

The figures of the second series (fig. 278) [fig. 336 of the present paper] are nearly all painted upon low, round nodes placed about the body of the alligator vases, and hence are inclosed in circles. The animal figure in the first example is coiled up like a serpent [fig. 334], but still preserves some of the well-known characters of the alligator. In the second example [fig. 336 *b*] we have a double hook near the center of the space which takes the place of the body, but the dotted triangles are placed separately against the encircling line. In the next figure the body symbol is omitted and

the three triangles remain to represent the animal. In the fourth there are four triangles, and the body device being restored in red takes the form of a cross. In the fifth
two of the inclosing triangles are omitted and the idea is preserved by the simple
dots. In the sixth the dots are placed within the bars of the cross, the triangles
becoming mere interspaces, and in the seventh the dots form a line between the two
encircling lines. This series could be filled up by other examples, thus showing by

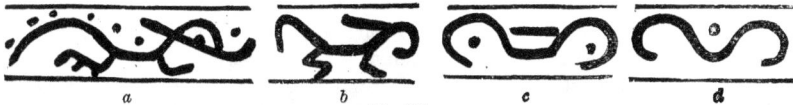

a   b   c   d
Fig. 335.

SERIES OF FIGURES OF ALLIGATORS SHOWING STAGES OF SIMPLIFICATION.

Chiriqui.

Sixth Annual Report of the Bureau of Ethnology, fig. 277.

what infinitesimal steps the transformations take place.   *   *   *

We learn by the series of steps illustrated in the annexed cuts that the alligator
radical, under peculiar restraints and influences, assumes conventional forms that
merge imperceptibly into these classic devices.

Professor Holmes's theory of the evolution of the cross from the alligator and its location in Chiriqui is opposed to that of Professor Good-

a   b   c   d

e   f   g
Fig. 336.

SERIES SHOWING STAGES IN THE SIMPLIFICATION OF ANIMAL CHARACTERS, BEGINNING WITH THE ALLI-
GATOR AND ENDING WITH THE GREEK CROSS.

Chiriqui.

Sixth Annual Report of the Bureau of Ethnology, fig. 278.

year, who, in his "Grammar of the Lotus," ascribes the origin of the
cross to the lotus and locates it in Egypt. I file what in law would be
an "interpleader"—I admit my want of knowledge of the subject
under discussion, and leave the question to these gentlemen.

INTRODUCTION OF THE CROSS INTO AMERICA.

Professor Holmes is, in the judgment of the author, correct when he insists upon the aboriginal character of the cross in America. We all understand how it is stated that the Spanish missionaries sought to deny this and to connect the apparition of St. Thomas with the appearance of the cross. Professor Holmes[1] says:

The first explorers were accompanied by Christian zealots who spared no effort to root out the native superstition and introduce a foreign religion of which the cross was the all-important symbol. This emblem was generally accepted by the savages as the only tangible feature of a new system of belief that was filled with subtleties too profound for their comprehension. As a result, the cross was at once introduced into the regalia of the natives, at first probably in a European form and material, attached to a string of beads in precisely the manner they had been accustomed to suspend their own trinkets and gorgets; but soon, no doubt, delineated or carved by their own hands upon tablets of stone and copper and shell in the place of their own peculiar conceptions.

There is sufficient evidence, and to spare, of the aboriginal use of the cross in some of its forms, without resorting to the uncertain and forced explanation of its introduction by Christian missionaries. It is possible that the priests and explorers were, like Colonel Mallery's missionary, mistaken as to the interpretation given to the cross by the Indians. Dr. Hoffman, in his paper on the "Midē'wiwin or Grand Medicine Society of the Ojibwa,"[2] states the myth of the re-creation of the world "as thrown together in a mangled form by Hennepin." Dr. Hoffman observes:

It is evident that the narrator has sufficiently distorted the traditions to make them conform as much as practicable to the Biblical story of the birth of Christ.

And on the same page he quotes from Père Marquette, who says:

"I was very glad to see a great cross set up in the middle of the village, adorned with several white skins, red girdles, bows, and arrows, which that good people offered to the Great Manitou to return him their thanks for the care he had taken of them during the winter, and that he had granted them a prosperous hunting."

Marquette [comments Dr. Hoffman] was, without doubt, ignorant of the fact that the cross is the sacred post, and the symbol of the fourth degree of the Midē'wiwin, as is fully explained in connection with that grade of society. The erroneous conclusion that the cross was erected as an evidence of the adoption of Christianity and, possibly as a compliment to the visitor was a natural one on the part of the priest, but this same symbol of the Midē' society had probably been erected and bedecked with barbaric emblems and weapons months before anything was known of him.

Most aboriginal objects bearing crosses are from localities along the Ohio River and through Kentucky and Tennessee, a locality which the early Christian missionaries never visited, and where the cross of Christ was rarely, if ever, displayed until after that territory became part of the United States. Per contra, the localities among the Indians in which the early missionaries most conducted their labors—that is to say, along the Great Lakes and throughout northern

---

[1] Second Ann. Rep. Bureau of Ethnology, p. 269.
[2] Seventh Ann. Rep. Bureau of Ethnology, p. 155.

Illinois—produce the fewest number of aboriginal crosses. This was the country explored by Fathers Marquette, Lasalle, and Hennepin, and it was the scene of most of the Catholic missionary labors. Professor Holmes seems to have recognized this fact, for he says:[1]

> The cross was undoubtedly used as a symbol by the prehistoric nations of the South, and, consequently, that it was probably also known in the North. A great majority of the relics associated with it in the ancient mounds and burial places are undoubtedly aboriginal. In the case of the shell gorgets, the tablets themselves belong to an American type, and are highly characteristic of the art of the Mississippi Valley. A majority of the designs engraved upon them are also characteristic of the same district.

The author agrees heartily with Professor Holmes's argument in this matter, and his conclusion, when he says of these objects (p. 270):

> The workmanship is purely aboriginal. I have not seen a single example of engraving upon shell that suggested a foreign hand or a design, with the exception of one (cross), that could claim a European derivation.

There have been numerous European or Catholic crosses, as well as many other objects of European manufacture or objects of civilized types, found among the Indians. There have been silver crosses found with images of the Virgin thereon, with Latin inscriptions, or of Roman letters; there have been glass beads, iron arrowheads, and divers other objects found in Indian graves which bore indubitable evidence of contact with the whites, and no one with any archæological experience need be deceived into the belief that these were aboriginal or pre-Columbian manufacture. As a general rule, the line of demarkation between objects of Indian manufacture and those made by the whites is definite, and no practiced eye will mistake the one for the other. There may be exceptions, as where the Indian has lived with the whites or a white man with the Indians, or where an object is made with intent to deceive. In such cases one may have more trouble in determining the origin of the object.

There were many Indians who died and were buried within a century past, whose graves might contain many objects of white man's work. Black Hawk and Red Jacket are examples, and, possibly, King Philip. Indian graves have been opened in New England and New York containing the gun or firelock of the occupant of the grave buried with him, and that this was evidence of European contact there can be no doubt. So there have been hundreds, possibly thousands, of Indians buried since the Columbian discovery down to within the last decade whose graves contain white man's tools or implements. But no person with any archæological experience need be deceived by these things. The theory that the Latin or Greek crosses or Swastikas shown on these gorgets, disks, and pottery furnish evidence of contact by the aborigines with Europeans in post-Columbian times is without foundation and inadmissible.

---

[1] Second Ann. Rep. Bureau of Ethnology, p. 269.

DECORATIVE FORMS NOT OF THE CROSS, BUT ALLIED TO THE SWASTIKA.

COLOR STAMPS FROM MEXICO AND VENEZUELA.

The aborigines of Mexico and Central and South America employed terra-cotta color stamps, which, being made into the proper pattern in

Fig. 337.

Fig. 338.

Fig. 339.

Fig. 340.

Fig. 341.

Fig. 342.

TERRA-COTTA COLOR STAMPS WITH DESIGNS SIMILAR TO THE SWASTIKA.
Mexico.
Cat. Nos. 99124, 99127, 27887, 99115, 99118, 99122, U. S. N. M.

the soft clay, were burned hard; then, being first coated with color, the stamp was pressed upon the object to be decorated, and so transferred its color, as in the mechanical operation of printing, thus giving the intended decoration. Patterns of these stamps are inserted in this paper in connection with the Swastika because of the resemblance—not in form, but in style. They are of geometric form, crosses, dots, circles (concentric and otherwise), lozenges, chevrons, fret, and labyrinth or meander. The style of this decoration lends itself easily to the Swastika; and yet, with the variety of patterns contained in the series of stamps belonging to the U. S. National Museum, shown in figs. 337 to 342, no Swastika appears; nor in the similar stamps belonging to other collections, notably that of Mr. A. E. Douglass, in the Metropolitan Museum of Natural History, Central Park, New York, are any Swastikas shown. Of the foregoing figures, all are from Tlaltelolco, Mexico (Blake collection), except fig. 339, which is from the Valley of Mexico, and was received from the Museo Nacional of Mexico.

Marcano says:[1]

The present Piaroas of Venezuela are in the habit of painting their bodies by a process different from that of the North American Indian. They make stamps of wood, which, being colored (as types are with ink), they apply to their bodies.

Fig. 343.

TERRA-COTTA COLOR STAMPS WITH DESIGNS SIMILAR TO THE SWASTIKA.

Piaroa Indians, Venezuela.

Tenth Annual Report of the Bureau of Ethnology, fig. 982.

Fig. 982 shows examples of these stamps. [See fig. 343 of the present paper.] The designs are substantially the same as some petroglyphs. They either copied the models they found carved on the rocks by peoples who preceded them, or they knew the meaning and preserved the tradition. The former is the only tenable hypothesis. Painting is to the Piaroas, both ornamentation and necessity. It serves, not only as a garment to protect them against insects, but becomes a fancy costume to grace their feasts and meetings.

These designs are not presented as Swastikas nor of any evolution or derivation from one. They show a style common enough to Central and South America, to the Antilles and the Canary Islands,[2] which might easily produce a Swastika. The aboriginal designer of these might, if we depend upon the theory of psychological similarity of culture among all peoples, at his next attempt make a Swastika. Yet, with the hundreds of similar patterns made during the centuries of aboriginal occupation and extending throughout the countries named, none of these seem ever to have produced a Swastika.

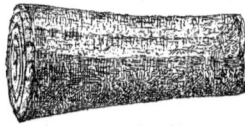

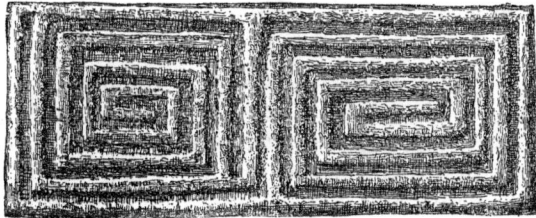

---

[1]Mem. Soc. d'Anthrop., Paris, 1890, p. 200.

[2]De Quatrefages, "Histoire Générale du Races Humaines," Introduction, p. 239, figs. 185-191, 193-194.

V.—SIGNIFICANCE OF THE SWASTIKA.

The origin and early history of the Swastika are lost in antiquity. All the author has been able to find on these subjects is set forth in the preceding chapters.

It is proposed to examine the possible uses of the Swastika in an endeavor to discover something of its significance. The Swastika might have served:

> I. As a symbol—
>> 1, of a religion,
>> 2, of a nation or people,
>> 3, of a sect with peculiar tenets;
> II. As an amulet or charm—
>> 1, of good luck, or fortune, or long life,
>> 2, of benediction, or blessing,
>> 3, against the evil eye;
> III. As an ornament or decoration.

It may have been (1) originally discovered or invented by a given people in a given country, and transmitted from one generation to the next, passing by migration from one country to another, and it may have been transmitted by communication to widely separated countries and among differently cultured peoples; or (2) it may have appeared in these latter countries by duplicate invention or by accident, and without contact or communication.

Positive evidence concerning its origin and earliest migration is not obtainable, and in its absence we are driven to secondary and circumstantial evidence. This will consist (1) of comparison of known facts directly concerning the subject; (2) of facts indirectly concerning it, and (3) reason, induced by argument, applied to these facts, presenting each truly, and giving to each its proper weight.

The possible migrations of the Swastika, and its appearance in widely separated countries and among differently cultured peoples, afford the principal interest in this subject to archæologists and anthropologists. The present or modern scientific interest in and investigation of the Swastika as a symbol or a charm alone are subsidiary to the greater question of the cause and manner of its appearance in different countries, whether it was by migration and contact or by independent invention. In arguing this question, we must keep continually in mind the rules of reason and of logic, and neither force the facts nor seek to explain them by unknown, imaginary, or impossible methods. There must be no dogmatic assertions nor fanciful theories. If we assume certain migrations of the Swastika, we must consider those things which might have (or must have) migrated with it; and we must admit the means necessary to the assumed end.

The history of the beginning and first appearance of any of the forms of the cross is also lost in antiquity, and it would be hazardous for any person to announce positively their origin, either as to locality or time. The Swastika was certainly prehistoric in its origin. It was in extensive use during the existence of the third, fourth, and fifth cities of the site of ancient Troy, of the hill of Hissarlik; so also in the Bronze Age, apparently during its entire existence, throughout western Europe from the Mediterranean Sea to the Arctic Ocean. It continued in use in Europe during the Iron Age, and also among the Etruscans, Greeks, and Trojans. The name " Swastika," by which it is recognized to-day in all literature, is a Sanscrit word, and was in common use among the Sanscrit peoples so long ago that it had a peculiar or individual pronunciation in Pânini's grammar prior to the fourth century B. C. Some authorities are of the opinion that it was an Aryan symbol and used by the Aryan peoples before their dispersion through Asia and Europe. This is a fair subject for inquiry and might serve as an explanation how, either as a sacred symbol or charm, an amulet, or token of good wishes or good fortune, the Swastika might have been carried to the different peoples and countries in which we now find it by the splitting up of the Aryan peoples and their migrations and establishment in the various parts of Europe. Professor Sayce is of the opinion that the Swastika was a Hittite symbol and passed by communication to the Aryans or some of their important branches before their final dispersion took place, but he agrees that it was unknown in Assyria, Babylonia, Phenicia, or among the Egyptians.

Whether the Swastika was in use among the Chaldeans, Hittites, or the Aryans before or during their dispersion, or whether it was used by the Brahmins before the Buddhists came to India is, after all, but a matter of detail of its migrations; for it may be fairly contended that the Swastika was in use, more or less common among the people of the Bronze Age anterior to either the Chaldeans, Hittites, or the Aryans. The additional facts in this regard have been set forth in the chapter on this subject, and need not be repeated here.

The question should, so far as possible, be divested of speculation, and the evidence accepted in its ordinary meaning "without prejudice or preconceived opinion."

A consideration of the subject in the light of the material here collected develops the following questions:

(1) Was the Swastika, in any of its forms, the symbol of an ancient religion or philosophy, or was it only the sign of a particular sect, tenet, faith, or idea; or was it both?

(2) Was it a charm or amulet to be used by anyone which derived its value from the signification given to it?

(3) What lesson can be gathered from it concerning the early migrations of the races of man?

Examples illustrating these questions are to be found in history as well as in everyday life. The Scarabæus of Egypt and Etruria was a symbol of eternity. The golden hoop on the lady's finger representing a snake swallowing its tail, is also a symbol of eternity. These represent a sentiment, and are symbols of that sentiment without regard to sect or organized body.

On the other hand, the Maltese cross was the symbol of the Knights of Malta, and has become, in later years, that of the Masonic fraternity; while the three links is the symbol of the Order of Odd Fellows. The Latin cross is a symbol of the Christian religion and, to a certain extent, of a Christian denomination.

Upon the evidence submitted, we must accept the Swastika first as a symbol of that sect of Jains within the Buddhist Church originally in Tibet, which spread itself in the Asiatic country under the names of Tao-sse, Tirthankara, Ter, Musteg, and Pon or Pon-po, the last signifying purity (ante, p. 774). This sect, or these sects, adopted the Swastika as their symbol, giving it the translation *su* "well," *asti*, "it is," the whole word meaning "it is well," or "so be it," implying resignation under all circumstances, the sect holding, in accordance with the meaning given to their symbol, that contentment and peace of mind were the chief objects of human life. In so far as it concerns this sect, the Swastika was a symbol of both kinds. It represented a religious or at least a moral and philosophic idea, and also the sect which held to this idea.

Among the Buddhists proper, the Swastika seems to have been employed as a holy or sacred symbol; its occurrence as one of the signs in the footprint of Buddha, their founder, with some relation either to the mystery of his appearance as a leader, a missionary, or of the holy and sacred object of his mission, causes this to be inferred. Their use of it on the bronze statues of Buddha, and associating it with solemn inscriptions in the caves of India, leaves no doubt as to its use as a symbol more or less of this character.

Again, the use in the early Christian times of different forms of the cross, coupled with the extensive use by the Christians of the "monogram of Christ" (fig. 6), shows how naturally there may have been a conflict of opinion in the selection of a cross which should be a representative, while we know from history that there was such discussion, and that different forms of the cross were suggested. Among other forms was the Swastika, but to what extent or with what idea the author is not informed. The Swastika was used, Burnouf says, a thousand times on Christians' tombs in the catacombs at Rome. This is evidence of its use to a certain extent in a sacred or solemn and funereal character, which would signify its use as the symbol of a religious idea.

Beyond these instances the author is unable to find evidence of the Swastika having served as a symbol of any religious or philosophic idea or of any sect or organization.

Whether among the Bronze Age people of western Europe—among the Trojans, Greeks, or Etruscans—whether among the semicivilized peoples of South or Central America, or among the savages (mound-builders) of North America, there is apparently no instance of the Swastika having been regarded as holy or used on a sacred object—that is, holy and sacred in the light of godliness, piety, or morality. It may have been or may yet be discovered that some of these wild men used the Swastika upon objects serving at ceremonies or festivals of their religion, or which had, in their eyes, a semi-sacred character. But it does not seem that it was used as a representative of a holy idea or of any god or supernatural being who stood for such an idea. The meal used in the Zuñi ceremony may have been regarded as sacred, and it may, indeed must, have been made on a stone metate, yet neither the metate nor the stone thereby obtained any holy or sacred character. So, also, it may have been decorated with a fret, chevron, herringbone, or any of the numerous styles, none of which would receive any sacred character from such use. So it is believed to have been with the Swastika found on these objects; it was not holy or sacred because of this use.

The author declines to discuss the possible relation of the Swastika to the sun or sun god, to the rain or rain god, the lightning, to Dyaus, Zeus or Agni, to Phebus or Apollo, or other of the mythological deities. This question would be interesting if it could be determined with certainty, or if the determination would be accepted by any considerable number of persons. But this is left for some one more competent and more interested than the author.

The most probable use of the Swastika among prehistoric peoples, or among Orientals other than the Buddhists, was as a charm or amulet signifying good fortune, good luck, long life, or benediction and blessing.[1] (See p. 780.)

Looking over the entire prehistoric world, we find the Swastika used on small and comparatively insignificant objects, those in common use, such as vases, pots, jugs, implements, tools, household goods and utensils, objects of the toilet, ornaments, etc., and infrequently on statues, altars, and the like. In Armenia it was found on bronze pins and buttons; in the Trojan cities on spindle-whorls; in Greece on pottery, on gold and bronze ornaments, and fibulæ. In the Bronze Age in western Europe, including Etruria, it is found on the common objects of life, such as pottery, the bronze fibulæ, ceintures, spindle-whorls, etc.

In addition to the foregoing, there were peculiar uses of the Swastika in certain localities: In Italy on the hut urns in which the ashes of the dead are buried; in the Swiss lakes stamped in the pottery; in Scandinavia on the weapons, swords, etc., and in Scotland and Ireland on the brooches and pins; in America on the metates for grinding corn; the Brazilian women wore it on the pottery fig leaf; the Pueblo Indian painted it on his dance rattle, while the North American Indian, at the epoch of the mound building in Arkansas and Missouri, painted it in spiral form on his pottery; in Tennessee he engraved it on the shell, and

---

[1] Goblet d'Alviella, "La Migration des Symboles," pp. 56, 57.

in Ohio cut it in its plainest normal form out of sheets of copper. So also among the modern Indians we find it employed on occasions of ceremony, as in the mountain chant by the Navajoes, and the war chant of the Kansas, on the necklace and ceremonial garters of the Sac woman, and on the war shields of the Pimas.

As we do not find it represented in America on aboriginal religious monuments, on ancient gods, idols, or other sacred or holy objects, we are justified in claiming that it was not here used as a religious symbol; while, as it is found only on trinkets, shells, copper plaques, spindle-whorls, metates, pottery bowls, jugs, bottles, or vases; as we find it sometimes square, sometimes spiral, now outside, now inside, of bowls and jars, etc.; at one time a small rectangular figure and at another of extensive convolutions covering the side of the vase; as we find it on the tools of the workmen, the objects in everyday use, whether in the house or the shop, used indiscriminately by men and women, or on gaming implements or dance rattles, the contention seems justifiable that it was used as an ornament or as a charm for good luck and not as a religious symbol. Yet we know it was used on certain ceremonial occasions which may themselves have had more or less a sacred character.

Thus, after the fullest examination, we find the Swastika was confined to the commoner uses, implements, household utensils, and objects for the toilet and personal decoration. The specimens of this kind number a hundred to one of a sacred kind. With this preponderance in favor of the common use, it would seem that, except among the Buddhists and early Christians, and the more or less sacred ceremonies of the North American Indians, all pretense of the holy or sacred character of the Swastika should be given up, and it should (still with these exceptions) be considered as a charm, amulet, token of good luck or good fortune, or as an ornament and for decoration.

VI.—THE MIGRATION OF SYMBOLS.

MIGRATION OF THE SWASTIKA.

The question of the migration of the Swastika and of the objects on which it was marked, which furnished its only means of transportation, remains to be considered. It is proposed to examine, in a cursory manner perhaps, not only the migration of the Swastika itself, but some of these objects, spindle-whorls especially, with a view to discover by similarity or peculiarity of form or decoration any relationship they may have had with each other when found in distant countries and used by different peoples. Thus, we may be able to open the way to a consideration of the question whether this similarity of Swastikas or other decorations, or of the objects on which they were placed, resulted from the migration of or contact or communication between distant peoples, or was it accidental and the result of independent discoveries and duplicate inventions—an evidence of the parallelism of human thought?

Dr. Brinton, in a communication before the American Philosophical Society,[1] starts out with a polemical discussion upon the subject of the migration of the Swastika and its possible American migration, as follows:

My intention is to combat the opinion of those writers who, like Dr. Hamy, M. Beauvois, and many others, assert that because certain well-known Oriental symbols, as the Ta Ki, the Triskeles, the Svastika, and the cross, are found among the American aborigines, they are evidence of Mongolian, Buddhistic, Christian, or Aryan immigrations previous to the discovery by Columbus, and I shall also try to show that the position is erroneous of those who, like William H. Holmes, of the Bureau of Ethnology, maintain "that it is impossible to give a satisfactory explanation of the religious significance of the cross as a religious symbol in America."

In opposition to both these views, I propose to show that the primary significance of all these widely extended symbols is quite clear, and that they can be shown to have arisen from certain fixed relations of man to his environment, the same everywhere, and hence suggesting the same graphic representations among tribes most divergent in location and race, and, therefore, that such symbols are of little value in tracing ethnic affinities or the currents of civilization.

I am sorry to be compelled to differ with Dr. Brinton in these views. I may not attempt much argument upon this branch of the subject, but whatever argument is presented will be in opposition to this view, as not being borne out by the evidence. Of course, the largest portion of the discussion of this subject must consist of theory and argument, but such facts as are known, when subjected to an analysis of reason, seem to produce a result contrary to that announced by Dr. Brinton.

It is conceded that the duplication of the cross by different or distant peoples is no evidence of migrations of or contact between these peoples, however close their relations might have been. The sign of the cross itself was so simple, consisting of only two marks or pieces intersecting each other at a right or other angle, that we may easily suppose it to have been the result of independent invention. The same conclusion has been argued with regard to the Swastika. But this is a *non sequitur*.

First, I dispute the proposition of fact that the Swastika is, like the cross, a simple design—one which would come to the mind of any person and would be easy to make. For evidence of this, I cite the fact that it is not in common use, that it is almost unknown among Christian peoples, that it is not included in any of the designs for, nor mentioned in any of the modern European or American works on, decoration, nor is it known to or practiced by artists or decorators of either country.[2] For the truth of this, I appeal to the experience of artists and decora-

[1] Proc. Am. Philosoph. Soc., xxvi, p. 177.

[2] For general lack of knowledge of Swastika in modern times, see Preface, p. 763.

tors, and would put the question whether, of their own knowledge, by their own inventions, they have ever discovered or made Swastikas, or whether their brother artists have done so, and if they answer in the affirmative, I would ask whether those cases were not rare. It may be granted that when the Swastika has been seen by an artist or decorator it is easily understood and not difficult to execute, but, nevertheless, I insist that its invention and use among artists and decorators during the centuries since the Rennaissance is rare.

It is argued by Zmigrodzki that the Swastika on so many specimens, especially the Trojan spindle-whorls, having been made regularly, sometimes turning one way, sometimes another, sometimes square, other times curved, goes to show the rapidity with which the sign was made, that it did not require an artist, that its use was so common that it had become a habit and was executed in a rapid and sketchy manner, as evidenced by the appearance of the marks themselves upon the whorls. He likens this to the easy and unconsidered way which men have of signing their names, which they are able to do without attention. He likens it also to the sign of the cross made by Roman Catholics so rapidly as to be unnoticed by those who are unaware of its significance. With this line of argument, Zmigrodzki reasons that the Swastika was in its time confined to common use and thus he accounts for the number of ill-formed specimens. This only accounts for the comparatively few ill-formed specimens, but not for the great number, the mass of those well formed and well drawn. Instead of the Swastika being a sign easily made, the experience of the writer is the contrary. A simple cross like the Latin, Greek, St. Andrew's, and other common forms may be very easy to make, but a really good specimen of the Swastika is difficult to make. Any one who doubts this has only to make the experiment for himself, and make correctly such a specimen as fig. 9. While it may be easy enough to make the Greek cross with two lines of equal length intersecting each other at right angles, and while this forms a large proportion of the Swastikas, it is at its conclusion that the trouble of making a perfect Swastika begins. It will be found difficult, requiring care and attention, to make the projecting arms of equal length, to see that they are all at the same angle; and if it is bent again and again, two or three turns upon each other, the difficulty increases. If a person thinks that the Swastika, either in the square or the ogee curves or the spiral volutes, is easy to make, he has but to try it with paper and pencil, and, if that is his first attempt, he will soon be convinced of his error. The artist who drew the spirals for this paper pronounces them to be the most difficult of all; the curves are parabolic, no two portions of any one are in the same circle, the circle continually widens, and no two circles nor any two portions of the same circle have the same center. To keep these lines true and parallel, the curve regular, the distances the same, and at the same time sweeping outward in the spiral form, the artist pro-

nounces a most difficult work, requiring care, time, and attention (fig.
295). Even the square and meander Swastikas (figs. 10, 11) require a
rule and angle to make them exact. All this goes to show the intention
of the artist to have been more or less deliberate; and that the object
he made was for a special purpose, with a particular idea, either as a
symbol, charm, or ornament, and not a meaningless figure to fill a vacant
space.

Yet it is practically this difficult form of the cross which appears to
have spread itself through the widest culture areas, extending almost
to the uttermost parts of the earth. All this is foundation for the
suggestion that the Swastika was not the result of duplicate invention
or independent discovery, that it is not an illustration of parallelism
in human thought, but that it was transmitted from person to person,
or passed from one country to another, either by the migration of its
people, by their contact or communication, or by the migration and
transmission of the symbol and the sign itself. Pushing the argument
of the difficulty of its making, to account for the rarity of the design,
it is alleged that in modern times the Swastika is practically unknown
among Christian peoples. It passed out of use among them nigh a
thousand years ago and has been supplanted by every other imaginable
geometric form. The fret, chevron, herringbone, crosses, and circles
of every kind, spirals, volutes, ogees, moldings, etc., have all remained
in use since neolithic times, but no Swastika. The latest use mentioned in the literature upon this subject appears to have been in the
arch-Episcopal chair in the cathedral at Milan, which bears the three
ancient Christian crosses, the Latin cross, the monogram of Christ, and
the Swastika, of which the first and last are carved in alternates around
the pedestal of the chair. Yet the knowledge of the Swastika has
been perpetuated in some countries and its use has not died out all
over the world; therefore, examples of its use in modern times should
be noted in order to prevent misapprehension and contradiction. The
double Greek fret made with two continuous lines (fig. 139) forms a
psuedo Swastika at each intersection, although we have seen that this
is not a real but only an apparent Swastika (p. 783). This is used in
modern times by carpet and linen weavers as borders for carpets and
tablecloths, and by tile makers in similar decoration. The Swastika
mark has continued in use among the Orientals; the Theosophists have
adopted it as a seal or insignia; the Japanese (fig. 30), the Koreans
(p. 799), the Chinese (fig. 31), the Jains (figs. 33, 34), and, among the
North American Indians, the Navajo (pl. 17), and those of the Kansas
Reservation (pls. 15 and 16). It is not used by European peoples in
modern times, except in Lapland and Finland. The National Museum
has lately received a collection of modern household and domestic
utensils from Lapland, some of which bear the marks of the cross and
one a churn, the lid of which bears a possible Swastika mark. Through
the kindness of Professor Mason and Mr. Cushing, I have received a

drawing of this (fig. 344). Theodor Schvindt, in "Suomalaisia koris-
teita,"[1] a book of standard national Finnish patterns for the embroideries of the country, gives the Swastika among others; but it is classed
among "oblique designs" and no mention is made of it as a Swastika
or of any character corresponding to it. Its lines are always at angles
of 45 degrees, and are continually referred to as "oblique designs."

The Swastika ornaments Danish baptismal fonts, and according to Mr. J. A. Hjal-
talin it "was used [in Iceland] a few years since as a magic sign, but with an
obscured or corrupted meaning." It arrived in that island in the ninth century
A. D.[2]

The Swastika mark appears both in its normal and ogee form in the
Persian carpets and rugs.[3] While writing this memoir, I have found
in the Persian rug in my own bedchamber sixteen figures of the Swastika. In the large rug in the chief clerk's office of the National Museum
there are no less than twenty-seven figures of the Swastika. On a
piece of imitation Persian carpet, with a heavy pile, made probably in

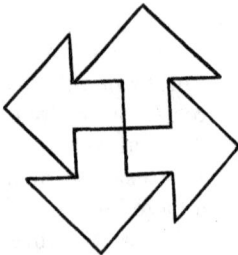

Fig. 344.
MODERN CHURN LID WITH DE-
SIGN RESEMBLING SWASTIKA.
Lapland.
U. S. National Museum.

London, I found also figures of the Swastika.
All the foregoing figures have been of the normal
Swastika, the arms crossing each other and the
ends turning at right angles, the lines being of
equal thickness throughout. Some of them were
bent to the right and some to the left. At the
entrance of the Grand Opera House in Washington I saw a large India rug containing a number
of ogee Swastikas; while the arms crossed each
other at right angles, they curved, some to the
right and some to the left, but all the lines increased in size, swelling in the middle of the
curve, but finishing in a point. The modern
Japanese wisteria workbaskets for ladies have
one or more Swastikas woven in their sides or covers.

Thus, it appears that the use of the Swastika in modern times is confined principally to Oriental and Scandinavian countries, countries
which hold close relations to antiquity; that, in western Europe, where
in ancient times the Swastika was most frequent, it has, during the
last one or two thousand years, become extinct. And this in the countries which have led the world in culture.

If the Swastika was a symbol of a religion in India and migrated as
such in times of antiquity to America, it was necessarily by human aid.
The individuals who carried and taught it should have carried with it
the religious idea it represented. To do this required a certain use of
language, at least the name of the symbol. If the sign bore among the

[1] Finnische Ornamente. 1. Stichornamente. Heft 1-4. Soumalaisen Kirjallis-
uuden Seura Helsingissä, 1894.
[2] Karl Blind, "Discovery of Odinic songs in Shetland," Nineteenth Century, June,
1879, p. 1098, cited by Alfred C. Haddon in "Evolution in Art," London, 1895, p. 285.
[3] Miss Fanny D. Bergen, in Scribner's Magazine, September, 1894.

aborigines in America the name it bore in India, Swastika, the evidence of contact and communication would be greatly strengthened. If the religion it represented in India should be found in America, the chain of evidence might be considered complete. But in order to make it so it will be necessary to show the existence of these names and this religion in the same locality or among the same people or their descendants as is found the sign. To find traces of the Buddhist religion associated with the sign of the Swastika among the Eskimo in Alaska might be no evidence of its prehistoric migration, for this might have occurred in modern times, as we know has happened with the Russian religion and the Christian cross. While to find the Buddhist religion and the Swastika symbol together in America, at a locality beyond the possibility of modern European or Asiatic contact, would be evidence of prehistoric migration yet it would seem to fix it at a period when, and from a country where, the two had been used together. If the Swastika and Buddhism migrated to America together it must have been since the establishment of the Buddhist religion, which is approximately fixed in the sixth century B. C. But there has not been as yet in America, certainly not in the localities where the Swastika has been found, any trace discovered of the Buddhist religion, nor of its concomitants of language, art, or custom. Adopting the theory of migration of the Swastika, we may therefore conclude that if the Swastika came from India or Eastern Asia, it came earlier than the sixth century B. C.

If a given religion with a given symbol, both belonging to the Old World, should both be found associated in the New World, it would be strong evidence in favor of Old World migration—certainly of contact and communication. Is it not equally strong evidence of contact to find the same sign used in both countries as a charm, with the same significance in both countries?

The argument has been made, and it has proved satisfactory, at least to the author, that throughout Asia and Europe, with the exception of the Buddhists and early Christians, the Swastika was used habitually as a sign or mark or charm, implying good luck, good fortune, long life, much pleasure, great success, or something similar. The makers and users of the Swastika in South and Central America, and among the mound builders of the savages of North America, having all passed away before the advent of history, it is not now, and never has been, possible for us to obtain from them a description of the meaning, use, or purpose for which the Swastika was employed by them. But, by the same line of reasoning that the proposition has been treated in the prehistoric countries of Europe and Asia, and which brought us to the conclusion that the Swastika was there used as a charm or token of good luck, or good fortune, or against the evil eye, we may surmise that the Swastika sign was used in America for much the same purpose. It was placed upon the same style of object in America as in Europe and Asia. It is not found on any of the ancient gods of America, nor on any of the statues, monuments, or altars, nor upon any sacred place or object, but rather upon such objects as indicate the common and everyday use, and on which the Swastika, as a charm for good luck, would be most appropriate, while for a sacred character it would be singularly inappropriate.

The theory of independent invention has been invoked to account for the appearance of the Swastika in widely separated countries, but the author is more inclined to rely upon migration and imitation as the explanation.

When signs or symbols, myths or fables, habits or customs, utensils, implements or weapons, industries, tools or machinery, have been found in countries widely separated from each other, both in countries bearing characteristics so much alike as to make them practically the same objects or industries, and which are made in the same way, they present a question to which there are only two possible solutions: Either they are independent discoveries or inventions which, though analogous, have been separately conceived, or else they have been invented or discovered in one of the countries, and passed to the other by migration of the object or communication of the knowledge necessary to form it, or by contact between the two peoples. Of these inventions or discoveries said to have been made in duplicate, each of which is alleged to have sprung up in its own country as a characteristic of humanity and by virtue of a law of physics or psychology, it is but fair to say that in the opinion of the author the presumption is all against this. Duplicate inventions have been made and will be made again, but they are uncommon. They are not the rule, but rather the exception. The human intellect is formed on such unknown bases, is so uncertain in its methods, is swayed by such slight considerations, and arrives at so many different conclusions, that, with the manifold diversities of human needs and desires, the chances of duplicate invention by different persons in distant countries, without contact or communication between them, are almost as one to infinity.

The old adage or proverb says, "Many men of many minds," and it only emphasizes the differences between men in regard to the various phenomena mentioned. There are some things sure to happen, yet it is entirely uncertain as to the way they will happen. Nothing is more uncertain than the sex of a child yet to be born, yet every person has one chance out of two to foretell the result correctly. But of certain other premises, the chances of producing the same result are as one to infinity. Not only does the human intellect not produce the same conclusion from the same premises in different persons, but it does not in the same person at different times. It is unnecessary to multiply words over this, but illustrations can be given that are satisfactory. A battle, a street fight, any event happening in the presence of many witnesses, will never be seen in the same way by all of them; it will be reported differently by each one; each witness will have a different story. The jurors in our country are chosen because of the absence of prejudice or bias. Their intellect or reason are intended to be subjected to precisely the same evidence and argument, and yet how many jurors disagree as to their verdict? We have but to consider the dissensions and differences developed in the jury room which are settled, sometimes by argument, by change of conviction, or by compromise. What would be the resources of obtaining justice if we were to insist upon unanimity of decision of the jury upon their first ballot or the first expression of their opinion and without opportunity of change? Yet these jurors have been charged, tried, and sworn a true verdict to render according to the law and evidence as submitted to them. There is no doubt but that they are endeavoring to fulfill their duty in this regard, and while the same evidence as to fact, and charge as to law, are presented to all of them at the same time, what different impressions are made and what different conclusions are produced in the minds of the different jurors. Illustrations of this exist in the decisions of our Supreme Court, wherein, after full argument and fair investigation, with ample opportunity for comparison of views, explanations, and arguments, all based upon the same state of facts, the same witnesses; yet, in how many cases do we find differences of opinion among the members of the court, and questions of the gravest import and of the most vital character settled for the whole nation by votes of 8 to 7 and 5 to 4? The author has examined, and in other places shown, the fallacy of the rule that like produces like. Like causes produce like effects is a law of nature, but when the decision rests upon the judgment of man and depends upon his reason and his intellect, our common knowledge testifies that this law has no application. When the proposition to be determined has to be submitted to individuals of widely separated and distinct countries between whom there has been neither communication nor contact, and who have received no suggestion as to their respective ideas or needs, or the means of satisfying them, it seems to the author that no rule can be predicated upon the similarity of human condition, of human reason, or of human intellect, certainly none which can be depended on to produce the same conclusion.

Consideration of the facility with which symbols, signs, myths, fables, stories, history, etc., are transmitted from one people to another and from one country to another, should not be omitted in this discussion. It may have slight relation to the Swastika to mention the migrations of the present time, but it will give an idea of the possibility of past times. In this regard we have but to consider the immense number of articles or objects in museums and collections, public and private, representing almost every country and people. We there find objects from all quarters of the globe, from the five continents, and all the islands of the sea. Some of them are of great antiquity, and it is a matter of wonderment how they should have made such long passages and have been preserved from destruction by the vicissitudes of time and space. We have but to consider how money passes from hand to hand and is always preserved to be passed on to the next. Every collection of importance throughout the world possesses a greater or less number of Greek and Roman coins antedating the Christian era. We have an excellent illustration of these possibilities in the word 'halloo," commonly rendered as " hello." A few years ago this word, was peculiar to the English language, yet an incident lately occurred in the city of Washington, within sight of my own residence, by which this word, " hello," has traveled the world around, has spread itself over land and sea, has attached itself to and become part of most every spoken language of civilization, and without much consideration as to its meaning; but being on the procrustean bed of imitation, there are people, foreigners, who believe that the telephone can be only made to respond when the demand is made "hello!"

MIGRATION OF CLASSIC SYMBOLS.

Count Goblet d'Alviella, in "La Migration des Symboles," traces many ancient symbols from what he believes to be their place of origin to their modern habitat. The idea he elucidates in his book is indicated in its title.

The sacred tree of the Assyrians.—This he holds to be one of the oldest historic symbols; that it had its origin in Mesopotamia, one of the earliest civilized centers of the world. Beginning with its simplest form, the sacred tree grew into an ornate and highly complex pattern, invariably associated with religious subjects. Two living creatures always stand on either side, facing it and each other. First they were monsters, like winged bulls or griffins, and after became human or semihuman personages—priests or kings, usually in the attitude of devotion. The Count says the migration of both these types can be readily traced. The tree between the two monsters or animals passed from Mesopotamia to India, where it was employed by the Buddhists and Brahmins, and has continued in use in that country to the present time. It passed to the Phenicians, and from Asia Minor to Greece. From the Persians it was introduced to the Byzantines, and during the early ages, into Christian symbolism in Sicily and Italy, and even penetrated to the west of France. The other type—that is, the tree between two semi-human personages—followed the same route into India, China, and eastern Asia, and, being found in the ancient Mexican and Maya codices, it forms part of the evidence cited by the Count as a pre-Columbian communication between the Old World and the New. He argues this out by similarity of the details of attitude and expression of the human figure, the arrangement of the branches of the sacred tree, etc.

The sacred cone of Mesopotamia.—This was worshipped by the western Semites as their great goddess, under the image of a conical stone.

Its figurative representation is found alike on monuments, amulets, and coins. On some Phenician monuments there is to be seen, super-added to the cone, a horizontal crossbar on the middle of which rests a handle. This shape bears a striking resemblance to the *Crux ansata* (fig. 4), and, like it, was a symbol of life in its widest and most abstract meaning. The resemblance between them is supposed to have caused them to have been mistaken and employed one for the other in the same character of symbol and talisman. It is alleged that the Ephesian Artemis was but the sacred cone of Mesopotamia anthropomorphized, although, with the halo added to Artemis, the allegation of relationship has been made in respect of the *Crux ansata.*

The Crux ansata, the key of life.—This is probably more widely known in modern times than any other Egyptian symbol. Its hieroglyphic name is *Ankh,* and its signification is "to live." As an emblem of life, representing the male and female principle united, it is always borne in the hands of the gods, it is poured from a jar over the head of the king in a species of baptism, and it is laid symbolically on the lips of the mummy to revive it. From Egypt the *Crux ansata* spread first among the Phenicians, and then throughout the whole Semitic world, from Sardinia to Susiana.

The winged globe.—This was a widely spread and highly venerated Egyptian symbol. From Egypt it spread, under various modifica-tions, throughout the Old World. It is formed by a combination of the representations of the sun that have prevailed in different locali-ties in Egypt, the mythology of which ended by becoming a solar drama. Two uræus snakes or asps, with heads erect, are twisted round a globe-shaped disk, behind which are the outstretched wings of a hawk, and on its top the horns of a goat. It commemorates the victory of the principle of light and good over that of darkness and evil. It spread readily among the Phenicians, where it is found sus-pended over the sacred tree and the sacred cone, and was carried wheresoever their art was introduced—westward to Carthage, Sicily, Sardinia, and Cyprus, eastward to Western Asia. Very early it pene-trated on the north to the Hittites, and when it reached Mesopotamia, in the time of Sargonidæ, the winged circle assumed the shape of the wheel or rosette, surmounted by a scroll with upcurled extremities and with a feathered tail opening out like a fan, or a human figure in an attitude sometimes of benediction, sometimes warlike, was inscribed within the disk. Then it was no longer exclusively a solar emblem, but served to express the general idea of divinity. From Mesopotamia it passed to Persia, principally in the anthropoid type. It was, however, never adopted by Greece, and it is nowhere met with in Europe, except, as before stated, in the Mediterranean islands. When Greece took over from Asia symbolic combinations in which it was originally repre-sented, she replaced it by the thunderbolt. But the aureole, or halo,

which encircles the heads of her divinities, and which Christian art
has borrowed from the classic, was directly derived from it.

The caduceus.—This is one of the interesting symbols of antiquity.
It appears in many phases and is an excellent illustration of the migration of symbols. Its classic type held in the hand of Mercury and used
to day as a symbol of the healing art—a winged rod round which two
serpents are symmetrically entwined—is due to the mythographers of
later times, and is very remote from its primitive form. In the Homeric
hymn it is called "the golden rod, three-petaled of happiness and
wealth," which Phœbus gave to the youthful Hermes, but on early
Greek monuments the three leaves are represented by a disk surmounted by an incomplete circle. In this shape it constantly appears
on Phenician monuments; and at Carthage, where it seems to have
been essentially a solar emblem, it is nearly always associated with the
sacred cone. It is found on Hittite monuments, where it assumes the
form of a globe surmounted by horns. Numerous origins and manifold
antecedents have been attributed to it, such as an equivalent of the
thunderbolt, a form of the sacred tree, or a combination of the solar
globe with the lunar crescent. Some examples seem to indicate a
transition from the sacred tree surmounted by the solar disk, to the
form of the caduceus of the Hittites. Our author believes it was
employed originally as a religious or military standard or flag, and that
it was gradually modified by coming in contact with other symbols.
Some Assyrian bas-reliefs display a military standard, sometimes consisting of a large ring placed upon a staff with two loose bandelets
attached, sometimes of a winged globe similarly disposed. This Assyrian military standard may be the prototype of the labarum, which
Constantine, after his conversion to Christianity, chose for his own
standard, and which might equally well have been claimed by the sun
worshipers. Under its latest transformation in Greece, a winged rod
with two serpents twined round it, it has come down to our own times
representing two of the functions of Hermes, more than ever in vogue
among men, industry and commerce. It has survived in India under
the form of two serpents entwined, probably introduced in the track of
Alexander the Great. It was also met with in that country in earlier
times in its simpler form, a disk surmounted by a crescent, resembling
our astronomical sign for the planet Mercury. This earliest type of
the caduceus, a disk surmounted by a crescent, appears at a remote
date in India, and seems to have been confounded with the trisula.

The trisula.—This form of the trident peculiar to the Buddhists was
of great importance in the symbolism of the Hindus; but whether it was
an imitation of the type of thunderbolt seen on Assyrian sculptures, or
was devised by them spontaneously, is uncertain. Its simplest form,
which is, however, rarely met with, is an omicron (*o*) surmounted by an
omega (*ω*). Nearly always the upper portion is flanked by two small
circles, or by two horizontal strokes which often take the appearance of

leaves or small wings. The points of the omega are generally changed into small circles, leaves, or trefoil; and the disk itself is placed on a pedestal. From its lower arc there fall two spires like serpents' tails with the ends curving, sometimes up and sometimes down. This is a very complex symbol. None of the Buddhist texts give any positive information in regard to its origin or meaning, and few symbols have given rise to more varied explanations. The upper part of the figure is frequently found separated from the lower; sometimes this is plainly a trident superposed upon a disk-shaped nucleus. The trident may possibly have symbolized the flash of lightning, as did Neptune's trident among the Greeks, but more probably it is the image of the solar radiation. Among the northern Buddhists it personifies the heaven of pure flame superposed upon the heaven of the sun. Though undoubtedly a Hindu emblem, its primitive shape seems to have early felt the influence of the caduceus, while its more complex forms exhibit a likeness to certain types of the winged globe. Still later the trisula was converted by Brahmanism into an anthropoid figure, and became the image of Jagenath. The vegetable kingdom was also laid under contribution, and the trisula came into a resemblance of the tree of knowledge. Although we have learned the probable signification of its factors in the creeds that preceded Buddhism, we know very little about its meaning in the religion that used it most, but it is a symbol before which millions have bowed in reverence. The plastic development of the trisula shows with what facility emblems of the most dissimilar origin may merge into each other when the opportunity of propinquity is given, and there is sufficient similarity in form and meaning.

The double-headed eagle on the escutcheon of Austria and Russia.— Count D'Alviella tells the history of the migration of the symbol of the double-headed eagle on the escutcheon of Austria and Russia. It was originally the type of the Garuda bird of southern India, found on temple sculptures, in carved wood, on embroideries, printed and woven cloths, and on amulets. It first appears on the so-called Hittite sculptures at Eyuk, the ancient Pteria in Phrygia. In 1217 it appeared on the coins and standards of the Turkoman conquerors of Asia Minor.

In 1227–28 the Emperor Frederick II undertook the sixth crusade, landing at Acre in the latter year, and being crowned King of Jerusalem in 1229. Within thirty years from these dates the symbol appeared on the coins of certain Flemish princes, and in 1345 it replaced the single-headed eagle on the armorial bearing of the holy Roman Empire. Thus, the historic evidence of the migration of this symbol, from the far east to the nations of the west by direct contact, would seem complete.

The lion rampant of Belgium.—This lion was incorporated into the Percy or Northumberland escutcheon by the marriage of Joceline of Louvain, the second son of Godfrey, the Duke of Brabant, to Agnes, the sister and heir of all the Percys. The Counts of Flanders, Brabant, and Louvain bore as their coat of arms the lion rampant facing to the left, which is the present coat of arms of the King of Belgium. The story is thus told in Burke's "Peerage" (1895): Agnes de Percy married Joceline of Louvain, brother of Queen Adeliza, second wife of Henry I, and son of Godfrey Barbalus, Duke of Lower Brabant and Count of Brabant, who was descended from the Emperor Charlemagne. Her ladyship, it is stated, would only consent, however, to this great alliance upon condition that Joceline should adopt either the surname or arms of Percy, the former of which, says the old family tradition, he accordingly assumed, and retained his own paternal coat in order to perpetuate his claim to the principality of his father, should the elder line of the reigning duke become extinct. The matter is thus stated in the old pedigree at Sion House: "The ancient arms of Hainault this Lord Jocelyn retained, and gave his children the surname of Percy."

The migration of this lion rampant is interesting. It was in the twelfth century the coat of arms of the King of Albania. Phillippe d'Alsace, the eldest son of Thierry d'Alsace, was Count of Flanders, sixteenth in succession, tracing his ancestry back to 621 A. D. The original and ancient coat of arms of the Counts of Flanders consisted of a small shield in the center of a larger one, with a sunburst of six rays. Phillippe d'Alsace reigned as Count of Flanders and Brabant from 1168 to 1190 A. D. He held an important command in two crusades to the Holy Land. During a battle in one of these crusades, he killed the King of Albania in a hand-to-hand conflict, and carried off his shield with its escutcheon of the lion rampant, which Phillippe transferred to his own shield, took as his own coat of arms, and it has been since that time the coat of arms of the Counts of Flanders and Brabant, and is now that of Belgium. The lion in the escutcheon can thus be traced by direct historic evidence through Northumberland, Flanders and Louvain back to its original owner, the King of Albania, in the twelfth century. Thus is the migration of the symbol traced by communication and contact, and thus are shown the possibilities in this regard which go far toward invalidating, if they do not destroy, the presumption of separate invention in those cases wherein, because of our ignorance of the facts, we have invoked the rule of separate invention.

Greek art and architecture.—It has come to be almost a proverb in scientific investigation that we argue from the known to the unknown. We might argue from this proverb in favor of the migration of the Swastika symbol and its passage from one people to another by the illustration of the Greek fret, which is in appearance closely related to the Swastika; and, indeed, we might extend the illustration to all Greek architecture. It is a well-known fact, established by numberless historic evidences, that the Greek architecture of ancient times migrated—that is, passed by communication and contact of peoples, and by transfer of knowledge from one man to another, and from one generation to the succeeding generation, until it became known throughout all western countries. The architects of Rome, Vicenza, Paris, London, Philadelphia, Washington, Chicago, and San Francisco derive their knowledge of Grecian architecture in its details of Doric, Ionic, and Corinthian styles by direct communication, either spoken, written or graphic, from the Greek architects who practiced, if they did not invent, these styles.

The Greek fret.—This has migrated in the same manner. As to its invention or origin, we have little to do in the present argument. Whether the fret was the ancestor or the descendant of the Swastika is of no moment to our present question. It has been demonstrated in the early part of this paper that both it and the Swastika had a common existence in early if not prehistoric Greece, and that both were employed in perfected form on the same specimen of Archaic Greek pottery. Figs. 133 and 134 demonstrate that these two signs migrated together from Greece to Egypt, for the particular specimen mentioned was found at Naukratis, Egypt. From this high antiquity the Greek fret has migrated to practically every country in the world, and has been employed during all historic time by the peoples of every civilization. The fret is known historically to have passed by means of teachers, either through speaking, writing, or drawing, and never yet a suggestion that its existence or appearance in distant countries depended upon separate invention or independent discovery.

Why strain at the gnat of independent invention of the Swastika when we are compelled to swallow the camel of migration when applied to the Greek fret and architecture? The same proposition of migration applies to Greek art, whether of sculpture, engraving, or gem carving. These ancient Grecian arts are as well known in all quarters of the civilized globe at the present day as they were in their own country, and this was all done by communication between peoples either through speaking, writing, or drawing. So far from being separate inventions, the modern sculptor or engraver, with full historic knowledge of the origin or, at least, antiquity of these arts, and with an opportunity for inspection and study of the specimens, is still unable to reproduce them or to invent original works of so high an order. The imaginary and newly invented theory that culture is the result of the psychologic nature of man manifesting itself in all epochs and countries, and among all peoples, by the evolution of some new discovery made to fit a human need—that as all human needs in a given stage are the same, therefore all human culture must, *per se*, pass through the same phases or stages—is a theory to which I refuse adhesion. It receives a hard blow when we take down the bars to the modern sculptor, requiring of him neither original invention nor independent discovery, but permitting him to use, study, adapt, and even servilely copy the great Greek art works, and we know that with all these opportunities and advantages he can not attain to their excellence, nor reach their stage of art culture.

VII.—PREHISTORIC OBJECTS ASSOCIATED WITH THE SWASTIKA, FOUND IN BOTH HEMISPHERES, AND BELIEVED TO HAVE PASSED BY MIGRATION.

SPINDLE-WHORLS.

Spindle-whorls are first to be considered. These are essentially prehistoric utensils, and are to be found in every part of the world where the inhabitants were sufficiently cultured to make twisted threads or cords, whether for hunting or fishing, games, textile fabrics, or coverings, either for themselves, their tents, or other purposes. In western Asia, all of Europe, in the pueblos of North America, and among the aborigines—by whatever name they are called—of Mexico, Central America, and the north and west coast of South America, wherever the aborigines employed cord, cloth, or fiber, the spindle-whorl is found. Where they used skins for the coverings of themselves or their tents, the spindle-whorl may not be found. Thus, in the Eskimo land, and among certain of the North American savages, spindle-whorls are rarely if ever found.

The spindle-whorl was equally in use in Europe and Asia during the Neolithic Age as in the Bronze Age. It continued in use among the peasants in remote and outlying districts into modern times. During the Neolithic Age its materials were stone and terra cotta; during the Bronze Age they were almost exclusively terra cotta. They are found of both materials. Recently a Gallo-Roman tomb was opened at Clermont-Ferrand and found to contain the skeleton of a young woman, and with it her spindles and whorls.[1]

The existence of spindle-whorls in distant and widely separated countries affords a certain amount of presumptive evidence of migrations of peoples from one country to another, or of contact or communication between them. If the people did not themselves migrate and settle the new country, taking the spindle-whorls and other objects with them, then the spindle-whorl itself, or the knowledge of how to make and use it, must in some other way have gotten over to the new country.

This argument of migration, contact, or communication does not rest solely on the similarity of the whorls in the distant countries, but equally on the fact of spinning thread from the fiber; and this argument is reenforced by the similarity of the operation and of the tool or machine with which it was done. It has been said elsewhere that the probability of communication between widely separated peoples by migration or contact depended for its value as evidence, in some degree, upon the correspondence or similarity of the object considered, and that this value increased with the number of items of correspondence, the closeness of similarity, the extent of the occurrence, and the difficulty of its performance. So we pass to the similarity in size, appearance, mode of manufacture, and, finally, the use of the whorls of the two continents.

---

[1] Bull. Soc. d'Anthrop., Paris, October, 1893, p. 600.

EUROPE.

Switzerland—Lake dwellings.—Figs. 345 and 346 show stone spindle-whorls from prehistoric Swiss lake dwellings. These are in the U. S. National Museum, and with them are dozens of others of the same kind

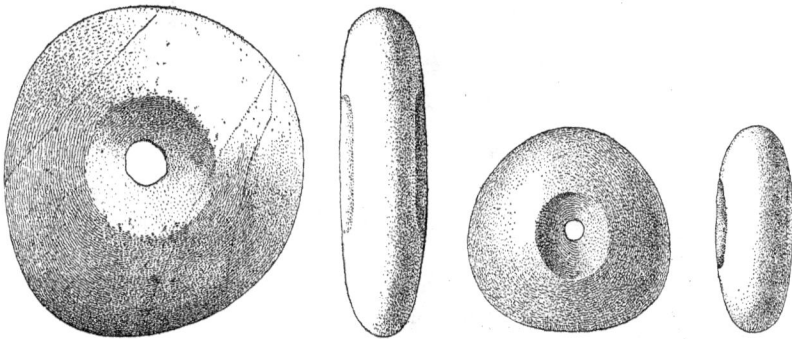

Figs. 345 and 346.
STONE SPINDLE-WHORLS.
Neolithic.
Swiss lake dwellings.
U. S. National Museum.

and style from all other parts of Europe. Fig. 347 shows a stone spindle-whorl from Lund, Sweden. It is in the U. S. National Museum and was contributed by Professor Jillson. Figs. 348, 349, and 350 represent terra-cotta spindle-whorls from the Swiss lakes. These specimens were

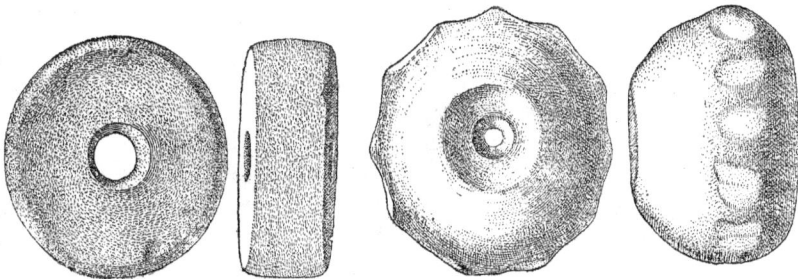

Fig. 347.
STONE SPINDLE-WHORL.
Neolithic.
Lund, Sweden.
Cat. No. 5281, U. S. N. M.

Fig. 348.
TERRA-COTTA SPINDLE-WHORL.
Neolithic or Bronze Age.
Swiss lake dwellings.
Cat. No. 100642, U. S. N. M.

selected to show the different patterns, to illustrate their unlikeness instead of their likeness, to give an understanding of the various kinds of whorls rather than that they were all one kind, a fad which should be kept in mind during this argument.

Italy.—Figs. 351, 352, and 353 show terra-cotta spindle-whorls from Orvieto, Italy, 78 miles north from Rome.   Figs. 354 and 355 represent

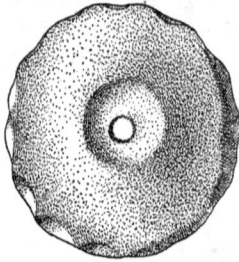

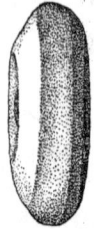

Fig. 349.

TERRA-COTTA SPINDLE-WHORL.

Neolithic or Bronze Age.

Swiss lake dwellings.

Cat. No. 100642, U. S. N. M.

Fig. 350.

TERRA-COTTA SPINDLE-WHORL.

Swiss lake dwellings.

Cat. No. 100647, U. S. N. M.

spindle-whorls from Corneto, Italy, 63 miles north from Rome.   As remarked above, they have been chosen to represent the different kinds.

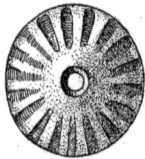

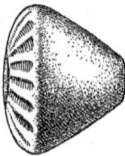

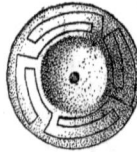

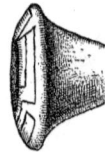

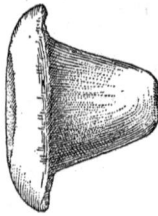

Figs. 351, 352, and 353.

PREHISTORIC TERRA-COTTA SPINDLE-WHORLS.

Orvieto, Italy.

Cat. Nos. 101671, 101672, U. S. N. M.

There are thousands of these whorls found in Italy.   In the Archæological Exposition at Turin, 1884, the number was so great that they were twined about the columns, thereby providing a place of storage as well as a place of display.

Wurtemburg.—Dr. Charles Rau procured for, and there is now in, the U. S. National Museum a spindle (fig. 356) with its whorl which had been in use for spinning from 1860 to 1870, and which he obtained in Wurtemburg, Germany, from the woman who had used it.

France.—The author has seen the French peasants in Brittany spin-

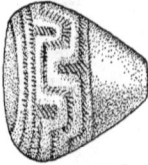

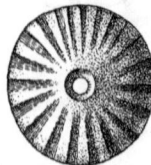

Figs. 354 and 355.

PREHISTORIC SPINDLE-WHORLS.

Corneto, Italy.

Cat. No. 101773, U. S. N. M.

ning their thread in the same way, and once took a photograph of one in the hamlet of Pont-Aven, Morbihan, but it failed in development.

PLATE 21.

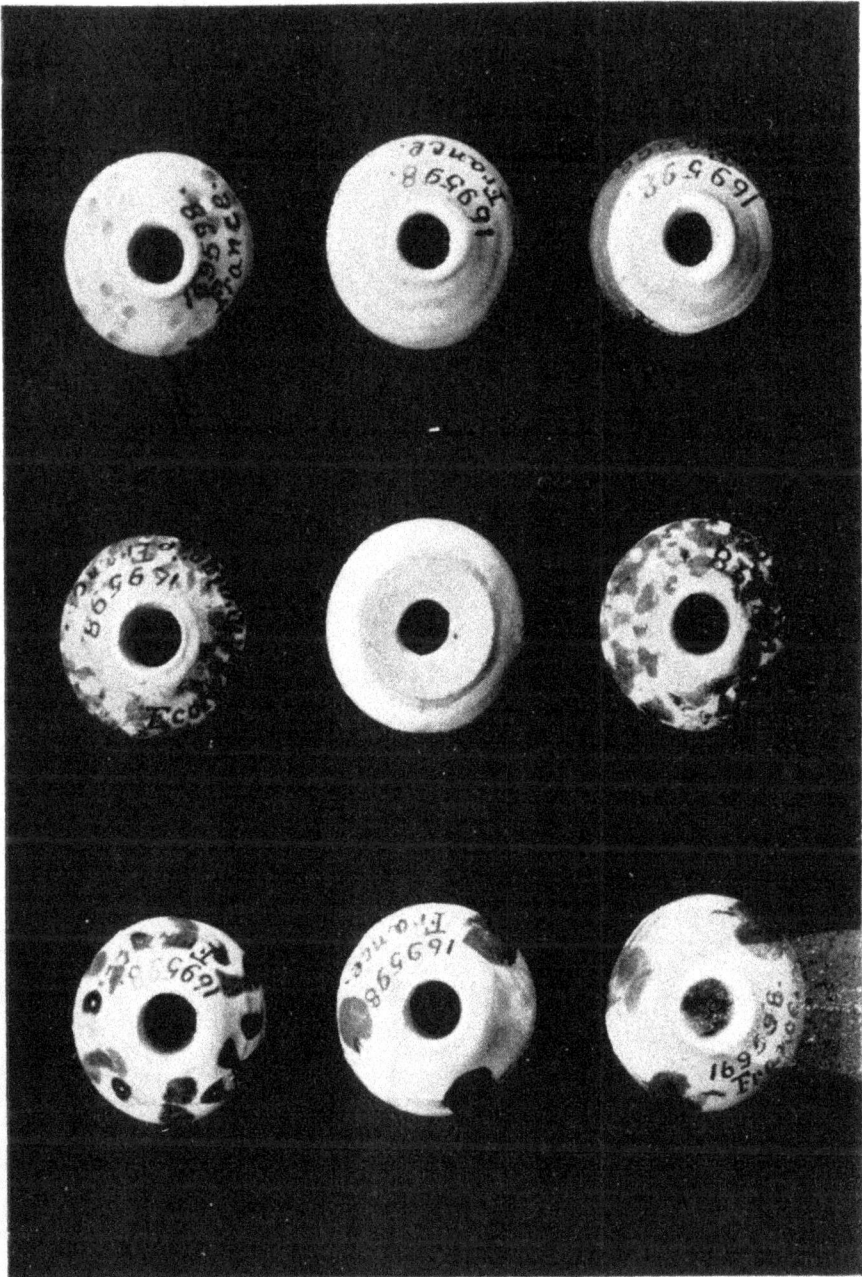

SPINDLE-WHORLS OF MODERN PORCELAIN FROM SOUTHERN FRANCE.

Cat. No. 169598, U. S. N. M.

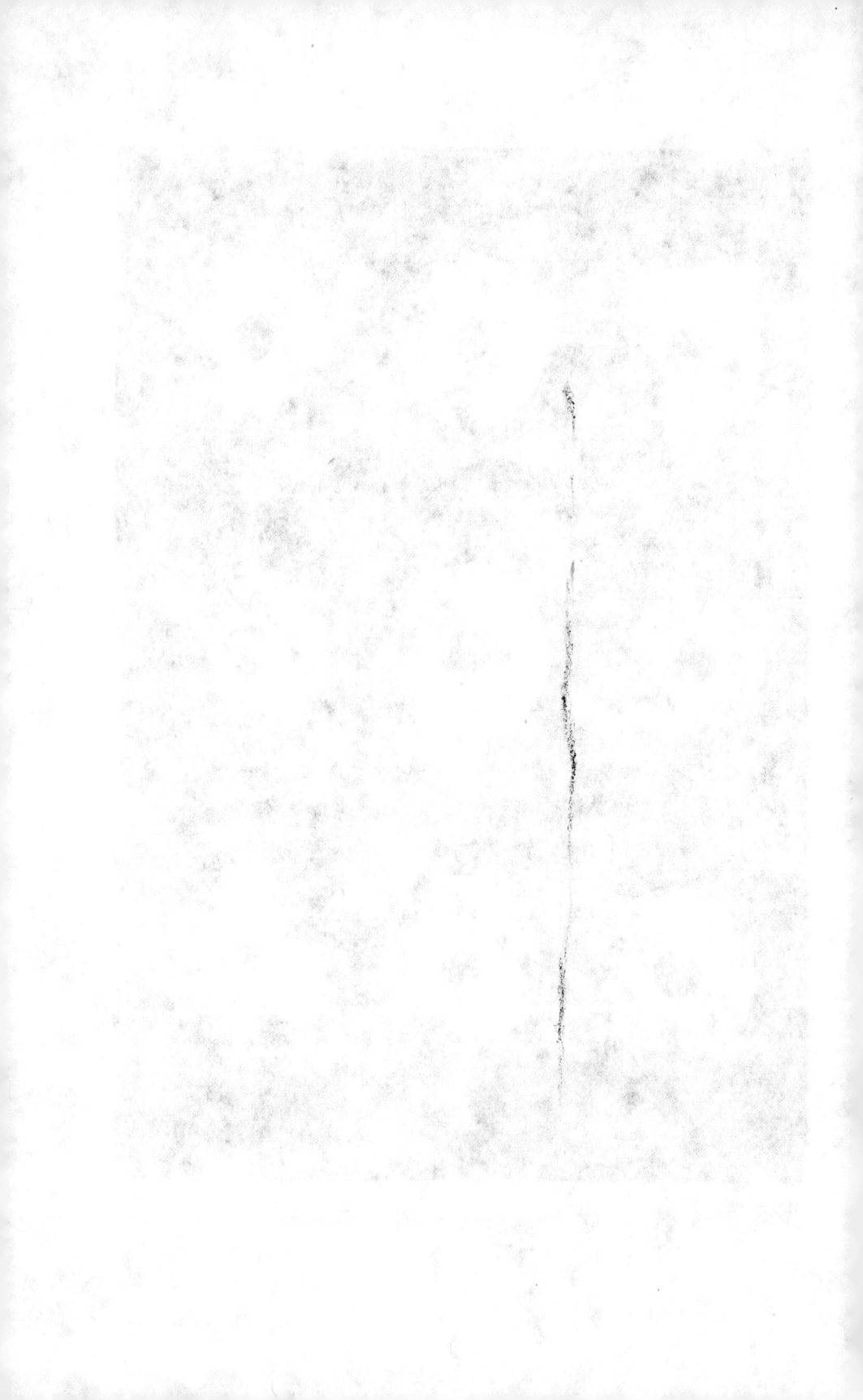

In 1893 Mr. Harle purchased at St. Gerons, Ardeche, a merchant's entire stock of modern porcelain spindle-whorls. The manufactory was located at Martres-Tolosane, and the trade extended throughout the Pyrenees. He presented a series to the Société d'Anthropologie at Paris, July, 1893.[1]

The U. S. National Museum has lately received, through the kindness of the École d'Anthropologie, a series of nine of these porcelain whorls (pl. 21). The wheel and modern machines for spinning have penetrated this corner of the world, and these whorls are the last emblem of an industry dating slightly after the advent of man on earth and already old in that locality when Roland crossed the mountain pass near there and sounded his "Oliphant," calling for help from Charlemagne. These are the death chant of the industry of hand spinning in that country.

NORTH AMERICA—PRE-COLUMBIAN TIMES.

The North American Indians employed rushes and animal skins as the principal coverings for themselves and their tents. They used sinews and thongs for thread and cord, and thus avoided largely the necessity for spinning fiber or making textiles; for these or possibly other reasons, we find few spindle-whorls among them compared with the number found in Europe. Yet the North American Indians made and used textile fabrics, and there are pieces of woven cloth from mounds in Ohio now in the Department of Prehistoric Anthropology, U. S. National Museum. The Pueblo Indians spun thread and wove cloth in pre-Columbian times, and those within the States of Colorado and Utah and the adjoining Territories of Arizona and New Mexico, particularly the Navajoes, have been long noted for their excellence in producing textile fabrics. Specimens of their looms and thread are on display in the National Museum and have been published in the reports. Special attention is called to that by Dr. Washington Matthews in the Third Annual Report of the Bureau of Ethnology, 1881–82. Dr. Matthews is of the opinion that the work of the Pueblo Indians antedated that of the Navajoes, that the latter learned the art from the former since the advent of the Spaniards; and he remarks that the pupils now excel their masters in the beauty and quality of their work. He declares that the art of weaving has been carried to greater perfection among the Navajoes than among any native tribe in America north of the Mexican boundary; while with none in the entire continent has it been less influenced by contact with Europeans.

Fig. 356

MODERN SPINDLE AND WHORL USED FOR SPINNING THREAD.

Wurtemburg, Germany.

---

[1] Bull. Soc. d'Anthrop., Paris, pp. 461–462.

The superiority of the Navajo to the Pueblo work results not only from a constant advance of the weavers' art among the former, but from a deterioration of it among the latter. This deterioration among the Pueblo Indians he attributes to their contact with the whites, their inclination being to purchase rather than to make woven fabrics, while these influences seem not to have affected the Navajoes. He represents a Navajo woman spinning (see pl. 22 of the present paper). She is seated, and apparently whorls the spindle by rubbing it on her leg. The spindle is of wood, as are all other spindles, but the whorl is also of wood. In this these people are peculiar and perhaps unique. The whorl, among most other savage or prehistoric peoples, as we have already seen, was of stone or clay. These wooden whorls are thinner and larger, but otherwise they are the same. An inspection of the plate will show that with it the spinning apparatus forms the same machine, accomplishes the same purpose, and does it in the same way. The sole difference is in the size and material of the whorl. The difference in material accounts for the difference in size. It is not improbable that the Indian discovered that the wooden whorl would serve as well as a stone or pottery one, and that it was easier made. The machine in the hands of the woman, as shown in the figure, is larger than usual, which may be accounted for by the thread of wool fiber used by the Navajo being thicker and occupying more space than the flaxen thread of prehistoric times; so it may have been discovered that a large whorl of wood served their purpose better than a small one of stone. Stone whorls of large size might be too heavy. Thus may be explained the change from small stone or pottery whorls to large wooden ones.

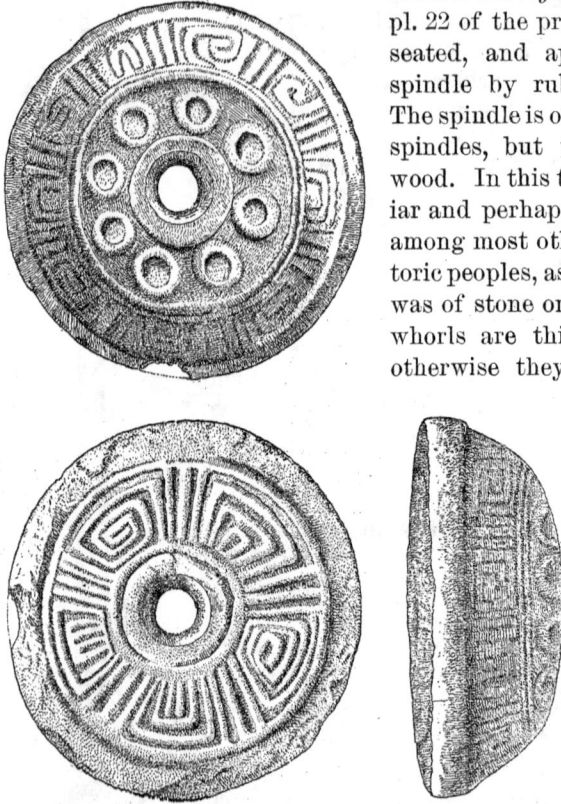

Fig. 357.

TERRA-COTTA SPINDLE-WHORL WITH DESIGN SIMILAR TO SWASTIKA.

Valley of Mexico.

Cat. No. 27875, U. S. N. M.

Mexico.—Fig. 357 represents the two sides and edge of a pottery terra-cotta spindle-whorl. It is the largest of a series of six (Cat. Nos.

PLATE 22.

NAVAJO WOMAN USING SPINDLE AND WHORL.

Dr. Washington Matthews, Third Annual Report of the Bureau of Ethnology, 1881-82, Pl. xxxiv.

27875–27880) from the valley of Mexico, sent to the U. S. National Museum by the Mexican National Museum in 1877. Fig. 358 also represents one of a series from Mexico, obtained by W. W. Blake, July, 1886 (Cat. Nos. 99051–99059). The National Museum possesses hundreds of these from Mexico, as well as the small ones from Peru.

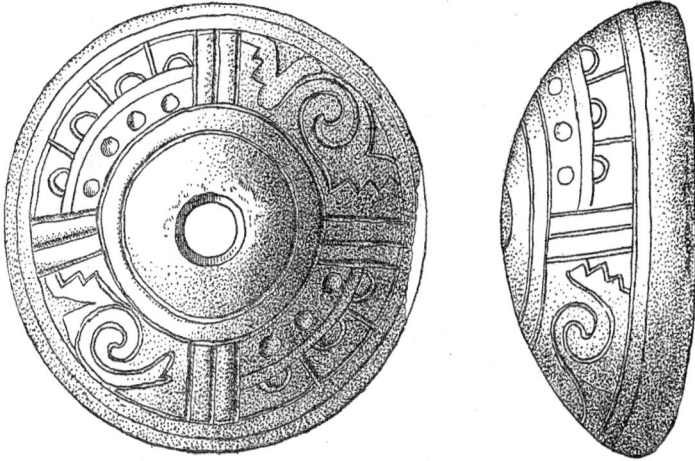

Fig. 358.
MEXICAN TERRA-COTTA SPINDLE-WHORL WITH DESIGN SIMILAR TO SWASTIKA.

These specimens are chosen because they are the largest and most elaborately decorated. It will be perceived at a glance how the style of decoration lends itself to the Swastika. It consists mostly of geometric figures, chief of which is the Greek fret, the labyrinth, the circle, and the volute, but as in the color stamps (pp. 946–947) there is no Swastika.

CENTRAL AMERICA.

Nicaragua.—The specimen shown in fig. 359, from Omotepe Island, Lake Nicaragua, is one of a series of pottery spindle-whorls, bearing,

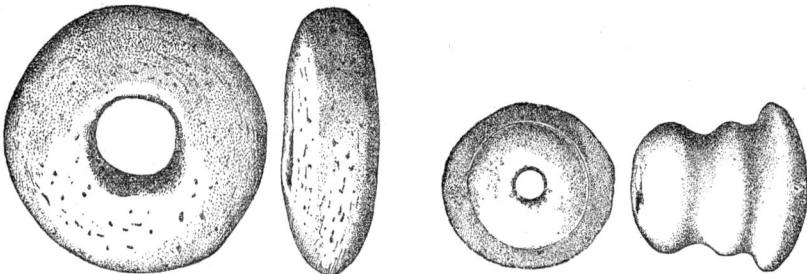

Figs. 359 and 360.
TERRA-COTTA SPINDLE-WHORLS.
Omotepe Island, Nicaragua.
Cat. Nos. 28898, 28899, U. S. N. M.

however, great resemblance to those of stone. Fig. 360 shows a specimen from the same locality. It is of pottery and bears much resemblance in form to the earliest whorls found by Schliemann on the site of Troy on the hill of Hissarlik. Both these were collected by Dr. J. F. Bransford, and are in the U. S. National Museum. Fig. 361 shows a specimen from Granada, Nicaragua. It is of the common shape of the European prehistoric spindle-whorl. Its flat surface is decorated

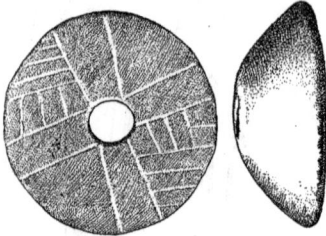

Fig. 361.

TERRA-COTTA SPINDLE-WHORL.

Granada, Nicaragua.

Cat. No. 23295, U. S. N. M.

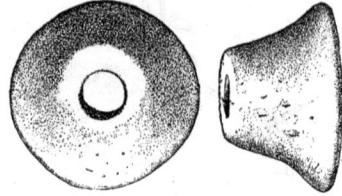

Fig. 362.

TERRA-COTTA SPINDLE-WHORL.

Malacate, Nicaragua.

Cat. No. 29009, U. S. N. M.

with a Greek cross in incised lines, two quarters of which are filled with hatch marks. Fig. 362 shows a terra-cotta spindle-whorl from Malacate, Nicaragua. It is cone-shaped. Both these specimens were collected by Dr. Earl Flint.

SOUTH AMERICA.

Chiriqui.—Figs. 363, 364, and 365 show terra-cotta spindle-whorls from Chiriqui, the most northern territory in South America and adjoining the Isthmus of Panama. They are engraved natural size, with ornamentation similar to that on the pottery of that country.

Colombia.—Fig. 366 shows a cone-shaped terra-cotta whorl from Manizales, Colombia, South America. It has a star-shaped design on the face and a three-line zigzag or chevron pattern.

Fig. 363.

SPINDLE-WHORL MADE OF GRAY CLAY AND DECORATED WITH ANNULAR NODES.

Chiriqui.

Sixth Annual Report of the Bureau of Ethnology, fig. 218.

Peru.—Plate 23 represents a series of spindles and whorls from Peru. They were furnished to the U. S. National Museum by I. V. Norton, of Plainville, N. Y. The whorls were originally considered to be beads, and were without further description. The spindles were not inserted in them as at present. The spindles, as well as whorls, are exceedingly small. Some of the whorls are decorated by incised lines in the clay, and many of the spindles are decorated in the middle with paint in different colors, in lines, scrolls, and chevrons. These are the only whorls from Peru which the U. S. National Museum has, though it possesses an extensive series of the spindles, several of which still have the spun thread wrapped upon them.

There are certain distinguishing peculiarities to be remarked when

PLATE 23.

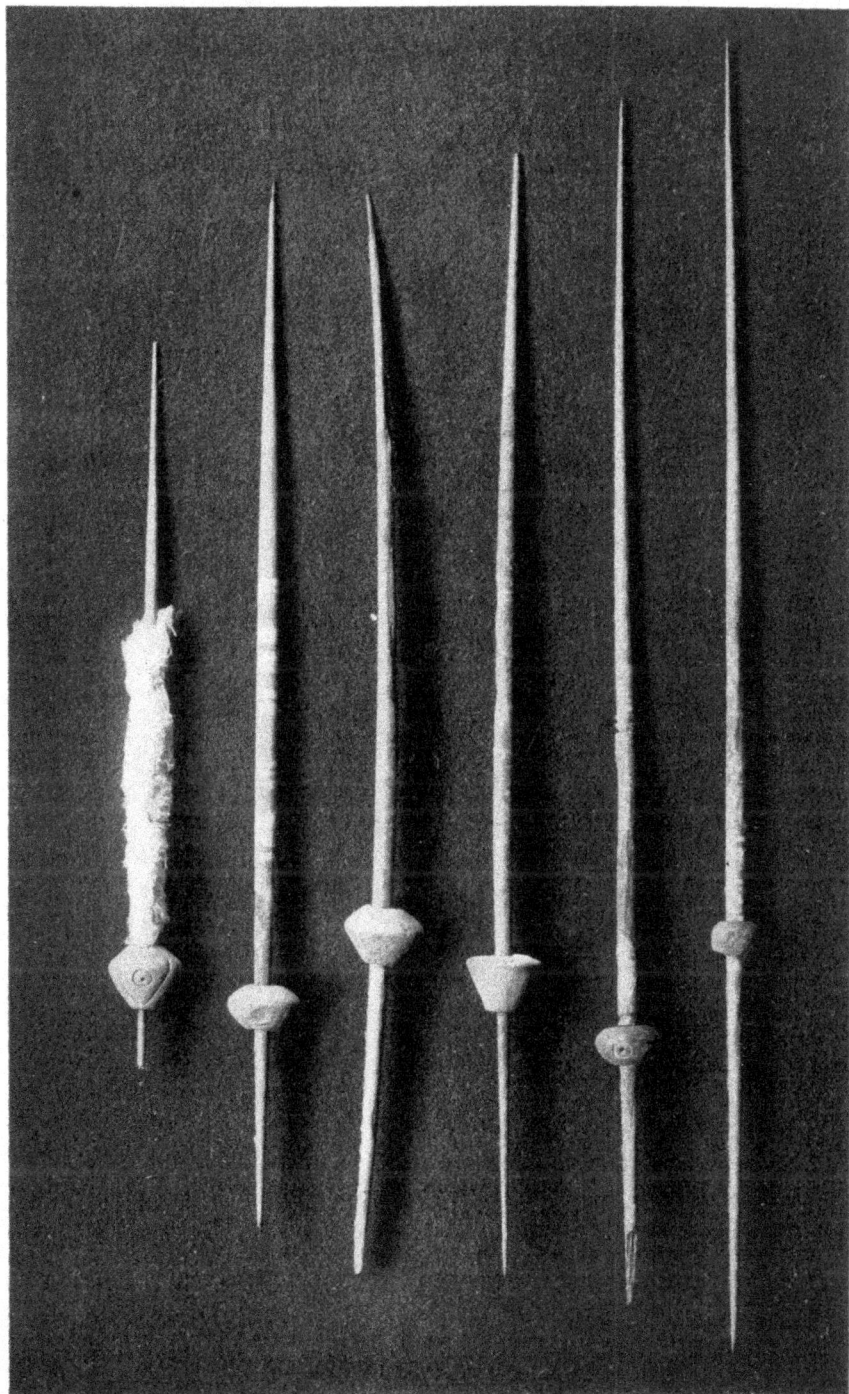

SERIES OF ABORIGINAL SPINDLES AND WHORLS FROM PERU.
Cat. No. 17510, U. S. N. M.

comparing the spindle-whorls from the Western Hemisphere with those from the Eastern Hemisphere. There is greater diversity in size, form, and decoration in the American than in the European whorls. A series of European whorls from any given locality will afford a fair represen-

Fig. 364.

SPINDLE-WHORL OF GRAY CLAY WITH
FIGURES OF ANIMALS.

Chiriqui.

Sixth Annual Report of the Bureau of Ethnology,
fig. 219.

Fig. 365.

SPINDLE-WHORL OF DARK CLAY WITH PER-
FORATIONS AND INCISED ORNAMENTS.

Chiriqui.

Sixth Annual Report of the Bureau of Ethnology,
fig. 220.

tation of those from almost every other locality. But it is different with the American specimens. Each section in America has a different style, not only different from the European specimens, but different from those of neighboring sections. Among the eighteen thousand whorls found by Dr. Schliemann on the hill of Hissarlik, there is

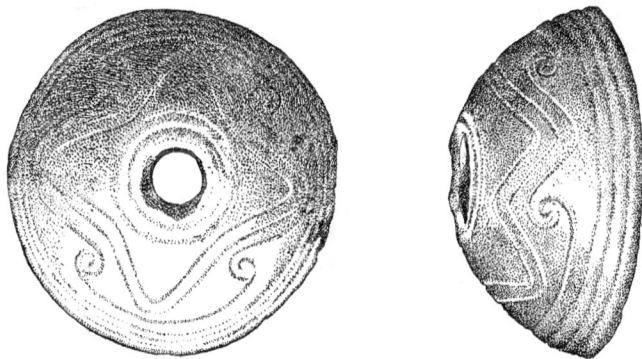

Fig. 366.

TERRA-COTTA SPINDLE-WHORL.

Manizales, Colombia.

Cat. No. 16838, U. S. N. M.

scarcely one so large as those here shown from Mexico, while, on the other hand, there were only a few as small as the largest of the series from Peru. The difference in size and material in the Pueblo whorls has already been noticed. The ornamentation is also peculiar in that it adopts, not a particular style common to the utensil, but that it adopts the styles of the respective countries. The Mexican whorl has a Mexican style of ornamentation, etc. The Nicaragua specimens resemble the European more than any other from America in their forms and the almost entire absence of decoration.

The foregoing are the differences; but with all the number and extent of these differences the fact remains that the whorls of the two hemispheres are practically the same, and the differences are insignificant. In style, shape, and manner of use they are so similar in the two hemispheres as to be the same invention. The whorls, when put upon their spindles, form the same machine in both countries. They were intended for and they accomplish the same purpose, and the method of their performance is practically the same. While the similarity of the art of spinning and the mechanism (*i. e.*, the spindle and whorl) by which it is accomplished may not prove conclusively that it migrated from the Eastern Hemisphere, nor yet show positive connection or communication between the two peoples, it goes a long way toward establishing such migration or communication. The similarity in the art and its mechanism appears to the author to show such resemblance with the like culture in the Eastern Hemisphere, and is so harmonious with the theory of migration or contact or communication, that if there shall be other objects found which either by their number or condition would prove to be a well-authenticated instance of migration from or contact or communication between the countries, the evidence of the similarity of the spindle-whorls would form a valuable addition to and largely increase the evidence to establish the main fact. Until that piece of well-authenticated evidence has been obtained, the question must, so far as concerns spindle-whorls, remain only a probability. The differences between them are of manner, and not of matter; in size and degree, but not in kind, and are not other or greater than might easily arise from local adaptation of an imported invention. Compare the Navajo spindle (pl. 22) with that from Wurtemburg, Germany (fig. 356), and these with the spindles and whorls from Peru (pl. 23). These facts are entirely in harmony with the possibility that the spindle and whorl, as a machine for spinning, was a single invention, and that its slight differentiations resulted from its employment by different peoples—the result of its intertribal migrations. For purposes of comparison, and to show the similarity of these objects in Europe, the author has introduced a series of spindle-whorls from Troy, Hissarlik (pls. 24 and 25). These belong to the U. S. National Museum, and form part of the valuable collection from Mme. Schliemann, the gift by her talented husband to the people of the United States as a token of his remembrance and grateful feelings toward them.

PLATE 24.

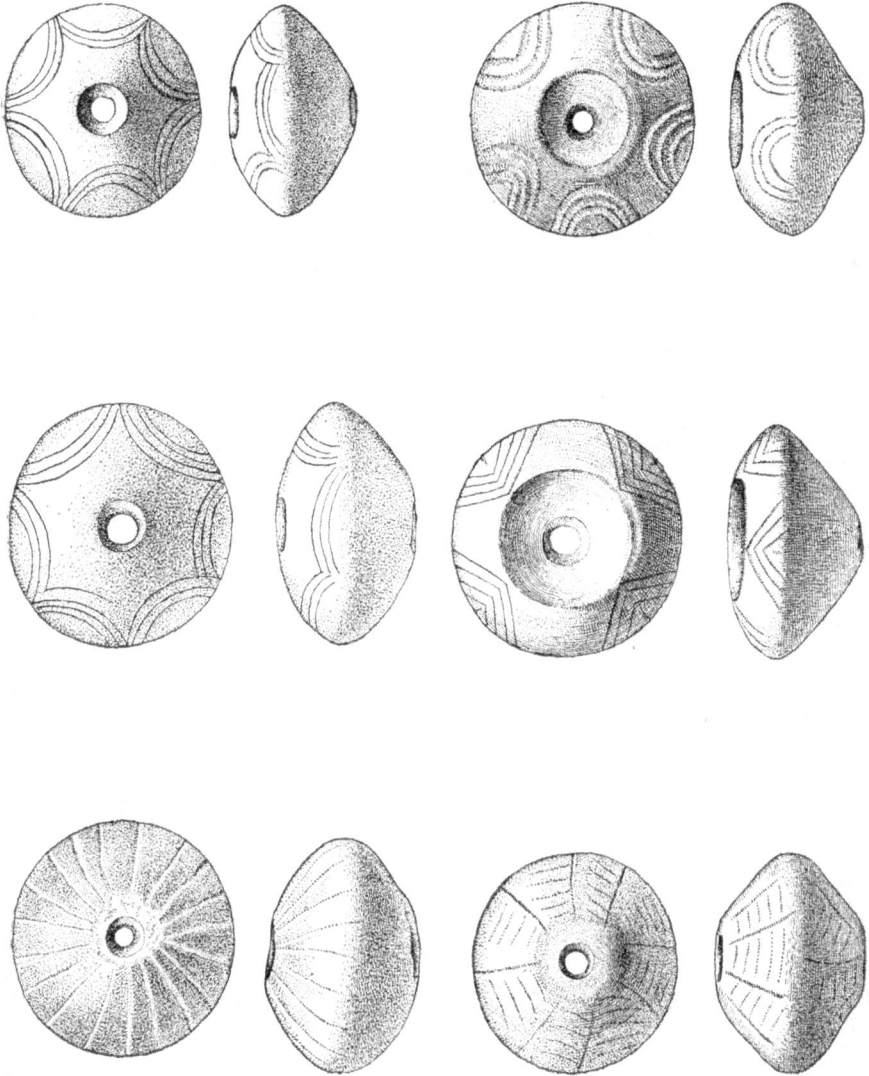

SELECTED SPECIMENS OF SPINDLE-WHORLS FROM THE THIRD, FOURTH, AND FIFTH CITIES
OF TROY.

U. S. National Museum.

PLATE 25.

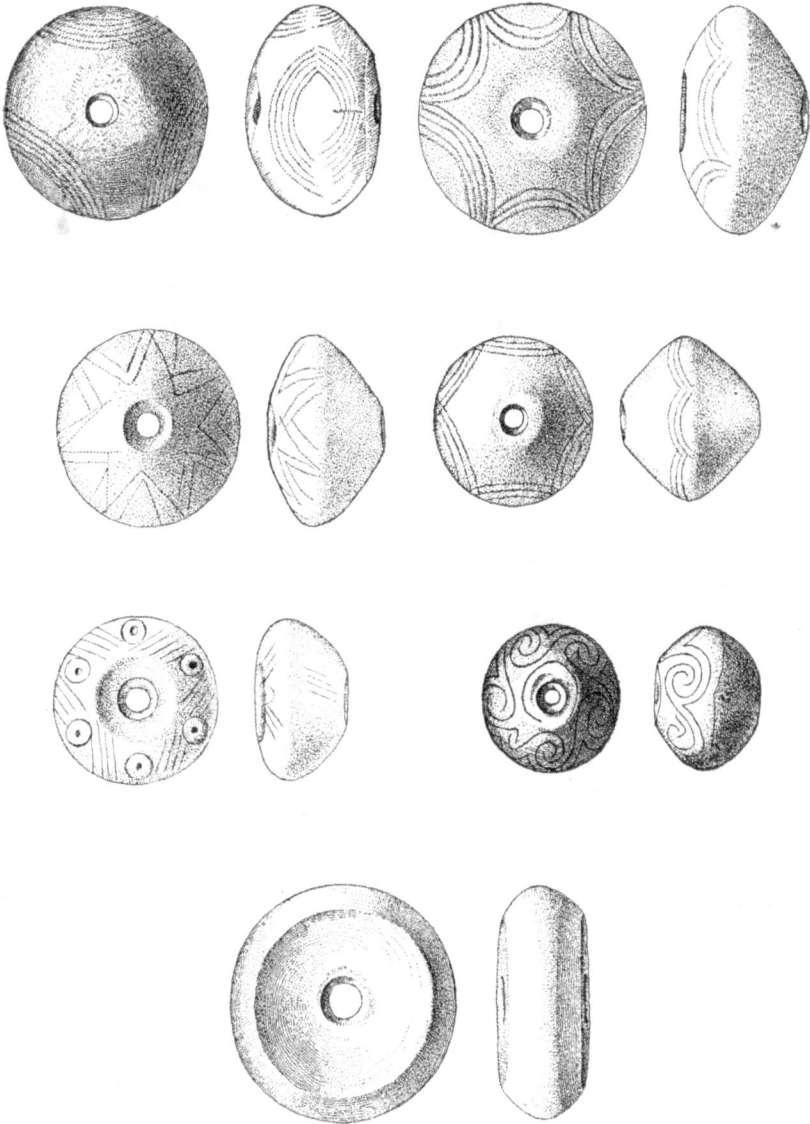

SELECTED SPECIMENS OF SPINDLE-WHORLS FROM THE THIRD, FOURTH, AND FIFTH CITIES OF TROY.

U. S. National Museum.

BOBBINS.

EUROPE.

We have already seen how an increase in the number of correspondences between objects from distant countries increases the weight
of their evidence in favor of contact or communication between the
peoples. If it should be found upon comparison that the bobbins
on which thread
is to be wound,
as well as the
spindle-whorls
with which it is
made, had been in
use during prehis-
toric times in the
two hemispheres,
it would add to
the evidence of
contact or commu-
nication. The U.

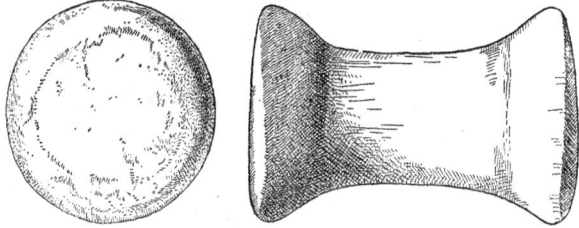

Fig. 367.

BOBBIN OR SPOOL FOR WINDING THREAD (?).

Type Villanova.

Corneto, Italy.

U. S. National Museum.

S. National Museum possesses a series of these bobbins, as they
are believed to have been, running from large to small, comprising
about one dozen specimens from Italy, one from Corneto and the
others from Bologna, in which
places many prehistoric spindle
whorls have been found (figs.
367 and 368). These are of the
type Villanova. The end as
well as the side view is represented. The former is one
of the largest, the latter of
middle size, with others smaller
forming a graduating series.

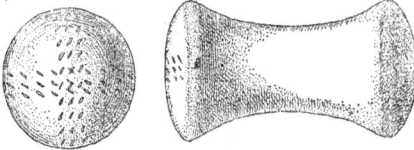

Fig. 368.

TERRA-COTTA BOBBIN OR SPOOL FOR WINDING
THREAD (?).

Type Villanova.

Bologna, Italy.

Cat. No. 101771, U. S. N. M.

The latter is engraved on the
end by dotted incisions in three parallel lines arranged in the form
of a Greek cross. A similar bobbin from Bologna bears the sign
of the Swastika on its end (fig. 193).[1] It was found by Count Gozzadini
and forms part of his collection in Bologna.

UNITED STATES.

The three following figures represent clay and stone bobbins, all
from the State of Kentucky. Fig. 369 shows a bobbin elaborately decorated, from a mound near Maysville, Ky. It has a hole drilled longi-

---

[1] De Mortillet, "Musée Préhistorique," fig. 1239.

tudinally through the center. The end shows a cross of the Greek form with this hole in the center of the cross. Fig. 370 shows a similar object from Lexington, Ky., sent by the Kentucky University. It

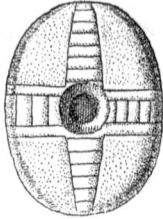

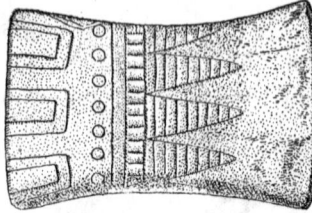

Fig. 369.

BOBBIN (?) FROM A MOUND NEAR MAYSVILLE, KENTUCKY.

Cat. No. 16748, U. S. N. M.

is of fine-grained sandstone, is drilled longitudinally through the center and decorated as shown. The end view shows a series of concentric circles with rows of dots in the intervals. Fig. 371 shows a similar object of fine-grained sandstone from Lewis County, Ky. It is also drilled longitudinally, and is decorated with rows of zigzag lines as shown. The end view represents four consecutive pentagons laid one on top of the other, which increase in size as they go outward, the hole through the bobbin being in the center of these pentagons, while the outside line is decorated with spikes or rays extending to the periphery of the bobbin, all of which is said to represent the sun. The specimen shown in fig. 372, of fine-grained

Fig. 370.

BOBBIN (?) FROM LEXINGTON, KENTUCKY.

Cat. No. 16691, U. S. N. M.

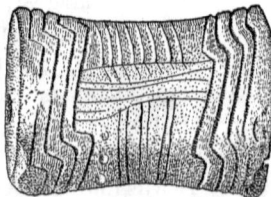

sandstone, is from Maysville, Ky. The two ends are here represented because of the peculiarity of the decoration. In the center is the hole, next to it is a rude form of Greek cross which on one end is repeated

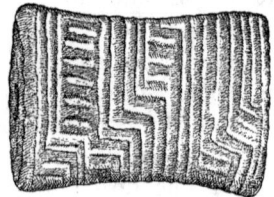

Fig. 371.

BOBBIN (?) OF FINE-GRAINED SANDSTONE.

Lewis County, Kentucky.

Cat. No. 59681, U. S. N. M.

as it goes farther from the center; on the other, the decoration consists of three concentric circles, one interval of which is divided by radiating lines at regular intervals, each forming a rectangle. Between the outer lines and the periphery are four radiating rays which, if completed all around, might form a sun symbol. Bobbins of clay have been lately discovered in Florida by Mr Clarence B. Moore and noted by Professor Holmes.

Thus we find some of the same objects which in Europe were made.

and used by prehistoric man and which bore the Swastika mark have migrated to America, also in prehistoric times, where they were put to the same use and served the same purpose. This is certainly no inconsiderable testimony in favor of the migration of the sign.

VIII.—SIMILAR PREHISTORIC ARTS, INDUSTRIES, AND IMPLEMENTS IN EUROPE AND AMERICA AS EVIDENCE OF THE MIGRATION OF CULTURE.

The prehistoric objects described in the foregoing chapter are not the only ones common to both Europe and America. Related to the spindle-whorls and bobbins is the art of weaving, and it is perfectly susceptible of demonstration that this art was practiced in the two hemispheres in prehistoric times. Woven frabrics have been found

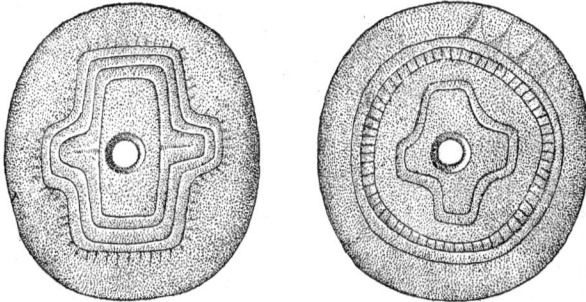

Fig. 372.

VIEW SHOWING BOTH ENDS OF A BOBBIN(?) OF FINE-GRAINED SANDSTONE.

Maysville, Kentucky.

Cat. No. 16747, U. S. N. M.

in the Swiss lake dwellings, in Scandinavia, and in nearly all parts of Europe. They belonged to the Neolithic and Bronze ages.

Figs. 373 and 374 illustrate textile fabrics in the Bronze Age. Both specimens are from Denmark, and the National Museum possesses another specimen (Cat. No. 136615) in all respects similar. While prehistoric looms may not have been found in Europe to be compared with the looms of modern savages in America, yet these specimens of cloth, with the hundreds of others found in the Swiss lake dwellings, afford the most indubitable proof of the use of the looms in both countries during prehistoric times.

Complementary to this, textile fabrics have been found in America, from the Pueblo country of Utah and Colorado, south through Mexico, Central and South America, and of necessity the looms with which they were made were there also. It is not meant to be said that the looms of the two hemispheres have been found, or that they or the textile fabrics are identical. The prehistoric looms have not been found in Europe, and those in America may have been affected by contact with the white man. Nor is it meant to be said that the textile fabrics of the two hemispheres are alike in thread, stitch, or pattern.   But these at best are only details.   The great fact remains that the prehistoric man of the two hemispheres had the knowledge to spin fiber into thread, to wind it on bobbins, and to weave it into fabrics; and whatever differences there may have been in pattern, thread, or cloth, they were finally and substantially the same art, and so are likely to have been the product of the same invention.

While it is not the intention to continue this examination among the prehistoric objects of the two hemispheres in order to show their similarity and thus prove migration, contact, or communication, yet it may be well to mention some of them, leaving the argument or proof to a future occasion.

The polished stone hatchets of the two hemispheres are substantially the same.   There are differences of material, of course, for in each country the workman was obliged to use such material as was obtainable.   There are differences in form between the polished stone hatchets of the two hemispheres, but so there are differences between different localities in the same hemisphere.   Some hatchets are long, others short, some round, others flat, some have a pointed end, others a square or nearly square or unfinished end; some are large, others small.   But all these differences are to be found equally well pronounced within each hemisphere.

Scrapers have also been found in both hemispheres and in all ages. There are the same differences in material, form, and appearance as in the polished stone hatchet.   There is one difference to be mentioned of this utensil—i. e., in America the scraper has been sometimes made with a stem and with notches near the base, after the manner of arrow-

Fig. 373.

WOMAN'S WOOLEN DRESS FOUND IN AN OAK COFFIN AT BORUM-ESHOI, DENMARK.

Bronze Age.

Report of the Smithsonian Institution (U. S. National Museum), 1892, pl. CI, fig. 2.

and spear-heads, evidently intended to aid, as in the arrow- and spear-head, in fastening the tool in its handle. This peculiarity is not found in Europe, or, if found, is extremely rare. It is considered that this may have been caused by the use of a broken arrow- or spear-head, which seems not to have been done in Europe. But this is still only a difference in detail, a difference slight and insignificant, one which occurs seldom and apparently growing out of peculiar and fortuitous conditions.

The art of drilling in stone was known over an extended area in prehistoric times, and we find innumerable examples which must have been performed in both hemispheres substantially in the same manner and with the same machine.

The art of sawing stone was alike practiced during prehistoric times in the two hemispheres. Many specimens have been found in the prehistoric deposits of both.

The aboriginal art of making pottery was also carried on in the same or a similar manner in both hemispheres. The examples of this art are as numerous as the leaves on the trees. There were differences in the manipulation and treatment, but the principal fact remains that the art was the same in both countries. Not only were the products greatly similar, but the same style of geometric decoration by incised lines is common to both. Greater progress in making pottery was made in the Western than in the Eastern Hemisphere during prehistoric times.

The wheel was unknown in both hemispheres, and in both the manipulation of clay was by hand. True, in the Western Hemisphere there

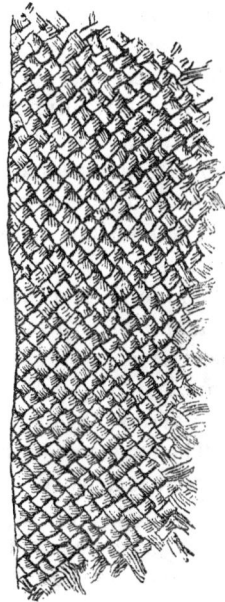

Fig. 374.

DETAIL OF DRESS SHOWN IN THE PRECEDING FIGURE.

was greater dexterity and a greater number of methods employed. For example, the vase might be built up with clay inside a basket, which served to give both form and decoration; it was coiled, the damp clay being made in a string and so built up by a circular movement, drawing the side in or out as the string of clay was laid thereon, until it reached the top; it may have been decorated by the pressure of a textile fabric, real or simulated, into the damp clay. A few years ago it would have been true to have said that pottery decorated in this manner was peculiar to the Western Hemisphere, and that it had never been found in the Eastern Hemisphere, but Prince Poutjatine has lately found on his property, Bologoje, in the province of Novgorod, midway between Moscow and St. Petersburg, many pieces of prehistoric pottery which bear evidence of having been made in this manner, and while it may be rare in the Eastern Hemisphere, it is similar in these respects to thousands of pieces of prehistoric pottery in North America.

One of the great puzzles for archæologists has been the prehistoric jade implements found in both countries. The raw material of which these were made has never been found in sufficient quantities to justify anyone in saying that it is indigenous to one hemisphere and not to the other. It may have been found in either hemisphere and exported to the other. But of this we have no evidence except the discovery in both of implements made of the same material. This material is dense and hard. It is extremely difficult to work, yet the operations of sawing, drilling, carving, and polishing appear to have been conducted in both hemispheres with such similarity as that the result is practically the same.

Prehistoric flint-chipping was also carried on in both hemispheres with such similarity of results, even when performing the most difficult and delicate operations, as to convince one that there must have been some communication between the two peoples who performed them.

The bow and arrow is fairly good evidence of prehistoric migration, because of the singularities of the form and the intricacies of the machinery, and because it is probably the earliest specimen of a machine of two separate parts, by the use of which a missile could be sent at a greater distance and with greater force than if thrown by hand. It is possible that the sling was invented as early as the bow and arrow, although both were prehistoric and their origin unknown.

The bow and arrow was the greatest of all human inventions—greatest in that it marked man's first step in mechanics, greatest in adaptation of means to the end, and as an invented machine it manifested in the most practical and marked manner the intellectual and reasoning power of man and his superiority over the brute creation. It, more than any other weapon, demonstrated the triumph of man over the brute, recognizing the limitations of human physical capacity in contests with the brute. With this machine, man first successfully made up for his deficiency in his contests with his enemies and the capture of his game. It is useless to ask anything of history about the beginnings of the bow and arrow; wherever history appears it records the prior existence, the almost universal presence, and the perfected use of the bow and arrow as a weapon. Yet this machine, so strange and curious, of such intricacy of manufacture and difficulty of successful performance, had with all its similarities and likenesses extended in prehistoric times almost throughout the then inhabited globe. It is useless to specify the time, for the bow and arrow existed earlier than any time of which we know; it is useless for us to specify places, for it was in use throughout the world wherever the world was occupied by neolithic man.

Imitative creature as was man, and slow and painful as were his steps in progress and in invention during his infancy on earth, when

he knew nothing and had everything yet to learn, it is sufficiently wonderful that he should have invented the bow and arrow as a projectile
machine for his weapons; but it becomes doubly and trebly improbable that he should have made duplicate and independent inventions
thereof in the different hemispheres. If we are to suppose this, why
should we be restricted to a separate invention for each hemisphere,
and why may we not suppose that he made a separate invention for
each country or each distant tribe within the hemisphere? Yet we are
met with the astonishing but, nevertheless, true proposition that
throughout the entire world the bow and arrow existed in the early
times mentioned, and was substantially the same machine, made in the
same way, and serving the same purpose.

CONCLUSION.

The argument in this paper on the migration of arts or symbols, and
with them of peoples in prehistoric times, is not intended to be exhaustive. At best it is only suggestive.

There is no direct evidence available by which the migration of symbols, arts, or peoples in prehistoric times can be proved, because the
events are beyond the pale of history. Therefore we are, everybody is,
driven to the secondary evidence of the similarity of conditions and
products, and we can only subject them to our reason and at last determine the truth from the probabilities. In proportion as the probabilities of migration increase, it more nearly becomes a demonstrated fact.
It appears to the author that the probabilities of the migration of the
Swastika to America from the Old World is infinitely greater than that
it was an independent invention.

The Swastika is found in America in such widely separated places,
among such different civilizations, as much separated by time as by
space, that if we have to depend on the theory of separate inventions
to explain its introduction into America we must also depend upon the
same theory for its introduction into the widely separated parts of
America. The Swastika of the ancient mound builders of Ohio and
Tennessee is similar in every respect, except material, to that of the
modern Navajo and Pueblo Indian. Yet the Swastikas of Mississippi
and Tennessee belong to the oldest civilization we know in America,
while the Navajo and Pueblo Swastikas were made by men still living.
A consideration of the conditions bring out these two curious facts: (1)
That the Swastika had an existence in America prior to any historic
knowledge we have of communication between the two hemispheres;
but (2) we find it continued in America and used at the present day,
while the knowledge of it has long since died out in Europe.

The author is not unaware of the new theories concerning the parallelism of human development by which it is contended that absolute
uniformity of man's thoughts and actions, aims and methods, is produced when he is in the same degree of development, no matter in
what country or in what epoch he lives. This theory has been pushed

until it has been said, nothing but geographical environment seems to modify the monotonous sameness of man's creations. The author does not accept this theory, yet he does not here controvert it. It may be true to a certain extent, but it surely has its limitations, and it is only applicable under special conditions. As a general proposition, it might apply to races and peoples but not to individuals. If it builds on the hereditary human instincts, it does not take into account the will, energy, and reasoning powers of man. Most of all, it leaves out the egoism of man and his selfish desire for power, improvement, and happiness, and all their effects, through the individual, on human progress. In the author's opinion the progress of peoples through consecutive stages of civilization is entirely compatible with his belief that knowledge of specific objects, the uses of material things, the performance of certain rites, the playing of certain games, the possession of certain myths and traditions, and the carrying on of certain industries, passed from one country to another by migration of their peoples, or by contact or communication between them; and that the knowledge, by separate peoples, of the same things, within reasonable bounds of similarity of action and purpose, and with corresponding difficulty of performance, may well be treated as evidence of such migration, contact, or communication. Sir John Lubbock expresses the author's belief when he says,[1] "There can be no doubt but that man originally crept over the earth's surface, little by little, year by year, just, for instance, as the weeds of Europe are now gradually but surely creeping over the surface of Australia." The word migration has been used by the author in any sense that permitted the people, or any number thereof, to pass from one country to another country, or from one section of a country to another section of the same country, by any means or in any numbers as they pleased or could.

The theory (in opposition to the foregoing) is growing in the United States that any similarity of culture between the two hemispheres is held to be proof of migration of peoples. It appears to the author that these schools both run to excess in propagating their respective theories, and that the true condition of affairs lies midway between them. That is to say, there was certain communication between the two hemispheres, as indicated by the similarities in culture and industry, the objects of which could scarcely have been the result of independent invention; while there are too many dissimilar arts, habits, customs, and modes of life belonging to one hemisphere only, not common to both, to permit us to say there was continuous communication between them. These dissimilarities were inventions of each hemisphere independent of the other.

An illustration of the migration to America is the culture of Greece. We know that Greek art and architecture enter into and form an important part of the culture of Americans of the present day; yet

---

[1] "Prehistoric Man," p. 601.

the people of America are not Greek, nor do they possess any considerable share of Greek culture or civilization. They have none of the blood of the Greeks, nor their physical traits, nor their manners, habits, customs, dress, religion, nor, indeed, anything except their sculpture and architecture. Now, there was undoubtedly communication between the two countries in so far as pertains to art and architecture; but it is equally true that there has been no migration of the other elements of civilization mentioned.

The same thing may be true with regard to the migrations of prehistoric civilization. There may have been communication between the countries by which such objects as the polished stone hatchet, the bow and arrow, the leaf-shaped implement, chipped arrow- and spear-heads, scrapers, spindle-whorls, the arts of pottery making, of weaving, of drilling and sawing stone, etc., passed from one to the other, and the same of the Swastika; yet these may all have been brought over in sporadic and isolated cases, importing simply the germ of their knowledge, leaving the industry to be independently worked out on this side. Certain manifestations of culture, dissimilar to those of the Old World, are found in America; we have the rude notched ax, the grooved ax, stemmed scraper, perforator, mortar and pestle, pipes, tubes, the ceremonial objects which are found here in such infinite varieties of shape and form, the metate, the painted pottery, etc., all of which belong to the American Indian civilization, but have no prototype in the prehistoric Old World. These things were never brought over by migration or otherwise. They are indigenous to America.

Objects common to both hemispheres exist in such numbers, of such infinite detail and difficulty of manufacture, that the probabilities of their migration or passage from one country to another is infinitely greater than that they were the result of independent invention. These common objects are not restricted to isolated cases. They are great in number and extensive in area. They have been the common tools and utensils such as might have belonged to every man, and no reason is known why they might not have been used by, and so represent, the millions of prehistoric individuals in either hemisphere. This great number of correspondences between the two hemispheres, and their similarity as to means and results is good evidence of migration, contact, or communication between the peoples; while the extent to which the common industries were carried in the two continents, their delicacy and difficulty of operation, completes the proof and forces conviction.

It is not to be understood in the few foregoing illustrations that the number is thereby exhausted, or that all have been noted which are within the knowledge of the author. These have been cited as illustrative of the proposition and indicating possibilities of the argument. If a completed argument in favor of prehistoric communication should be prepared, it would present many other illustrations. These could be found, not only among the objects of industry, utensils, etc., but in the modes of manufacture and of use which, owing to their number and the extent of territory which they cover, and the difficulty of accomplishment, would add force to the argument.

BIBLIOGRAPHY OF THE SWASTIKA.

ABBOTT, CHARLES C. Primitive Industry: | or | Illustrations of the Handiwork, | in stone, bone and clay, | of the | Native Races | of | the Northern Atlantic Seaboard of America. | By Charles C. Abbott, M. D. | Cor. Member Boston Soc. Nat. Hist., | Fellow Royal Soc. | of Antiq. of the North. Copenhagen,etc.,etc., | Salem,Mass.: | George A. Bates. | 1881.

8°, pp. v–vi, 1–560, fig. 429.
Grooved ax, Pemberton, N. J. Inscription of Swastika denounced as a fraud, p. 32.

ALLEN, E. A. The | Prehistoric World | or | Vanished Races | by | E. A. Allen, | author of "The Golden Gems of Life." | Each of the Following well-known Scholars reviewed one or more | Chapters, and made valuable suggestions: | C. C. Abbott, M. D., | Prof. F. W. Putnam, | A. F. Bandelier, | Prof. Chas. Rau, | Alexander Winchell, LL. D., | Cyrus Thomas, Ph. D. | G. F. Wright. | Cincinnati: | Central Publishing House. | 1885.

8°, pp. i–vi, 1–820.
Swastika regarded as an ornament in the Bronze Age, p. 233.

AMERICAN ANTIQUARIAN and Oriental Journal.

Vol. VI, Jan., 1884, p. 62.
Swastika found in a tessellated Mosaic pavement of Roman ruins at Wivelescombe, England; reported by Cornelius Nicholson, F. G. S., cited in Munro's "Ancient Scottish Lake Dwellings," note, p. 132.

AMERICAN ENCYCLOPEDIA.
Title, Cross.

AMERICAN JOURNAL of Archæology and of the History of Fine Arts.

Vol. XI, No. 1, Jan.–March, 1896, p. 11, fig. 10.
Andokides, a Greek vase painter (525 B. C.), depicted Athena on an amphora with her dress decorated with many ogee and meander Swastikas. The specimen is in the Berlin Museum.

ANDERSON, JOSEPH. Scotland in Early Christian Times.
The Swastika, though of Pagan origin, became a Christian symbol from the fourth to the fourteenth century, A. D. Vol. II, p. 218.
Cited in "Munro's Ancient Scottish Lake Dwellings," note, p. 132.

BALFOUR, EDWARD. Cyclopædia of India | and of | Eastern and Southern Asia, | Commercial, Industrial, and Scientific: | Products of the | Mineral, Vegetable and Animal Kingdoms, | Useful Arts and Manufactures; | edited by | Edward Balfour, L. R. C. S. E., | Inspector General of Hospitals, Madras Medical Department, | Fellow of the University of Madras, | Corresponding Member of the Imperial Geologic Institute, Vienna. | Second Edition. | Vol. V. | Madras: | Printed at the Lawrence and Adelphi Presses, | 1873. | Copyright.

8°, pp. 1–956.
Title, Swastika, p. 656.

BARING-GOULD, S. Curious Myths | of | the Middle Ages. | By | S. Baring-Gould, M. A., | New York: | Hurst & Co., Publishers, | No. 122 Nassau street.

12°, pp. 1–272.
Title, "Legends of the Cross," pp. 159–185.

BERLIN SOCIETY for Anthropology, Ethnology, and Prehistoric Researches, Sessional report of—.
III, 1871; VIII, July 15, 1876, p. 9.

BLAKE, WILLSON W. The Cross, | Ancient and Modern. | By | Willson W. Blake. | (Design) | New York: | Anson D. F. Randolph and Company. | 1888.
8°, pp. 1–52.

BRASH, RICHARD ROLT. The | Ogam Inscribed Monuments | of the | Gaedhil | in the | British Islands | with a dissertation on the Ogam character, &c. | Illustrated with fifty Photolithographic plates | by the late | Richard Rolt Brash, M. R. I. A., | F. S. A. Scot. | Fellow of the Royal Society of | Ireland; and author of "The Ecclesiastical | Architecture of Ireland." | Edited by George M. Atkinson | London: | George Bell & Sons, York street, Covent Garden | 1879.

4°, pp. i–xvi, 1–425.
Swastikas on Ogam stone at Aglish (Ireland), pl. XXIV, pp. 187–189; on Newton stone Aberdeenshire, (Scot.), pl. XLIX, p. 359; Logie stone, (Scot.), pl. XLVIII, p. 358; Bressay, (Scot.), pl. XLVII.

BRINTON, Daniel G. The Ta Ki, the Swastika, and the Cross in America.

Proceedings American Philosophical Society, XXVI, 1889, pp. 177-187.

—— The | Myths of the New World: | A treatise | on the | Symbolism and Mythology | of the | Red Race of America. | By | Daniel G. Brinton, A. M., M. D., | Member of the Historical Society of Pennsylvania, of the Numismatic | and Antiquarian Society of Philadelphia; Corresponding Member | of the American Ethnological Society; Author of "Notes | on the Floridian Peninsula," etc. | (Design) | New York: | Leypoldt & Holt. | 1868.

8°, pp. i–viii, 1–307.
The cross of Mexico, pp. 95–97, 183–188.

—— American | Hero-Myths. | A study of the Native Religions | of the Western Continent. | By | Daniel G. Brinton, M. D., | Member of the American Philosophical Society; the American | Antiquarian Society; the Numismatic and Antiquarian | Society of Phila., etc.; Author of "The Myths of | the New World;" "The Religious Senti- | ment," etc. | Philadelphia: | H. C. Watts & Co., | 506 Minor Street, | 1882.

8°, pp. i–xvi, 1–251.
Symbol of the cross in Mexico. The rain god, the tree of life, and the god of strength, p. 122; in Palenque, the four rain gods, p. 155; the Muscayas, light, sun, p. 222.

BROWNE, G. F. Basket-work figures of men on sculptured stones. Triquetra.

Archæologia, Vol. L, 1887, pt. 2, p. 291, pl. XXIII, fig. 7.

BURGESS, James. Archæological Survey of Western India. Vol. IV. | Report | on the | Buddhist Cave Temples | and | Their Inscriptions | Being Part of | The Results of the Fourth, Fifth, and Sixth Seasons' Operations | of the Archæological Survey of Western India, | 1876–77, 1877–78, 1878–79. | Supplementary to the Volume on "Cave Temples of India." | By | Jas. Burgess, LL. D., F. R. G. S., | Member of the Royal Asiatic Society, of the Société Asiatique, &c. | Archæological Surveyor and Reporter to Government | for Western and Southern India. | Lon-

BURGESS, James—continued.
don: | Trübner & Co., Ludgate Hill. | 1883. | (All rights reserved.)

Folio, pp. 140.
Inscriptions with Swastika, vol. IV, pls. XLIV, XLVI, XLVII, XLIX, L, LII, LV; vol. V, pl. LI.

—— The | Indian Antiquary, | A Journal of Oriental Research | in | Archæology, History, Literature, Languages, Folk-Lore, &c., &c., | Edited by | Jas. Burgess, M. R. A. S., F. R. G. S. | 3 vols., 1872–74, | Bombay: | Printed at the "Times of India" Office. | London: Trübner & Co. Paris: E. Leroux. Berlin: Asher & Co. Leipzig: F. A. Brockhaus. | New York: Westermann & Co. Bombay: Thacker, Vining & Co.

4°, Vols. I–III.
Twenty-four Jain Saints, *Suparsva,* son of Pratishtha by Prithoi, one of which signs was the Swastika. Vol. II, p. 135.

BURNOUF, Emile. Le | Lotus de la Bonne Loi, | Traduit du Sanscrit, | Accompagné d'un Commentaire | et de Vingt et un Mémoires Relatifs au Buddhisme, | par M. E. Burnouf, | Secrétaire Perpétuel de l'Académie des Inscriptions et Belles Lettres. | (Picture) | Paris. | Imprimé par Autorisation du Gouvernement | à l'Imprimerie Nationale. | MDCCCLII.

Folio, pp. 1–897.
Svastikaya, Append. VIII, p. 625.
Nandavartaya, p. 626.

—— The | Science of Religions | by Emile Burnouf | Translated by Julie Liebe | with a preface by | E. J. Rapson, M. A., M.R. A. S. | Fellow of St. John's College, Cambridge | London | Swan, Sonnenschein, Lowrey & Co., | Paternoster Square. | 1888.

Swastika, its relation to the myth of Agni, the god of fire, and its alleged identity with the fire-cross, pp. 165, 253–256, 257.

BURTON, Richard F. The | Book of the Sword | by | Richard F. Burton | Maître d'Armes (Brevette) | (Design) | With Numerous Illustrations | London | Chatto and Windus, Piccadilly | 1884 | (All rights reserved).

4°, pp. 299.
Swastika sect, p. 202, note 2.

CARNAC, H. Rivett, Memorandum on Clay Disks called "Spindle-whorls" and votive Seals found at Sankisa,

CARNAC, H. Rivett—continued.
Behar, and other Buddhist ruins in the Northwestern provinces of India. (With three plates).
Journal Asiatic Society of Bengal, Vol. XLIX, pt. 1, 1880, pp. 127-137.

CARTAILHAC, ÉMILE. Résultats d'Une Mission Scientifique | du | Ministère de l'Instruction Publique | Les | âges Préhistoriques | de | l'Espagne et du Portugal | par | M. Émile Cartailhac, | Directeur des Matériaux pour l'Histoire primitive de l'homme | Préface par M. A. De Quatrefages, de l'Institut | Avec Quatre Cent Cinquante Gravures et Quatre Planches | Paris | Ch. Reinwald, Libraire | 15, Rue des Saints Pères, 15 1886 | Tous droits réservés.
4°, pp. i-xxxv, 1-347.
Swastika, p. 285.
Triskelion, p. 286.
Tetraskelion, p. 286.
Swastika in Mycenæ and Sabraso.—Are they of the same antiquity ?, p. 293.

CENTURY DICTIONARY.
Titles, Swastika, Fylfot.

CESNOLA, Louis Palma Di. Cyprus: | Its Ancient Cities, Tombs, and Temples. | A Narrative of Researches and Excavations During | Ten Years' Residence in that Island. | By | General Louis Palma Di Cesnola, | * * * | * * | With Maps and Illustrations. * * | New York: | Harper Brothers, Publishers, | Franklin Square. | 1877.
8°, pp. 1-456.
Swastika on Cyprian pottery, pp. 210, 300, 404, pls. XLIV, XLV, XLVII.

CHAILLU, Paul B. Du. The Viking Age | The Early History | Manners and Customs of the Ancestors | of the English-Speaking Nations | Illustrated from | The Antiquities Discovered in Mounds, Cairns, and Bogs, | As Well as from the Ancient Sagas and Eddas. | By | Paul B. Du Chaillu | Author of "Explorations in Equatorial Africa," "Land of the Midnight Sun," etc. | With 1366 Illustrations and Map. | In Two Volumes * * | New York: | Charles Scribner's Sons. | 1889.
8°, I, pp. i-xx, 1-591; II, pp. i-viii, 1-562.
Swastika in Scandinavia. Swastika and triskelion, Vol. I, p. 100, and note 1; Vol. II, p. 343. Swastika, Cinerary urn, Bornholm, Vol. I, fig. 210, p. 138. Spearheads with runes, Swastika

CHAILLU, Paul B. Du—continued.
and Triskelion, Torcello, Venice, fig. 335, p. 191. Tetraskelion on silver fibula, Vol. I, fig. 567, p. 257, and Vol. II, fig. 1311, p. 342. Bracteates with Croix swasticale, Vol. II, p. 337, fig. 1292.

CHANTRE, Ernest. Études Paléoethnologiques | dans le Bassin du Rhône | Âge du Bronze | Recherches | sur l'Origine de la Métallurgie en France | Par | Ernest Chantre | Première Partie | Industrie de l'Âge du Bronze | Paris, | Librairie Polytechnique de J. Baudry | 15, Rue Des Saints-Pères, 15 | MDCCCLXXV.
Folio, pp. 1-258.

—— Deuxième Partie. Gisements de l'Âge du Bronze. pp. 321.

—— Troisième Partie. Statistique. pp. 245.
Swastika migration, p. 206. Oriental origin of the prehistoric Sistres or tintinnabula found in Swiss lake dwellings, Vol. I, p. 206.
Spirals, Vol. II, fig. 186, p. 301.

—— Notes Anthropologiques: De l'Origine Orientale de la Métallurgie. In-8, avec planches. Lyon, 1879.

—— Notes Anthropologiques. Relations entre les Sistres Bouddhiques et certains Objets Lacustres de l'Age du Bronze. In-8. Lyon, 1879.

—— L'Âge de la Pierre et l'Âge du Bronze en Troade et en Grèce. In-8. Lyon, 1874.

—— L'Âge de la Pierre et l'Âge du Bronze dans l'Asie Occidentale. (Bull. Soc. Anth., Lyon, t. I, fasc. 2, 1882.)

—— Prehistoric Cemeteries in Caucasus. (Nécropoles préhistoriques du Caucase, renferment des crânes macrocéphales.)
Matériaux, seizième année (16), 2° série, XII, 1881.
Swastika, p. 166.

CHAVERO, D. ALFREDO. Mexico | A Través de los Siglos | Historia General y Completa del Desenvolvimiento Social, | Político, Religioso, Militar, Artístico, Científico, y Literario de México desde la Antigüedad | Más Remota hasta la Época Actual | * * | Publicada bajo la Dirección del General | D. Vicente Riva Palacio | * | * | * | * | * | Tomo Primero | Historia Antigua y de la Conquista | Escrita por el Licenciado | D. Alfredo Chavero. | México | Bal-

CHAVERO, D. ALFREDO—continued.
lesca y Comp.ⁿ, Editores | 4, Amor de
Dios, 4.

Folio, pp. i–lx, 1–926.

Ciclo de 52 años. (Atlas del P. Diego Duran,
p. 386.) Swastika worked on shell (Fains
Island), "*labrado con los cuatro puntos del
Nahui Ollin.*" p. 676.

CLAVIGERO, C. F. Storia Antica del
Messico. Cesena, 1780.

Swastika, II, p. 192, fig. A. Cited in Hamy's
Decades Américanœ, Première Livraison, 1884,
p. 67.

CONDER, Maj. C. R. Notes on Herr
Schick's paper on the Jerusalem Cross.

*Palestine Exploration Fund, Quarterly State-
ment,* London, July, 1894, pp. 205, 206.

CROOKE, W. An Introduction | to
the | Popular Religion and Folk-lore |
of | Northern India | By W. Crooke,
B. A. | Bengal Civil Service. | Honor-
ary Director of the Ethnographical
Survey, Northwestern | Provinces and
Oudh | Allahabad | Government
Press | 1894.

8°, pp. i–ii, 1–426.
Swastika, pp. 7, 58, 104, 250.

CROSS, The. The Masculine Cross, or
History of Ancient and Modern Crosses,
and their Connection with the Mys-
teries of Sex Worship; also an account
of the Kindred Phases of Phallic Faiths
and Practices.

In Cat. 105 of Ed. Howell, Church street,
Liverpool.

D'ALVIELLA, LE COMTE GOBLET. La |
Migration des Symboles | par | Le
Comte Goblet d'Alviella, | Professeur
d'Histoire des Religions à l'Université
de Bruxelles, | Membre de l'Académie
Royale de Belgique, | Président de la
Société d'Archéologie de Bruxelles |
(Design, Footprint of Buddha) | Paris |
Ernest Leroux, Editeur | Rue Bona-
parte, 28 | 1891.

8°, pp. 1–343.

Cross, pp. 16, 110, 113, 164, 250, 264, 330, 332.

Crux ansata, pp. 22, 106, 107, 114, 186, 221, 229,
250, 265, 332.

Cross of St. Andrew, p. 125.

Swastika cross, Cap. II, passim, pp. 41–108,
110, 111, 225, 271, 339.

Tetraskelion. Same references.

Triskele, triskelion, or triquetrum, pp. 27, 28,
61, 71, 72, 83, 90, 100, 221–225, 271, 339.

Reviewed in *Athenæum,* No. 3381, Aug. 13,
1892, p. 217.

D'ALVIELLA, LE COMTE GOBLET—cont'd.

Favorably criticised in Reliquary Illustrated
Archæologist (Lond.), Vol. I, No. 2, Apr. 1895,
p. 107.

DAVENPORT.——Aphrodisiacs.

The author approves Higgins' views of the
Cross and its Relation to the Lama of Tibet.

DENNIS, G. The | Cities and Cemeter-
ies | of | Etruria. ⌐ Parva Tyrrhenum
per aequor vela darem. Horat. | (Pic-
ture) | By George Dennis. | Third
Edition. | In two volumes | * * * |
With maps, plans, and illustrations. |
London: | John Murray, Albemarle
Street. | 1883.

8°, two vols.: (1), pp. i–cxxviii, 1–501; (2)
pp. i–xv, 1–579.

Archaic Greek vase, British Museum. Four
different styles of Swastikas together on one
specimen. Vol. I, p. xci.

Swastika, common form of decoration, p.
lxxxix.

Primitive Greek Lebes, with Swastika in
panel, left, p. cxiii, fig. 31.

Swastika on bronze objects in Bologna foun-
dry. Vol. II, p. 537.

D'EICHTAL, G. Etudes sur les origines
bouddhiques de la civilization améri-
caine, 1ʳᵉ partie. Paris, Didier, 1862.

Swastika, p. 36 et suiv. Cited in Hamy's
Decades Américanœ, Première Livraison, 1884,
p. 59.

DICTIONNAIRE DES SCIENCES AN-
THROPOLOGIQUES. Anatomie, Crâniolo-
gie, Archéologie Préhistorique, Ethnographie (Mœurs, Arts, Industrie), Dé-
mographie, Langues, Religions. Paris,
Octave Doin, Éditeur, 8, Place de
l'Odéon, Marpon et Flammarion, Li-
braires 1 à 7, Galeries de l'Odéon.

4°, pp. 1–1128.

Title, Swastika, Philippe Salmon, p. 1032.

DORSEY, J. OWEN. Swastika, Ogee
(tetraskelion), symbol for wind-song on
Sacred Chart of Kansa Indians.

Am. Naturalist, XIX (1885), p. 676, pl. XX,
fig. 4.

DULAURE, J. A. Histoire Abrégée | de
| Différens Cultes. | Des Cultes | qui
ont précédé et amené l'Idolatrie | ou |
l'Adoration des figures humaines | par
J. A. Dulaure; seconde édition | revue,
corrigée et augmentée | Paris | Guil-
laume, Libraire-Editeur | rue Haute-
feuille 14. | 1825.

Two vols.: (1), pp. i–x, 11–558; (2), pp. i–xvi,
17–404.

DULAURE, J. A.—continued.

Origin of symbols, works of art and not natural things, Vol. I, pp. 25, 26. Another result of a combination of ideas, p. 45.

The cross represents the phallus, Vol. II, pp. 58, 59, 167, 168.

DUMOUTIER, Gustave Le. Swastika et la roue Solaire en Chine.

Revue d'Ethnographie, Paris, IV, 1885, pp. 327-329.

Review by G. De Mortillet, Matériaux pour l'Histoire Primitive et Naturelle de L'Homme, II, p. 730.

EMERSON, Ellen Russell. Indian Myths | or | Legends, Traditions, and Symbols of the | Aborigines of America | Compared with those of other Countries, including Hindostan, Egypt, Persia | Assyria and China | by Ellen Russell Emerson | Member of the Société Américaine de France | illustrated | Second Edition | London | Trübner & Company | Ludgate Hill | Printed in the U. S. A.

8°, pp. i-x, 1-425.

ENCYCLOPÆDIC DICTIONARY.

Titles, Ansated Cross (Crux ansata), p. 230, Vol. I; Cross, p. 1362, Vol. II; Crux, p. 1378, Vol. II; Fylfot, p. 2240, Vol. II; Gammadion, p. 2256, Vol. II.

ENCYCLOPEDIA BRITANNICA.

Title, Cross. 4°, pp. 539-542.

ENGLEHARDT, C. Influence Classique sur | le Nord Pendant l'Antiquité | par | C. Englehardt. | Traduit par | E. Beauvois. | Copenhague, | Imprimerie de Thiele. | 1876.

8°, pp. 199-318.
Solar disks, fig. 44, p. 240. Crosses, figs. 64, 65, p. 252.

ETHNOLOGY, Reports of the Bureau of.
Second Annual Report, 1880-81.

Art in Shell of the Ancient Americans, by W. H. Holmes. pp. 179-305, pls. XXI-LXXVII.

Collections made in New Mexico and Arizona in 1879, by James Stevenson. pp. 307-422, figs. 347-697.

Third Annual Report, 1881-82.

Catalogue of Collections made in 1881, by W. H. Holmes. pp. 427-510, figs. 116-200.

Fourth Annual Report, 1882-83.

Ancient Pottery of the Mississippi Valley, by W. H. Holmes. pp. 361-436, figs. 361-463.

Fifth Annual Report, 1883-84.

Burial Mounds of Northern Sections of the United States, by Cyrus Thomas. pp. 3-119, pls. I-VI, figs. 1-49.

The Mountain Chant, by Washington Matthews. pp. 379-467, pls. X-XVIII, figs. 50-59.

ETHNOLOGY, Reports of the Bureau of—continued.

Sixth Annual Report, 1884-85.

Ancient Art in the Province of Chiriqui, by W. H. Holmes. pp. 3-187, pl. I, figs. 1-285.

Tenth Annual Report, 1888-89.

Picture writing of the American Indians, by Garrick Mallery. pp. 3-807, pls. I-LIV, figs. 1-1290.

Twelfth Annual Report, 1890-91.

Mound Explorations, by Cyrus Thomas. pp. 3-730, pls. I-XLII, figs. 1-344.

EVANS, John. The Ancient | Bronze Implements, | Weapons, and Ornaments, | of | Great Britain | and | Ireland. | By | John Evans, D. C. L., LL. D., F. R. S., | F. S. A., F. G. S., Pres. Num. Soc., &c., | London: | Longmans, Green & Co. | 1881. | (All rights reserved.)

8°, pp. i-xix, 1-509.

—— The Ancient | Stone Implements, | Weapons, and Ornaments, | of | Great Britain, | by | John Evans, F. R. S., F. S. A. | Honorary Secretary of the Geological and Numismatic Societies of | London, etc., etc., etc. | London: | Longmans, Green, Reader, and Dyer. | 1872. | (All rights reserved.)

8°, pp. l-xvi, 1-640.

FAIRHOLT, F. W. A Dictionary | of | Terms in Art. | Edited and Illustrated by | F. W. Fairholt, F. S. A. | with | Five Hundred Engravings | On Wood | (Design) | Daldy, Isbister & Co. | 56, Ludgate Hill, London.

12° pp. i-vi, 1-474.
Titles, Cross, Fret, Fylfot, Symbolism.

FERGUSSON, James. Rude Stone Monuments | in | All Countries; | Their Ages and Uses. | By James Fergusson, D. C. L., F. R. S, | V. P. R. A. S., F. R. I. B. A., &c. | (Picture.) | With Two Hundred and Thirty-four Illustrations. | London: | John Murray, Albemarle Street. | 1872. | The Right of translation is reserved.

8°, pp. i-xix, 1-559.
Crosses, Celtic and Scottish, pp. 270-273.

FORRER, R. Die | Graeber- und Textilfunde | von | Achmim-Panopolis. | von | R. Forrer | mit 16 Tafeln: 250 Abbildungen | in Photographie, Autographie, Farbendruck und theilweisem

FORRER, R.—continued.

Handcolorit, nebst Clinché-Abbildungen | im Text; Text und Tafeln auf Cartonpapier. | Nur in wenigen nummerirten Exemplaren hergestellt. | (Design.) | Strassburg, 1891 | Druck von Emil Birkhäuser, Basel. | Photographie von Mathias Gerschel, Strassburg. | Autographie und Farbendruck von R. Fretz, Zürich. | Nicht im Buchhandel.

Folio, pp. 1-27.

Swastika, ornament at Achmin-Panopolis, Egypt, p. 20, pl. XI, fig. 3.

FRANKLIN, Colonel. [Swastika an emblem used in the worship of specified sects in India.]

The Jeyrees and Boodhists, p. 49, cited in "Ogam Monuments," by Brash, p. 189.

FRANKS, AUGUSTUS W. Horæ ferales. Pl. 30, fig. 19.

GARDNER, ERNEST A. Naukratis. Part II. | By | Ernest A. Gardner, M. A., | Fellow of Gonville and Caius College, Craven student and formerly Worts student of the University of Cambridge; | Director of the British School of Archæology at Athens. | With an Appendix | by | F. L.L. Griffith, B. A., | of the British Museum, formerly student of the Egyptian Exploration Fund. | Sixth Memoir of | the Egypt Exploration Fund. | Published by order of the committee. | London: etc.

Folio, pls. 1-24, pp. 1-92. Swastika in Egypt, Pottery, Aphrodite. Pl. V, figs. 1, 7; pl. VI, fig. 1; pl. VIII, fig. 1.

GREG, P. R. Fret or Key Ornamentation in Mexico and Peru.

Archæologia, Vol. XLVII, 1882, pt. 1, pp. 157-160, pl. VI.

—— Meaning and Origin of Fylfot and Swastika.

Archæologia, Vol. XLVIII, 1885, pt. 2, pp. 293, 326, pls. XIX, XX, XXI.

GOODYEAR, WILLIAM H. The Grammar of | the Lotus | A new History of Classic Ornament | as a | development of Sun Worship | with Observations on the Bronze Culture of Prehistoric Europe as derived | from Egypt; based on the study of Patterns | by | Wm. H. Goodyear, M. A. (Yale, 1867) | Curator Department of Fine Arts in the Brooklyn Institute of Arts and

GOODYEAR, WILLIAM H.—continued.

Sciences | * * * | London: | Sampson, Low, Marston & Company | Limited | St. Dunstan's House, Fitter Lane, Fleet Street, E. C., | 1891.

Chapters on Lotus and Swastika.

GOULD, S. C. The Master's Mallet or the Hammer of Thor.

Notes and Queries, (Manchester, N. H.), Vol. III (1886), pp. 93-108.

HADDON, ALFRED C. Evolution in Art: | As Illustrated by the | Life-Histories of Designs. | By | Alfred C. Haddon, | Professor of Zoology, Royal College of Science, Corresponding | Member of the Italian Society of Anthropology, etc. | With 8 Plates, and 130 Figures in the Text. | London: | Walter Scott, Ltd., Paternoster Square. | Charles Scribner's Sons, | 153-157 Fifth Avenue, New York. | 1895.

The meaning and distribution of the Fylfot, pp. 282-399.

HAMPEL, JOSEPH. Antiquités préhistoriques de la Hongrie; Erstegom, 1877. No. 3, pl. XX.

—— Catalogue de l'Exposition préhistorique des Musées de Province; Budapest, 1876, p. 17.

HAMY, Dr. E. T. Decades Américanæ | Mémoires | d'Archéologie et d'Ethnographie | Américaines | par | le Dr. E.-T. Hamy | Conservateur du Musée d'Ethnographie du Trocadéro. | Première Livraison | (Picture) | Paris | Ernest Leroux, Editeur | Libraire de la Société Asiatique | de l'École des Langues Orientales Vivantes, etc. | 28, Rue Bonaparte, 28 | 1884.

8°, pp. 1-67.

Le Svastika et la roue solaire en Amérique, pp. 59-67.

HEAD, BARCLAY V. Synopsis of the Contents | of the | British Museum. | Department of | Coins and Medals. | A Guide | to the principal gold and silver | Coins of the Ancients, | from circa B. C. 700 to A. D. 1. | With 70 Plates. | By | Barclay V. Head, Assistant Keeper of Coins. | Second Edition. | London: | Printed by order of the Trustees. | Longmans & Co., Paternoster Row; B. Quaritch, 15, Piccadilly; | A. Asher & Co., 13, Bedford Street, Convent Gar-

HEAD, BARCLAY V.—continued.

den, and at Berlin; | Trübner & Co., 57 and 59, Ludgate Hill. | C. Rollin & Feuardent, 61, Great Russell Street, and 4, Rue de Louvois, Paris. | 1881.

8°, pp. i–viii, 1–128, pl. 70.

Triskelion, (Lycian coins), three cocks' heads, pl. 3, fig. 35.

Punch-marks on ancient coins representing squares, etc., and not Swastika. Pl. 1, figs. 1, 3; pl. 4, fig. 24; pl. 4, figs. 7, 8, 10; pl. 5, fig. 16; pl. 6, figs. 30, 31; pl. 12, figs. 1, 3, 6.

HIGGINS, GODFREY. Anacalypsis | or | attempts to draw aside the veil | of | the Saitic Isis | or, | an inquiry into the origin | of | Languages, Nations, and Religions | by | Godfrey Higgins, Esq. | F. S. A., F. R. Asiat. Soc., F. R. Ast. S. | of Skellow Grange, near Doncaster. | London | Longman, &c., &c., Paternoster Row | 1836.

Vols. I, II.

Origin of the Cross, Lambh or Lama; official name for Governor is Ancient Tibetan for Cross. Vol. I, p. 230.

HIRSCHFELD, G. Vasi arcaici Ateniesi. Roma, 1872. Tav. XXXIX and XL.

HOLMES, W. H. Art in Shell of the Ancient Americans.

Second Ann. Rep. Bureau of Ethnology 1880–81. The cross, pls. XXXVI, LII, LIII. Spirals, pls. LIV, LV, LVI. Swastika, (shell gorget, the bird,) pls. LVIII, LIX. Spider, pl. LXI. Serpent, pls. LXIII, LXIV. Human face, pl. LXIX. Human figure, pls. LXXI, LXXII, LXXIII. Fighting figures, pl. LXXIV.

—— Catalogue of Bureau Collections made in 1881.

Third Ann. Rep. Bureau of Ethnology, 1881–82. Fighting figures, fig. 128, p. 452. Swastika in shell, from Fains Island, fig. 140, p. 466. Spider, same, fig. 141. Spirals on pottery vase, fig. 165, p. 484.

—— Ancient Pottery of the Mississippi Valley.

Fourth Ann. Rep. Bureau of Ethnology, 1882–83. Spirals on pottery, figs. 402, p. 396; 413, p. 403; 415, 416, p. 404; 435, p. 416; 442, p. 421; in basketry, fig. 485, p. 462. Maltese cross, fig. 458, p. 430.

—— Ancient Art in the Province of Chiriqui.

Sixth Ann. Rep. Bureau of Ethnology, 1884–85. Conventional alligator, series of derivations showing stages of simplification of animal characters, figs. 257 to 528, pp. 173–181. Spindle-whorls, Chiriqui, figs. 218–220, p. 149.

HOLMES, W. H.—continued.

—— The Cross used as a Symbol by the Ancient Americans.

Trans. Anthrop. Soc., Washington, D. C., II, 1883.

HUMPHREYS, H. NOEL. The | Coin Collector's Manual, | or guide to the numismatic student in the formation of | A Cabinet of Coins : | Comprising | An Historical and Critical Account of the Origin and Progress | of Coinage from the Earliest Period to the | Fall of the Roman Empire; | with | Some Account of the Coinages of Modern Europe, | More especially of Great Britain. | By H. Noel Humphreys, | Author of "The Coins of England," "Ancient Coins and Medals," | etc., etc. | With above one hundred and fifty illustrations | on Wood and Steel. | In two volumes. | London : | H. G. Bohn, York Street, Convent Garden. | 1853.

12°, (1), pp. i–xxiv, 1–352; (2), pp. 353–726.

Punch-marks on ancient coins, Vol. I, pls. 2, 3, 4. Triquetrum, triskele or triskelion on coins of Sicily, Vol. I, p. 57, and note.

KELLER, FERDINAND. The | Lake Dwellings | of | Switzerland and Other Parts of Europe. | By | Dr. Ferdinand Keller | President of the Antiquarian Association of Zürich | Second Edition, Greatly Enlarged | Translated and Arranged | by | John Edward Lee, F. S. A., F. G. S. | Author of Isca Silurum etc. | In Two Volumes | Vol. I. (Vol. II) | London | Longmans, Green and Co. | 1878 | All rights reserved.

8°, Vol. I, text, pp. i–xv, 1–696; Vol. II, pls. CCVI.

Swastika, Lake Bourget, pattern-stamp and pottery imprint, p. 339, note 1, pl. CLXI, figs. 3, 4.

LANGDON, ARTHUR G. Ornaments of Early Crosses of Cornwall.

Royal Institute of Cornwall, Vol. X, pt. 1, May, 1890, pp. 33–96.

LE PLONGEON, AUGUSTUS. Sacred Mysteries | Among | the Mayas and the Quiches, | 11,500 Years Ago. | Their Relation to the Sacred Mysteries | of Egypt, Greece, Chaldea and India. | Free Masonry | In Times Anterior to The Temple of Solomon. | Illustrated. | By Augustus Le Plongeon, | Author of "Essay on | the Causes of Earthquakes;" "Religion of Jesus Compared

LE PLONGEON, AUGUSTUS—continued. with the | Teachings of the Church;" "The Monuments of Mayas and | their Historical Teachings." | New York: | Robert Macoy, 4 Barclay Street. | 1886.

8°, pp. 163.
Cross and Crux ansata, p. 128.

—— Mayapan and Maya Inscriptions.

Proc. Am. Antiq. Soc., Worcester, Mass., April 21, 1881.
Also printed as a separate. See pp. 15, 17, and figs. 7, 13, and frontispiece.

LITTRÉ'S FRENCH DICTIONARY. Title, Svastika.

MCADAMS, WILLIAM. Records | of | Ancient Races | in the | Mississippi Valley; | Being an account of some of the Pictographs, sculptured | hieroglyphics, symbolic devices, emblems, and tra- | ditions of the prehistoric races of America, with | some suggestions as to their origin. | With cuts and views illustrating over three hundred objects | and symbolic devices. | By Wm. McAdams, | Author of * | * | * | * | * | St. Louis: | C. R. Barns Publishing Co. | 1887.

4°, pp. i–xii, 1–120.
Mound vessels with painted symbols, sun symbols, cross symbols, cross with bent arms (Swastika), etc., Chap. xv, pp. 62–68.
Cites Lord Kinsborough, "Antiquities of Mexico," for certain forms of the cross, of which the first is the Swastika and the third the Nandavartaya Chap. xvii, pp. 62–68.

MACRICHIE, DAVID. Ancient | and | Modern Britons: | A Retrospect. | London: | Kegan Paul, Trench & Co., | 1 Paternoster Square. | 1884.

Two vols., 8°. (1), pp. i–viii, 1–401; (2), i–viii, 1–449.
Sculptured stones of Scotland (p. 115), the Newton stone, a compound of Oriental and western languages (pp. 117–118). Ethnologic resemblances between old and new world peoples considered. Vol. II (app.).

MALLERY, GARRICK. Picture writing of the American Indians.

Tenth Ann. Rep. Bureau of Ethnology, 1888–89, pp. 1–807, pls. I–LIV, figs. 1–1290.
Sun and star symbols, figs. 1118–1129, pp. 694–697. Human form (cross) symbols, figs. 1164–1173, pp. 705–709. Cross symbols, figs. 1225–1234, pp. 724–730. Piaroa color stamps, fret pattern, fig. 982, p. 621.

MARCH, H. COLLEY. The Fylfot and the Futhorc Tir.

Cited in Transactions of the Lancashire and Cheshire Antiquarian Society, 1886.

MASSON, ——. [The Swastika found on large rock near Karachi.]

Balochistan, Vol. IV, p. 8, cited in Ogam Monuments, by Brash, p. 189.

MATÉRIAUX pour l'Histoire Primitive et Naturelle de l'Homme. Revue mensuelle illustrée. (Fondée par M. G. De Mortillet, 1865 à 1868.) Dirigée par M. Émile Cartailhac. * * *

Swastika, Vol. XVI, 1881.
Prehistoric Cemeteries in Caucasus, by E. Chantre, pp. 154–166.
Excavations at Cyprus, by General di Cesnola, p. 416.
Signification of the Swastika, by M. Girard de Reale, p. 548.
Swastika, Vol. XVIII, 1884.
Étude sur quelques Nécropoles Halstattiennes de l'Autriche et de l'Italie. By Ernest Chantre, Swastika on Archaic Vase, fig. 5, p. 8. Croix Gammée, figs. 12 and 13, p. 14. Cross, p. 122. Swastika, pp. 137–139. Swastika sculpté sur pierre, Briteros, Portugal, fig. 133, p. 294.
Necropolis of Halstatt, pp. 13, 14; p. 139, fig. 84; p. 280, Report of spearhead with Swastika and runic inscription, found at Torcello, near Venice, by Undset.
Swastika, Vol. XX, 1886.
Frontispiece of January number. Swastika from Museum, Mayence.

MATTHEWS, WASHINGTON. The Mountain Chant.

Fifth Ann. Rep. Bureau of Ethnology, 1883–84, pp. 379–467, pls. X–XVIII, figs. 50–59.
Swastika in Navajo Mountain Chant. Second (?) Dry Painting, pl. XVII, pp. 450, 451.

MONTELIUS, OSCAR. The | Civilization of Sweden | in Heathen Times | by | Oscar Montelius, Ph. D. | Professor at the National Historical Museum, Stockholm. | Translated from the Second Swedish Edition | Revised and enlarged for the author | by | Rev. F. H. Woods, B. D. | Vicar of Chalfont St. Peter. | With Map and Two Hundred and Five Illustrations. | London | Macmillan and Co. | and New York. | 1888.

pp. i–xvi. 1–214.
The wheel with cross on many monuments of the Bronze Age became almost unknown during the Age of Iron (in Scandinavia). It was the contrary with the Swastika. Compte-Rendu, Cong. Inter. d'Anthrop. et d'Arch. Préhistorique. 7me session, 1874, I, pp. 439, 460

MOOREHEAD, Warren K. Primitive Man | In Ohio | by | Warren K. Moorehead | Fellow of the American Association for the Advancement of Science | Author of "Fort Ancient, the Great Prehistoric | Earthwork of Ohio," etc. | G. P. Putnam's Sons | The Knickerbocker Press, | 1892.

pp. i–xii, 1–246.
Discoveries in Hopewell Mound, Chillicothe, Rose County, Ohio, pp. 184–196.
Swastika, p. 193.

MORGAN, J. De. Mission Scientifique | au Caucase | Etudes | Archæologiques et Historiques | par | J. De Morgan | Tome Premier | Les Premiers Ages Des Métaux | Dans l'Arménie Russe | Paris | Ernest Leroux, éditeur | 28, Rue Bonaparte, 28 | 1889.

8°, (1), pp. i–iii, 1–231; (2), pp. i–iv, 1–305.
Swastikas on bronze pin-heads from prehistoric Armenian graves, Vol. I, p. 160, figs. 177, 178, 179.

MORTILLET, Gabriel et Adrien de. Musée | Préhistorique | par | Gabriel et Adrien de Mortillet | Photogravures Michelet | Paris | C. Reinwald, Libraire-Editeur | 15, Rue des Saints-Pères, 15 | 1881 | Tous Droits Réservés.

4°. Planches C, figs. 1269.
Tintinnabulum and Buddha with Swastika, pl. xcviii, fig. 1230. Swiss Lake pottery, fig. 1231. Swastika, many representations, pl. xcix, figs. 1233, 1234, 1235, 1239, 1240, 1241, 1244, 1246, 1247, 1248, 1249; pl. c, figs. 1255, 1256, 1257, 1261, 1263, 1264, 1265, 1266, 1267. Crosses—divers, pl. xcix, etc.

MORTILLET, Gabriel de. Le Préhistorique | Antiquité de l'Homme | par Gabriel de Mortillet | Professeur d'anthropologie préhistorique | à l'École d'anthropologie de Paris. | 64 figures intercalées dans le texte. | Paris | C. Reinwald, Libraire-Éditeur | 15, Rue des Saints-Pères, 15 | 1883 | Tous droits réservés.

12°, pp. 1–642.
Communications between Europe and America, pp. 186, 187.

—— Le Signe | de la Croix | Avant | le Christianisme | par ǀ Gabriel de Mortillet | Directeur des Matériaux pour l'Histoire positive et philosophique | de l'homme | avec 117 gravures sur bois. | Paris | C. Reinwald, Libraire-

MORTILLET, Gabriel de—continued.
Éditeur | 15, rue des Saints-Père, 15 | 1866 | Tous droits réservés.
See p. 182.

MÜLLER, F. Max. Chips | from | A German Workship. | By Max Müller, M. A., | Fellow of All Souls College, Oxford. | Essays on * * | New York : | Scribner, Armstrong & Co. | Successors to Charles Scribner & Co.

Essays on Mythology, Traditions, and Customs. Svasti, Sanscrit, meaning joy or happiness. Vol. II, p. 24.
Swastika. Letter to Dr. Schliemann, "Ilios," pp. 346–349.
Swastika, Review of, Athenæum (Lond.), No. 3332, Aug. 20, 1892, p. 266.

MÜLLER, Ludwig. [Swastika.]
Proc. Royal Danish Academy of Science, Fifth series, Section of History and Philosophy, Vol. III, p. 93.

MUNRO, Robert. Ancient | Scottish Lake Dwellings | or Crannogs | with a Supplementary Chapter on | Remains of Lake Dwellings in England | by | Robert Munro, M. A. | M. D., F. S. A. Scot. | (Design) | Edinburgh: David Douglas | 1881 | All rights reserved.

8°, pp. i–xx, 1–326.
Swastika on pin and triskelion on plank, crannog of Lochlee, figs. 144 and 149, pp. 130–134.
Note by Montelius, figs. 11 and 12, p. 131.

—— The | Lake Dwellings | of | Europe : | Being the | Rhind Lectures in Archæology | for 1888. | By | Robert Munro, M. A., M. D., | Secretary of the Society of Antiquaries of Scotland; Author of | "Ancient Scottish Lake Dwellings or Crannogs." | Cassell & Company, Limited : | London, Paris & Melbourne. | 1890 | (All rights reserved).

4°, pp. i–xl, 1–600.
Swastika in Lake Bourget (Savoy), fig. 195, Nos. 11 and 12, pp. 532 and 538; in Lisnacroghera (Ireland), fig. 124, No. 20; triskele, fig. 124, No. 22, pp. 383, 585.

NADAILLAC, Marquis de. Prehistoric America | by the | Marquis de Nadaillac | Translated by N. D'Anvers | Edited by W. H. Dall | (Design of Vase) | with 219 illustrations | New York and London | G. P. Putnam's Sons | The Knickerbocker Press | 1884.

8°, pp. i–vii, 1–566.

NADAILLAC, Marquis de—continued.

Swastika (?) alleged to be on the Pemberton hammer from New Jersey, pp. 22, note 1, citing Professor Haldeman, Sept. 27, 1877, Rep. Peabody Museum, 1878, p. 255. Dr. Abbott denounces this inscription as a fraud. Primitive Industry, p. 32.

NEWTON, JOHN. History of Migration of the Triskelion from Sicily to the Isle of Man, through Henry III of England and Alexander III of Scotland.

Athenæum, No. 3385, Sept. 10, 1892, pp. 353, 354.

NICHOLSON, CORNELIUS. Report of Swastika found in recently explored Mosaic pavement in Isle of Wight, Munro's "Ancient Scottish Lake Dwellings," note, p. 132.

PETRIE, W. M. FLINDERS. Naukratis (Greek inscription). | Part I, 1884–85) by | W. M. Flinders Petrie. | With Chapters by | Cecil Smith; Ernest Gardner, B. A.; | and Barclay V. Head. | (Design, two sides of coin.) | Third Memoir of | The Egypt Exploration Fund. | Published by Order of the Committee. | London: | Trübner & Co., 57 & 59, Ludgate Hill. | 1886.

Folio, pp. 1–100, pls. 1–28.
Swastika in Egypt, fourth and fifth centuries B. C., pl. IV, fig. 3. Meander Swastikas, pl. V, figs. 15, 24.

PRÄHISTORISCHE BLÄTTER. | Von | Dr. Julius Nau, in München. | VI. Jahrg., 1894. München. Nr. 5. Mit Taf. XI–XV.

Söderberg, Sven. Die Thierornamentik der Völkerwanderungszeit. | Mit Tertabildungen und Tafel XI–XV. | Lund, Sweden. Figs. 12, 13, p. 73.

PRIME, WILLIAM C. Pottery and Porcelain | Of All Times And Nations | With Tables of Factory and Artists' Marks | For the Use of Collectors | by William C. Prime, LL. D. | (Design) | New York | Harper & Brothers, Publishers | Franklin Square | 1878.

8°, pp. 1–531.
Symbolic marks on Chinese porcelain. Tablet of honor inclosing Swastika. Fig. 155, p. 254; fig. 33, p. 61.

QUEEN LACE BOOK, The. A | Historical and Descriptive Account of the Hand-Made | Antique Laces of All Countries. | * * | with | Thirty Illustrations of Lace Specimens, and seven

QUEEN LACE BOOK, The—continued.
Diagrams of | Lace Stitches. | London: | "The Queen" Office, 346, Strand, W. C. | 1874. | All rights reserved.

pp. i–viii, 1–38.
Swastika design in linen embroidery and cutwork (Sixteenth Century). Geometric Style). pl. 1, fig. 2.

RAWLINSON, GEORGE. The Religions | of | the Ancient World. | By | George Rawlinson, M. A. | Author of "The Seven Great Monarchies of the Ancient | Eastern World," etc. | New York: | Hurst & Co., Publishers, | 122 Nassau Street.

12°, pp. 1—180.
Religion of the Ancient Sanscrit Indians. Agni, the god of Fire, described pp. 87, 89. Sun, Wind, Dyaus (Heaven), and Prithivi (Earth). Nothing said about Swastika or Solar circle.

RICHTER, MAX OHNEFALSCH. Excavations in Cyprus.

Bull. Soc. d'Anthrop., Paris, Vol. XI (ser. III), pp. 669–682.

ROBINSON, DAVID. A Tour | through | The Isle of Man: | To which is subjoined | A Review of the Manx History. | By David Robertson, Esq. | London: | Printed for the Author, | by E. Hodson, Bell-Yard, Temple-Bar. | Sold by Mr. Payne, Mews-Gate; Messrs. Egertons, Whitehall; | Whites, Fleet Street; and Deighton, Holborn. | 1794.

4° narrow, pp. 235.
Triskelion—Coat of arms of Isle of Man.

ROCKHILL, WILLIAM WOODVILLE. Diary of a Journey | through | Mongolia and Tibet | in | 1891 and 1892 | by | William Woodville Rockhill | Gold Medalist of the Royal Geographical Society | (Design.) | City of Washington | Published by the Smithsonian Institution | 1894.

4°, pp. i–xx, 1–413.
Swastika (yung-drung) tattooed on hand of native at Kumbum, p. 67.

SACHEVERELL, WILLIAM. An | Account | of the | Isle of Man, | its | Inhabitants, Language, Soil, re- | markable Curiosities, the Succession | of its Kings and Bishops, down to | the present Time. | By way of Essat. | With a | Voyage to I-Columb-kill. | By William Sacheverell, Esq.: | Late Governour of

SACHEVERELL, William—continued. Man. | To which is added, | A Dissertation about the Mona of Cæsar and | Tacitus; and an Account of the Antient | Druids, &c. | By Mr. Thomas Brown, | Address'd in a Letter to his Learned | Friend Mr. A. Sellars. | London: | Printed for J. Hartley, next the King's Head Tavern. | R. Gibson in Middle Row, and Tho. Hodgson over a- | gainst Gray's-Inn Gate in Holborn, 1702.

12mo, pp. 175.
Triskelion—Coat of arms of Isle of Man.

SCHICK, Herr Baurath von. The Jerusalem Cross.

Palestine Exploration Fund, Quarterly Statement, July, 1894, pp. 183–188.

SCHLIEMANN, Heinrich. Atlas Trojanischer Alterthümer. | Photographische Abbildungen | zu dem | Berichte | über die Ausgrabungen in Troja | von | Dr. Heinrich Schliemann. | (Design) | Leipzig: | In Commission bei F. A. Brockhaus. | 1874.

Folio, pp. 1–57, plates, 1–217.
Spindle whorls—*passim*. Swastikas on many specimens from fig. No. 142 to 3468. No. 237 is in U. S. National Museum as part of Mme. Schliemann's collection.

SCHLIEMANN, Henry. Ilios | The City and Country | of | the Trojans | The Results of Researches and Discoveries on the Site of Troy and | Throughout the Troad in the Years 1871–72–73–78–79 | Including an | Autobiography of the Author | By Dr. Henry Schliemann | F. S. A., F. R. I. British Architects | Author of "Troy and Its Remains," "Mycenæ," etc. | With a Preface, Appendices, and Notes | By Professors Rudolf Virchow, Max Müller, A. H. Sayce, J. P. Mahaffy, H. Brugsch-Bey, P. Ascherson, M. A. Postolaccas, M. E. Burnouf, Mr. F. Calvert, and Mr. J. A. Duffield. | (Greek Verse) | With Maps, Plans, and About 1,800 Illustrations. | New York | Harper & Brothers, Franklin Square | 1881. |

8°, pp. i–xvi, 1–800.
Swastika: Introduction, p. xi, and pp. 229, 231, 303, 349, 353, 416, 518, 571, 573.
"Owl-faced" (?) vases, figs. 227, 1293, 1294. Fig. 986 (not owl, but human, Virchow), pp. xiii, xiv.
Figures of Swastika on spindle-whorls—*passim*—fig. 1850 is in the U. S. National Museum.

SCHLIEMANN, Henry—continued.
——Mycenæ; | A Narrative of Researches and Discoveries | at Mycenæ and Tiryns. | By Dr. Henry Schliemann, | Citizen of the United States of America, | Author of "Troy and Its Remains," "Ithaque, Le Peloponnèse et Troie," | and "La Chine et le Japon." | The Preface | By the Right Hon. W. E. Gladstone, M. P. | Maps, Plans, and Other Illustrations. | Representing more than 7,000 Types of the Objects Found in the | Royal Sepulchres of Mycenæ and Elsewhere | In the Excavations. | New York: | Scribner, Armstrong & Company. | 1878. | (All Rights Reserved.)

8°, pp. i–lxviii, 1–384, Swastika, pp. 77, 165, 259, figs. 383, 385, and many others.

—— Troja | Results of the Latest | Researches and Discoveries on the | Site of Homer's Troy | And in the Heroic Tumuli and Other Sites | Made in the Year 1882 | and a Narrative of a Journey in the Troad in 1881 | by | Dr. Henry Schliemann | Hon. D. C. L., Oxon., and Hon. Fellow of Queen's College, Oxford | F. S. A., F. R. I. B. A. | Author of " Ilios," " Troy and its Remains," and "Mycenæ and Tiryns " | Preface by Prof. A. H. Sayce | with 150 Woodcuts and 4 Maps and Plans | (Quotation in German from Moltke: Wunderbuch, p. 19, Berlin, 1879) | New York | Harper & Brothers, Franklin Square | 1884.

8°, pp. 1–434.
Swastika, preface xviii, xxi, pp. 122, 124, 125, 126, 127, 128.
Spiral form, pp. 123.
Lycian coins—triskelion, pp. 123, 124.

SCHVINDT, Theodor. Vihko 1–4 | Suomalaisia koristeita. | 1. Ompelukoristeita. | Finnische Ornamente. | 1. Stickornamente. | Heft 1–4 | Suolalaisen Kirjallisuuden Seura Helsingissa. | 1894.

Description of Finnish national ornamental embroidery in which the Swastika appears as a pattern made by oblique stitches, pp. 14, 15, figs. 112–121.

SIMPSON, William. Swastika.

Palestine Exploration Fund, Quarterly Statement, January, 1895, pp. 84, 85.

SNOWDEN, James Ross. A Description | of | Ancient and Modern Coins, | in the | Cabinet Collection | at the Mint

SNOWDEN, JAMES ROSS—continued. of the United States. | Prepared and arranged under the Direction of | James Ross Snowden, | Director of the Mint. | Philadelphia: | J. B. Lippincott & Co. | 1860.

8°, pp. i–xx, 1–412.

Punch-marks on ancient coins, and how they were made. Introduction, pp. ix–xiv, and figures.

SQUIER, E. GEORGE. Peru | Incidents of Travel and Exploration | in the | Land of the Incas | By E. George Squier, M. A., F. S. A. | Late U. S. Commissioner to Peru, Author of "Nicaragua," "Ancient Monuments | of Mississippi Valley," etc., etc. | (Design) | With Illustrations | New York | Harper Brothers, Publishers | Franklin Square | 1877.

8°, pp. i–xx, 1–599.

Mythologic representations of earth, air, and water. The cross not mentioned as one, p. 184.

STEVENS, GEORGE L. The Old Northern | Runic Monuments | of Scandinavia and England | Now first | collected and deciphered | by | George Stevens, Esq., F. S. A. | Knight of the Northern Star and other titles, | with many hundreds of fac-similes and illustrations partly in gold, silver, bronze and colors. | Runic alphabets; introductions; appendices; word-lists, etc. | London, John Russell Smith. | Kobenhaven, Michaelsen and Tillge. | Printed by H. H. Thiele, 1866–67.

8°, pp. i–xi, 1–625.

STEVENSON, JAMES. Collections made in New Mexico and Arizona, 1879, by James Stevenson.

Second Ann. Rep. Bureau of Ethnology, 1880–81, pp. 307–465, figs. 347–697.

Spiral in basketry, fig. 542. Swastika (dance-rattle), fig. 562, p. 394. Maltese cross, fig. 642. Greek cross, fig. 708, p. 453.

SYKES, Lieut. Col. Notes on the religious, moral, and political state of India before the Mohammedan invasion, chiefly founded on the travels of the Chinese Buddhist priest, Fa-Hian, in India, A. D. 399, and on the commentaries of Messrs. Klaproth, Burnouf, and Landresse.

Journal Royal Asiatic Society of Great Britain and Ireland, Vol. VI, pp. 248, 299, 310, 334.

THOMAS, CYRUS. Burial Mounds of Northern Sections of the United States.

Fifth Ann. Rep. Bureau of Ethnology, 1883–84, pp. 3–119, pls. I–VI, figs. 1–49.

Excavations in Little Etowah Mounds. Human figures on copper plates, repoussé work, figs. 42, 43, pp. 100, 101.

Eagle (copper) Mound near Bluff Lake, Union County, Illinois, fig. 48, p. 105.

—— Report on the Mound Explorations of the Bureau of Ethnology.

Twelfth Ann. Rep. Bureau of Ethnology, 1890–91, pp. 1–730, pls. I–XLII, figs. 1–344.

Human figures (copper), repoussé work, figs. 186, p. 304; 189, p. 306.

Eagle Mound in Illinois, fig. 192, p. 309. Swastika on shell, Big Toco Mound, Tennessee, fig. 262, p. 383.

THOMAS, G. W. Excavations in Anglo-Saxon Cemetery, Sleaford, Lincolnshire. Swastika.

Archæologia, Vol. L, 1887, pt. 2, p. 386, pl. XXIV, fig. 2.

TYLOR, EDWARD B. Anthropology: | An Introduction to the Study of | Man and Civilization. | By | Edward B. Taylor, D. C. L., F. R. S. | With Illustrations. | New York: | D. Appleton and Company, | 1, 3, and 5 Bond Street. | 1881.

12°, pp. 1–448.

Spinning and spindle whorls, pp. 247, 248.

—— Primitive Culture | Researches into the Development of | Mythology, Philosophy, Religion, | Language, Art and Custom | by | Edward E. Tylor, LL. D., F. R. S., | Author of "Researches into the Early History of Mankind," etc. | (Quotation in French) | First American, from the Second English Edition | In Two Volumes | (Design) | Boston | Estes & Lauriat | 143 Washington Street | 1874.

8°, (1), pp. i–xii, 1–502; (2), pp. i–viii, 1–470.

WAKE, C. S. The Swastika and Allied Symbols.

Am. Antiquarian, 1894, Vol. XVI, p. 413.

The writer cites Prof. Alois Raimond Hein, Meander, etc., Worbelornamente in Amerika. Vienna, 1891.

WARING, J. B. Ceramic Art | in | Remote Ages; | With Essays on the Symbols of | the Circle, the Cross and Circle, | the Circle and Ray Ornament, the Fylfot, | and the Serpent, | Showing their Relation to the Primitive

WARING, J. B.—continued.

Forms | of | Solar and Nature Worship, | by | J. B. Waring, | Author of "Stone Monuments, Tumuli, and Ornament of Remote Ages," "Illustrations of Architecture and Ornament," | "The Art Treasures of the United Kingdom," &c., &c. | London: | Printed and Published by John B. Day, | Savoy Street, Strand | 1874.

Folio, pp. 1-127, pls. 1-55.
Swastika; Triskelion; Ancient coins. Plates 2, 3, 7, 27, 33, 41-44.

WIENER, CHARLES. Pérou | et Bolivie | Récit de Voyage | suivi | d'Études Archéologiques et Ethnographiques | et de Notes | Sur l'Écriture et les Langues des Populations Indiennes | par | Charles Wiener | Ouvrage Contenant | 100 Gravures, 27 cartes et 18 plans | (Design) | Paris | Librairie Hachette et Cie. | 79, Boulevard Saint-Germain, 79 | 1880 | Droits de Propriété et de traduction réservés.

8°, pp. i-xi, 1-796.
Christian cross in America.—Means used to implant it. Chap. VII, pp. 716-730.

WOOD, J. G. The | Natural | History of Man; | Being | an Account of the Manners and Customs of the | Uncivilized Races of Men. | By the Rev. | J. G. Wood, M. A., F. L. S. | etc., etc. | With New Designs by Angas, Danby, Wolf, Zwecker, etc., etc. | Engraved by the Brothers Dalziel. | London: | George Routledge and Sons, The Broadway, Ludgate. | New York: 416 Broome Street. | 1868.

2 vols., 8°, pp. 774, 864.
The Gurani Indians wear the queyu or bead apron; Vol. II, p. 620, but the Waraus wear only a triangular bit of bark, p. 623.

WRIGHT, T. F. Notes on the Swastika.

Palestine Exploration Fund, Quarterly Statement, London. October, 1894, p. 300.

ZMIGRODZKI, MICHAEL V. Zur | Geschichte der Suastika | von | Michael V. Zmigrodzki | Mit Vier Figuren im Text und Vier Tafeln. | Braunschweig, | Druck und Verlag von Friederich Vieweg und Sohn. | 1890.

—— Histoire du Suastika.

Congrès International d'Anthrop. et Archéol. Préhist. Compte Rendu de la dixième session à Paris, 1889 pp. 473-490.

LIST OF ILLUSTRATIONS.

PLATES.

---

[1] The Basáltæ and Orrescii were Thracian tribes who dwelt in the valleys of the Strymon and the Angites, to the north of the Pangæan Range.

TEXT FIGURES.

www.ingramcontent.com/pod-product-compliance
Lightning Source LLC
Chambersburg PA
CBHW062201270326
41930CB00009B/1612